PRAISE FOR
WORK WON'T LOVE YOU BACK

"*Work Won't Love You Back* brilliantly chronicles the transformation of work into a labor of love, demonstrating how this seemingly benign narrative is wreaking havoc on our lives, communities, and planet. By pulling apart the myth that work is love, Jaffe shows us that we can reimagine futures built on care, rather than exploitation. A tremendous contribution."

—Naomi Klein, author of *On Fire: The Burning Case for a Green New Deal*

"Sarah Jaffe gives us engrossing stories of how ordinary people in familiar jobs navigate the precarious and all-consuming conditions of work and fight back against them. How did we come to this? Through sharp analyses of the recent history and social contours of each occupation, Jaffe helps us understand the contemporary landscape and provides tools to contest how we are put to work. The result is a marvelously lucid, thoroughly readable, and wonderfully engaging book."

—Kathi Weeks, author of *The Problem with Work: Feminism, Marxism, Antiwork Politics, and Postwork Imaginaries*

"Sarah Jaffe's months in the library have built the kind of analysis that you'd find in an institute of advanced study. Her years as a labor reporter have let her see frontlines where others have failed to look. And a lifetime of elegant writing has produced a prose style that pulls you through a book of rare importance. You'll find it on the picket-lines of sports, non-profits, art, retail, teaching, domestic work, gaming and the academy. And once you've finished it, you'll find it close to your heart, too."

—Raj Patel, author of *Stuffed and Starved: The Hidden Battle for the World Food System*

"*Work Won't Love You Back* is a tremendous achievement. Jaffe's committed, on-the-ground engagement, historical range, and ferocious gathering of revolutionary thought combines to create something genuine and profound. I cannot think of another book that ranges so widely, and yet so attentively, through the variegated landscape of our current condition, and the conflicts and struggles that have composed it. Without hyperbole, this book is a gift to its reader, and to a possible future. To put it in Marxish: Jaffe has achieved a prismatic and elusive goal, combining a generality of historical scope, the particularity of relation between different moments and movements, and the aching specificity of what it means to endure capitalism and dream of something better, more connected, more alive."

—Jordy Rosenberg, author of *Confessions of the Fox*

"Many of us write books to make people think. Sarah Jaffe writes books to make you act. I can honestly say that *Work Won't Love You Back* has caused me to re-think my entire relationship to how I work and live. Read it and it will change you too."

—David Dayen, author of *Chain of Title* and *Monopolized*

"As she swaggers through history, theory, and journalism in her newest book, Sarah Jaffe has written a dazzling takedown of the myth of working for love, and a call to arms for workers to invest their love and solidarity not in their jobs but in each other. This is a big book, in terms of intellectual scope, ambition, and impact."

—Molly Crabapple, artist and author of *Drawing Blood* and coauthor of *Brothers of the Gun*

"In *Work Won't Love You Back*, our finest labor journalist raises her game. Sarah Jaffe charts a path through the most painful realities of working-class life in the twenty-first century, taking readers on an eye-opening journey through a remarkably varied number of industries. It's an indispensable addition to labor journalism, labor history, and much more broadly, our understanding of what resistance looks like—and could look like—in these difficult times. It's part Barbara Ehrenreich, part Studs Terkel, and all Sarah Jaffe, one of the most unique voices writing today. Remember, 'the problem is not you, it's work itself.'"

—Dave Zirin, author of *A People's History of Sports in the United States*

"Sassy and big-hearted, learned and astute, this chronicle of late capitalism warns against the expropriation of bodies, minds, and spirits when we confuse work with love. Through vivid portraits of service and creative workers—including home aids, interns, teachers, gamers, adjuncts, and athletes—Sarah Jaffe more than indicts jobs that promise pleasure. She shows ordinary people fighting back for recognition, rights, and living wages. A stunning achievement!"

—Eileen Boris, Hull Professor of Feminist Studies, University of California, Santa Barbara

"Sarah Jaffe's *Work Won't Love You Back* stages a much-needed intervention into a bad relation: our employment. The scope of Jaffe's wonderful book is stunning, covering the gamut of our modern economy, from the field to what's left of the factory, from the home to the Amazon distribution center and university. Jaffe's analysis of how capitalism learned to use affective sentiment to organize labor relations is nuanced and profound. Neoliberalism, it turns out, is a vast gaslighting project, manipulating emotions, promising not better wages but self-fulfillment in exchange for ever greater rates of value extraction. That project is collapsing, and you'll find no better guide to help sift through the wreckage than this book. Fusing critical theory and on-the-ground reporting, Jaffe reminds us that capitalism can't love us back. But, if we force it, it can provide the material conditions that will help us love each other."

—Greg Grandin, C. Vann Woodward Professor
of History, Yale University

"Sarah Jaffe is asking, and helping to answer, fundamental questions at the exact right time. Read this book to help clarify the demands list for a far better society. Jaffe's decades of shrewd and discerning journalism helped her produce this excellent book. It is a multiplex in still life; a stunning critique of capitalism, a collective conversation on the meaning of life and work, and a definite contribution to the we-won't-settle-for-less demands of the future society everyone deserves."

—Jane McAlevey, author of *A Collective Bargain: Unions,
Organizing, and the Fight for Democracy*

"Illuminating and inspiring . . . *Work Won't Love You Back* is ultimately an optimistic book. Jaffe is clear-eyed about all the ways employers exploit workers' goodwill, but because she has spent so much time reporting on labor actions across the world, she has also seen how workers use love to their advantage in organizing."

—*The New Republic*

"An extremely timely analysis of how we arrived at these brutal inequalities and of some of the ways in which a deliberately atomised workforce is beginning to organise to challenge them."

—*The Guardian*

"The book is also both structurally ambitious, combining essays on very specific industries such as domestic work, teaching, retail, nonprofits, art, academic, tech, sports, and of particular note, interns as it is a narrative feat. . . . The most lucid moments in Jaffe's writing come in the form of her blunt redefinitions of commonplace ideas. There are several of these brilliant sentences throughout the pages: 'The labor of love, of short, is a con'; 'Charity is a relationship of power'; and 'programming, a field currently dominated by young men, was invented by a woman,' to name a few."

—*The Progressive*

"Jaffe and the workers she interviews help us make sense of the messy tangle of emotions so many of us feel about our professional lives; when the lines are blurred between work and play, as Jaffe so astutely explains and historicizes for us, they are simply the messy tangle of emotions about our lives, full stop. The final chapter of *Work Won't Love You Back* is at once a brilliant contribution to the growing canon of anti-work political theory and a moving ode to human connection."

—*The Baffler*

"The prose is crisp and compulsively readable . . . a deeply engaging work."

—*Indypendent*

"An important, timely reminder of the meaning of work."

—*The Los Angeles Review of Books*

WORK
WON'T
LOVE YOU
BACK

WORK WON'T LOVE YOU BACK

How Devotion to Our Jobs Keeps Us
Exploited, Exhausted, and Alone

SARAH JAFFE

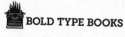

BOLD TYPE BOOKS

New York

Bold Type Books
116 East 16th Street, 8th Floor New York, NY 10003
www.boldtypebooks.org
@BoldTypeBooks

Printed in the United States of America

First Edition: January 2021
First Trade Paperback Edition: January 2022

Published by Bold Type Books, an imprint of Perseus Books, LLC, a subsidiary of Hachette Book Group, Inc. Bold Type Books is a co-publishing venture of the Type Media Center and Perseus Books.

The Hachette Speakers Bureau provides a wide range of authors for speaking events. To find out more, go to www.hachettespeakersbureau.com or call (866) 376-6591.

The publisher is not responsible for websites (or their content) that are not owned by the publisher.

Print book interior design by Amy Quinn

Library of Congress Cataloging-in-Publication Data
Names: Jaffe, Sarah, 1980– author.
Title: Work won't love you back : how devotion to our jobs keeps us exploited, exhausted, and alone / Sarah Jaffe.
Description: First edition. | New York, NY : Bold Type Books, [2021] | Includes bibliographical references and index.
Identifiers: LCCN 2020031919 | ISBN 9781568589398 (hardcover) | ISBN 9781568589381 (ebook)
Subjects: LCSH: Quality of work-life. | Job satisfaction. | Work-life balance. | Work—Psychological aspects. | Labor.
Classification: LCC HD6955 .J34 2021 | DDC 331.2—dc23
LC record available at https://lccn.loc.gov/2020031919

ISBNs: 9781568589398 (hardcover), 9781568589381 (e-book), 9781568589374 (trade paperback)

LSC-C

Printing 1, 2021

For Melissa and Peter

CONTENTS

Preface to the Paperback Edition   *ix*

Introduction. Welcome to the Working Week   1

PART ONE: WHAT WE MIGHT CALL LOVE

Chapter 1. Nuclear Fallout: The Family   21
Chapter 2. Just Like One of the Family: Domestic Work 55
Chapter 3. We Strike Because We Care: Teaching   83
Chapter 4. Service with a Smile: Retail   111
Chapter 5. Suffer for the Cause: Nonprofits   139

PART TWO: ENJOY WHAT YOU DO!

Chapter 6. My Studio Is the World: Art   175
Chapter 7. Hoping for Work: Interns   207
Chapter 8. Proletarian Professionals: Academia   231
Chapter 9. Playbor of Love: Technology   263
Chapter 10. It's All Fun and Games: Sports   291
Conclusion. What Is Love?   321

Acknowledgments   *337*
Notes   *343*
Index   *403*
Reading Group Guide   *421*

PREFACE TO THE PAPERBACK EDITION

"Nobody Wants to Work Anymore"

I<small>T'S HARD TO TELL WHEN THE FIRST SIGN POPPED UP, ONLY THAT THEY</small> were suddenly ubiquitous in the spring of 2021. The viral photos shared on social media showed the homemade paper announcements, taped up presumably by managers, on drive-thru menus or restaurant doors. The signs were often misspelled, but that wasn't what made them so repulsive, though it contributed to the air of crude class snobbery they projected. They all seemed to say some version of the same thing: because unemployment benefits were too high, those ungrateful service workers just wouldn't come back to their jobs.

Those were the same workers, of course, who had been laid off early on in the Covid-19 pandemic, sent home to collect unemployment benefits so the bosses could lower costs. Precious Cole, a McDonald's employee in Durham, North Carolina, shrugged off the idea that expanded unemployment benefits were some kind of problem. "Why would people go back to a job that doesn't treat them fairly, that's paying them poverty wages, that doesn't want to hear anything that they have to say?" she asked.

She and so many other workers, deemed "essential" while their managers retreated behind office doors, had continued to show up to serve food. They were the ones who ran the business and who had been briefly lauded for their courage during the terrifying early pandemic days. They were the ones who were exposed to risk—Cole had to quarantine because one of her coworkers tested positive for the virus. Yet she wasn't offered sick pay and, on top of that, she was living with and supporting her mother, whose failing health prevented her from working herself. Cole and her coworkers walked off the job in protest, forcing the restaurant to close for the day. It took two strikes, but they eventually won ten days of paid sick time.

To Cole, it was obvious that people like her had given much more to their jobs than their jobs had ever given back. "We are the ones in the trenches making the decisions for your company, we're making the food for your company, we're dealing with your nasty, rude customers, with a smile on our face. We're the ones that go home every day tired, because we ran our bodies out but we're only making minimum wage or maybe a little bit more. It's still not enough to live on, still not enough to feed our kids, still hardly enough to put gas in our car to get back and forth to work."

People like Precious Cole, who prepared food for strangers to eat, were those most likely to die of Covid-19. While the pandemic changed working conditions for nearly everyone, some were able to work safely from home; Cole and her coworkers, meanwhile, did not have that option, and it was their labor that allowed others to barricade themselves indoors. Black workers like Cole, along with other people of color, were even more likely to fall ill than white workers in the same position.[1]

When the first edition of this book went to press, we were in what we did not know would just be the early days of a pandemic that would be ongoing a year and a half later, as this edition went to press. Everywhere, governments were leaping to unprecedented action, expanding unemployment benefits, subsidizing employers, even sending out checks to every citizen. Employers were offering $2 an hour "hazard" or, more bombastically, "heroes" pay to those, like Cole, who were still reporting to work. But as the pandemic stretched on past the first couple of months, the extra pay began to be yanked back, and the workers formerly lauded as heroes were admonished to get back into the workplace. Governors across the US began to cut unemployment benefits, even refusing to take the expanded federal funding that had been provided by the Biden administration. And Covid protections were being cut back long before a level of vaccination that could approximate the much-discussed "herd immunity" had been reached, even in the world's richest countries.[2]

The pandemic, I noted even in those early days, had peeled back the veil draped over work to hide its coercive core. Even as the world sank into a nightmare, most people were expected to keep working as normal. The sheer horror of this worldview occasionally spilled from the mouth of some overeager politician; Texas's Lieutenant Governor Dan Patrick suggested that "lots of grandparents" would be willing to risk death to keep the economy going. He later doubled down, saying, "There are more important things than living." Keeping up the fantastic accumulation of wealth for a very few—America's billionaires pocketed some $1.2 trillion between January 2020 and April 2021, and Britain added twenty-four new billionaires during the pandemic—was, apparently, more important than breathing. Of course, the Lieutenant Governor wasn't on the front lines doing dangerous service work alongside Precious Cole, and therefore didn't personally face the choice: would he, a grandfather of five himself, really have risked his life to keep the economy going?

The burden of the pandemic would be borne not by elected officials or fast food magnates or Amazon executives. Rather, it would be borne by people like Ann Marie Reinhart, whose story I was lucky to hear in 2020. You will meet her in these pages, and I tried to capture the twinkle in her eye when she told a joke and the way she choked up remembering the way her customers at Toys "R" Us sometimes mistreated her and her coworkers. Reinhart invited me into her home and told me her story of battling alongside other Toys "R" Us workers abandoned by the company when it was driven into bankruptcy; she shared tales from her decades in retail, where she was still working in 2021 as the economy began to reopen. She died on February 17, 2021, of Covid-19. She was 61.

I joined a Zoom memorial for her, hosted by the labor organization United for Respect. The numerous video chats brought on by the pandemic were never more hollow and haunting than when we used the technology to hold the funerals we couldn't have in person. But that day Reinhart's family—her husband and sons—and her lifelong friends got to meet the people who knew her through her labor activism, and share stories of her humor, her warmth, and her fierceness. She was one of over six hundred thousand people to die in America of Covid, and like all of them, she deserved so much better. When you read her story in the pages to come, remember that there are so many like her, people who were treated as expendable in the service of reopening the economy, and that they had full, valuable lives that should not have been sacrificed in order to make someone else rich.

It is not surprising that, surrounded by all of this horror, people are rethinking their relationship to the workplace. Now that our bosses have, in so many cases, shown us that there is no level of catastrophe that will alleviate the demand for productivity, is it any wonder that "nobody wants to work anymore"?

One writer called it the "Great Resignation," noting that the quit rate in March of 2021 was higher than it had been in that month for twenty years. A report from the job search site Monster.com found that 95 percent of workers were considering changing jobs, and 92 percent even considering changing industries. Another survey found that 63 percent of respondents valued working from home two or three days a week as much as they would a raise. Many who weren't immediately quitting decidedly preferred working from home. A US survey found that just 21 percent of white workers wanted to return to the office full time, and a minuscule 3 percent of Black workers did. Yet working from home can be its own burden, as workers shoulder the costs of doing business and are isolated from the coworkers with whom they could challenge the boss, collectively. British employers complained of "the worst staff shortages since the late 1990s," and data found that Londoners were spending more time in the park and less time in the office—visitors to parks were at prepandemic levels, but central London saw only about 30 percent of its normal worker traffic.[3]

And in China, slacking off reached social-movement status as young people embraced "lying flat." Luo Huazhong, a former factory worker, quit his job five years ago and embraced a lifestyle of doing as little work as possible. His blog post manifesto, titled "Lying Flat Is Justice," was taken down by censors but embraced by millennials, and in the summer of 2021, reached trend piece status in US media outlets. Xiang Biao, a professor of social anthropology at Oxford University, told the *New York Times*, "Young people feel a kind of pressure that they cannot explain and they feel that promises were broken. People realize that material betterment is no longer the single most important source of meaning in life." And to Luo, a "slow lifestyle" was his right. "Do we have to work twelve hours a day in a sweatshop, and is that justice?"[4]

Like Luo, so many people already felt their relationship with work was toxic before the pandemic, and the upheaval of the moment provided the catalyst for change. And yet the results of that changed relationship are still to be decided. Simply changing jobs isn't enough for many people, who are organizing to demand political change that would allow everyone more freedom from work. In Iceland, prepandemic trials of a four-day, thirty-five- or thirty-six-hour work week, down from forty hours over five days were deemed an "overwhelming success." The experiment took place across a range of workplaces, from preschools to offices to hospitals and social service providers. In the UK, following the publication of a study on the Iceland experiment, 64 percent of those polled by Survation said they'd support a government-backed trial of a four-day work week. Support in the US and UK for a universal basic income also increased during the pandemic—one study found that 71 percent of Europeans now backed the idea, and of course in the US the stimulus checks sent to all were wildly popular under Presidents Trump and Biden. Biden's expansion of the child tax benefit into a monthly payment was also hailed by some as a reversal of the harshness of 90s-era welfare reform and a recognition that childcare is in fact work. In Germany, millions of people applied for a basic income trial study that would give participants a monthly income of €1,200 ($1,423). The Welsh government was holding a twenty-four-month trial where five thousand residents would get an income of £213.59 per week for working-age adults (slightly less for children and the elderly). Austria, on the other hand, launched a pilot job guarantee program.[5]

Big changes in the workplace (and the home office), in other words, might indeed be forthcoming. But what will ultimately decide the future of work are the struggles waged by working people, ourselves. Many of those struggles are detailed in the book in front of you; many more of them are still ongoing.

My first reporting trip after my second vaccine shot was to central Massachusetts, to the city of Worcester, where nurses at St. Vincent Hospital, owned by the Texas-based Tenet Healthcare corporation, a for-profit entity, had been on strike for fifty-five days. (As I write this, they're now on day 120 of the strike, the longest such strike in the US in at least a decade.) The nurses I met told me of inadequate protective equipment, pervasive understaffing, constant disrespect. Despite worsening conditions, they'd worked through two waves of Covid. "It's a community hospital," nurse Marlena Pellegrino, called "Mother Marlena" by her colleagues, told me. "We have always had a very high standard of care. To be a nurse at St. Vincent Hospital, it's not just a job."[6]

But they'd finally reached a breaking point, and the issue that drove them to the picket lines during a Northeastern winter, masked and swathed in layers to keep warm, was staffing levels. The hospital, nurse Marie Ritacco explained, had received almost $3 billion from the federal government's Covid emergency funds, yet the union had spent its own money buying masks and other protective gear for the nurses. And yet, Ritacco said, on the very day the nurses took their strike vote, the hospital announced that they had made over $414 million in profit in the previous year.

"Now we've worked through a pandemic, we're exhausted, we've seen patients die, they feel we're probably vulnerable," Pellegrino said. "I think they saw an avenue to exploit and make more money off the pandemic and off of nurses who they felt probably were weakened. I think that they really underestimated the strength of nurses, their character. Because we are a compassionate profession, I think they construed that as weakness."

But the nurses at St. Vincent were holding firm as this edition went to press, and they echoed something that I had heard over and over again while writing this book, and heard even more in the months since it first hit shelves. Pressed during ordinary times, then squeezed even more during a pandemic, they had had enough, and they were no longer willing to shoulder the burden in the workplace while their bosses walked away with even more money. They were going to demand better, for themselves, and for the people around them.

It is their determination to fight, and of millions of others around the world to join them, that will really determine the future of work.

INTRODUCTION

WELCOME TO THE WORKING WEEK

I LOVE MY WORK.

Technically, I don't have a job. I haven't had one in a few years, since I left the last magazine that hired me full-time for a one-year stint as a staff writer. Since then, I have supported myself as a freelance journalist, to varying degrees of success. I travel, I report, I give the occasional talk, and mostly, I write. I meet fascinating people and get to share their stories with the world, and I actually, at least at the moment, make a living at it.

I also make about $15,000 less a year than the average woman my age with my level of education.[1]

I am the poster child for work in today's economy. I'm flexible, working on the fly from a laptop in coffee shops around the country and occasionally the world. I don't have an employer that pays for my health insurance, and forget about retirement benefits. Vacation? What's that? I have none of the things that used to signify a stable adult life—no family, no property, just me and a dog. (On the upside, I don't have a boss, either.)

This book isn't about me, though. It is about the millions of people around the world who share some or even most of my working conditions, even if they've managed to snag a good old-fashioned full-time job. So many features of what people used to consider "employment security" are gone, melted into air. Instead, as a thousand articles and nearly as many books have told us over and over, we're all exhausted, burned out, overworked, underpaid, and have no work-life balance (or just no life).

At the same time, we've been told that work itself is supposed to bring us fulfillment, pleasure, meaning, even joy. We're supposed to work for the love of it, and how dare we ask questions about the way our work is making other people rich while we struggle to pay rent and barely see our friends.

Like so many things about late capitalism, the admonishment of a thousand inspirational social media posts to "do what you love and you'll never work a day in your life" has become folk wisdom, its truthiness presumably everlasting—stretching back to our caveperson ancestors, who I suppose *really enjoyed* all that mammoth hunting or whatever. Instead of "never working," the reality is that we work longer hours than ever, and we're expected to be available even when technically off the clock. All this creates stress, anxiety, and loneliness. The labor of love, in short, is a con.[2]

But the expectation that we will love our jobs isn't actually all that old. Once upon a time, it was assumed, to put it bluntly, that work sucked, and that people would avoid it if at all humanly possible. From the feudal system until about thirty or forty years ago, the ruling class tended to live off its wealth. The ancient Greeks had slaves and *banausoi*—a lower class of workers, including manual laborers, skilled artisans, and tradespeople—to do the work so that the upper classes could enjoy their leisure time and participate in community life. If you've ever read a Jane Austen novel and wondered how those people who don't seem to do much of anything (except hem and haw about whom to marry) got by, you get the general picture. Work, to the wealthy, was for someone else to do.[3]

Since the 1970s and 1980s, there has been a shift. The ownership class these days does tend to work, and indeed, to make a fetish of its long hours. But the real change has come in the lives of those of us who don't make millions. It's become especially important that we believe that the work itself is something to love. If we recalled why we work in the first place—to pay the bills—we might wonder why we're working so much for so little.[4]

People have long considered the question of whether work should be enjoyable. In the 1800s, socialist and artisan William Morris wrote of the three hopes that might make work worth doing—"hope of rest, hope of product, hope of pleasure in the work itself." Morris acknowledged that the idea of pleasurable work might seem strange to most of his readers, but argued that the inequality that capitalism had wrought meant that some who did no work lived off the labor of others, who were condemned by this system to "useless toil." Modern industry had taken away what little independence and power craftspeople might have had and reduced them to interchangeable, robotic wage laborers. No one cared whether the proletariat liked its work—it wasn't given a choice in the matter.[5]

But those proletarians, too, usually tried their hardest to escape work. The labor movement's earliest demands were usually for *less* work—shorter working hours, down to twelve, then eleven, then ten, then eight, plus days off. The strike, the workers' best weapon, is, after all, a refusal of work, and for a while they wielded it effectively, winning some concessions on the length of the working day and week as well as on wages. Capitalists would give up a little here and there to keep the profits flowing, but they also sought new strategies to keep workers on track beyond simple brute force.[6]

The carrot that was eventually offered to the industrial working class was what is often called the Fordist compromise, named, of course, after Henry Ford's Ford Motor Company. Workers would give up a large chunk of their time, but a manageable one—generally five eight-hour days of work a week—to the boss and in return they would get a decent paycheck, health care (either provided by the company, in the United States, or, in other countries, provided by the state), and maybe some paid holidays and a pension to retire on. It was Morris's "hope of rest"—and, if not actually the hope of controlling one's product, at least some financial remuneration—that provided workers with some ability to support themselves, and maybe a family, and to enjoy themselves in their time off the shop floor.[7]

This might be hard for some of us to imagine, now, as we sneak in time to read between checking work emails or waiting on call for the next shift. And it's certainly not something to romanticize—work was often both grinding and dull, and workers often too tired to enjoy their hard-won free time. But it allowed for a brief period of stability, from the end of the Great Depression until the 1960s, nostalgia for which still haunts us today.

Like most compromises, the Fordist bargain had left both sides vaguely unsatisfied, and it was held steady largely by repeated strikes from the workers on one side and repeated attempts by the bosses to unpick it on the other. But it was a deal that the ownership class had more or less gone along with when times were good and profits high enough that they didn't mind the sharing too much. It was less appealing when crisis struck in the 1970s. "By the 1970s, the dynamism the system had displayed in the immediate postwar decades was exhausted, worn down by multiple political challenges and institutional sclerosis," explained economist James Meadway. The solution to this problem, for capital, was to squeeze labor harder. Companies closed factories in high-wage countries and moved them to places where they could pay a fraction of the rates workers commanded in the United States or the United Kingdom. Working hours began to creep upward, and incomes down; more families relied on two incomes, and with two working parents, no one had time to do the housework.[8]

By 2016, the United States had hemorrhaged enough industrial jobs that Donald Trump made them a focus of his pitch to "Make America Great Again." In 2017, after he became president, I went to Indianapolis to visit the Carrier plant. The factory, which had been slated to shut down in 2016, had been a campaign focal point for Trump's promise to bring good jobs back. When he won, he returned to Carrier to declare "Mission

Accomplished," telling the workers that he'd cut a deal to keep their plant open. But when I arrived, the Rexnord plant around the corner was closing. Those workers didn't get a visit from the president as their jobs disappeared; nor did the workers in Lordstown, Ohio, where the General Motors plant closed in March 2019.

The workers I spoke to in Indiana and Ohio all wanted to keep the plants open, but none of them waxed lyrical about their jobs. They hadn't taken those positions to find fulfillment; they took them to find a paycheck. They took them for the weekends they'd have off, the homes they'd be able to buy. When I asked what they'd miss about their jobs, none of them said the work itself—they spoke of coworkers so close they'd become like family, of after-shift beers at the bar across the street, and of the solidarity that came from being active in their union (solidarity that brought them to the picket lines in GM's 2019 strike even after the plant had been closed for months). But mostly, they spoke of money, of the reality that losing a $26-an-hour job (plus overtime) meant a serious downgrade in their standard of living.

Looming outside the Carrier plant were Amazon and Target distribution centers, the likely future of work for some of the folks let go from their union jobs. The distribution center or warehouse job has become synonymous with misery these days: stories abound of workers having to urinate into bottles because they're not allowed enough restroom breaks, being tracked around the facility via GPS, or popping Advil like candy to deal with the aches and pains. Yet even Amazon, in denying the reports of hellish conditions written up by journalist Emily Guendelsberger, touts its "passionate employees, whose pride and commitment are what make the Amazon customer experience great."[9]

The global pandemic in 2020 just made the brutality of the workplace more visible. The amount of people employed in manufacturing worldwide has shrunk, but still the work is done, and more and more of it for pennies and without union protections. Women and children labor in deadly conditions in factories in places like Bangladesh, where the Rana Plaza garment factory collapse in 2013 killed 1,132 workers and injured more than 2,000 more. The day-to-day conditions of Bangladeshi garment workers—or, say, the workers who assemble iPhones at the Foxconn plant in China—range from tedious to backbreaking to deadly. Few seriously expect such workers to like their jobs, though they might face pressure to smile for the factory inspectors on the rare occasions they come around.[10]

Coal miners and factory workers have been described in many an article, laden with stereotypes, as Trump's base, layering a thick sheen of romance over what was and remains miserable work. George Orwell famously described the coal mines of Wigan, outside Manchester, England, as "like hell, or at any rate like my own mental picture of hell." GM workers at the Linden plant in New Jersey told sociologist Ruth Milkman that the place was "like prison"; at Lordstown, they called management "the little SS or the Gestapo." Chuckie Denison, recently retired from Lordstown, told me "on the plant floor, there was basically a war on the workers." Those jobs, Milkman explained, had been good because they had been union jobs, not because workers' actual day-to-day experience was anything other than "relentless and dehumanizing."[11]

That process of standardization and control was designed to reduce workers down to interchangeable cogs—so interchangeable that shutting down a factory in Indianapolis and opening it in Mexico or Bangladesh, where labor is cheaper, is easy. Or interchangeable enough to be replaced utterly by machines.

But the process of outsourcing or automating these jobs out of expensive locations like the United States and Western Europe has shifted the nature of work in those rich countries and resulted, strangely enough, in employers seeking out those very human traits that industrial capitalism had tried so hard to strip away. Those human traits—creativity, "people skills," caring—are what employers seek to exploit in the jobs we're supposed to love. Exercising them is what is supposed to make work less miserable, but instead it has helped work to worm its way deeper into every facet of our lives.[12]

The political project that brought us here is known as neoliberalism, though it sometimes goes by other names: post-Fordism, maybe, or just "late capitalism." As political philosopher Asad Haider explained, "neoliberalism . . . is really two quite specific things: first, a state-driven process of social, political, and economic restructuring that emerged in response to the crisis of postwar capitalism, and second, an ideology of generating market relations through social engineering." The success of the latter part of the project depended on twisting those desires for liberation articulated in the 1960s and 1970s, redefining "freedom" away from a positive concept (freedom *to* do things) and toward a negative one (freedom *from* interference). Neoliberalism encourages us to think that everything we want and need must be found with a price tag attached.[13]

Neoliberalism didn't just happen; it was a set of choices made by the winning side in a series of struggles. The victors remade the state to subject everything to competition; to enforce private property rights; and to protect the right of individuals to accumulate. Public services were sold off to private profiteers. Citizens became customers. Freedom was there, the neoliberals argued, you just had to purchase it.[14]

Neoliberalism was born in Chile in 1973, when Augusto Pinochet overthrew the democratic socialist Salvador Allende and, with the advice of American economists, reorganized the economy by force. That year also brought oil shocks and a global downturn, a collapse in asset values, and the beginnings of a crisis for capitalism—unemployment and inflation were both rising, and social movements were demanding change. In that context, Pinochet cleared the way for neoliberalism with brutality and torture, despite the claims of "freedom."[15]

Despite the violence at its heart, neoliberalism would spread from Chile with the support of democratically elected governments. Margaret Thatcher, who became prime minister in the United Kingdom in 1979, set out to crush unions and destroy the very idea of solidarity. She sold off public utilities and state-owned enterprises and turned public housing into private condos. To people who had little, Thatcherism offered the pleasures of cruelty, the negative solidarity of seeing others made even worse off than themselves by cuts to the welfare state. "Economics are the method: the object is to change the soul," Thatcher said.[16]

Thatcher is most famous, perhaps, for her declaration that "there is no alternative." She meant it as a preference—communism was still kicking at the time, and social democracy still had a grip on much of Europe. But

TINA was the foundation of the phenomenon the British theorist Mark Fisher called "capitalist realism"—the idea that it is impossible to imagine any other way that the world could be organized. Neoliberalism relies on such realism, even when—or perhaps especially when—it is faltering.[17]

In the United States, Federal Reserve chair Paul Volcker's "shock" in 1980, limiting the money supply and hiking interest rates, put tens of thousands of companies out of business. Cities like Youngstown, Ohio, saw more than one in five people out of work. Thatcher's buddy Ronald Reagan won office that year and followed her path, slashing tax rates and breaking the air-traffic controllers' union. The economic and political crisis of the 1970s had begun the process of deindustrialization, and Thatcher, Volcker, and Reagan stepped on the accelerator. Production was shut down in the rich countries and shipped elsewhere or automated. Autoworkers, used to calling strikes to halt production to make demands, were suddenly put in the position of calling for plants to be kept open. Joshua Clover, in his book *Riot, Strike, Riot*, called this "the affirmation trap": a situation where "labor is locked into the position of affirming its own exploitation under the guise of survival." It is a short step from the affirmation trap to the labor of love.[18]

The jobs that replaced the factory jobs were in retail, in health care, and in services and technology. We hear a lot about the knowledge economy, about the exciting creative work we could be doing, but we're all far more likely to be in some sort of service job. These jobs come with their own affirmation trap: you must show up with a smile on your face or be tossed out.[19]

The ideals of freedom and choice that neoliberalism claims to embrace function, paradoxically, as a mechanism for justifying inequality. The choice is yours, but so are the costs for choosing wrong. Cuts to the welfare state mean that those costs can be deadly. This kind of freedom, as political theorist Adam Kotsko wrote, is also a trap, an "apparatus for generating blameworthiness."[20]

This dynamic is always individualizing—your situation in life must be the result of choices that *you* made, and thus no one else has any reason to sympathize, let alone to help, if you fall. Privatization, as Fisher noted, has brought with it the privatization of stress, the proliferation of depression, and a rise in anxiety. If you cannot get a job, it must be because you failed to do enough (unpaid) work to acquire the correct skills; if you get that job and it makes you miserable, just get another! Such discourse justifies the constant job-hopping that provides companies with what they want: just-in-time labor, easily hired and fired, easily controlled.[21]

There's another famous Thatcherism for this process, usually paraphrased as "There is no such thing as society," though what she actually said was: ". . . who is society? There is no such thing! There are individual men and women and there are families." Without a society, with the lines between the family and the workplace blurring, with little time for a personal life anyway, we are even more likely to try to make work more pleasurable, even to seek in it a replacement for the love we lack elsewhere. Over and over again while reporting this book, I spoke to workers who told me that their bosses described the workplace as "like a family." One video-game company even brands itself a "fampany." If we fail to love our work, it becomes another form of individual shame. Love, after all, is supposed to be an unlimited resource that lives within us: If the workplace is a family, shouldn't we *naturally* love it?[22]

Turning our love away from other people and onto the workplace serves to undermine solidarity. Thatcher's statement that there was no such thing as society came after she had crushed labor unions, those vehicles not just of shop-floor action but off-the-clock sociality. If workers have a one-on-one love relationship with the job, then the solution for its failure to love you back is to move on or to try harder. It is not to organize with your coworkers to demand better. Collective action is unthinkable; the only answer is to work harder on yourself or to leave.[23]

Yet the coercion behind the mask of love is becoming more visible these days, and workers are beginning to act again. The popularity of the concept of "burnout"—for what is burnout but the feeling experienced when one's labor of love is anything but—reminds us of this. Repeated cycles of layoffs, steady low wages, and cutbacks to the private sector have made jobs harder and harder to love. The conditions under which "essential" workers had to report to the job during the coronavirus pandemic revealed the coercion at the heart of the labor relation. We are being punished for all the choices we have made even as we have continued to do what we are told—racking up student debt, working longer hours, answering work emails on our phones from parties, funerals, and bed, and doing more, always, with less.[24]

Neoliberalism relies on the labor of love ideology to cover up the coercion that was in fact required to push people into the workplace at the origin of capitalism. Yet these days the violence is more visible, and the rebellions—from Chile to Quebec to Chicago, and including climate strikes on every continent—are louder, too. Neoliberalism tried to sell us on freedom not from work but *through* work. But a glance at today's streets would seem to imply that we are no longer buying.[25]

The simple reality of work under capitalism is that the worker doesn't control much of anything on the job. That fact doesn't change if the job is more or less pleasant, or if wages increase by a dollar an hour or by ten dollars an hour. The concept of alienation isn't about your feelings; it's about whether you have the power to decide where and how hard you will work, and whether you will control the thing you make or the service you provide.[26]

Labor is required for value to be produced and capital accumulated, but that labor, as we've noted, is all too often likely to rebel against the process. Labor, after all, is *us*: messy, desiring, hungry, lonely, angry, frustrated human beings. We may be free to quit our jobs and find ones that we like better, as the mantra goes, but in practice that freedom is constrained by our need to eat, to have someplace to sleep, to have health care. Our place in the hierarchy of capitalist society is decided not by how hard we work but by any number of elements out of our control, including race, gender, and nationality. Work, as political theorist Kathi Weeks wrote, is a way that we are produced as social and political subjects.[27]

Work, in other words, helps to tell us how to be. And changes in the shape of the workplace, in the shape of capitalism itself, have changed our expectations for what our lives will be like, for where and how we will find fulfillment. The concept of a "good" job is one that has changed over time and through struggle, a point we would do well to remember.

THE IDEA THAT WORK SHOULD BE A SOURCE OF FULFILLMENT HAS BE-
come common sense in our world, to the extent that saying otherwise is
an act of rebellion. The Italian theorist Antonio Gramsci reminded us that
common sense itself is a product of history, that popular beliefs are in fact
material forces, and they change when material conditions change. His
concept of hegemony explains to us how one group comes to arrange the
world in its own interests, through culture and ideas as well as material
forces. Hegemony is the process by which we are made to consent to the
power structures that shape our lives.[28]

The thing about common sense is that it's often wrong. And we may
even be aware on some level that it's wrong. You are, after all, reading this
book because something told you that maybe, just maybe, the problem is
not you, it's work. But we don't have to truly believe in order to consent.
Many of us simply act as if we believe, and that is enough.[29]

Max Weber famously wrote of the *Protestant Ethic and the Spirit of
Capitalism*, the way that the rise of Protestantism lent a belief in hard
work as a calling and deferred gratification (in Heaven) to the developing
capitalism of the time. The first spirit of capitalism valued above all the
accumulation of more and more money for its own sake, not for the sake
of consumption. Consumption and other forms of pleasure were, in fact,
to be avoided. One worked to be *good*, not to be happy. This process may
have started with the church, but it had long since become common sense,
Weber wrote. "The Puritan wanted to work in a calling; we are forced to
do so."[30]

French scholars Luc Boltanski and Eve Chiapello have built on Weber to argue that the spirit of capitalism has changed over time, bringing
with it new versions of the work ethic. The spirit of capitalism of each age,
they wrote, must answer three questions: How will people secure a living
for themselves and their families? How do they find enthusiasm for the
process of accumulation, even if they are not going to pocket the profits?
And how can they justify the system and defend it against accusations of
injustice?[31]

Justification of capitalism is necessary because people do challenge it.
People look at its processes and see the inequality that has resulted. They

rebel: they strike, they riot, they refuse to go quietly to work. Those challenges then force crises and changes in the system, which has to adapt, to find new justifications, new mechanisms by which we will consent to keep working. Those struggles spill over from the workplace into the rest of our lives. Political philosopher Nancy Fraser calls them "boundary struggles," battles over the lines between economy and society, production and reproduction, work and family.[32]

In the shifts created by these struggles, new work ethics and new spirits of capitalism emerge. We know the spirit of the Fordist bargain—it's the one depicted in a thousand nostalgic stories, where workers like Chuckie Denison went to the factory and came home to a family and had weekends off, vacations, and decent benefits. That family could afford to buy nice things on one income: a worker in the factory would have a wife in the home who did the work of looking after the children and shopping for the things the family needed. This was the era of the family wage, the "organization man," the suburbs. Unlike the Protestant ethic, the industrial ethic promised at least some goods to workers now, rather than what the Industrial Workers of the World used to call "pie in the sky when you die." Work was a path to social mobility, but whether people enjoyed doing it was still beside the point.[33]

Something had to shift to get us from the industrial work ethic to today's labor-of-love ethic, where we're expected to enjoy work for its own sake. Today's ideal workers are cheery and "flexible," networked and net-savvy, creative and caring. They love their work but hop from job to job like serial monogamists; their hours stretch long and the line between the home and the workplace blurs. Security, the watchword of the industrial ethic, where workers spent a lifetime at one job and earned a pension on their way out the door, has been traded for fulfillment. And the things we used to keep for ourselves—indeed, the things the industrial workplace wanted to minimize—are suddenly in demand on the job, including our friendships, our feelings, and our love.[34]

Working people didn't just wake up one day and decide that this was how they wanted to be; the new work ethic was born from shifts in global capitalism. The spread of "globalization" meant that the unpleasant work could be shoved out of the rich countries into the poor ones, where labor was cheaper and governments easier to bully out of regulation. Boltanski and Chiapello argued that capitalism changed, too, in response to the struggles of its critics, the social movements of the 1960s and 1970s. They identified two critiques: the "artistic" critique, which challenged the conformity of midcentury capitalism, decrying its fundamental *boringness* as oppressive; and the "social" critique, which focused on the fundamental inequalities of capitalist life, the way a few have their needs catered to while so many others, as geographer Ruth Wilson Gilmore put it, face "organized abandonment."[35]

The social and artistic critiques mirror the two halves of the labor-of-love ethic: the caring and the creative work. Those halves together are the partial, inverted concessions to demands made by workers who rebelled against the factory and the social hierarchy, against the suburban bourgeois family and a world where everything was commodified. The movements of the 1960s had trouble integrating the two critiques: the demands simultaneously for more security and more autonomy. Into the cracks, capitalism was able to send tendrils that blossomed into a new spirit and a new shape of work.[36]

In the 1970s, demands for workers' control had sprung up across the industrialized world, from the Fiat factories in Italy to Lordstown, Ohio. In these workplaces the merging of the social and the artistic critique was most pronounced: workers, facing forty years breaking their bodies on an assembly line before retirement, struck back. Wildcat strikes were common in Lordstown in the early 1970s, where a diverse group of young workers rebelled against the very idea of work. They did not just demand more money, or even a share of the profits; they challenged the idea that anyone ought to spend their lives on an assembly line. But in the end, those workers wound up trading autonomy for security.[37]

On the flip side of the rebellion against the Fordist factory was the rebellion against the suburban home. Women kicked against what Betty Friedan famously dubbed the "feminine mystique" of the suburban housewife, and what many of them demanded was more fulfilling, waged work. As they began to earn enough to be economically self-sufficient, a husband looked less necessary—a shift in the family form itself, which was destabilized even as the workplace was.[38]

The difference between what the movements of the 1970s wanted and what they got was telling. They wanted democratic control over the firm; they got employee stock ownership plans. They wanted less work, a life less dominated by demands of the boss; they got fewer jobs and work fragmented into gigs. They wanted less hierarchical trade unions; they got union-busting. They wanted freedom for creative pursuits; they got, in Fisher's terms, "managerialism and shopping." They wanted to change their relationship to the patriarchal nuclear family; they got admonitions to see coworkers as family and the need to be constantly networking. They wanted more interesting work; they got simply more work. They wanted authentic human connection; they got demands to love their jobs.[39]

WE ARE NOW LIVING WITH THE CONSEQUENCES OF A HISTORIC LOSS FOR working people, a shift in the global order that splintered the working class, pitting workers against each other while power and wealth reconsolidated in the hands of a few staggeringly wealthy folks at the top. Our current common sense about work has the story backward. It is not a victory to have work demand our love along with our time, our brains, and our bodies. The wild fantasies of those movements of the 1960s and 1970s for freedom and plenty were subverted; nothing, as the feminist activist and scholar Silvia Federici wrote, "so effectively stifles our lives as the transformation into work of the activities and relations that satisfy our desires."[40]

With industrial jobs waning, more and more of us are falling into jobs that require some version of the labor-of-love ethic. In the United States, the fields adding the most jobs are nursing, food service, and home health care, all gendered jobs where the worker is expected to care for other people. These kinds of service positions draw on the skills presumed to come naturally to women; they are seen as extensions of the caring work they are expected to do for their families. High on the job-growth list, too, are computer programmers, who might earn higher salaries but are also expected to demonstrate passion for their work—though they show it through their long hours more than in outpourings of emotion. Their work is closer to the jobs of other creatives—entertainers, perhaps, or journalists like myself—rooted in our old notions of artistic work.[41]

If caring work is familial love, based in the all-sacrificing love of the mother, creative work is romantic love, based in a different kind of self-sacrifice and voluntary commitment that is expected, on some level, to love you back. Yet work never, ever loves you back.

The compulsion to be happy at work, in other words, is always a demand for emotional work from the worker. Work, after all, has no feelings. Capitalism cannot love. This new work ethic, in which work is expected to give us something like self-actualization, cannot help but fail. Most jobs will not make us happy, and even the ones that do will often be a source of deep frustration—I am writing these words, for example, at 8:00 p.m., eating microwaved soup from its plastic container, having now spent twelve hours in front of a computer screen, and I have it pretty good. We might have the best possible boss in the world, one who does genuinely care about us, but they will remain a boss, and financial concerns will come first for them.[42]

Capitalism shapes all of our lives—even under Fordism it reached well past the bounds of the workplace—and its disciplinary processes extend beyond what is necessary simply for extracting profits. Domination and subordination at work, as Kathi Weeks argued, are central to capitalism, and the workplace is where most people face the reality of how little freedom they have. As we look to the future, where debates over automation, a pandemic, and the climate crisis loom large, it is becoming increasingly clear that fewer of us than ever are needed to produce what is necessary for human flourishing. Our current world of work is helping to doom the Earth. Yet it remains nearly impossible to imagine a world where we have what we need whether or not we have jobs. Call it "workplace realism."[43]

How do we begin to break the love spell that work has us under? We might begin by understanding that love is a thing that happens between *people*. It is necessarily reciprocal, like solidarity. Love was once considered potentially subversive precisely because it encouraged people to value something other than work. No wonder the workplace had to absorb it. Work cannot offer it, but other people can. And it is precisely those bonds of solidarity that extend beyond the transactional relationships of the workplace that can help us break free.

Solidarity is another name for the bond between people that is forged in class struggle. Class is not a set of characteristics that inhere in certain people; it comes into existence, as historian E. P. Thompson wrote, "when some men, as a result of common experiences (inherited or shared), feel and articulate the identity of their interests as between themselves, and as against other men whose interests are different from (and usually opposed to) theirs." The irritants of class are felt often though not exclusively in the workplace, and it is often in the workplace that working people come to understand their power—or lack thereof.[44]

The working class is not a stable entity or a fixed category. It is, rather, a thing that changes as conditions change, as capitalism changes and produces new work ethics to match its demands. The process we call "class composition" occurs as the workers whose labor and lives have been organized by capitalism begin to understand themselves as a class and to act accordingly in their collective interests. We can see that process happening now, as workers who might have assumed themselves middle-class start to understand that their relationship to power means they're still workers. The video-game programmer might have more in common with the Uber driver than she previously thought.[45]

If the working class, broadly, consists of people who, when they go to work, are *not the boss*, who have little individual power to set the terms of their labor—even if, like an Uber driver or a freelance journalist, there's no one peering over their shoulder each moment—that is a huge swath of society.[46]

Today's working class is more diverse in race and gender than our image of the hard-hatted worker of the recent past, or even the "he" of Thompson's framing. Trump's trip to the Carrier plant, where he posed for a photo op with young Black women workers, reminds us that those women make up plenty of even what's left of the industrial workforce. The working class has never been all male or all white or all industrial, but, as historian Gabriel Winant noted, it is these days defined by "feminiza-tion, racial diversification, and increasing precarity: care work, immigrant work, low-wage work, and the gig economy." Working-class life is shaped as well by the world outside the workplace, where housing is harder to come by and education and health care more costly, where policing is harsher and care responsibilities double on top of the demands of the paid workplace, where immigration agents hound workers out of the country. Technology allows bosses to slice and dice schedules for retail workers, to demand that office staffers work from home at all hours, and to supervise app-based workers from a distance to squeeze more out of them. And one of the key things that many of these workers have in common is that they are whipsawed by the labor-of-love myth.[47]

The workers you will meet in this book have challenged the idea that their work should be provided solely out of love and draw our atten-tion to a key concept that is too often forgotten or misused: the idea of exploitation.

Exploitation is not merely extra-bad work, or a job you particularly dislike. These are the delusions foisted on us by the labor-of-love myth. Exploitation is wage labor under capitalism, where the work you put in produces more value than the wages you are paid are worth. Exploitation is the process by which someone else profits from your labor. This is true whether you're a nanny making $10 an hour, allowing your employer to make much more money at her higher-paid job, or a programmer at Goo-gle making $200,000 a year while Google rakes in over $7 billion. The labor of love is just the latest way that this exploitation is masked. But increasingly, workers are stripping away that mask.[48]

In these pages, you will meet many of the new laborers of love. They are video-game programmers and high school history teachers, artists and Toys "R" Us employees. They have organized collective spaces, national campaigns, and unions; lobbied for legislation; and gone on strike to de-mand better treatment *as workers*. Through their stories, we will trace the way the labor-of-love ethic has expanded, moving outward from narrow parts of the working world to encompass more and more of the jobs avail-able in today's workplaces in our postindustrial nations.

In Part One, we will follow the labor of love as it moves from women's unpaid work in the home through paid domestic work, teaching, retail work, and the nonprofit sector. Other forms of work that could just as easily have gone into this section include nursing, grocery store work, restaurant work, and call center jobs. It is worth noting that much of this work is the "essential" or "key" work of the coronavirus pandemic: these workers are the people expected to risk their lives to keep going to work in order for the rest of us to survive. In these jobs workers are expected to provide service with a smile or genuine, heartfelt care; they are expected to put themselves second to the feelings and needs of their customers or charges.

In the second half of the book, we'll move to the other half of the story. We'll see how our myth of the starving, devoted artist has leapt from art workers to unpaid interns, precarious academics, computer programmers, and even professional athletes. We could also add TV producers and actors, illustrators, musicians, and writers to that list—these are workers who are expected to find the work itself rewarding, as a place to express their own unique selves, their particular genius. In these jobs, we're likely to be told that we should be grateful to be able to work in the field at all, as there are hundreds of people who wish they had the opportunity to do jobs half as cool.

These workers have pushed back against the idea that their work should be provided solely out of love, though many of them still do genuinely enjoy their work. They have discovered the pleasures that are to be found in rebellion, in collective action, in solidarity, in standing shoulder to shoulder on the picket line, in carving out spaces and times to be with other working people and to change the conditions of their labor. They have laid claim to their time and their hearts and minds outside of the workplace.

I invite you to join them.

PART ONE

WHAT WE MIGHT CALL LOVE

CHAPTER 1

NUCLEAR FALLOUT
The Family

Rᴀʏ Mᴀʟᴏɴᴇ ꜰᴏᴜɴᴅ ᴏᴜᴛ sʜᴇ ᴡᴀs ᴘʀᴇɢɴᴀɴᴛ ᴡʜɪʟᴇ sʜᴇ ᴡᴀs ᴡᴏʀᴋɪɴɢ on her first musical theater project.

She was in her late twenties at the time, living in London, and finding her political voice. "It was 2014, like six days before I found out I was pregnant," she said, when she saw an ad to apply to perform at a feminist arts festival. It was in the days before Brexit, when the UK Independence Party (UKIP) was in the news agitating against immigration and the European Union. "UKIP seemed like such a joke, and [its leaders] were constantly saying such ridiculous things," Malone said. Their obsession with traditional gender roles convinced her to design a UKIP swing dance performance, so she joined forces with another theater-maker who was planning a UKIP-themed cabaret.

It had been a shock to discover her pregnancy. "It was quite violent," she explained. "They thought I had an ectopic pregnancy because I was in so much pain. I had a cyst that turned out to be the size of an orange." She also learned she had endometriosis, and with that discovery came the realization that this pregnancy might be her only chance to have the child she knew she wanted.

Malone is a slight woman, pale and petite, with artist's hands that are usually moving, occupied—embroidering, gesturing. She lights up when she's telling a story, and you can see the charisma she'd project onstage.

She danced through her pregnancy, in a big wig and exaggerated feminine silhouette, embodying and mocking all the stereotypes of womanhood she'd lived with all her life. "My daughter is really musical—that's why," she laughed. It was her first political theater project, and she worked alongside activist groups, adding numbers to go along with outrageous things that politicians said. "There was a UKIP councilor that said that floods were caused by gay people, so we had a troupe of gay men singing, 'It's Raining Men.'" They took the cabaret to the hometown of Nigel Farage, UKIP's founder and public face, and tried to conga into the pub across the street one night when he turned up there. They were chased off. But Farage came out to confront them—and then told the press he'd been harassed by leftists chasing his children. Farage was in the *Daily Mail* "calling us scum," Malone said.[1]

Back in London after the event, the performers gathered to hold a debrief, and the white nationalist group Britain First turned up and attempted to intimidate them. "I remember thinking, 'Don't get stressed out because it would be really bad for the baby,'" she said. "The Britain First people were like, 'We're going to teach you to scare people's kids!' 'You're the lefty witch who is chasing good children,'" she said. But her friends shouted back, "There's a pregnant woman in here!" "We were like, 'No, I'm the good woman.'"

"This has been my journey of being a mother," she said. She felt haunted by these tropes: good mother, bad mother. She'd worried about being a single parent because of her own upbringing in what she described as "quite a patriarchal family, really." She struggled too with the presumption that working-class women have children solely in order to get benefits.

Malone was born in North Wales; she's the youngest of six children by several years. By the time she came along, her parents were more economically secure than they'd been early on, though they described themselves, she said, as working class. Her father was an English teacher and a climbing instructor; her mother had left school young and taken an arts job. "We're all quite creative, and I think we all get it from my mom working in this art shop when she was sixteen," she said. Her father, too, had a creative influence—the poet John Cooper Clarke credited her father's teaching with inspiring him to write. John Malone would tell his students, "Write like the greats, but write about what you know"—a line Malone has taken to heart in her own art practice.

Being an artist, she noted, is insecure work. She asked herself, "Am I kidding myself to think I could raise a child by doing this? You can feed yourself beans on bread for a week, but you can't have an undernourished child because you want a career in the arts."

The father of her baby was someone she'd been close to for a while—they'd run a theater company together—and so they decided to try co-parenting, but their relationship didn't last. Realizing she would need more support once the baby arrived, and looking at London rents, in her eighth month of pregnancy she decided to move to Sheffield to be near her sister.

Her sister helped support her, bringing her food parcels; in turn, Malone helped with her sister's kids. "You are so vulnerable when you've just had a child," she noted. "You see a health visitor once in a while that asks, 'Are you all right? Is your baby sleeping through the night?' They are not going to ask, 'How have you coped moving two hundred miles away from where you know anybody, with a young child, and when you don't know what you're doing for the rest of your life?'" The political situation didn't help. The United Kingdom had become incredibly polarized around Brexit. She missed the community of the cabaret.

Just before her daughter Nola's first birthday, a friend from the theater called with an offer to do a show in Greece. Malone directed a performance of Shakespeare's *The Tempest* for an all-women theater company on the island of Lesbos with Nola on her hip. It was idyllic: "I was surrounded by this big group of women who would look after my daughter all the time, I was directing theater in the sunshine."

But at the end of the show, she and Nola returned to a cottage in "pretty much the middle of nowhere." Manchester was a twenty-minute train ride away, but getting there with a small child was difficult. "It was really isolating." The cottage was free and she was out of work, but being completely alone was getting to her. "Not everybody has a child in the 'right' way," she noted, with a partner and a mortgage. "Being an artist, you often feel that your occupation is a luxury and your whole identity, then, feels like you are playacting being something." She'd studied theater through graduate school, and didn't want to give it up after all that investment. But, she noted, "it is a big question for lots of actors: How long do you keep going with it?" She'd worked in Russia, briefly, years earlier, as a governess for a wealthy family, and seeing that wealth had given her more resolve to want to continue making art. "There are less and less working-class voices in the art world," she said.

So when the chance came to do *The Tempest* again, this time in London, she was thrilled. Nola could be closer to her father, and Malone could get paid to do theater. At first, though, making ends meet in London was nearly impossible. "I lived in a shared house for a while that turned out to be a nightmare, living in a bedsit type of situation with a two-year-old." From there, she wound up essentially homeless, hopping from house-sitting gig to house-sitting gig. "It was really, really stressful," she said. "We don't know where we're going to be. We've got no money. We're on our own."

She was living on Universal Credit, the United Kingdom's new benefits system, while taking on occasional gigs—"any old job"—and getting some support from her daughter's father. Living close to him, though, means being "a very poor person living in a very wealthy pocket of London." Receiving Universal Credit comes with stigma—especially, she noted, in that wealthy area—and people don't consider raising a daughter to be work. "I tried to get my daughter into a different nursery," Malone said. "They were like, 'Oh, you have to pay £150 a month.'" The woman at the nursery asked more questions about money, and Malone explained that she was on Universal Credit but her ex was a teacher. "The woman on the phone at the nursery was like, 'We do find that people are rewarded if they work.' It was like a knife in the stomach, like, 'You're not a proper member of society.'"

When she was house-hopping, Malone said, the local council offered to rehouse her in Birmingham. With the housing benefit capped below market rental rates, for many people the only option is to leave London— but in London, Malone has the support of her former partner. "We waste so much money in rent," she said. "I have to think, 'God, what else could that be spent on? Could my daughter have music lessons? Could we have a holiday if we weren't spending so much money on rent?'"

Searching for a full-time job, though, presented even more problems. To keep receiving Universal Credit, she had to make periodic visits to the job center, and the program's requirements get stricter as your child grows older. By the time Nola was three, Malone was expected to be looking for full-time work and required to turn up at the job center regularly for meetings with a "work coach." But child care, even with Nola in school, is hard to come by, and it made her question whether it was worth it to get a job. The stress that parents are under, she noted, is constant. "Women are having their kids taken off them because of a variety of stresses that they are under because of poverty, because of austerity, because the situation that we're in is awful. I'm somebody with a postgraduate education that has still found a huge amount of struggle. It is a really difficult thing to talk about. You don't want to seem like a bad mother."[2]

LOVE IS WOMEN'S WORK. THIS IS THE LESSON YOUNG GIRLS ARE TAUGHT from the time they are born; girl babies are dressed in pink, the color of Valentine's Day. As they grow up they are encouraged in a thousand tiny ways to pay close attention to the needs of the people around them, to smile and to be pleasing to the eye. Gender roles are reinforced first and foremost in the family, and the family, even in this supposedly postfeminist era, revolves around the unpaid work of taking care of others. Failure to do that work properly, as Ray Malone said, results in the charge of "bad mother," which often just translates to "bad woman."[3]

The labor of love begins, then, in the home. We are still told that the work of cleaning and cooking, of nursing wounds, of teaching children to walk and talk and read and reason, of soothing hurt feelings and smoothing over little crises, comes naturally to women. These things are assumed not to be skills, not to be learned, as other skills are, through practice. And this assumption has crept from the home into the workplaces of millions of people—not all of them women—and has left them underpaid, overstretched, and devalued. Our willingness to accede that women's work is love, and that love is its own reward, not to be sullied with money, creates profits for capital.

None of this is natural. The family itself was and is a social, economic, and political institution. It developed alongside other such institutions— capitalism and the state—and, like them, developed as a mechanism of controlling and directing labor, in this case, the labor of women. As historian Stephanie Coontz wrote, to mourn the decline of the two-heterosexual-parent nuclear family is to be nostalgic for "the way we never were," for a situation that never included everyone and by which few were well served. It is to lament the crumbling of an edifice designed to keep women's labor cheap or free.[4]

The work ethic and the family ethic developed together and they are still intertwined. When we hear of "work-life balance," it is all too often in stories of women trying to find time outside of the office to spend with their families. The family, in other words, is presented as being in competition with the demands of capitalism. But theorists as far back as Karl Marx and Friedrich Engels have pointed out that the family as we know it actually serves to smooth the functioning of capitalism: it reproduces workers, without whom capitalism can't function. This is why we call all of that caring, cooking, and soothing, along with the literal process of bearing children, "reproductive labor." If the family is in crisis, it is because capitalism is in crisis—and if we can see the cracks now, it is because the stories we have been told about these institutions have ceased to paper over reality.[5]

There is nothing natural about a two-parent, two-point-five-child picket-fence household, any more than there is anything natural about the car that carts it around. It is a creation of history, a history that involves plenty of violence and struggle as well as what we think of as evolution. The one "natural" fact of reproduction, Coontz and anthropologist Peta Henderson wrote, is that the people we came to think of as women were "society's source of new members." A division of reproductive labor, though, did not automatically mean that one type of labor would end up paid, valorized, and mythologized while the other was devalued and presumed not to be work at all.[6]

Scholars disagree on the exact causes of male dominance, or what we might call patriarchy. But they have given us clues as to how we ended up in a world where women still do most of the unpaid labor. As early humans began to produce more than they could consume, individually or as a group, they began to exchange products with other groups, as well as to exchange members, in some version of what we now call marriage. As those products became private property, to be handed down through the family line, control of reproduction—as well as the other labors women were expected to perform—became more important to men. Women were not simply oppressed, in other words, but *exploited.*[7]

This exploitation, the subordination of women's work, was accomplished in part through violence but upheld through ideology. As the institution matured, the "family" shrank down to something like what we think of now as the nuclear family. By the time of ancient Greece, the household was central, and women's place had been established as in the home.[8]

That doesn't mean that work and the family looked in Plato's Athens the way they did in 1950s America. For one thing, Athenian prosperity was based in the labor done by slaves, not white men working union jobs. But the subordination of women and the diminishing of the value of their work was firmly established at the birth of the state as an institution, long before the advent of capitalism.[9]

With capitalism, though, came a whole new set of practices for dividing and controlling household work. The division between "home" and "workplace" didn't exist in feudal Europe in the way it began to exist under capitalism. In early medieval cities, women worked as doctors, butchers, teachers, retailers, and smiths. They had gained a degree of freedom. In precapitalist Europe, Silvia Federici wrote, "women's subordination to men had been tempered by the fact that they had access to the commons and other communal assets." Under capitalism, though, "*women themselves became the commons*, as their work was defined as a natural resource, laying outside the sphere of market relations."[10]

This rearranging of reproductive labor was ushered in with blood. Specifically, the bloodshed that birthed modern domestic relations came through witch-hunts. Women were deprived of rights they'd previously held, of access to wages, and allowed neither to gather in groups nor to live alone. The only safe place for a woman to be was attached to a man. Although women who refused to marry, women who owned a little property, and particularly midwives, healers, and other women who exercised some control over reproduction, and who may have carried out abortions, were especial targets of the witch-hunts, the terror worked precisely because nearly anyone could be accused. This terror helped create the thing we now think of as gender.[11]

The witch-hunts not only served to force women off the common land being enclosed and back into the home. They also reminded entire populations what might happen if they refused to work. Eliminating popular belief in magic, Federici wrote, was central to the creation of the capitalist work ethic: magic was "an illicit form of power and an instrument to *obtain what one wanted without work*, that is, a refusal of work in action." The discipline (and at times torture) of the body during the witch-hunts helped lay the ground for the discipline of the body by the boss during the workday, not only the discipline of the time-clock but also of sore muscles, tired joints, and worn-out minds that it now became a woman's job to soothe.[12]

Thus the dichotomy between "home" and "work" was created, and along with it so many other binary oppositions that continue to shape our assumptions about the world: "mind" and "body," "technology" and "nature," and, of course, "man" and "woman." This, too, was the period when the concept of race as we know it began to take shape—along with the designation of certain races as natural slaves, and of societies penalizing nonreproductive forms of sex. At the end of this period of up-heaval, women were not simply firmly ensconced in the home, unwaged and rightsless, but the history of violence that had created that situation was simply wiped away. "Women's labor began to appear as a natural re-source," Federici wrote, "available to all, no less than the air we breathe or the water we drink." Even women's sexuality, she argued, had been trans-formed into work. Jason W. Moore and Raj Patel, in their book *A History of the World in Seven Cheap Things*, referred to this period as the "Great Domestication."[13]

This, then, is the beginning of the double bind that mothers like Ray Malone are still trapped in: the work of parenting is not considered im-portant enough to pay for, yet if you demonstrate that you have other priorities beyond the home, you'll be castigated as a bad mother. The lines have always been permeable and shifting, but that has only made stigma harder to evade.

Even with these divisions now firmly in place, capitalists were happy to send plenty of women and children to work in the mills and mines alongside or in place of the men—a preference for nimble little fingers could be expressed with no sense of shame, and these workers could be paid less than men. In the early days of wage labor, there was no pretense that such work was enjoyable: the choice was to do it or starve. When misery was known to be the condition of the wage worker, people would do nearly anything to avoid such labor, so bosses—and the state—had to ensure that people's lives without waged work would be even more miser-able than with it.[14]

From this necessity arose the tradition of poor relief that still shapes social welfare policy today. The working classes rebelled frequently: Lud-dite machine-breaking, early forms of trade unionism, and riots roiled early capitalist England. And while nonproductive activities were met with harsh punishments—begging could be punished by "public whip-ping till the blood ran"—the authorities also acceded to pressure to create a sort of safety valve in the form of poor relief. But the English Poor Laws were designed to serve the bosses. Relief payments were low enough and punishing enough that any job at all was preferable to being on the dole;

often one had to live and labor in a workhouse in exchange for the scraps of relief on offer. In this way, the work ethic was reinforced by the state under the guise of magnanimity, the idea that one should be grateful for a job inculcated. The Poor Laws live on today in Universal Credit's punitive structures—the same punitive structures that Ray Malone faced.[15]

The Poor Laws also enforced the idea of family responsibility—that relatives had a duty to and should be compelled to support their relations before public monies would be handed out. Later versions of relief were instituted specifically for people with disabilities and, importantly, for widows and mothers—for people excluded from the work relationship on account of ability or gender. The family ethic and the work ethic were thus shaped by the state in parallel.[16]

Capitalism continued its march throughout the world, bringing with it the family, often at the tip of the sword. In the colonies and then the new United States, for example, Native people's ways of living were reorganized, violently, by the colonizers into something they recognized as a family, with land formerly owned in common turned into inheritable private property. Even as the family was imposed from without, though, its existence was described as natural, inevitable, a way of living and working that benefited all.[17]

⣿

TODAY'S LABOR-OF-LOVE MYTH REQUIRED NOT JUST THE GLOSSING OVER of the brutality of the family and the workplace, but the addition of a romantic sheen. Marriage, for its first few centuries, had little to do with love. As that changed, the ideal of marriage-for-love brought with it its own mystifications of work.

If marriage was done out of love, after all, then the labors subsumed into it must also be done for love. Marriage and housework alike, in this way, become things that women, in particular, are expected to find fulfilling and self-actualizing. Centuries' worth of popular entertainment, from the novels of Jane Austen to the Oscar-winning 2019 film *Marriage Story*, take love and marriage as their narrative material, and mommy blogs and lifestyle Instagrammers, as journalist Kelli María Korducki wrote, still uphold signifiers of romance that date back to the post-Enlightenment era. These signifiers were popularized through the new women's magazines and novels depicting women's separate sphere as a space of pleasure, not of work.[18]

The family as romantic escape from the burdens of work was a bourgeois ideal that trickled downward; like most such gifts, it was anything but. The middle classes were able to marry for love rather than simply for money; the white middle-class housewife could hire help to do the hard physical labor of housework, thus devoting herself to the romanticized emotional work. But working-class women still had to do it all.[19]

There is also real love in a family, which is precisely what makes it and its surrounding ideologies so sticky. As Angela Davis observed in *Women and Capitalism*, the family fulfills very real human needs, needs "which cease to demand at least minimal fulfillment only when human beings have long since ceased to be human. In capitalist society, the woman has the special mission of being both reservoir and receptacle for a whole range of human emotions otherwise banished from society."[20]

The emotional support, care, sexual expression, and real love that exist within families are not figments of our imagination, nor false consciousness, yet they are also shaped by a regime that exists to produce profits rather than human fulfillment. As bell hooks wrote, it has been the job of the wife "to produce this love by herself in the factory of the home and offer it to the man when he returned." The family absorbs the violent anger that a male worker cannot safely vent at his boss; at other times, it teaches real emotional connection that, as theorist and organizer Selma James noted, is the same skill that is necessary to build movements for change.[21]

Sexuality is valorized by capitalist society primarily within marriage, where it is presumably producing children who will grow up to be new workers. At the same time, the weight placed on the family under capitalism ensures that heterosexual love is incredibly difficult to maintain—that even as more expectations are placed on it, as the couple's relationships with other people outside of their marriage thin and fade, marriage threatens to collapse on itself. The pressure, James wrote, makes marriage such a hostile environment that "what's astonishing is that men and women even talk to each other, let alone live together and even love each other."[22]

Marriage is an institution constantly shifting, absorbing the critiques thrown at it and the needs placed on it by societies, embedded in a set of historical power relations. It has proved incredibly difficult to strip away the old "separate spheres" ideology holding that the home is women's domain, the workplace that of men. But this idealized way of living has never been universal.[23]

If the nuclear family—and society, which, as Engels wrote, "is a mass composed of . . . individual families as its molecules"—is a recent development, it was even more recently that the working classes were able to live this way, with a man working outside the home and a woman, unwaged, within it. This shift meant that even more people were subject to the pressures of which Ray Malone spoke—of being held to an ideal of feminine perfection, often with little support.[24]

Up until and into the twentieth century, working-class women worked in factories and mills; they took in laundry and did piecework while cooking, cleaning, and caring for children. The term "housewife" used to connote this sort of woman, who was both earning cash income and oriented toward the home; the term "homemaker" arose around 1890 to denote a wife who "was fully immersed in domestic activities." This new definition came along with new expectations—that the home not only be a place to eat and sleep but a place that was the opposite of work, where the homemaker saw to every comfort for her husband and children. Whether her comfort was seen to was a question she wasn't supposed to ask. In this way, changes in the structures of work produced changes in our understanding of gender, of what it meant to be a woman.[25]

While at first, homemakers were for the well-off, eventually even wage laborers could aspire to have a full-time wife. Labor movements began to demand the so-called "family wage": a pay rate high enough that a male worker could support his wife and children. It was first implemented in Australia in 1896, with a law allowing the setting of minimum wage rates with the assumption that men needed a wage that allowed them to be the breadwinner for a family. Protective legislation, too, banning child labor and limiting women's working hours, began to be enacted around this time, giving workers some of their demands cloaked in the idea that women were too weak for the workplace—a surprise to the millworkers of Manchester or Lowell—and that their place was in the home.[26]

The family-wage ideal spread rapidly. While labor liked it as a way to raise pay, it also served to bolster gender roles within the family. Becoming a "provider" was a way for working-class men to take pride and power in the home that they didn't have on the assembly line; it allowed them to define their manliness against those who did not bring home a decent wage. And, particularly in the United States, that also meant, for white men, defining their masculinity against workers of color. Black workers in the United States first labored as slaves, their marriages and reproduction directly appropriated by the slaveholder. When they were emancipated, a new set of laws encouraged former slaves into "traditional" families. As historian Tera Hunter has noted, under the conditions of slavery, where blood kin or spouses could be sold off at any moment on the slaveholder's whim, African Americans "transformed the strict definition of kinship," understanding the family in a more expansive way. But institutions like the Freedmen's Bureau aimed to condition Black workers into the patriarchal family even as it was unlikely that Black men would be paid anything like a family-sustaining wage.[27]

It was in the wake of the New Deal and World War II, as labor laws finally put in place some protections for the right of workers to unionize, that the family wage—and with it, the white working-class family—became institutions. This was what was known as the Fordist compromise. Henry Ford himself was deeply invested in implementing his idea of the correct family. In order to get the "family" wage, employees had to qualify—and Ford had an entire department of investigators, called the Sociological Department, who would interrogate workers on the job and show up at their homes to ensure that wives were working hard too. "Full-time domesticity on the part of the wife was required," sociologist Andrew J. Cherlin wrote. "Anything less would run afoul of the investigators."[28]

The American New Deal order that made possible the family-wage ideal explicitly excluded certain workers—agricultural and domestic workers were left out of the protections of the Fair Labor Standards Act (FLSA) and the National Labor Relations Act (NLRA). This meant that most Black men and women were left out of the family wage system. The Fordist family wage not only served to normalize gender and the nuclear family; it also defined race and class by who was in and who was out of the public-private partnership that was the US welfare state.[29]

This period gave us the thing we think of as the "traditional" family: the suburban two-point-five-kid picket-fence white nuclear household, the June Cleaver mom at home making dinner in high heels and waiting for her husband to come home from his eight-hour day in his five-day workweek. Yet this period was not traditional in the slightest: it was a historical exception, created by a compromise between capital and labor that was never stable, but overseen by a state that saw stabilizing business as its prime goal. And it was nothing to romanticize—the jobs that paid a family wage were alienated and boring. Women alone had no access to the higher wages paid to men; domestic violence was considered a man's prerogative. Indeed, as many have pointed out, for men, violence in the home was a way both to demonstrate masculinity in a world where they had little control and to discipline the labor of their wives. The labor contract, like the marriage contract, presumed a legal equality between parties that hid immense actual inequalities of power between boss and worker, husband and wife. Masculinity and femininity themselves were shaped by these experiences of power and powerlessness.[30]

There has always been a tension hidden within this ideology: whether women were needed at home because their work in the home was indispensable, or whether women should stay home because they were simply too pure, too good, or too weak for the world of wage labor. Women were encouraged, in the twentieth century, to improve their domestic skills—learning from women's magazines or through the new home economics courses in schools. Even the question of whether women should be paid for housework was on the table in one way or another—feminists struggled for mother's pensions and pay, for family aid, and for what in 1946 became the

Family Allowance in the United Kingdom. Yet they were still reminded in a thousand ways that this work wasn't "real" work, not like what men did.[31]

It was in the attempts at building a socialist society, though, that the real challenges to the family came about. Utopian socialists argued for raising children communally rather than in nuclear families, and this idea, as anthropologist Kristen Ghodsee has observed, influenced those who took power in the Soviet Union and elsewhere. In the early USSR, Alexandra Kollontai was made people's commissar for social welfare; the only woman in the cabinet, she took special interest in policies that would give women equal rights. She argued that "maternity was to be appraised as a social function and therefore protected and provided for by the state." Domestic work would be socialized through public nurseries, kindergartens, laundries, and cafeterias; abortion was legalized in 1920. Rather than assuming that women's work would be subsidized by men's wages, the socialist state would provide services to all, freeing women from economic dependence on men.[32]

But socialist men weren't always comfortable with changes to the family structure; they, too, had been raised to believe that it was natural for women to work in the home. Kollontai struggled with her comrades to implement her ideas; in 1936 many of her successes were overturned as Stalin reinstated support for the patriarchal family. Still, state socialist and social democratic governments in Eastern and Western Europe outpaced the United States in terms of family policies, allowing for maternity leave and other supportive measures and even officially encouraging men to take on more of the housework.[33]

In most of the capitalist world, child-rearing was presumed to be a private responsibility, to be taken on in a couple or, if not, done at one's own risk. Even as women argued for the value of their work in the home, they came up against the myth of the labor of love. Their work, which they had studied for, and at which they labored for longer hours than their husbands did at their paid jobs, was supposed to be the most fulfilling thing a woman could do. But this work, supposedly freely provided out of love, was in fact coerced at all levels, from the state down to the individual, and plenty of women continued to point out that they didn't love the work, not at all.[34]

The suburban home, supposed to be the pinnacle of achievement for the new middle class, often felt more like a trap and a prison than anything else. Women were isolated in the home, which was also their workplace, constantly alone, surrounded by reminders of the work that was always left to do. This realization began to leak into the mainstream consciousness in the 1960s. The stay-at-home housewife had only been a widespread phenomenon for about a decade, but she was already over it.[35]

Betty Friedan's book *The Feminine Mystique* was a meteoric best-seller when it dropped in 1963. Friedan detailed the "problem that has no name" of women trapped in the home doing housework and sparked a feminist rebellion. Her concerns, though, seemed to be for educated women consigned to do work she thought beneath them and more suited to "feeble-minded girls." For those educated women, getting a job would be a form of liberation.[36]

Yet careers outside the home, the solution Friedan offered to the problem of housework's tedium, did not actually improve the lives of all women. While well-off women could hire help to do the work in the house while they went off to decently paid jobs, many working-class women had never been or had only recently become able to choose to stay home. The jobs that were on offer for them should they leave the house were often low-paid versions of what they were doing at home—preparing food and serving it, cleaning, or caring. Some women certainly entered the paid labor force as an alternative to housework, but the very idea that women were doing so to amuse themselves, rather than out of necessity, helped employers justify paying women less. Meanwhile, many more of those who took paid work did so out of real need.[37]

The new labor-of-love myth was bolstered by the idea that leaving the home to go to a job constituted empowerment. Even as the old story—that housework, and particularly mothering, was inherently satisfying—hung on, the new myth, of work-as-liberation, grew up around it. The clash between these two narratives fueled clashes between women.

The class divisions between women became fault lines for other clashes, particularly over abortion and so-called welfare reform. Abortion, which had been key to the witch-hunts and hovered in the background ever since, became an explosive political issue in the 1960s and 1970s. As women fought back against the position of homemaker, they demanded the power to choose to parent or not. The feminist writer and activist Shulamith Firestone, in *The Dialectic of Sex*, argued that eliminating "sexual classes" meant "the seizure of control of *reproduction*: not only the full restoration to women of ownership of their own bodies, but also their (temporary) seizure of control of human fertility."[38]

But even before Firestone's literary bomb landed, women were arguing that control over their fertility was essential to their ability to control their destinies. Abortion, wrote sociologist Kristin Luker, was a "symbolic linchpin" for an entire set of assumptions about women's roles and women's work. On one side of the debate were people who presumed that women should be seen not as potential mothers but as individual humans, capable of independent decisions and lives; on the other were women and men who thought that women's primary role was in the home. Some of the latter, particularly the women, feared that abortion rights would not only upend those roles but devalue women's role in reproduction. But that ground was already shifting, and it wasn't abortion that ended the brief idyll of the working-class family. It was ending because of changes in the global economy.[39]

Against a backdrop of shifting material conditions, the Supreme Court's 1973 *Roe v. Wade* decision was a momentous shift, and for some it was too much. After *Roe*, a new group of activists—most of them women in nuclear families who did not work outside the home—joined the antiabortion cause. Fearing that by devaluing the fetus, the Court had also devalued women, these women plunged into activism. Their options in the job market were limited, but their work in the home, guarding "tenderness, morality, caring, emotionality, and self-sacrifice," at least received lip service. "As I see it, we were on a pedestal, why should we go down to being equal?" one woman asked. They feared, Luker wrote, motherhood demoted from a sacred calling to just another job.[40]

Feminists bristled when conservatives accused them of being out to destroy the family, insisting that they just wanted to give people choices. Yet destabilizing the reproductive role, making motherhood optional, and marriage something one could change one's mind about, did in fact put the family on shaky ground. Radicals like Firestone considered that all to the good, but mainstream feminism was more likely to focus on women "having it all"—the job *and* the family. That is perhaps why many mainstream feminists failed to join the fight of another group of women who were challenging traditional roles: the welfare rights activists, whose struggle centered, as historian Premilla Nadasen wrote, on "the work ethic, faith in the market economy, compassion for the less fortunate, models of motherhood, mores about sexuality and reproductive rights."[41]

The welfare rights movement was a relatively small group of women with very little social power, yet they collectively managed nevertheless to win some control for themselves over their lives. They rejected both the family ethic and the work ethic to demand the right to parent as they saw fit, refusing the discipline of the Poor Law tradition that was baked into the roots of Aid to Families with Dependent Children (AFDC), the program commonly called "welfare" in the United States.[42]

The National Welfare Rights Organization (NWRO) was founded in 1966 as a coordinating body for local groups, some of which had already been in existence for years. Those groups used direct action, often sitting in in welfare offices, and agitating for an end to discriminatory policies. They combined this strategy with political organizing and a legal effort challenging the surveillance policies associated with AFDC. Though Black women were never a majority of the women on AFDC, they led the welfare rights movement; their presence on the welfare rolls had provoked handwringing from politicians—often the same ones who argued that white women belonged at home with their children. Welfare rights organizers, as Nadasen wrote, "adopted political positions based on a material understanding of the hierarchies of race, class, gender, and sexuality and the way in which these realities were intertwined and inseparable for all people."[43]

Black women had long been expected to work, first as slaves and then as low-wage workers. The welfare panic exposed the tension between these two beliefs: that women's "natural" place was home taking care of children, and that Black people were getting away with something if they stayed home to parent. Pushing Black women—and by extension other women—off of welfare meant pushing them into taking a job, any job, no matter how low paid. This was, as sociologists Frances Fox Piven and Richard Cloward wrote, another way of coercing labor.[44]

The welfare rights groups, though, argued that welfare mothers were already working—that what they did in the home was important work deserving of support, and that they shouldn't have to be married to get it. "If the government was smart it would start calling AFDC 'Day and Night Care,' create a new agency, pay us a decent wage for the service work we are doing now," one organizer said, "and say that the welfare crisis has been solved, because welfare mothers have been put to work." For a while, they succeeded—in the 1960s, AFDC rolls increased 107 percent as organizing brought more people to claim the benefits to which they were legally entitled. "NWRO buttons are well known at the welfare department," said another organizer. "Our members find that when they go down to the department with buttons on, they receive prompter and better service."[45]

The welfare rights organizers posed a sweeping challenge to American ideas about work and who did it, and about the family and who was in charge of it. Mothers for Adequate Welfare (MAW), according to one reporter, believed that marriage, with its "fixed rules and obligations," was a "means for domination more than a means for expressing love." MAW favored "responsibility toward other persons, and freedom to whatever extent that responsibility allows," instead of the traditional family. Johnnie Tillmon, director of the NWRO, wrote, in an article for *Ms.* magazine, "Welfare is like a super-sexist marriage. You trade in a man for the man. But you can't divorce him if he treats you bad. He can divorce you, of course, cut you off anytime he wants. But in that case, he keeps the kids, not you. The man runs everything. In ordinary marriage, sex is supposed to be for your husband. On A.F.D.C., you're not supposed to have any sex at all. You give up control of your own body."[46]

The women of the NWRO argued for a guaranteed minimum income rather than jobs programs, challenging the idea that one must go to a job in order to make a living. Milwaukee WRO organizer Loretta

Domencich, of Native descent, noted that guaranteed income was similar to the way things had been done before colonization: "The dignity of the individual says that no matter what a person's capabilities are, whether he is the leader or whether he is a person who is crippled or elderly or can't do anything, he still has a place in the tribe." And under the administration of Richard Nixon, the NWRO nearly got its wish—Nixon's Family Assistance Plan, which, while lower than the NWRO's demand of $5,500 a year for a family of four (over $35,000 in today's dollars), would have given a basic income to more than ten million people.[47]

That the welfare rights movement came within a fingertip of seeing a law that would have guaranteed income for anyone regardless of marital status or employment enacted by a conservative president should remind us that it is possible to imagine work and the family differently. But in the 1970s, the pendulum swung the other way. The profitability crisis, the beginnings of outsourcing, and inflation meant that everyone was suddenly competing for a piece of a shrunken pie. Instead of guaranteed income and rights, we got the "welfare queen" stereotype. Women were considered immoral if they had abortions, but also if they had children outside of the prescribed social conditions, and they were demonized for getting state support. Seeming to underscore the long history of such demonization, Ronald Reagan told a story about the need to cut benefits premised on "a young lady . . . who on the basis of being a student is getting food stamps, and she's studying to be a witch."[48]

Turning presumably Black women on welfare into a hate object—claiming that they undermined both the family, by daring to be single mothers, and the work ethic, by not taking a waged job—created a wedge that was slowly driven in to dismantle the entire welfare state and usher in the neoliberal moment. The left, having embraced the idea that going to work was liberation, had little with which to counter this turn.[49]

But one group of feminists, inspired by the NWRO and the Italian Marxist *operaismo* (workerism) movement of the 1970s, put forward a different analysis, one that challenged popular ideologies of both work and the family. While the Wages for Housework Campaign, as a demand and a political perspective, didn't spread as far as its founders would have liked, its organizers continue to struggle and to inspire others to this day.[50]

Wages for Housework picked up the idea from *operaismo* that capitalist production has subsumed every social relation, collapsing the distinction between "society" and "workplace" and turning all of those relations into relations of production. To the organizers of Wages for Housework, the "social factory" began in the home, and the work done in the home was necessary for the functioning of capitalism because it reproduced workers for capital. They argued, therefore, that this work was worthy of pay. Selma James, one of the founding theorists of the movement, wrote, "To the degree that we organize a struggle for wages for the work we do in the home, we demand that work in the home be considered *as* work which like all work in capitalist society is forced work, which we do not for love but because, like every other worker, we and our children would starve if we stopped."[51]

Central to these demands was the idea that refusing housework— striking from it, the same way workers in a factory would strike—was a way that house-workers would have power. Women leaving the home for the workplace were refusing housework, but for too many women, going to a waged job was anything but liberating—it often meant still more low-paid drudgery similar in form to what they still had waiting for them at home when they returned after a long workday. Demanding a wage for the work was a way to point out that housework *was* work, and that work was a thing they would like to do less of. It was a way to say, *"We are not that work."*[52]

Additionally, it was a way for them to refuse the identity that had been forced upon them, the very way that gender had been constructed. The assumption that housework, and reproductive work, came naturally to women and satisfied some deep inner feminine need, they argued, shaped the experiences of all women, even those who were wealthy enough to hire others (usually also women) to do their housework.[53]

The women of the Wages for Housework Campaign took from the women of the welfare rights movement the understanding that neither the workplace nor the family was a site of freedom. They wanted, instead, time for themselves, freedom to discover what love and sexuality might look like outside of relations of power and labor. Queer women in the movement noted that the stigma on lesbianism served to enforce the patriarchal family and the work done in it. Women who worked in child care and hospitals noted that the devaluing of work in the home led to a devaluing of their work outside of it. Violence against women, they argued, was a form of work discipline, a boss keeping his subordinates in line. Wages for Housework was a perspective that could be applied to all political struggles—it added an angle that was missing in most analyses of capitalism and gender.[54]

Though many people laughed (and continue to laugh) at the idea of wages for housework, it is inarguably true that housework, in many instances, is in fact paid. As economist Nancy Folbre wrote, echoing those welfare rights organizers, "if two single mothers, each with two children under the age of five, exchanged babysitting services, swapping children for eight hours a day, five days a week, and paying one another the federal minimum wage of $7.25 an hour, they could both take full advantage of [the Earned Income Tax Credit], receiving a total of more than $10,000 for providing essentially the same services they would provide for their own children." The women of Wages for Housework noted that the state pays foster parents, and that courts had granted damages to men whose wives had been injured to pay for "lack of services."[55]

The new discourse of the labor of love was being knitted together as wages were dropping and factories were closing, moving, and automating. Those in the Wages for Housework movement were some of the first to see what was happening in the 1970s. The shifts in the economy became visible in New York and other cities, where a fiscal crisis laid the groundwork for later austerity politics. Wages for Housework proponents warned, Cassandra-like, that feminists were going into the workplace just as the bottom was falling out of it. Women were expected to pick up the slack by taking up paid work while not reducing the amount of work they did in the home. The new social conservatives, hand in hand with the ascendant neoliberals, aimed to reinforce the traditional nuclear family at the same time that policies were being put in place to wring more work out of everyone, reinstituting the Protestant work ethic by law if not by choice.[56]

The end result of all this was "welfare reform," a multi-decade process that culminated in President Bill Clinton's Personal Responsibility and Work Opportunity Reconciliation Act of 1996, a law that in its very text does the double duty of upholding the work and family ethics. Welfare reform was a reminder of the ruthless cruelty that disguises itself in pretty words about love, care, and concern, and it was a project that spanned the political spectrum. Neoliberals like Clinton and social conservatives like Reagan alike mobilized racist beliefs about Black women's unwillingness to work (thick with irony in a country built by the enslaved labor of Black people) and exploited newly working women's resentment of those who didn't have to do the double shift. They pitted women against one another and turned everyone against a program that should have been an option for anyone who needed it—as activist Johnnie Tillmon had written, "Welfare's like a traffic accident. It can happen to anybody, but especially it happens to women."[57]

Welfare reform was begun by conservative governors in states like Wisconsin and California but it was finally implemented nationally by a Democratic president. Clinton had become president in a three-way split election by promising a "third way" for American politics—a third way that involved turning his back on the movements of the 1960s that he had credited with awakening his political consciousness, and embracing both "free markets" and "personal responsibility." Clinton's program did away with AFDC in favor of a series of block grants to states, which had wide discretion in how to use the funds. Many of them instituted work requirements and put a lifetime cap on benefits. The 1996 law also included money for "marriage promotion" programs and funds for states that could lower the number of "illegitimate" births without increasing the abortion rate. It diverted money into funds to track down biological fathers and extract child support funds from them, whether the mother wished to have anything to do with the father or not. The preamble of the law included the line, "Marriage is the foundation of a successful society." It was, in political scientist Melinda Cooper's words, "a state-enforced system of private family responsibility," built on the old Poor Law tradition but expanding its punitive nature.[58]

Despite all the politicians' professions that they wanted to help women, the new law surveilled and punished Black women in disproportionate numbers. (All of this happened alongside the growth of mass incarceration, itself a bipartisan project of the 1980s and 1990s.) The flood of new, desperate workers into the low-wage labor market—often, once again, into jobs mirroring the work they were expected to do in the home—helped to hold wages down for all while improving profits for those at the top.[59]

In the decades following welfare reform, labor in the paid workplace has been made cheaper because certain work remains unwaged and in the home. In Kathi Weeks's words, neoliberalism's "romance of the capitalist market" as the site of freedom "is coupled with a revived romance of the privatized family as the necessary locus of social reproduction and a haven in a heartless world." The collapse of communism and the triumph of capitalist realism has led to diminished imaginings, too, of how domestic work could be done differently. Instead, in the age of the "two-earner family," we hear a lot about "work-life balance," but not enough about how, for everyone, "life" (code for "family") often means "unpaid work."[60]

And only some people even get to consider such balance. Marriage is increasingly a track for the upper middle class, while the working class is now more likely to opt instead for less legally binding relationships. Conservative opponents of same-sex marriage rights have argued that allowing queer people to marry would destroy the institution of marriage. But, as gender and sexuality professor Laura Briggs and others have noted, it's not gay marriage that has blasted open the family. Instead, it is economic inequality helping to splinter the family as we knew it. The birth rate itself has fallen since the 1970s: as Silvia Federici archly wrote, "the only true labor saving devices women have used in the '70s have been contraceptives." She also noted that the assault on abortion rights underway in much of the world has been an attempt to regulate the labor supply.[61]

The children who are born are increasingly being born outside of the family. By the 2000s, in the United States, just 59 percent of children were born to married mothers, a steep drop compared to the late 1950s, when 95 percent of children were. (In this sense, it seems, welfare reform has failed.) For many working-class women, it is obvious that marriage is becoming too much work—in the words of one single mother who decided to leave her child's father, "I can support myself. I always have. I can support myself and our kid. I just can't support myself, the kid, and him." Far from being the "bad mother" of the stereotype, she was making a decision to put her child's welfare first.[62]

But while the nuclear family might be mutating and falling apart, gendered assumptions around unpaid work—and who will do it—have not changed nearly enough. The pesky, persisting gender pay gap is explained in part by women's continuing responsibility for doing unpaid care work. What sociologist Arlie Russell Hochschild called the "second shift" remains in effect. Research in the United Kingdom in 2016 found that women still did nearly twice as much housework as men. US-based research showed that mothers working outside the home these days spend just as much time caring for children as mothers did in the 1970s, when their only job was in the home. Others have estimated that "the size of the paid labor force would double if all unpaid caregivers were paid for their work." During the coronavirus lockdown, one survey found that nearly half of men with young children reported splitting domestic duties equally—but their wives disagreed. Only 2 percent of women agreed that men were responsible for most of the housework during lockdown. Globally, United Nations researchers estimated in 1999 that all unpaid reproductive labor, if paid, would cost $16 trillion, a third of the world's total economic activity—$11 trillion of which would be women's share.[63]

For the working class, it's the impossibility of paying for help that forces the squeeze. But the middle and upper classes also face the new ideological pressure of "attachment parenting"—something the writer Heather Abel described as a horror story. "Mama gives birth to Baby, and she must not put her down," Abel wrote. "She cannot do sedentary work or even read for pleasure because Baby prefers movement—although Mama can, while Baby is strapped to her, perform housework."[64]

Such ideological pressure is jacked up to 11 on the far right, where a new generation of women calling themselves "tradwives" have become Internet celebrities. These women make the inherent fascist potential of the family explicit. They combine tips on child-rearing and husband-pleasing with white-supremacist rants; one woman issued what she called "the white baby challenge" to other wives, daring them to reproduce faster than nonwhite people. They are the curdled side of the unfinished feminist revolution: frustrated with limited career prospects and a shredded social safety net, they retreat to the home and blame feminism—and nonwhite people—for their plight. Today's far right relies on the libidinal energy generated by this tension even as it pretends to simply defend what has been. But there is no turning back. The only option, as theorist Jordy Rosenberg wrote, is to ride "the supernova of the family's destruction" through to something new.[65]

Even as the old order crumbles, magazines and the Internet are loaded with articles about the ongoing quest for women to "have it all." We rarely hear about men trying to "have it all," because just asking the question seems ludicrous. Yet, with the opening up of the public gaze to queer families (at least, as long as they still fit comfortably into the nuclear model) and some flexibility on gender roles, we have new entries into the field of discussion: men writing about their attempts to parent better, queer couples on the impossibility of doing all the work even without strict gender divisions. There's also new high-tech fixes for the problem, including egg freezing, which some companies are starting to offer to their valued employees. At bottom, though, so much of the conversation is individual: we must simply figure out a "balance" that works for us personally. Yet there's another way to look at things. As Briggs wrote, these seemingly individual battles "are where neoliberalism lives in our daily lives." The point of Wages for Housework is not for individual men to pay individual women, like the "wife bonuses" paid by wealthy husbands to their wives, described in Wednesday Martin's *Primates of Park Avenue*. The point is to demand wages in order to break the system.[66]

After all, there are so many ways that the system breaks us. It's not just that, as Hochschild pointed out, continued struggles over housework—and who will do it—mean that "many [straight] women cannot afford the luxury of unambivalent love for their husbands," that sex within the family is often just another type of labor. The presumption that unpaid care—for elders, for incapacitated spouses, and for children—will be provided by women in families is not only exhausting for women. In the United States, for example, health-care access—which necessitates health insurance—is still largely tied to the workplace, such that many people only have access to care through a spouse's job. How does that affect one's freedom to leave an unsatisfying or even abusive relationship? And what about those who do not have a partner at all?[67]

In a society that presumes that intimacy, and sometimes life-sustaining care, will be provided by partners in a romantic couple or other family members—and where 84 percent of the measurable 21.5 billion hours of noninstitutional personal care still is—what happens to those without partners or families? "Caring means giving more than you get, or giving without hope of receiving," wrote nurse Laura Anne Robertson. "But in order to receive this supposedly immeasurable care, you must first make yourself sufficiently loveable." Such a need to be loved—not just emotionally, but in order to survive—is a powerful form of discipline. To ensure that everyone in a society is equitably cared for, we are going to need more than, in Robertson's words, "love and guilt."[68]

Despite the turn toward gay marriage and "homonormativity," queer relationships have also long pointed the way toward something more expansive than families. Experiments with collective households took on new meaning during the AIDS crisis, when people locked out of the traditional family (and health insurance), and often shunned by the families of their birth, banded together to nurse one another and organize together to demand a political response to the epidemic. They fought for relationships marked not by legal contracts and state approval but by free choice, love, and care.[69]

People with disabilities have also turned the need for care and support into radical political demands, communities of care, and a defense of the idea that there are things more important than one's ability to hold a job. Unable to work in the ways that capitalism values, disability theorist

Sunaura Taylor wrote, "disabled people have to find meaning in other aspects of their lives and this meaning is threatening to our culture's value system." Elders, too, are often devalued by a society that attaches worth to work and work alone: a story about declining life expectancy in 2017 was summed up by Bloomberg News as, "We're dying younger. That could be really good news for our employers." When care is framed simultaneously, by capitalist society, as both exchange and altruistic gift, when exchange under capitalism is always unequal anyway, how do we think of value and relationships otherwise?[70]

During the coronavirus pandemic, Taylor's words took on new meaning. Politicians and the wealthy began to be less subtle about their demands that the economy be reopened, even if some people had to die. Grandparents, said Lieutenant Governor Dan Patrick of Texas, would be willing to die to save the economy for their grandchildren—certainly a perverse twist on the caring labor of the family. In the moment of the virus, staying home from work became itself an act of care and of social reproduction, a reminder that despite Patrick and his ilk, most of us do in fact recognize our intertwined lives and care for one another.[71]

Philosopher Eva Kittay suggested the concept of "doulia" (a play on the title "doula," used by caregivers who assist new parents during and after the birth of a child) as one that could replace exchange. She sees it as an understanding that interpersonal relationships will likely never be equal but can occur in a framework that sees care obligations as nested. In other words, we care for others understanding that we will one day be cared for, if not likely by the same person. But to have that understanding, we need to create structures to ensure that will be the case without relying on uncompensated work in the family. To do so, we must create a society that values and cares for those who need care and also for those who do the work.[72]

To pull apart the notion of the family, then, is not to say that the labor done within the household (the cleaning and cooking as well as the caring) is without value—a topic I'll address more in the next chapter. It is, rather, to claim the revolutionary potential of care, community, and relationships. It is to ask, as Selma James did, "What if [relationships] became the social priority which material production would serve?" Because women have been forced to do most of such work in society, they have also, Kittay noted, been the ones to lead political struggles to revalue it. In recent years, even as witch-hunts have returned in some places around the world, political struggles have led to wins: Wages for Housework proposals were revived by Mexico's ruling MORENA party, for example, and pensions for homemakers were instituted in Venezuela.[73]

Claiming the work done in the home *as work* is a way to begin to think beyond the double bind of "work-family balance," perhaps to begin reclaiming the old demand of the shorter-hours movement for time "for what we will." It is a way to begin envisioning a different society. After all, as Raj Patel and Jason W. Moore put it, "to ask for capitalism to pay for care is to call for an end to capitalism."[74]

IT WAS DURING A THEATER MEETING THAT RAY MALONE FIRST REALIZED she could turn her political gaze on her own life. A friend of hers had trained in Theater of the Oppressed techniques. This approach, developed by the Brazilian practitioner Augusto Boal, encourages dialogue between actors and audience with an aim of promoting political change. So Malone joined her friend and a group of theater-makers to discuss housing issues in London.

She found herself telling the story of the nursery where she'd been told she'd be "rewarded" if she got a job. The people in the room began riffing on her story, playing with every angle. "This conversation that I'd kept to myself, that I was a little bit embarrassed about," Malone said, suddenly became a way to get at deeply political issues of work and care.

That was one of the launch points for what became Fallout Club—"Fallout from the nuclear family," Malone laughed. Fallout Club was a way to create space for single parents—mostly single mothers—to gather and find ways to discuss and politicize their situation. "Where do we go with these feelings? Where is there a place for our anger to be heard about these situations? There is a lot that we should be angry about," Malone said.

There had been, she said, a "bit of an explosion" recently in groups for adults to talk about mothering, parenting, and being in the arts. Many of those groups felt like therapy—there were lots of tears, lots of sharing, akin to the consciousness-raising groups of the 1960s and 1970s. "We would often talk about the fact that we had specific barriers to accessing art workshops, yoga workshops. I said, 'Let's start a group for single mothers and low-income parents. I think there is something, specifically, that needs addressing here politically.'"

It was the theater that helped Malone open up, and so in her Fallout Club workshops there is always something creative to do. Crafting, she noted, has long been considered women's work, but it is also a way to focus and yet to be reflective. Lots of political meetings, she said, are noisy places full of argument, but what if they could be something else? The question, she said, was, "How do people realize the systems of their oppression? How do you get people to talk about the situation they are in and realize what underpins it?"

Embroidery artist Milou Stella became her collaborator on Fallout Club, and Malone began her own art project about the experience of Universal Credit. As Nola grew older, Malone was expected to spend more time at the job center, attempting to prove she was working hard enough not to lose her benefits. "As soon as your child is one year old they want to see your CV," she said. "If you don't have a job when your child is three years old, they could be threatening you with sanctions and taking your money away. It is a very punitive environment and a very difficult thing to have a toddler [there with you]. It is demeaning. It is really badly set up for actually getting a job." She began to notice other parents there with children in tow—highlighting, once again, the tensions between child care and paid work. Here were parents trying to soothe their children in this punitive space. She began doing embroidered renditions of photos she took of parents in the job center.[75]

Her daughter has picked up on the implications of the job center as well. Malone recalled showing Nola the photo she was working from. "I said to my daughter, who is four, 'Do you know what it's of?' She said, 'It's a woman and she is poor.' I said, 'How do you know she is poor?' She said, 'Because she is worried. Look at her face.'"

The embroidery project and the art workshops, she said, are ways of getting people to feel comfortable and open up. "If I said, . . . 'Are you on benefits?' or, 'Are you affected by the housing benefit cap?' people would be like, 'Whoa! I don't want to tell you that. That is really nosy.'" But when she leads with her own story, she said, people understand it differently, and if they can work together on creative projects about their experience, then they can have a discussion about it.

Malone has also started to think about solutions. She's drawn to the idea of universal basic income—the opposite of the Orwellian-named Universal Credit, which is laden with catch-22s, traps, and sanctions and rooted in the old punitive Poor Laws. Basic income, as the mothers of the welfare rights movement argued, would provide a floor for everyone, allowing single parents to take time with their children, or artists to cobble together a living doing creative work. For one workshop, Malone bought a child's playhouse to use as a prop and called it the Basic Income House. "We created loads of tiles for the house and we get people to embroider onto the tiles. We have a discussion about 'What do mothers need to survive and what do mothers need to thrive?'" They also do a presentation on the history of basic income, the United Kingdom's child benefit, and the importance of money that is paid to the mother, not to the family. "Child benefit actually allowed women to escape domestic violence situations because they had a bit of money that was paid to them," she noted. "But it hasn't continued at the rate of inflation. It is 80 quid a month [£80, equivalent to about US$100]. What can you do with 80 quid a month?"

At the end of the workshop, they asked attendees, "If you had an extra £1,000 [about US$1,200] a month, what would you do with the money?" The group was diverse: wealthier people said they'd spend their money on their grandchildren or give it to charities. To others, that amount would be life-changing. "Some people were like, 'I would escape my housing situation.' A disabled person was like, 'I can't chop food properly. I would bring somebody in to chop food.' You realize loads of people's basic needs are not being met." She planned to take the Basic Income House on the road to different communities, and to talk to people, particularly mothers, about their needs. "You feel punished for having a child by yourself as a single woman. Motherhood is throwing a lot of women into poverty. Or, a lot of women just make the decision, 'I can't afford to have a child.'"

Living in London, Malone felt the inequality acutely. "You always hear that people have got to work, they can't be given something for nothing. But something like 60 percent of wealth in this country is inherited wealth," she pointed out. That means a lot of people are, in fact, living on money they didn't work to earn. And Malone was working quite hard, but it was at a job that was deemed worthy of only £80 a month: raising a child.[76]

When she met Barb Jacobson, who had come out of Wages for Housework to coordinate the UK basic income network, Jacobson asked her if she wanted to help run a London group. Malone agreed, and at the group's first meeting, people raised questions that she had long been asking. The expectation of constant work, she said, created a "culture of just surviving without giving ourselves the breathing room to ask, 'What would the lives that we really wanted be like? If we could be as creative as we wanted to be? If we could spend more time with our children?'"

It remained hard for her, though, to be public about her own situation. At one of the basic income workshops, she and her collaborator, Stella, made badges to wear on the bright red jumpsuits they donned. "I made a badge that said, 'Universal credit survivor.' It was actually quite a difficult thing to put online and to be like, 'I'm telling everybody that I claim benefits.'" But, she said, she also felt, "This shouldn't be. I need to be able to be bold about it and say, 'There is no shame in this.'" She challenged the notion that she should feel ashamed of her life. "What is contributing to society better? Is it working at Wetherspoon's or is it raising the next generation and making sure that your child is securely attached and happy?"

Malone's organizing work—allowing people space to tell their stories without shame and articulating solutions that would eliminate that shame—kept her going, even if it, too, might never be recognized as real work. "Nobody really wants to be, 'Pity me!' But we still need to create a space where people explore the barriers that they are facing."

When the coronavirus hit, Malone was just about to start a new job—her first office job since Nola's birth. The job, a creative project on London's historic queer community, would entail a lot of research, and so they wanted her to start right away. But then she came down with a cough. And then the lockdown was called and she had to figure out how to do her new job from home. "I was immediately trying to cope with being on my own, having a really busy work schedule, and then being really public facing a big queer audience that I haven't met before."

She'd grown comfortable running meetings in a room where people could connect with one another, but Zoom calls were more difficult. It's been lonely and stressful at times, she said. She missed having a significant other. When her ex was the only person she saw in person besides her daughter, it heightened the strain, negotiating a co-parenting relationship with someone who no longer provided the same kind of care for her. "You need people that love you and like you and want to listen to your opinion, not somebody who has already marginalized you," she said.

Working from home during lockdown had its own stresses—she may not have needed to pay for child care, but she worried that she was not able to devote as much time to Nola as she wanted. She found herself comparing herself to her upstairs neighbors, whose child—a little older than Nola, but a year ahead in school—was reading and writing. Some people in lockdown, she noted, were able to lavish their children with attention, while others found their working hours eating up family time. Would a basic income have prevented this anxiety, she wondered. "Could I decide, 'Actually, my day is better spent making a slide for my daughter and that is what me and my kid need right now'?"

As an art practice during isolation, Malone had started doing video interviews with women about objects in their homes, and many of them, she said, had talked about their mothers, their grandmothers, and the work they did. "The small-scale stuff is where you actually build the biggest relationships with the people in your life," she said, "and they remember you when you're just cooking or you're just chatting or you're just doing the constant low-level care." She added, "It is the thing that is making us human and the people that are teaching us to be human. This is so undervalued, but it's the most important thing in the world."

With a basic income—something that has attracted more and more attention during the pandemic—she saw "massive transformative potential." It could take away the worry about money and allow her to spend time with her daughter. "It would allow us to focus on things that are better for us as humans," she said. "We would be more creative and we would be able to think more about the stuff that actually matters."

CHAPTER 2

JUST LIKE ONE OF THE FAMILY

Domestic Work

Mila is having a grabby phase. She is wrapping her tiny six-month-old fingers around Adela Seally's cheek when I first meet her. Seally closes her eyes to protect them from tiny fingernails and smiles, giving the baby more cheek to cling to. Mila presses her own baby cheeks against Seally's and grins big.[1]

Seally is Mila's nanny. Before Mila was born, she cared for Mila's older sister Ava until she was old enough to go to school. "I was part time for a bit," Seally explained, "but we still had our little thing going on. She used to take dance classes, and when she had her performances she would insist that I come. When she was moving up from preschool to kindergarten, she wanted me to be there to see her perform on stage."

With the birth of Mila, Seally was back at the family's house—a pleasant stand-alone home with a wraparound porch in New Rochelle, New York, about an hour's bus ride from where Seally lives in the Bronx—five days a week, from nine o'clock in the morning until four, five, or sometimes six in the evening. Most of the six years she's spent as a professional nanny have been with Ava and Mila's family. When she began work, she said, it was the family's first time having a nanny as well as her first time being one. "I just knew I was going to go into work and get paid. I didn't know anything about benefits or working hours and all of that. We were just learning as we went along."

Despite the learning curve, she has a good relationship with the family, one that is evident when her employer stops by to cuddle Mila before heading off to pick up the older girls (Ava and Mila have an older sister, Donna) from school. But it is the girls who make her light up. She beams when she sings to Mila; of Ava, she said, "We just clicked from when she saw me the first time." Every child is different, she explained—she has seven of her own, and she worked as a preschool teacher before coming to New York from St. Lucia. As a baby, Ava had gained a reputation in the neighborhood for crying a lot. When Seally took her for a walk through the neighborhood, to the park or the library, Seally said, "parents or nannies would come up to me and say, 'Isn't that the crying baby? She used to cry all the time.' But she wasn't doing it with me for some reason."

Seally dresses comfortably for work—today, she's wearing an orange T-shirt emblazoned with "Care in Action" and skinny jeans, her long black twists pulled back out of reach of Mila's grabbing fingers. Most of her day is spent sprawled on the floor playing with Mila, whose toys include a fluffy white stuffed bunny that sings and laughs a child's laugh straight out of a horror movie, though it delights the baby. There are also various gadgets that light up and play music when buttons are pushed. Seally names the colors for Mila as she pushes the buttons, and Mila obliges with an occasional shriek of glee. She takes special pleasure in making noise, Seally said, when her older sisters are around, as if to say, "I may not be the oldest, but I can be the loudest!"

In between Ava and Mila, Seally cared for another baby whose family lived in Queens. She adored him as well, but it was stressful, she said, because he had several serious allergies. "I had to be really careful with him when we would go to the park, or if we hung out with other kids. It is always on your mind. Even if you are CPR certified, that's one thing you have that you never really want to use."

When she returned to care for Mila, she explained, she was able to negotiate a better contract than she'd had previously. "You hear stories about how there is no promotion within nanny work, but I would say there is. You can negotiate for something better than what you had. Maybe it might be monetary—more pay—but it also might mean you get more vacation with pay or more sick or personal days."

Seally always knew she wanted to work with children. Before it was her full-time job, even when she was young, she would care for others' children. She recalled being part of a drama club, and writing plays for the children in the community to do. She had her own first child young, while she was still in St. Lucia, and after a couple of years at home with her child she became a preschool teacher. "That, for me, was in itself fun. It is learning through play. You get to release that little inner child that should be in all of us."

Seally's older children were her primary job for much of their youth. She was a deeply involved parent, going to school activities, trips, workshops, and parent association meetings. It was, she said, her way of giving back to her community. Now that she's working full time, her youngest son—he's ten—misses out on some of that, though she makes sure to still get time off for parent-teacher conferences. "Sometimes, the challenge is you have to leave your child and go take care of somebody else's child and you miss out on your child as much as they miss out." Some of the families, she said, have cameras in the home (just try a Google search for "Nanny cam" and count the results) that allow them to relive milestones they missed—first words said to a caregiver rather than a parent, first steps taken to the nanny's arms—but she has no such luxury at home. There have been times when her child has been ill and she has had to leave him with someone else in order to be there for the charges she is paid to care for. "That in itself can really take a toll. It makes you feel guilty," she said. There's also the reality, particularly for New York City nannies—who often live far from the wealthier families they work for—of long commutes that add to the workday, even if they're not technically spent on the clock.

On a typical day, Seally wakes up at 6:30 a.m.—though, she laughed, she often hits the snooze button for ten minutes. She starts the coffee maker, wakes up her kids, and makes sure they're getting ready for school before she leaves to catch her bus. Once at work, she feeds the baby, and if it's nice out, she takes her for a walk in the stroller or maybe on the bus up to the library, where there are children's programs and a playground. Mila naps for short periods of time, but she resists sleeping—Seally and I watch her eyelids droop several times, but she rights herself and lets out an indignant wail when Seally attempts to lay her down, then a piercing shriek straight into Seally's ear when she picks her back up. The best way to get her to sleep, Seally explains, is to put her in the stroller and walk her in little circles in the living room, or rock her back and forth until she nods off. Nanny work is constant and demanding, requiring a thousand tiny decisions about how to proceed, how to soothe, amuse, and teach the baby for long hours alone all day.

Other forms of domestic work didn't suit Seally so well. She tried housecleaning for a while, but found it frustrating and repetitive. "I remember once cleaning for somebody in Manhattan and whenever I was done, she would come back and ask me to do it over." A clogged drain meant hours of extra scrubbing. "It is a very tough job. I don't think I am cut out for that part of domestic work."

Caring for children has had its bothersome sides, too. Employers, she says, sometimes come home to undo the hard work the nanny has done, of setting routines for the children or enforcing rules that the parents have asked for but then cheerily ignore when they are home with their kids. "Then, [the children] see you as the bad guy. When you are not on the same page with the parents it can be really frustrating." She has also found it disheartening when they don't treat her as a skilled worker who has professional experience with children. "They see you as just the nanny," she said, and don't always trust her knowledge about when the best time is to introduce solid foods, or some other change. "Then, they struggle with that situation and take the child to a doctor, and then they come back and tell you the doctor said the same thing you said before."

Children, though, are her life's work. It's the little differences in the behavior of children that fascinate Seally. She advises the parents she works for not to compare their children to each other, not to expect that because it was a certain way with Ava, that Mila will like the same things or progress at the same rate. Ava was an independent child who liked to figure things out for herself, though she wanted her caregiver where she could see her in case she needed help—in that way she was different from most of the children Seally had cared for, who often wanted her to be hands-on.

"For me, taking care of Ava was really fulfilling, although I had to leave [my own children] behind and go to somebody else," she said. "I love to see them grow, discover, be curious and achieve their milestones and do a complete puzzle or something on their own and be very excited about completing it. I like to see the look on their face when they start walking and make a few steps and walk across the room without falling, or tying their shoelaces on their own. Even if I have kids of my own, still every time you see a child, a baby, growing and learning how to walk, or saying their first word, it still makes you feel so happy and fulfilled just to see the progress."

Seally's commitment was tested when the coronavirus pandemic came to New York. "I chose to become a live-in. I was thinking that it would be safer staying over for the week instead of taking public transportation or doing Uber or Lyft." She began spending Monday through Friday at her employers' home with their children; her employers pick her up Monday morning and drop her off Friday so she doesn't have to take public transit.

Her employers have mostly been working at home during the pandemic, so Seally's job is to keep the children occupied during the day. "They had a very busy schedule outside of their home, so for them it is a little more difficult because there are no after-school activities." Their father helps the older children with their schoolwork when he's done working, so most of her focus is on the smaller ones.

Seally had been lucky, she said, in that no one close to her had died of the virus. But all around her people were sick, as the Bronx was one of the hardest-hit places in the entire country. And spending most of the week at her employers' meant it was even trickier for her to balance her responsibility for her own children and the ones she was paid to care for. "The teenagers can be tricky," she said. "Sometimes we have been going for little walks here and there, but not an everyday thing. Pretty much they are inside all the time so that, in itself, can be a challenge." She worried about them with online schooling: Were they doing their work? "I always think, 'If I was home, I would be on top of them to do it more.' At least I call and say, 'Make sure you do your work.'"

Nannies and other domestic workers, she noted, have a hard time maintaining social-distancing protocols at work. "We just take precautions, wear our protective gear, especially because of the close proximity with the kids. You wear masks when you are in close proximity to other people. You make sure you wash your hands."

But the pandemic had underscored something that Seally already knew all too well: "If domestic workers don't show up for work, then the majority of the workforce can't show up for work," she said. "I love my work because my work is the silk thread that holds society together, making all other work possible."

⣿

THE HOME HAS BEEN A WORKPLACE FOR AS LONG AS THERE HAVE BEEN homes; for only slightly less long, homes have also been workplaces for those who don't live in them. The lines of work and non-work are blurred constantly in the home, and this happens even when there are wages involved.

Scholars Eileen Boris and Rhacel Salazar Parreñas came up with the term "intimate labor" to describe the range of work that entails closeness with others. That work can include knowledge of personal information as well as bodily contact and touch. Sometimes it involves having another person's life in your hands; other times the stakes are lower. But what all intimate labor has in common is that it brushes up against the line between what we think should be done for love and what we think should be done for money.[2]

Such "separate spheres" thinking is based in the ideology of the home that crystallized in the nineteenth and twentieth centuries. Atop that is built the idea that the home and workplace are not just separate but "hostile worlds": that any contact between them will corrupt both, introducing messy feelings into the workplace and unnecessary greed into the home. It assumes that care that is paid for—like Seally's—cannot also be genuine, and that paying for work done out of love will somehow serve to take the love away.[3]

What intimate labors of various kinds also have in common is that they are expected to be the province of a certain kind of worker—almost always female, working class, and very often racialized as outsiders. This is especially true of what we call domestic work—the cooking and cleaning and caring work done in the home by paid or coerced non-family members. It has long been the most common form of employment for women—in sixteenth- and seventeenth-century Europe, one-third of the female population worked as domestics, and even after the Industrial Revolution, domestic servants in fact made up the single largest group of working people. The coercion, low pay, and lack of respect for these workers is often covered up with an essentialist narrative that certain people are "naturally" better at domestic labor. For much of history that has included immigrant workers—the Irish in England, for example—and in the United States, it is a history that is deeply rooted in slavery.[4]

Such ideas about race and domestic work have their roots in the Enlightenment-era splits between mind and body, man and nature, human and animal. Closeness to dirt and to bodies rendered one too close to nature for comfort, and so the ruling classes preferred that such work be done by groups of people they considered closer to animals. This principle applied to women generally and particularly to racialized people and outsiders. The tradition of using slaves for domestic work goes back to the ancient world, where the women on the losing side of war or conflict were regularly enslaved to work in the homes of the victors. Indentured servants, paying their way from Europe to the United States by selling the rights to their labor for a term of years, often did housework before the turn to chattel slavery. When the people who would create the thing we now call the United States began kidnapping African people and enslaving them, the narrative they constructed to justify their actions was that these people were racially destined to do such dirty work, whether on the farm or in the home.[5]

For Black women under slavery, there was no "home" that was free of the demands of the enslaver. Their very reproduction was controlled as a source of profit; their biological families were regularly torn apart and sold away; and the enslaver's opulent home was the site of their unfree work. Black women, even as they fought to create a home that might be a space of love, saw white femininity defined against them, as something far too delicate for work. In order to exploit Black women's labor to the utmost, Angela Davis noted, the enslaving class had to release them from "the chains of the myth of femininity," yet such release did not include freeing them from the perception that they were naturally good at caring for (white) children.[6]

During the Civil War, sensing the end of slavery approaching, enslaved people stepped up myriad forms of resistance, from the small and domestic—challenging white women's monopoly on feminine beauty by wearing their enslavers' accessories or cosmetics—all the way up to running away to Union lines in what W. E. B. Du Bois characterized as a massive general strike. White women may have found themselves having to do more housework, but after the war they quickly resumed handing that work over to Black women, even if they had to pay them this time around. This historical tension—between the wealthy employers of domestics and the women who did the work—has continued to divide women and women's movements right up to the present, giving well-off women a material investment in ignoring divisions of race and class.[7]

Freed from slavery, Black women fought to control the conditions of their labor. Just as importantly, they fought for time away from work—"to 'joy my freedom," as historian Tera Hunter wrote in her book of the same title. They refused work conditions not to their liking—notably, despite the wishes of employers, many refused live-in domestic work—and quit jobs that didn't suit. They rejected anything that smacked of slavery, even as employers desperately tried to re-create it. Any time away from work that formerly enslaved people had was seen, by the white still-ruling class, as idleness, laziness, and "vagrancy," and they began writing such beliefs into law. Vagrancy, wrote historian and literary scholar Saidiya Hartman, "was a status, not a crime. It was not doing, withholding, nonparticipation, the refusal to be settled or bound by contract to employer (or husband)." And when the law was insufficient to discipline Black workers, groups like the Ku Klux Klan were always happy to use extralegal violence.[8]

Such limitations meant that the work options open for Black workers were limited mainly to domestic work for women and farmwork for men—the same forms of work associated with dirt and nature that whites considered beneath them. In Atlanta in the 1880s, some 98 percent of Black women wage-earners did domestic work of various kinds, from child care to general housework to cooking and laundering. Laundry, before the days of automatic washing machines, was a tremendous chore, but the women who worked as laundresses preferred it because they could do it at their own pace, in their own spaces. It gave them some freedom—and even the opportunity to again resist white women's monopoly on femininity, by "borrowing" some clothing. And it could be done communally, which made it easier to organize to protect their hard-won working conditions; it's not surprising that some of the earliest strikes of domestic workers were laundry workers' strikes. By striking, the laundry workers asserted not only the need for a minimum wage for their work, but also the notion that *they were not that work*.[9]

It was a struggle they had to continually wage. The idea that Black women deserved any non-work time was not one that former enslavers accepted easily. Slavery may have ended, but they still considered it "natural" that Black workers were at the bottom of the hierarchy. Indeed, Black women were paid so little that even the poorest white worker could usually afford some domestic help. Black workers' pleasure was actively threatening to such a hierarchy. Dance, in particular, something deeply important to Black people as a form of enjoyment and of resistance, was something whites tried to forbid, arguing that it took physical energy that should have been solely focused on work. Yet, Hunter wrote, "dancing hard, like laboring hard, was consistent with the work ethic of capitalism." It was anything but lazy—but it was "work" that the employer couldn't capture.[10]

The process of criminalizing Black workers through vagrancy laws and other Black Codes was an unveiled attempt at coercing labor and forcing people into socially prescribed roles—one woman was arrested and put in the stockade because she worked as a domestic for a Black family. "It was not enough to work as a servant if one did not labor for whites," Hunter observed. Two young women who were arrested for refusing to work as servants shattered windows in the jail, declaring, "You cannot make us work." They were sentenced to sixty days working in the prison laundry. In New York, women sent to reformatory were released only to labor as domestics in the upstate homes of white families, separated from the freedom the city had offered. The prison, then, served as the final punishment for women who were, in Angela Davis's words, marked as "undomesticated and hypersexual, as women who refuse to embrace the nuclear family as a paradigm."[11]

Meanwhile, at the end of the nineteenth century and the beginning of the twentieth, the nuclear family was solidifying around a conception of the middle-class white housewife. She would presumably have a domestic servant or two to help maintain the illusion of the home as a space of love and free of work. White women might work outside the family until they were married, but once wed they were expected to stay home. The majority of women, in surveys of the US population, listed themselves as "housewife" up until 1980, but many women were still working in other women's homes—"Personal Service: Private Household" remained the largest category of outside-the-house labor for women until 1950. Gender roles might have been calcifying in this time, but within those gender roles there was an equally calcified race and class divide.[12]

Tensions between employers and domestics were particularly high around child care. Children, unlike other aspects of housework, required constant attention and made emotional demands; employers expected that their hired workers would shower their children with as much affection as possible and find the job pleasurable. "You gave as much love to their children that you would give to yours almost," said Dorothy Bolden, a longtime domestic worker. Yet the worker seldom received such love in return. And if she did, it was often expected to be accepted in lieu of cash wages.[13]

While child-care workers were expected to pour their love into their work, many of them had families of their own at home who were neglected while they cared for others. The "second shift" was a reality for them long before the term was coined, and they did the same grinding work at home unwaged that they did elsewhere for pay. At a time—the 1930s and 1940s—when the demands of organized industrial labor and the inception of the New Deal meant that most other workers were making gains in wages and successfully shortening their working day, domestic workers' schedules remained grueling, with workweeks of up to eighty or ninety hours. As a result, like Seally, they spent much more time with their employers' families than with their own.[14]

DOMESTIC WORKERS' RESISTANCE WASN'T A NEW THING, BUT IN THE wake of the New Deal and with the rise in worker organizing that it brought, domestic workers, too, began to consider unionizing. Like Seally, they wanted firmer boundaries between work and home, they wanted to draw limits on what their employers could demand, and they wanted to make clear that the labor they did in others' homes was work, not something they did out of love.

Because the New Deal was constructed as a compromise between crusading liberals and racist southerners within the Democratic Party, domestic work, along with farmwork—the two kinds of work done mostly by Black workers—were carved out of the Fair Labor Standards Act (FLSA), which set minimum wages and overtime, as well as from Social Security. The New Deal's Depression-relief programs, meanwhile, continued to place Black women in domestic service and care, upholding the idea that this was their natural role. Domestic workers hoped for some sort of enforceable protections under the National Recovery Administration (NRA), but they remained on the outside. There were some reformers among the employing classes, but even they mostly balked at the idea of government regulations intruding on private homes. In response to calls to regulate paid domestic work, A. R. Forbush, the NRA's correspondence chief, wrote, "The homes of individual citizens cannot be made the subject of regulations or restrictions and even if this were feasible, the question of enforcement would be virtually impossible."[15]

And so the workers began to organize. The roots of such organizing can be traced back to those early washerwomen's strikes, when laundry workers demanded recognition for their work and its value. The domestic workers also sought the right to be separated from their work, to be seen as people with lives apart from the floors to be scrubbed and children to be minded. They deliberately evoked the legacy of slavery when demanding better conditions, and that legacy was never far away. In New York, women stood outside at street corners that were dubbed "Bronx Slave Markets," waiting for employers to come by and pick out a worker for the day's labor. Ella Baker and Marvel Cooke wrote of the market, "Not only is human labor bartered and sold for slave wage, but human love also is a marketable commodity. But whether it is labor or love that is sold, economic necessity compels the sale." The degrading conditions inspired women to organize, and to insist that they no longer be treated like chattel.[16]

Their work went hand in hand with civil rights organizing. Domestic workers were key to the Montgomery bus boycott in 1955 and 1956, raising funds, organizing their neighbors, and of course trudging to and from work rather than taking the bus. They led, as historian Premilla Nadasen explained, by mobilizing other workers to boycott, and they developed a notion of "collective community" that "became absolutely essential to the ways in which household workers could then challenge their employers." The questions of dignity at the heart of the bus boycott were also at the heart of their conflicts at work. And the buses, across the South, were centers where they could also meet to agitate for change on the job.[17]

Through organizations such as the National Domestic Workers Union, which Dorothy Bolden created in 1968 in Atlanta, the workers rallied around the idea that their work was skilled labor, not just their "natural" role. They fought for minimum wages, yes, but they also demanded to be called *household technicians*, a term of respect for their work, rather than maids; they built training programs to further emphasize (and improve) their skills. They listed chores they would not do—scrubbing on their knees among them. Training for household labor wasn't new: the home economics movement had always seen itself in part as a way to teach future domestic workers to uphold certain standards. But the workers' control of training sent a very different message about respect.[18]

By insisting that they were skilled employees, the domestic workers emphasized that the home was a workplace and that they were not simply "part of the family." This claim had always been a double-edged sword for household employees. They were not treated like equal family members—they were expected to use the back door, and to make themselves scarce, or to quietly serve, when company came. Said domestic worker Carolyn Reed, "I don't want a family. I need a job." Yet in order to improve their conditions, domestic workers often had to negotiate individually—a task that itself took considerable skill, and a skill that domestic worker organizations worked to teach.[19]

They won, too, through their organizing and political lobbying, some legal recognition for their work, such as some inclusion in labor protections under the FLSA. But the industry would remain largely unregulated, and Black women left it as soon as other job options opened up to them, opting for waged work that wasn't shot through with all the intimate conflicts of the family.[20]

Those intimate conflicts, after all, were blowing up—as domestic workers quit, middle-class women began to understand just how hard housework was, and to make such recognition political. The National Organization for Women, launched by Betty Friedan of *Feminine Mystique* fame, supported the extension of the FLSA to household workers, arguing that it would increase the supply of domestic workers—a necessary thing so that more middle-class women could get fulfilling careers.[21]

Housework, and who should do it, was a fraught question. For decades, for the housewife, keeping a tidy, loving home had been a task deeply tied up with her identity. To fail to keep a good home was *to fail to be a good woman*. It was therefore difficult to admit that the lion's share of that work was being done by someone else. The intimacy, too, of inviting a stranger into the home—the possibility that the employee would learn deeply personal secrets—had always seemed threatening. All of this, historian Phyllis Palmer noted, contributed to the need for employers to see their employees as lesser, as non-people. Hiring Black or immigrant women helped the employer to do this, but it's worth pointing out that this is more or less how all management appropriates the proceeds of labor. And the middle-class housewife did see herself as management; she was the "mind" while her employee was the "body." She needed to see herself as the ultimate performer of all the work, even if just as overseer.[22]

Cleaning was dirty work for dirty women. The conscription of working-class women to do it allowed the housewife's hands to stay clean. As sociologist Erin Hatton wrote, "narratives of immorality and privilege" painted housewives as non-workers because of their purity, their blessedness. And meanwhile, the people who cleaned up after them were assumed to be themselves impure—as in Ireland's Magdalene laundries, where, in the eighteenth to the late twentieth centuries, women who misbehaved were punished by being put to work doing laundry for strangers—an assumption that affects the women who now serve as personal care attendants for the ill and elderly.[23]

Home care work, like the broader field of domestic work, remained associated with both intimacy and dirt, and wrapped up in changing ideas about womanhood and care. In the early New Deal days of state-funded home care, most home care workers were seen as a sort of "substitute mother," doing general housework and care. But their services soon became more focused on caring for the elderly, even as they themselves were excluded from Social Security coverage that could have supported them in old age. After World War II, historians Eileen Boris and Jennifer Klein wrote, the job was reshaped into something that "took place in the home but performed the public work of the welfare state," and as countries face an "elder boom" in the coming decades, these jobs will continue to proliferate.[24]

The work of caring for the ill and elderly was something that, before the Depression, had been done in the family, by private charity (often the church), or relegated to the workhouse or poorhouse. New Deal relief programs turned such care into a distinct profession, as much to create work for women as to fulfill needs. The War on Poverty in the 1960s expanded the program, and then it grew further in the 1970s, as the disability and elder rights movements organized for home-based assistance as an alternative to institutions. Funding, bumped up in the 1960s, began to be sliced back in response to economic crises in the 1970s, however.[25]

For many years, home care was dominated by Black women, and they had to constantly struggle against the assumption that they were simply state-funded maids. On the other side, they were also squeezed by registered nurses, whose defined standards allowed them to portray themselves as skilled laborers and reinforced the idea that home care workers were "unskilled." Despite this perceived lack of skill, as Ai-jen Poo, director of the National Domestic Workers Alliance (NDWA), wrote, home care workers "often served as nutritionists, teachers, physical therapists, psychotherapists, emergency responders, drivers, personal organizers, and nurses." They also provided the all-important (and taxing) emotional support of listening to their clients and offering compassion. The definition of "skill," though, continued to have more to do with who the workers were than what they did. Black women were considered "unskilled" no matter how much training they had, or how many lives had rested in their hands. As immigrant women began to fill the ranks of home care and domestic work during the 1980s and 1990s, similar assumptions were made of them.[26]

In 1974, just after organized domestic workers won inclusion in FLSA protections, the US Department of Labor revoked that coverage from "persons employed in domestic service employment to provide companionship services for individuals who (because of age or infirmity) are unable to care for themselves." Such workers, even if they were employed through a private agency and had previously been protected by the law, now were exempt from minimum wage and overtime. Despite the fact that home care and other domestic work had long been done by the same people—and public perceptions of both kinds of labor were wrapped up in the same stereotypes—many home care workers were now being stripped of the title of worker. Now they were not only "unskilled" laborers—their work wasn't considered work at all.[27]

US policy continues to assume that family will be the primary caregivers or assistants for people with disabilities or elders. Medicaid now pays for such services for low-income recipients who qualify; when Medicaid won't pick up the bill, families are stuck finding the money to pay private carers or agencies. Ronald Reagan, proclaiming an official Home Care Week in 1988, declared that the "death of the family ha[s] been greatly exaggerated," and his official statement noted that "in the home, family members can supply caring and love." Such association with "family responsibility" was further solidified by Bill Clinton's welfare reform program passed in 1996. When former AFDC recipients were forced into paid work, many of them wound up doing home care.[28]

One of the biggest struggles that such care workers face is that their interests are constantly pitted against those of their clients. The idea that the work is provided for love serves to paper over the fact that sometimes workers have needs that cannot or should not be subsumed by those of the people they serve. Personal attendants, after all, provide a kind of independence—by helping with or performing certain tasks for their clients, they allow the clients to remain in their homes, rather than to be institutionalized, and to have control over their lives. But for the clients to feel independent, care workers have to effectively make themselves invisible, so that clients can feel themselves to be the ultimate performers of their tasks.[29]

Paid attendants can be invisible in a way that family members or friends cannot be. In order to perform this labor that they are told is a labor of love to the best satisfaction of their clients, the attendants must accept, at some level, this invisibility. "I'm like an extension of his body," one attendant told researcher Lynn May Rivas. Another, whose client referred to him as "just the caregiver," told Rivas that such dismissal of his humanity hurt. The perceived low status of these workers helps to foster such invisibility: immigrant women, for example, are easily made invisible on the job because our society already considers them socially invisible, erasing their skills by claiming that what they do simply comes naturally. To Rivas, even when the worker allows such erasure out of genuine care, it is still harmful: "To be made invisible is the first step toward being considered nonhuman."[30]

One of the ways home care workers have challenged such invisibility and attempted to improve their material conditions—real wages fell for home care workers between 1999 and 2007 even as demand for their services increased—has been by organizing into unions. The state's involvement helped lay the groundwork for a different way to do that. By declaring the state the ultimate employer of the home care worker (since it pays for the work through Medicaid), rather than the recipient of services, the state allowed home care workers to become a collective workforce and bargain collectively. But getting the right to do this was a struggle; while some states agreed to the policy, others fought granting even this right to home care workers, and they remained outside of federal labor protections. The Service Employees International Union (SEIU) challenged this on behalf of Evelyn Coke, a Jamaican immigrant woman who worked in home care on Long Island. The case reached the Supreme Court in 2007, but the Court's disappointing decision focused on the costs to the state and to clients in upholding home care workers' exclusion. Coke's livelihood and that of other workers like her was dismissed. "I feel robbed," Coke told reporters, though she was glad people were at least paying attention: "People are supposed to get paid when they work."[31]

Publicly employed home care workers continued to organize in states where they had been granted the right. SEIU represented something like seven hundred thousand of them around the country in 2020—a scale that compares with the big industrial union drives of the 1900s. They are, in other words, a huge swath of the organized working class, even while their work continues to be misunderstood and devalued. The Supreme Court dealt them another blow in 2014 with the *Harris v. Quinn* decision, where Justice Samuel Alito created the special designation of "partial public employees" to yet again exclude these workers from labor protections. The lead plaintiff in that case, Pamela Harris, received Medicaid funds to care for her own severely disabled son, and argued that, in essence, she did not want the state or the union interfering with her family decisions—a version of the "part of the family" argument that erased the hundreds of thousands of home care workers who are not, in fact, part of the family.[32]

The rights of home care workers matter because, as Poo pointed out in her 2015 book *The Age of Dignity*, many Western countries are facing an "elder boom" on the heels of a decade of severe austerity. Several more decades of neoliberal restructuring have also hacked away at many of the institutions on which elders rely. In Germany and Japan, Poo noted, new universal programs have been implemented that provide for long-term care based on need rather than income or the availability of family members. In the United Kingdom, care workers face many of the same struggles as they do in the United States: their long hours and unpaid travel time leave them exhausted. In the iconic industrial city of Manchester, one writer described a working class that had turned from factory labor to care work; in fact, many of the carers are looking after the very men and women who worked in those factories, but for lower wages and fewer benefits than the factory workers once had.[33]

In late capitalism, as more and more people have had to take on paid work, more and more of the work previously done in the home has been commodified and is now done for a wage. And in an increasingly global-ized world, much of this work is done—not just in the United States but in many other wealthy countries as well—by immigrants from the Global South. This has changed the power dynamics, particularly in the United States, where undocumented migration has only become more stigma-tized and vulnerable even as we rely on it more. A period of decline in paid domestic work has been followed by a dramatic spike, and home care, in particular, is one of the fastest-growing and largest US occupations. "The terrain of political struggle for domestic workers has shifted dramat-ically," Premilla Nadasen explained. In the 1970s, the movement fought for citizenship-based rights; in the 2010s, it has to struggle around the very issue of citizenship status.[34]

Immigrant women, who have few employment options outside of of-ten under-the-table domestic work, wind up at the very bottom of the la-bor market: they are paid the least and expected to put up with the most. Their low wages have subsidized the middle-class family; their caring has made sure that middle-class families do not have to go without. For many employers, a worker like Adela Seally with a family nearby is less desirable than an immigrant worker in the United States who has left her family at home in her country of origin and can devote all her love to the client's children. Those workers leave their own families in the care of others, in a form of "offshore reproduction." And the remittances they send back home rival oil company revenues in terms of international flows of money.[35]

The workers are also vulnerable because of immigration policy. The current migration apparatus in the United States has its roots in the 1990s—it was put together alongside welfare reform, by the same bipartisan coalition. The Antiterrorism and Effective Death Penalty Act and the Illegal Immigration Reform and Immigrant Responsibility Act of 1996 built on the foundation of the Reagan-era Immigration Reform and Control Act, which had allowed three million undocumented migrants to become "legal," but also heightened enforcement. As the prison system expanded, migrants found themselves criminalized just for existing.[36]

It is the very gray area in which many undocumented workers operate that allows the worst employers to take advantage of them, as workers who attempt to escape an abusive boss can be vulnerable to deportation. Migrant workers who leave their own families behind are often more willing to live with their employers, making their jobs a 24/7 commitment. Domestic workers have reported physical and sexual violence, and even human trafficking. As historian Laura Briggs pointed out, it was important that the immigration crackdown made migrants more vulnerable but did not halt immigration entirely. The supply of exploitable labor was too important.[37]

The vulnerability created by various systems of legal and extralegal migration is not limited to the United States, either—in Europe, non–European Union migrants, from Asia and North Africa and even the former Communist bloc—do a significant portion of the domestic labor, and they, too, are vulnerable to immigration crackdowns in an increasingly hostile climate. What all these workers have in common is that, as researcher Carmen Teeple Hopkins wrote, "the precarious citizenship that these women experience often interlocks their place of employment with their place of home."[38]

These workers are so often displaced from their homes, and yet they are expected to provide love where they land, in what Arlie Russell Hochschild called "the global capitalist order of love." And the fact that many of them do have genuine feelings for their clients, particularly when they care for children or elders, makes the work even harder. Eva Kittay, whose own daughter Sesha relied on the services of a longtime care worker, wrote poignantly of the challenges they all faced as Sesha and Peggy, her caregiver, grew older. How does one retire from such a longtime "relationship with no name"?[39]

For many of the women, in particular, who benefit from migrant women's caring work, the entire situation is fraught. Feminists, as noted above, may have fought for domestic workers' inclusion under labor laws, but many of their high-flying careers are subsidized by low-wage women in the home. This situation replicates an age-old power dynamic that has roots in systems of oppression those same women vehemently oppose. Yet there is no way to avoid the power differentials inherent in the employer-employee relationship. As author and social critic Barbara Ehrenreich wrote, "To make a mess that another person will have to deal with—the dropped socks, the toothpaste sprayed on the bathroom mirror, the dirty dishes left from a late-night snack—is to exert domination in one of its more silent and intimate forms." Researchers Seemin Qayum and Raka Ray pointed out that claims of friendship between boss and worker are just an "egalitarian" version of the "rhetoric of love."[40]

These problems came into sharp focus when the coronavirus pandemic locked many of us in our homes to work and to be surrounded by housework. When the United Kingdom moved to lift restrictions on movement, some well-off feminists celebrated the ability to hire cleaners once again—even as the rules appeared to imply that it was acceptable to bring a new person into your house to clean it, but not for a visit. "Cleaning is work, and it's work that I'd rather not do myself or negotiate with my household. I already have a job," wrote Sarah Ditum in *The Spectator*. *The Telegraph*, meanwhile, said the quiet part out loud: "The argument appears to come down to which women you want to defend—those who hire cleaners, or the cleaners themselves." Cleaning is indeed work, but the spat over hiring a cleaner reminded us that a woman's solution to the problem that has no name still often relies on a less well-off woman picking up the slack. Some of those who defended their decision to hire help insisted, in their defense, that their cleaners loved their work.[41]

The bonds of love can be so easily weaponized against domestic workers. "You're just like one of the family," an employer told a worker named Elvira. When Elvira responded that she had her own family—and that family did not treat her badly—the employer snapped, "Remember, you're just a maid." Yet the family narrative has also become so routine for workers that they make a joke of its insincerity. Filipina domestic workers in Hong Kong often wound up gripe sessions about overwork, curfews, and controlling employers by cracking, "So you're a member of the family too, eh?"[42]

If one can buy love and family so easily, where does it end? In perhaps its zenith, Ishii Yuichi and his Japan-based company, Family Romance, provide actors, including Yuichi himself, to fill family roles for a wage. While often he is hired to be a stand-in boyfriend at social events, Yuichi began his company portraying a father for a friend of his who was a single mother; another client of his hired him to play the father for her daughter, who had never met her biological parent. "I am the only real father that she knows," he explained. "If the client never reveals the truth, I must continue the role indefinitely. If the daughter gets married, I have to act as a father in that wedding, and then I have to be the grandfather. So, I always ask every client, 'Are you prepared to sustain this lie?'" Relationships like this one, Yuichi said, have made his "real" relationships feel like work. "I'm full of family," he said.[43]

It is a paradox of domestic labor that something that is so intimate, personal, and specific also relies so heavily on a few tropes. Thus it is perhaps not surprising that there are attempts, particularly as domestic workers assert their rights but also as the elder boom looms and low wages mean that few families can afford a stay-at-home parent, to try to find technological fixes. On the flip side of Yuichi's love-for-hire model in Japan is the institution of interactive robots to do some of the caring labor. While it is possible to imagine robots being a desirable option for those who want to be independent, the idea of "companion robots" paying attention to lonely elders feels every bit as dystopian as a parent-for-hire, particularly if human companionship is only available to those who can pay.[44]

Even without robots, employers have sought to standardize domestic work in order to eliminate some of those pesky intimate tensions. As

Barbara Ehrenreich wrote of her time working as a housecleaner, "For better or worse, capitalist rationality is finally making some headway into this preindustrial backwater." There is no pretense at family with Merry Maids; the employer pays the service, the service hires the maids and brags of their willingness to shine floors on their knees. Yet even these companies demand a certain performance of love. Author Miya Tokumitsu found "a maid-service company advertising on Craigslist . . . looking for 'a passionate individual' to clean houses."[45]

And then there are the apps. TaskRabbit and its competitors allow people to hire a one-off assistant at the click of a button. Care.com will find you a babysitter or care attendant. According to one TaskRabbit executive, 60 percent of its users are women, many of them mothers searching for just a little help around the edges. In his sunny view, this piecework approach to hired domestic labor is making women's lives easier. More cynically (and perhaps accurately, given that programming is still male dominated), one *Harvard Business Review* article called these apps the "Internet of 'Stuff Your Mom Won't Do for You Anymore.'"[46]

The labor exchanged via app is atomized, casual, precarious, and often personalized—just like paid domestic work has long been. It is less that these apps create a new form of unreliable, low-wage work, and more that new technology is facilitating a very old type of work arrangement. Yet domestic workers have also been some of the first to figure out how to collectively organize app-based work. In Denmark, the 3F union managed to win a collective bargaining agreement with a platform that provides cleaning workers to private homes. Workers will be considered employees of the platform—something that most of the bigger app-based services have fought strenuously against—and gain minimum-wage protections, job security, and unemployment benefits in case of illness, as well as something crucial for app-based workers, often called out at the touch of a button: 50 percent pay if the job is canceled less than thirty-six hours before it begins.[47]

Organizing has been difficult for domestic workers precisely because they have individual, one-on-one relationships with employers; the standardization of services like Merry Maids or the apps at least offers some hint of a way that the workers can come together to pressure the boss, something like the way home care workers have been able to bargain with governments at the state level. But for those who are still working in individual relationships, it has been necessary to rethink what organizing could look like.[48]

For workers who perform intimate labors, it may be necessary to create what historian Dorothy Sue Cobble called "more intimate unions," unions that understand the worker in a holistic sense and focus not simply on wages and benefits but on a deeper understanding of the interpersonal relationships that structure the work relation. Such organizations would see it as their job to meet the workers' needs on many levels—they would organize, for example, around immigration reform, fight deportations, and take their members' daily experiences of racism and sexism on the job seriously. Legal assistance and training, too, would be an important part of these organizations. Personal service jobs are only growing more common, particularly in deindustrialized nations where less production is now done: they are harder to automate, so far, and the relationships that these workers build with their clients can be sources of power as well as abuse.[49]

In the United States in 2010, New York's Domestic Workers United and its outgrowth, the National Domestic Workers Alliance, won the country's first Domestic Worker Bill of Rights. The bill put into law overtime and minimum-wage protections, a guaranteed day of rest, paid time off after three years, and protection against arbitrary employer deductions from wages. Subsequent state- and city-level bills in Massachusetts, Illinois, Seattle, and California have improved on the New York law, adding provisions for enforcement, notice of termination, and harassment protections. But one of the biggest challenges has remained: making sure domestic workers know their rights under the law, and feel empowered enough to demand that they are respected. Without a shop floor and a break room in which to post notifications of rights, workers, particularly when they are new immigrants, are often in the dark. Finding out about the law and making demands under it can be a daunting task.[50]

The National Domestic Workers Alliance stresses that the work its members do "is the work that makes all other work possible." It is an argument for the importance of that work not just on a personal level but as a key part of the economy. The Alliance consists of sixty affiliate organizations in more than thirty cities that organize with nannies, housekeepers, and caregivers. The affiliates also lobby for legislation and provide training, legal support, and guidance, and even engage in direct action on behalf of abused workers. The Alliance also puts out original research relying on the testimony of domestic workers about their conditions and their needs. "Our journey," said Ai-jen Poo, the founder and director of NDWA, "[took us] through realizing how much at the core of this was about a devaluing of the work that women have historically done to care for families across generations. . . . That was at the heart of it, in addition to the structural racism that has led to the exclusion of this workforce being written into the law and shaping our framework for how we value work in this country."[51]

In recognizing these key facts, Poo said, the organization has recognized that its fight is about more than legal protections. It's about "the values that will shape the economy of the future, what the social contract will look like and who it will include, and who it will uplift and what kind of opportunity it will create."

⁙

ADELA SEALLY FOUND HER WAY TO NDWA IN 2014, WHEN SHE ATTENDED a National Nanny Training Day event. There, she met Allison Julien, who was at the event to speak about the New York Domestic Worker Bill of Rights. Julien invited the attendees to a monthly organizing meeting, and once Seally went, she was hooked.

The monthly meetings, she said, provided more than just a space in which to talk about grievances. There are more opportunities for training, and also writing workshops and arts and crafts projects. Through NDWA she has taken expanded training modules on nutrition and on effective communication with parent-employers. She has also become a peer leader—something like a shop steward in a more traditional union setup. She leads training sessions on her own and makes sure that other nannies and domestic workers know their rights under the law.

To Seally, giving up Saturdays for training sessions and being a peer leader is another way of giving back to her community—a community of workers who are often very isolated on the job. It has also given her a sense of the challenges that other domestic workers face. She and the other volunteers, she explained, spend time calling other workers to check in, find out how their work relationships are going, offer support, and invite them to workshops. The workshops range from "know your rights" training to resume-building or immigration law. Seally is also a part of a group within NDWA called We Dream in Black, a group of domestic workers who identify as Black. Within that group, they have a space to discuss the specific issues of racism that they face on the job. "Nannies in New York City, getting them to come together is really difficult," she laughed. "We have so many different backgrounds. It is challenging. Sometimes we have meetings and then like five people show up. You always have doubts. 'Are we getting across to them?'"

"We have been talking about the challenges of getting our nannies to organize," she explained. "Being a domestic worker, most times there is just one of you in the house. If you do live up in the suburbs or somewhere, you hardly see another domestic worker or nanny. We try to get them to come at least once a month and we can talk about whatever is going on, how to organize, and how they can negotiate their contract for their working conditions."

She has spoken with workers who have gone in and at the end of the day, had the employer simply say, "We don't need you anymore." Part-time nannies sometimes get a phone call saying, "We don't need you today," and don't get paid. Parents will scream about minor things, she said, like the nanny giving the child the wrong snack. "Then, the mom goes off. That is not the reason why. Maybe she is feeling guilty [because the nanny is the one spending time with her children]." But, Seally noted, nannies have the same problem as the employer: they, too, must leave their families at home in order to go to work. "Whatever is going on in your personal life," she said, "you have to leave it at the door when you get there and put on your brightest, happiest face for the baby and the employer. No matter how you are feeling, you have to suppress your emotions just to keep that job."

Domestic workers sometimes find themselves caught between employers—one parent may come home, get angry, and fire the worker, and then the other parent tries to come in and smooth things over because they need the worker back. "Being a nanny is the only profession I would say where you have two employers to one worker," Seally said. Then, if the nanny wants to move on, the parents mobilize their emotional bonds to try to keep her. "Why are you leaving the kids? The kids love you so much," they'll say. "Some nannies will give them a month's notice and then, one or two weeks after, they get so mad because she is trying to move on, they fire her." This leaves the nannies feeling betrayed.

One woman Seally spoke to while phone-banking for an NDWA event was a live-in worker who had been sexually harassed on the job. "She was telling me sometimes when she goes to bed, she will take her dresser and put it behind the door, and that is how she would feel safe because there was no lock on the door." The room she slept in was the children's playroom with a sofa bed, not a real bedroom. With Seally and NDWA's support, the woman was able to find a better position.

Nannies find employers sneaking in extra duties. "They tell you light cleaning, but then it becomes heavy cleaning. You have to take care of the child, but then you have to do the family's laundry, and all of these things take away from being able to provide optimal care for the child," she continued. "I think because they are the employer, they feel that it is okay to disrespect and look down on you."

Through NDWA, Seally learned about the early washerwomen's strikes, and about Dorothy Bolden and the organizers of domestic workers' unions in the 1960s and 1970s. Those stories inspire her to keep organizing. "With all of this technology and access," she said, "we really have no excuse not to organize and be seen."

Seally has also taken part in protests and political actions. She traveled to Washington, DC, to stand alongside women farmworkers who had been sexually harassed and assaulted, and to speak about domestic workers' similar exclusion from legal protections against such violence. While she was there, she also made some lobbying visits to senators to ask them to support a federal Domestic Worker Bill of Rights that was introduced in Congress in the summer of 2019. "We are going to start working on getting all workers included in the law so they can work for a living wage," she said. They talk about a "living wage," not just "minimum wage," these days, she said, because the goal is to make sure workers are not choosing between paying rent and paying the other bills.[52]

New York domestic workers, Seally said, are also working on expanding the Bill of Rights there to incorporate some of the protections won in other states. "The thing with having a Bill of Rights is that enforcing it can be really tricky and difficult," she said. "Some individuals can negotiate a really good contract when they go in for an interview. Some are very laid back. For me, when I started, I had no idea about that. Sometimes, we sell ourselves short." Because their work can be so unreliable, domestic workers often feel pressure to take whatever job is offered, even if they know the pay will not actually cover their bills. After a little while with NDWA, Seally was able to return to her employers and negotiate paid time off when they take vacations, and other improvements to her contract when she returned to full-time work.

When the coronavirus pandemic hit, all of the issues around which the nannies were organizing became more urgent. Seally's situation changed, but she was able to keep her job; other workers lost their jobs when the families they worked for decided to leave New York. As of this writing, many of them still didn't know whether their employers would return. "Some of the nannies have been paid while all of this is happening. Some of them are getting full pay. Some of them are getting half pay. Some of them are getting no pay at all," she said. "Some of them are actually doing a little bit of virtual nannying [over video chat]," engaging with the children so that parents can do something else. "This is new to everybody, so everybody is just trying to see how they can do something to ease all of the stress."

Deciding to go back to work, for the nannies, is difficult. Employers have been making outsized demands in some cases, while often being unwilling to reciprocate or compromise. One of Seally's colleagues was asked to come back to work, but to refrain from all other social contact, she said. Another nanny's clients were in Florida for a while, and upon their return they asked her to provide proof that she'd been tested and was COVID-free. But when she asked the family for the same proof, they became angry. "I think she ended up leaving her job," Seally said. "The sudden demands of nannies are unacceptable, I would say. Everybody wants to stay safe. Nobody wants to get sick. I know that I may be taking precautions, but I don't know what the other person is doing."

It is not enough to rely on employers to do the right thing, Seally noted. "Paid sick leave and paid family leave are very important because everybody has their families to take care of, and bills are still expected to be paid. Domestic workers do deserve better health care, like any other sector of workers. We contribute to society just as any other profession. I think we should be paid and treated the same."

Seally feels that her time organizing has helped her to grow as a person and to learn about her work, about the law, and about how to be an effective political actor. Organizing work, she said, is challenging, but fighting the stigma on domestic workers is worth it even if it adds up to just a drop at a time. "Society has seen nannies as being dumb, not informed, and that is so far from the truth," she said. "A nanny is a nurse, she is the doctor, she is the mom, she is [the] therapist, she is the miracle worker. All of these things come into your responsibility." The most important thing, to her, is to continue to make her work visible and respected. "I always tell my nannies, 'You have to demand respect because nannying is a profession. You have to be proud to say that you are a domestic worker. You are the pillars of society. You hold up society.'"

CHAPTER 3

WE STRIKE BECAUSE WE CARE

Teaching

Rosa Jimenez's smile lights up her whole face. The twelve-year teacher can often seem pensive, but when something pleases her, the feeling is infectious. And when I met her, in January 2019, despite the miserable and very un-Los-Angeles-like rainstorm that had poured on the striking teachers' picket lines for four days, she was still smiling, even bundled in a purple raincoat and rain boots, her glasses misty.

Teachers like Jimenez in the United States make something like 21 percent less than workers with similar education levels in other fields, and yet for all that they sacrifice—for all that they love their work—they are still often blamed when students fail to transcend the circumstances in which they live. Teachers tend to stick it out, staying on the job even as budget cuts mean class sizes grow and resources shrink—and even as they buy toilet paper and food for their students out of their own paychecks. When they dare to make demands for themselves—and especially when they strike, as Jimenez and her coworkers in the United Teachers Los Angeles (UTLA) did that January—they are often told that they are greedy, that they are only in it for the money. Being on the picket lines in that driving rain, Jimenez said, was "really visceral" for her. It brought home to her how hard it was to make ends meet in a rapidly gentrifying city. It's a struggle for her, and it's an even bigger struggle for many of her students, who face homelessness, a hostile immigration system, and violent policing in their neighborhoods and in the schools. It sunk in, she said, that first day: "Wow, this is about fighting for ourselves and our families. And this is also for our students and our community. And this is much bigger than us, as well."

Jimenez teaches history to the upper grades—high school juniors and seniors—at the University of California Los Angeles Community School, which is one of six schools that share the Robert F. Kennedy Community Schools campus in LA's Koreatown neighborhood. She became a teacher, she told me, because, "I realized I need to do something where I am serving the community, but I also have an opportunity to be an organizer. I don't see any other places, other than teaching, to be able to do that, where you are in the middle of a community, you are able to grow those relationships with parents, with students, with other teachers, and really try to build something big and powerful."

Building that power is important because of whom she serves. Her school alone has over eight hundred students in kindergarten through twelfth grade. It is located in one of the most densely populated areas in a mostly spread-out city (the district spans some 960 square miles, from mountains to valleys to waterfront). Many of her students are recently arrived immigrants from Central America, Mexico, and Southeast Asia, and her school is bilingual—she teaches in English and Spanish.

"We consider ourselves a social justice school," she explained, and when I asked what that meant, she laughed, her face lighting up again. "We have had lots of internal debates about that, but the idea was both that the teachers and the way that we teach are reflective of the needs of our students and that we are building an environment and building spaces for learning that support students to become agents of change."

That means, for instance, that the school is taught in multiple languages because teachers and the community believe it is valuable and just that students learn in the language in which they are most familiar. It means a commitment to antiracism and to teaching the students curricula that are relevant to their lives.

The school is also, as the name implies, a "community school," a model that teacher activists like Jimenez have committed to as an alternative to the wave of privatization that has swept through urban school districts in the past few decades. Teachers are involved in making school decisions democratically, parents are invited to feel comfortable inside the school building and to be part of those decisions, and students' thoughts on how the school should be run are valued.

The social justice dimension of Jimenez's work hits close to home. Her parents were immigrants from Mexico who both worked in factories; her father, a shop steward in his union, she said, "always talked about the importance of standing up for your rights as a worker." Her activism meshed with her teaching from her first days in the classroom. She was part of a wave of new teachers who were laid off in the days of budget cuts driven by the 2007–2008 financial crisis, and the fight to save funds for the schools was the first glimmer of the movement that would find her on that soggy picket line twelve years later. She was part of a big civil disobedience action against budget cuts, but it was unsuccessful, and she realized, "We have a long way to go if we want to really shift and challenge the situation—otherwise, it is not going to change."

The schools were crumbling and overcrowded, she said, when she was brought back into the classroom. When she got the opportunity to move to the new RFK campus to help build the community school, it was a chance for her to put some of her ideas into practice in the classroom as well as outside of it, to create a space that could be a model for the rest of the district.

At her school, she has a number of responsibilities on top of teaching. She has regular meetings with students and parents, of course. She is on committees to help with professional development. And she makes time for organizing meetings each week—bringing together teachers who want to support students' organizing, or meeting with community groups that work alongside the union. All of this is on top of being a single mother, so her eleven-year-old daughter's commitments—to softball, playing guitar, or other activities—also take up a lot of her time.

Things had only become more challenging with the coming of the Trump administration and its crackdown on immigrants. "Every week, we see new students and we recognize that those students have experienced a lot of trauma," she said. "We have kids who are coming from detention centers, and we do not have the capacity to support them and their social-emotional needs." Part of the challenge, she said, is trying to do more with what they have—resources she is grateful for at her school, but that she recognizes are still insufficient.

"We really need more therapists, more psychiatric social workers," she told me. "We need people who can support that aspect that we just don't have the capacity for. Teachers are doing it every day and our counselors are doing the best they can, but . . ." she trailed off.

The challenge of being an authority figure, a counselor, an adviser, and a friend to her students is a big one, and it is complicated further by punitive school disciplinary practices. When students face random searches in school, she pointed out, it's not by school police (of which there are plenty—Los Angeles has a dedicated school police force), but administrators and counselors. "The very same people that you are supposed to trust and you are supposed to feel safe with are the ones that are making kids feel unsafe." For teachers to really build trust, she noted, they have to change this disciplinary framework. "What are alternatives to traditional school discipline that pushes kids of color out of the schools?" she asked.

It is a daily challenge to make the school feel like a place of safety. Migrant students and other students of color have justified fears of state authorities, and fears of the school shootings so prevalent across the United States today. But Jimenez believes that all the threads of her work come together, that none of them work without the other parts. The students have to feel comfortable, safe, and valued in the school; parents have to be a part of that space; and teachers have to have the support they need to make sure all of this happens.

To that end, it's the idea of sanctuary that she returns to. "What would it mean to be a sanctuary school?" she asked. "It would be a community school with all the things that a community school has and it would be free of ICE [US Immigration and Customs Enforcement] and it would be free of police and it would have all the things that students need to feel safe. It would be a place that could be a center of organizing for the community. So if the community is experiencing issues around police, around housing, whatever the case may be, that these schools are not just here to protect, but we are also able to go out and support whatever organizing is happening in the community."

"I don't think such a place exists yet," she said dreamily. "But that is the vision."

⁂

TEACHERS LIKE ROSA JIMENEZ HAVE LONG BEEN EXPECTED TO TREAT their job as more than just a job. From the beginning of publicly funded schooling in the United States (and Europe), teachers have been pressed to treat their work as a calling, to dedicate long hours outside of the classroom to it, and to do this out of care for their students. Yet such expectations have existed in tension with the idea that teachers' skills are little more than a "natural" inclination to care for children, rooted in a love that is simultaneously too big and too unimportant to be fairly remunerated. Like the work done in the home—paid or unpaid—teachers' work is considered both necessary and not really work at all.

Teachers thus occupy an uneasy place in our understanding of the world: expected to be a reservoir of emotional and intellectual support for new generations, they become a receptacle for all the blame when their teaching does not manage to overcome all the obstacles placed in their students' way. They exist on the edge of a class boundary, not quite granted the respect given to doctors or lawyers, but not quite perceived as the working masses, either. Teaching has been the professional occupation most accessible to immigrants and to Black people, a fact that has also contributed to its complicated status both as a path to upward mobility and as an easy place to lay blame. For a long time teaching was considered a stopgap job, either on the way to a real career (for men), or on the way to having one's own children (for women). The teaching profession is still overwhelmingly female, teachers' labor considered similar to mothering—an essential job nevertheless to be done out of sheer love. Teacher and author Megan Erickson pointed out, "Thus the failure of teachers is like the failure of mothers—unthinkable, monstrous, disgusting, the final antisocial act that threatens not only the fabric of the political economy but its perpetuation."[1]

Teachers are, in other words, perhaps the ultimate laborers of love. Expected to do more with less every time budgets need tightening, and yet to take the blame every time those budget cuts do harm, teachers epitomize the trap that has all laborers of love in its grip. If they demand better conditions for themselves, they're called selfish, even as their demands are often ones that would improve their students' lives as well. Yet teachers have a long history of militant organizing, of challenging the boundaries placed around them by politicians and administrators, and of bringing their communities along with them.

Teaching was not always or inevitably women's work, though. In the early days, before the institution of compulsory public education, teaching was a young man's job, often a part-time one. Students were clumped together in a one-room schoolhouse or tutored privately, and teachers sometimes traveled between multiple teaching gigs. Women teachers began to appear with the first "Dame" schools, an English transplant to the colonies where children were educated by women in their private homes—a type of work close enough to mothering to be considered an acceptable occupation for women.[2]

The "feminization" of teaching began in earnest as publicly funded schools expanded. The first generation of school reformers explicitly advocated it. Catharine Beecher, the sister of Harriet Beecher Stowe of *Uncle Tom's Cabin* fame and a prominent social activist, opened a training school for women teachers in 1830 and became the loudest voice calling for women to enter the field. Women, by teaching (and Beecher herself, by teaching the teachers), could gain "influence, respectability, and independence," she wrote, while maintaining their womanly virtues. Teaching could also, Beecher noted in a somewhat more forward-thinking moment, give women an alternative to marrying out of economic necessity. In speeches, she extolled the ability of women teachers to prevent uprisings like the French Revolution, where the "common people" had taken it upon themselves to overthrow their leaders. Women teachers, akin to ministers or missionaries, could soothe such fires and instill moral values in the nation's youth with their boundless love for children.[3]

But it wasn't just women's angelic goodness that led to them being hired en masse as schoolteachers. There was the simple fact that staffing schools was expensive, states wanted to keep pay low, and men could find higher-paying work elsewhere. Women, meanwhile, had few options. They were perceived not to need a wage—they would be supported by their fathers before marriage, and their husbands after it, with teaching as an interlude. Advocates explicitly called for the hiring of women to keep budgets down. Even if, as Beecher intimated, some women saw teaching as an escape hatch from marriage and the family, it was hard to fully get free. Teachers who lived away from their families often boarded in the homes of school board members, leaving them under 24/7 supervision from the boss. And most school districts explicitly banned married women from teaching—another implication that the work done in schools and the work done in the home were equivalents, neither deserving of pay.[4]

The weight fell even harder on the teachers in schools for Black children, where every dollar spent was begrudged by white people and where teachers had an even more urgent mission. Teachers of Black children held in their hands not just individual children's futures but the need to prove that Black children as a group could achieve just as much as white youth, given half a chance. And half a chance—or a third of a chance—was often all they were given, with segregated Black schools receiving sometimes as little as a third as much funding as white schools. More than any other teachers, Black teachers were expected to perform miracles out of pure love.[5]

By 1900, nearly three-quarters of all American teachers were women, and that number was even higher in urban areas. In European countries, teaching held closer to a 50/50 gender split, and pay and benefits were comparatively higher. The percentage of male teachers increased as students grew older (and the work, presumably, less like mothering and more intellectual), and most administrators were male. But despite all the stereotypes of saintly, self-sacrificing "motherteachers," women teachers were in fact acutely aware of the less-than-optimal conditions in which they often worked, and they were getting angry.[6]

The resistance began in the 1890s in the same city where it would restart a century later: in Chicago. Schools had been formalized, though battles over taxation still meant they were often underfunded. Public employees in many places had won benefits such as pensions, which, as historian Marjorie Murphy wrote, offered women teachers "an attractive alternative to the adulation of the feminine, which would give them no financial solace in their old age." Money, not love, after all, paid the bills. Still, male administrators retained control, and male-dominated legislatures—elected by male voters (women did not yet have that right)—decided where schools would be and how much would be spent on them. These men had no intention of letting women teachers have a say.[7]

Without the right to vote, and without the legal, formalized collective bargaining that would come much later, teachers needed the support of the broader community behind their demands. They were able to use the close relationships they built with students, as well as their reputation for selflessness, to build bonds inside and outside of the classroom that enabled them to win improvements in the schools. It was a lesson that teachers like Rosa Jimenez later drew upon as they rebuilt their unions in the 2000s. These teacher activists took the responsibility of care seriously. Rather than chasing the respectability politics of professionalism, a path they had been denied in any case by virtue of their gender, they decided that if they were going to be treated as women first and workers second, they would use those stereotypes to build power.[8]

In the early years of public schooling, teachers had been told that it was their femininity, not their brains or carefully honed skills, that was important in the classroom. Asking for higher wages, though, made them seem less feminine. Teachers were highly trained and heavily supervised and yet told their work was a product of natural talent. To all of that, Margaret Haley and the early Chicago Teachers Federation (CTF) said, "Enough!"[9]

Haley and the other Chicago teachers taught in cramped classrooms with up to sixty students in them, many of those students freshly arrived immigrants who among them spoke half a dozen different languages. (Conditions, in other words, not too dissimilar from those faced by Rosa Jimenez today.) But Haley and the CTF scoured the tax rolls to catch those who weren't paying taxes and campaigned to have the city recover that money and spend it on schools. Their work earned the teachers a major raise in 1899, and the federation—not yet a union—national attention.[10]

The National Education Association (NEA)—a professional organization dominated by (male) administrators, who resented the incursion of women classroom teachers on their professional prerogatives—had existed for a number of years at that point. But the CTF teachers drew on their experience in the classroom and their skills as communicators (also honed on the job) to build an organization that fought for teachers and their working-class students along class lines. Haley was a fierce critic of industrial elites, telling a crowd, "Two ideals are struggling for supremacy in American life today; one the industrial ideal dominating through the superiority of commercialism, which subordinates the worker to the product and the machines; the other, the ideal of democracy, the ideal of the educators, which places humanity above all machines, and demands that all activity shall be the expression of life." The joys of teaching, Haley argued, would only exist if teachers were preparing their students for a world in which they would be full democratic participants, not merely drudges.[11]

In response to the rabble-rousing Chicago teachers, the NEA reached out to women's clubs and social organizations—the forerunners of today's nonprofits. But these women were mostly bourgeois activists rather than working schoolteachers. Haley and her colleagues preferred to rally alongside the working class, bringing together teachers from several cities to form the American Federation of Teachers (AFT). They also allied with the Chicago Federation of Labor to help organize women factory workers; the AFT joined the national American Federation of Labor (AFL) in

1916. Yet the teachers' relationship with organized labor was fraught—officially, the AFL supported the "family wage," which assumed workers were men with a wife at home doing housework. The teachers, meanwhile, demanded equal pay for women, even married women, who were still too often banned from the classroom.[12]

There were still tensions within the teaching profession, too. Despite all of Haley's leadership, a man, Charles Stillman of the Chicago Federation of Men Teachers, was elected founding president of the new AFT. Power struggles remained between men and women teachers over issues of professionalism, privileges for high school teachers, and even support for the world war then raging around them. Black teachers were admitted in segregated locals, but the specific challenges they faced teaching Black students in separate and most definitely unequal facilities were often ignored in favor of other debates. Were teachers workers like any other, or were they members of the professional middle class? Were they to be troublemaking trade unionists, or lobbying wheeler-dealers? And always at the bottom of such questions: Was the work done for love or money?[13]

WHERE TEACHERS HAD AT FIRST BEEN EXPECTED TO CARE FOR THEIR students, once they'd unionized, administrators found such caring workers unruly. Instead of saints, they had become hell-raisers. School officials began to look to the new "science" of management, Frederick Winslow Taylor's ideas about compartmentalizing and deskilling work, to control their troublesome workers. Teachers' interpersonal skills had never been recognized as such, and now those skills were being defined out of existence entirely. Standardized testing, the bête noire of today's teachers' unions, first arose at this time, along with the idea of tracking students by class background into vocational or more elite programs.[14]

With the advent of the first Red Scare, after the Communist revolution in Russia, administrators found a new way to control educators who might have ideas about running schools. The first loyalty oaths for teachers appeared in New York in 1917 and had spread to two-thirds of the states by the 1930s. As the teachers' unions fought for academic freedom in the classroom, they also joined their communities in organizing outside of it—some advocated freedom for leftists like Nicola Sacco and Bartolomeo Vanzetti, or for members of the Industrial Workers of the World, who had been accused of violence but railroaded for their political beliefs. It was often the women teachers who led the charge for these causes, against World War I, and for racial equality in schooling, while male teachers were more likely to hew to the ideology of professionalism. The progressive women teachers—these early Rosa Jimenezes—were still holding to a caring ideal, but they expanded the range of things that they cared about. And for that, they began to lose their jobs.[15]

The first teacher to go on trial—not technically a legal trial but certainly conducted and publicized like one—was a Quaker, Mary Stone McDowell, who opposed the loyalty oath in keeping with her faith. She was fired in 1918 for "conduct unbecoming a teacher." There would be many more like her after World War II, when, the fight against the Nazis over, Americans turned all their energy toward the Cold War with the Communist USSR.[16]

During the Depression of the 1930s, the teachers being hired were more educated than ever, and more diverse than ever—particularly, as journalist Dana Goldstein wrote in *The Teacher Wars*, in New York, where many of the teachers (a majority of new hires by 1940) were Jewish. Jews were newly able to access higher education through the City University system, but unlikely to be hired outside of the public sector even with their degrees. New teachers, politically radicalized by circumstances and paid through President Franklin Roosevelt's temporary relief programs, had flocked to the unions, and young leftists in turn flocked to the Communist Party. The Depression pressed teachers to their limits: public budgets in places like Chicago were so stretched that teachers were paid in scrip or sometimes not paid at all. Yet the teachers were still targets of rage from the public for being relatively well off (which, in that era, often meant having a job at all).[17]

After the Depression, the economy was growing again, the Baby Boom was on, and the schools were expanding. Yet that resentment remained, and teachers remained a politically soft target. They were easy to paint as radicals undermining America while sponging off the public dime, in a preview of the language later used to demonize the "welfare queen."[18]

Some of them—though certainly not all of them—were in fact radical, though their ideas were far from the caricatures promoted by the red-baiters. Communist teachers emphasized organizing alongside the community, particularly the working-class and underserved Black and Latinx communities in the cities where they taught. They fought for improved working conditions, but similar to the reform movement headed by teachers like Jimenez in the 2010s, they understood those working conditions to also be their students' learning conditions.[19]

In New York, Communist members ran the Teachers Union (TU), which argued that an "organization like ours cannot confine itself to a narrow line of economic activity only. Teachers, like other humans, do not live by bread alone." It pledged to end "discrimination in education on account of sex, color, race, religion, or political beliefs, or affiliations" in the 1940s, well before *Brown v. Board of Education* put an end to legal separate-but-equal schooling. The union lobbied for smaller class sizes, for recreational spaces for children, and for special attention to underserved areas like Harlem and Bedford-Stuyvesant in Brooklyn, where children of color attended crumbling segregated schools. The leftist teachers advocated for culturally relevant curricula that taught Black history and immigrant history and grappled honestly with the American legacy of racism.[20]

The Teachers Union fought, too, for the rights of women teachers, including the right to marry and remain in the classroom, something that was banned in many states up until World War II. In 1941, Bella Dodd, spokeswoman for the TU, proposed the creation of publicly funded nursery schools (more than sixty years before New York mayor Bill de Blasio made universal prekindergarten his central campaign plank). The union wanted to both create jobs for teachers and to "aid working women with small children."[21]

The Red Scare sprang from the top down—it was Washington-led fearmongering in support of US foreign policy—but locally it became a useful whip with which to discipline teachers who were making trouble.

The first teacher to feel its sting in the postwar era was Louis Jaffe (no relation), a Brooklyn high school social studies teacher who was driven from his post despite the support of ninety of his colleagues. Jaffe was punished for teaching about the Soviet Union in a way that upset his supervisor. Another New York teacher, Minnie Gutride, was dragged from her class and questioned in a "surprise hearing"; a cancer survivor, Gutride was so traumatized by the event that she committed suicide.[22]

Despite the bad press that Gutride's death gave the district, administrators continued the witch hunt, eventually purging 378 teachers from New York schools. A TU lawyer commented, "These were people well along in years and careers. Many became menial salesmen, burdens on friends and families, moving about like beggars. Some were totally shattered. And they had all been good teachers, some great." Parents coming forward, telling administrators, as they did of one Harlem teacher, "We love Alice Citron because she has fought for us and our children," had no effect. Citron, who had taught in Harlem for nineteen years, was known for "writing an African American history curriculum, inviting students to her home, and using her own money to buy needy children eyeglasses, books, shoes, and food."[23]

In other words, the teachers who were purged were doing what they had been recruited to do: care for the children in their charge, fight for them, put those children before themselves. They built connections with the local families and used their power as a union to make those families' demands heard.[24]

In response to the Red Scare, the Teachers Union went deeper into the community, demanding desegregation, construction of schools and play spaces in Black neighborhoods, and the hiring of Black teachers. This was in spite of spying, police infiltration, and sometimes racialized hate mail—one anti-Semitic hate letter "juxtaposed a loyal and patriotic 'American mother' to Godless Jewish Communists." It was in spite of the threat, for immigrant teachers, of deportation (one administrator was on the lookout for those whose citizenship might be "amenable to cancellation," presaging the Trump administration's attempts to get rid of those it considered undesirable), and constant attempts to find proof that

Communist teachers were plotting to overthrow the US government. All the spies found during their snooping were debates about racism, gender bias, and US foreign policy.[25]

The Cold War also led, at least for a while, to increased funding for schools. The launch of the first satellite, Sputnik 1, by the Soviets in 1957 made American officials realize that the Communist teachers had been right about one thing, at least. As Megan Erickson wrote, "education and space are both metonyms for the future," and it appeared that the USSR was pulling ahead in both. Americans were nervous about the future, and the schools, then as now, were a locus for those conflicting anxieties—people feared that Communist teachers might be indoctrinating students, but the schools also needed more funding in order for American kids to catch up to the Communists.[26]

The pattern was repeated the decade after the *Brown v. Board of Education* decision in 1954. While teachers' unions broadly supported the school desegregation process, the fallout from the fight largely hit Black educators, many of whom lost jobs when Black schools were closed. Black students might be going to previously all-white schools, but white parents were damned if they were going to have their kids taught by Black teachers. Black teachers, who had gone above and beyond the ill-funded school system in which they had taught, who had marched and organized and fought for desegregation and served as anchors and caretakers for the Black middle class, lost their jobs as payment for all their care. Once again they were caught in the trap: too much love will cost you.[27]

Teacher tenure laws were one major target for segregationists determined to find a facially race-neutral strategy for getting rid of Black teachers. Across the South, after *Brown*, seven states moved to change their tenure laws, and North Carolina placed all teachers on one-year contracts. These attacks had the desired effect of making it easier to fire or drive out Black teachers, but also made it easier to fire any and all teachers. Punishing teachers for failing to solve all the world's problems with their care became that much easier. Black teachers who retained jobs were often set up to fail, as in the case of one Black home economics teacher assigned to teach second grade after integration. She—and many others—were fired for "incompetence" at jobs they had never done before. At the same time, the Lyndon Johnson administration moved to recruit students from elite schools to do short-term teaching stints, a strategy that flipped the earlier image of teachers on its head: rather than committed, caring educators, all this strategy offered students was a brief encounter with the highly educated, who would then presumably move on.[28]

The tensions within the teaching profession came to a head in Ocean Hill–Brownsville in Brooklyn in 1968, where the old Teachers Union style of community organizing came up against a new style of unionism. Militant and surging unions were winning collective bargaining rights, and the hard-charging United Federation of Teachers (UFT), having won the right to represent all of New York City's teaching force through a strike, wound up clashing with Black community activists. The UFT was focused on the "bread-and-butter" needs of teachers. Meanwhile, frustrated with desegregation efforts implying that Black children were deficient and Black teachers incompetent, Black community organizers were agitating for community control of schools, arguing that it was racism, not Black deficiency, that left Black students underachieving. Teachers who had pulled back from the community found themselves deemed uncaring by activists, who argued that Black communities already had the ability to improve the schools, if officials would just get out of the way.[29]

The UFT at the time was designed to make teaching more professional, more like "work" and less like "home." It was led by Al Shanker, who, according to educator and scholar Lois Weiner, didn't acknowledge "the inevitable contradictions that arise between teachers' personal and individual responsibility for children, the ways their work continues the functions of the family, and the location of these functions in a bureaucracy as paid labor." The disconnected professionalism—which had always been gendered masculine—of the new UFT brought it into conflict with Black parents and education activists who embraced their role as caretakers for Black children. The arguments of professionalism grated on parents, who felt condescended to by those who had never seemed to care for Black children. During the UFT's strike against the community-driven firing of white and Jewish teachers in Ocean Hill–Brownsville, many teachers—the descendants of the old TU—crossed picket lines as well. Where the Teachers Union model had worked side by side with those parents and had fought to bring more Black educators into the schools, the UFT stressed the division between "work" and "home," which ended up pitting them against parents. This strategy would weaken the newly powerful teachers' unions, leaving them vulnerable to attacks that they did not care enough about children.[30]

This conflict also showed up in Chicago, during the then white-dominated Chicago Teachers Union's 1969 strike. Many Black teachers who had been organizing for better schools crossed picket lines and continued to work. Others participated in the strike, seeing it as a way to bring more resources to the children of color they taught. These moments seemed to raise the same few questions: Was a strike by teachers an inherently selfish thing? Or was the problem that the teachers were disconnected from the parents and students in the communities where they taught? The embrace of such a disconnect was what administrators had wanted—a point beaten into teachers with the crushing of the TU—but the distance also served as a weapon to then turn against "uncaring" teachers. And the school districts were only too happy to fire more people.[31]

The success of teachers' unions in this time, then, was a double-edged sword. They won improved conditions through collective bargaining and strikes, including protections, Marjorie Murphy noted, that would have "saved the jobs of hundreds if teachers had had such rights before McCarthyism." But it also set them up as a labor aristocracy—people more concerned with their own wages and job security than for the students for whom they were responsible—and left them on their own in crucial fights. When the economy as a whole turned downward in the 1970s, teachers and their unions were an easy target for tax-cutting conservatives. When the corporate reformers came in, waving their own banner of care for children while finding new ways to make profits off the public schools, the teachers' unions were unprepared.[32]

The same people who demanded that teachers be held accountable for perceived declining standards were those who advocated slashing taxes and making teachers do more with less. This trend began in the 1970s but was ramped up in the 1980s with the neoliberal revolution. Class sizes grew and, particularly in urban schools, programs like art and music were stripped away. Public schools in the United States have always been hampered by the fact that they are mostly funded through local property taxes, meaning that the richer communities have more money to pour into schools, and poor neighborhoods suffer from less money per child. The inequality now rampant in American life shows up in public education in dramatic fashion.[33]

⁛

FOR A WHILE, TEACHERS ACQUIESCED TO THE CHANGES. "WE'RE USED TO being like, 'OK, whatever you want me to do, I'll do it, because we all care about what's best for kids,'" said Karen Lewis, the president of the Chicago Teachers Union during its 2012 strike. But that kind of caring didn't help them against a corporate-backed education "reform" movement that wedged itself into the cracks between teachers and the communities they served; no matter how much the teachers conceded, the reformers continued to insist that teachers' selfishness was the problem.[34]

The creation of charter schools was at first itself an initiative of the AFT, but the union quickly realized its mistake when neoliberal reformers seized on the charters as a way to open new, nonunion, privately run schools with public dollars. The schools targeted for closure or privatization, and the teachers targeted for removal, tended be to those responsible for educating Black and Latinx children. "Choice" was a sleight-of-hand turn away from "community control." Instead of schools that parents could be involved in—like the schools Rosa Jimenez works to create— charter schools gave parents a "choice" of the underfunded, overcrowded public school or a shiny new program with experimental (and often draconian) disciplinary policies and claims of improved test scores. Implicit in the rhetoric of choice, as Adam Kotsko noted, is the acceptance of personal responsibility—and the attendant blame if your choice doesn't work out. It echoes in the line we're often given about "choosing" a job we love—as if work were a thing we decided to do for fun.[35]

Teachers were used to accepting blame by now, but even the reformers had to admit—as they did in the Reagan administration's 1983 report on the situation, called *A Nation at Risk: The Imperative for Educational*

Reform—that teachers were being asked not just to make up for underfunded schools, but, with their care, to make up for the cuts to the entire welfare state. The report still, even admitting this fact, blamed schools for the nation's economic problems. But the real problem was that, like the home care workers who filled in the gaps of social care, teachers were expected to solve problems caused by homelessness, hunger, and a lack of health care in their communities. Just as the cuts pushed responsibilities back onto individual parents, they also forced teachers—those whose work was assumed to be closest to that of mothers—to make up for massive cuts elsewhere.[36]

In order to better "hold teachers accountable," the reformers relied heavily on standardized testing. George W. Bush's No Child Left Behind Act, passed with bipartisan support in 2002, introduced a strict testing regime and made federal funds—which were desperately needed in poor districts where property tax money was insufficient—dependent on the schools submitting to a range of new regulations and privatization schemes. As Lois Weiner noted, the law brought home the reforms that had been imposed on Global South countries through the United States' dominance of international institutions like the World Bank and the International Monetary Fund. The intent behind the reforms, Weiner suggested, can be seen most clearly in those international documents, which state explicitly that most students are destined for menial work and need neither a well-rounded education nor skilled (or particularly caring) teachers.[37]

The Obama administration made noises about changing No Child Left Behind, but its own program, Race to the Top, doubled down on testing students and firing teachers. The language that Education Secretary Arne Duncan and his allies in the now-sprawling private education reform industry used was "putting students first," the implication being that selfish teachers and their unions did the exact opposite.[38]

Yet these reforms were designed in fact to produce less-caring teachers. Whether it was bringing in short-term outsider teachers, from programs like Teach for America, or imposing weeks of standardized testing, the reformers deskilled teachers while denying they were doing so. After all, teachers' concern and care had never been recognized as skills to begin with. They were just attributes of naturally caring workers.[39]

Schools are the hinge point of neoliberalism, a place where it has been imposed and where the blame is placed for its harms. If teachers were simply adequate, the thinking goes, then all of this inequality would go away. Yet when this line of argument is pursued to its end, the lie is evident: even if every single child received a top-notch education, and "learned to code," as the cliché has it, all this would do is produce more competition for those relatively few highly paid knowledge-economy jobs, and drive down their wages. It's almost like that's the point.[40]

But in 2012, the Chicago teachers' strike upended these power dynamics. Black teachers like Karen Lewis were at the forefront of the reform movement within teacher unions around the country, drawing on the history of Black and leftist teachers' community involvement in places like Chicago and New York. With the CTU's confrontation with Mayor Rahm Emanuel, Lewis and the union sent a shot across the bow. "We're supposed to think that the elite, who are very wealthy and very well educated and don't send their children to public schools, care more [than we do] about black and brown children they don't know?" Lewis said. They were the ones with the children day in and day out, and with the community by their side, they were going to fight for the kinds of public schools their students deserved.[41]

This new organizing strategy is based in the teachers' relationships in the community, harking back to the old days of the Communist organizers, and to Margaret Haley and the origins of the Chicago union. It avoids the trap imposed on teachers—strike, and get called selfish by administrators, and alienate parents who depend on the schools—by reclaiming the mantle of caring about the students and the broader community. In working alongside parents and students to make demands of the school administrators, teachers gain the space to make demands for themselves.[42]

And they need that space. As economist Kate Bahn explained, teachers and other caring workers face a pay penalty when compared to other workers with similar education levels, and a big part of that is because they care. Teachers are less pay sensitive when compared to other work-ers, meaning they're less likely to pack up and leave for a better-paid job, and indeed, they have accepted cut after cut. The Economic Policy In-stitute calculated that "teachers' weekly wages in 2018 were 21.4 percent lower than their nonteaching peers." Teacher Kevin Prosen wrote, "This love is supposed to be part of the compensation of doing our job. But people are less comfortable considering that love is not compensation; love is work. . . . It's exhausting, loving and working so much, for such little pay—which explains why over 32,000 mid-career teachers have left the system over the past eleven years. We can't live on these wages, and we have only so much love, and time, to give."[43]

Their opponents have not stopped, after all. The year after the CTU strike, Emanuel retaliated by closing forty-nine public schools, mostly in Black and Brown neighborhoods. And then in 2018, the Supreme Court, building off the *Harris v. Quinn* decision of 2014, that took rights away from home care workers, ruled, in *Janus v. AFSCME*, that the entire pub-lic sector was now "right-to-work." That meant that a union that has won the right to represent a particular workforce no longer has a right to collect a fee for its costs. The backers of *Janus*, a who's who of anti-union orga-nizations, expected the public sector, and particularly teachers' unions, to hemorrhage members, though so far the damage has been blunted—largely, it appears, by the willingness of teachers to fight.[44]

When the teachers in West Virginia organized a strike in 2018, clos-ing every public school in the state to demand fair pay, they kicked off a strike wave that spread to at least fourteen states, further changing the cal-culus about public schools. Their slogan, taken from Chicago, "Our work-ing conditions are our students' learning conditions," was written across protest signs, printed on T-shirts, and included on lists of demands. And as Los Angeles struck, as Chicago struck again in 2019, and as the St. Paul Federation of Teachers struck in the spring of 2020, the teachers contin-ued to further their demands, adding safe housing, restorative justice pro-grams, moratoria on charter schools, and mental health care for students to the list of victories won by teachers for their communities. The frame-work begun in Chicago is now known as "Bargaining for the Common

Good." It provides a way for unions—not just teachers but many different kinds of unions—to bring demands to the bargaining table that benefit the community at large.[45]

That kind of union ethos served teachers well when the COVID-19 pandemic began. In New York, as it became clear that the virus was spreading across the city, teachers mobilized to pressure the city's Department of Education to close schools. Organizing networks that had begun as a reform movement within the union sprang into action, using video calls to discuss what to do. The idea of a sick-out, as teacher Ellen Schweitzer explained, came up relatively early. "Many rank and filers, who hadn't necessarily been that involved before, just sprang into action seeing that this was urgent, that others needed to step in and take charge and that a sick-out would work." As the momentum for the sick-out built, and as teachers spoke out and parents joined them, the DOE announced that schools would close.[46]

The teachers have had enough, and because of the work of reformers like Lewis, Schweitzer, and Rosa Jimenez, the public is once again on their side. From the strikes to their mobilizations against police violence that sparked in late May 2020, these organizers demonstrated a point that radical teachers have long known: teachers' fraught location in public life can be an immensely powerful one if they use the skills they've honed on the job—caring, communicating—and their ability to disrupt the day-to-day functioning of a city or state to see that their demands are met.[47]

THE RAIN ENDED IN LOS ANGELES ON A FRIDAY IN JANUARY 2019, AFTER four straight days of downpour on more than thirty thousand UTLA member teachers who turned out to the picket lines in ponchos and borrowed rain boots, carrying umbrellas painted with strike slogans such as "Red for Ed," "Students First," and "Lower class sizes now!" Many carried signs with some version of the slogan "We strike because we love our students." They had held dance parties and sing-alongs in the rain; with the sun, they poured into Grand Park downtown for a rally and concert with another thirty thousand or so of their friends, students, and allies.

"UTLA, do you feel your power?" boomed the union's president, Alex Caputo-Pearl, from the stage, and the crowd roared back at him.

In the afternoon, in the sun, the picket line outside of RFK Community Schools was raucous, even before the hotel workers' union showed up. Rosa Jimenez joined her coworkers in marching alongside the UNITE HERE members, taking over the streets in a red-clad mass of solidarity that culminated at the LINE Hotel on Wilshire, where the hotel workers also sought a contract. In her red UTLA shirt, her daughter at her side, Jimenez grabbed a bullhorn and addressed the crowd in Spanish and English from the back of a pickup truck. "It is important that we are together!" she told them. "We're all workers, we all need good health care, we all deserve a good wage." The rest of her comments were drowned out in cheers.

That weekend, the district gave in, agreeing to a contract that would lower class sizes, put a nurse in every school, reduce standardized testing by 50 percent, hire more counselors, invest in more green space on campus, cut back on random searches, cap charter schools, and give the teachers a 6 percent raise.

On the phone that night, Jimenez told me, "It's way more than I could have ever imagined." The district had threatened to take the union to court over its demands, arguing that things like green space and policing were outside the realm of what the union could ask for. But the teachers had known that they had the support of the community, the students, and their parents, and had held firm. The contract also included a commitment to creating more community schools like the one Jimenez had helped build, as well as a fund for defending immigrant students—things that had been priorities not just for her, but for the student activists with whom she had crafted demands.

"We went out on this idea that we're not going out for ourselves, we're going out for our students," she said, but nevertheless, it was important to remember the teachers' own needs too. "Seventy percent of us teachers are women. We're asked to do feminized labor even more than we have to. I think it's worth acknowledging how much work and care go into being a teacher." To have a nurse in every school, a counselor, meant that some of that work could be shared.

"It's not the end," she continued. "We now have a sturdy ground to stand on with what we've learned from this, what we've learned about organizing, to build coalitions, to work with students and parents in a meaningful way. Whatever we imagined was possible, it's now bigger. Now our imagination can run wild, and that's what we need to really build justice in our communities."

Getting to that point of victory in the massive strike (Los Angeles is the United States' second-largest school district; only New York City has more teachers and more students) had taken years of preparation. For Jimenez, the struggle had begun with the budget battles of her early years teaching. "When the budget cuts hit, we were really looking to the union to help and a lot of people's opinions were that it didn't do enough to protect all of these young teachers of color. So there were a lot of young teachers of color who were organizing on their own."

Some of those teachers went on to found a caucus within the union called Progressive Educators for Action. It was made up of teachers, like Jimenez, who wanted the union to be more active on issues of racial justice in the schools, whether on policing or immigration issues or in the fight for more ethnic studies courses and other relevant curricula. They also built a coalition outside of the union, the Coalition for Educational Justice, that began to bring teachers together with parents and students who wanted to change conditions in the schools. The coalition's grassroots organizing expanded, challenging so-called school reconstitutions at supposedly failing schools in low-income areas. In bringing teachers together with parents and students, they began to challenge the narrative that blamed teachers' lack of care for the problems in public schools.

After the CTU strike in 2012, the Los Angeles teachers began to think more seriously about what it would look like to take power in the union, and built a new caucus, called Union Power, around the demands they had been shaping alongside parents and students. When Union Power won control of UTLA in 2014's union election, it kept its promises to build an organizing department, a political department, a research department, and a parent/community division—the teachers even voted to increase their own dues to do so. They built into the union, Jimenez said, a shift in how they thought about organizing. The new union was all about rank-and-file teachers like her stepping up to take on new roles, and so she became part of what was initially called the Parent Community Organizing Committee. She then helped build a bigger coalition called Reclaim Our Schools LA with other community organizations, including the Alliance of Californians for Community Empowerment (ACCE).

Jimenez and her counterparts in the groups she began working with thought it was important to recognize that the union must use the power it had at the bargaining table to bring demands originating with the students and the parents before the district. This kind of bargaining for the common good expands on the strategy of the old radical unions, blending community work with the power of collective bargaining. Jimenez's work within the union has been "to think strategically about how to use this body, this space, to push out a different narrative about what it means to have a labor-community alliance, and what it is capable of doing." That means monthly sessions where members of the union and the different groups meet up to talk about plans and desires. It means communicating back to members the decisions that were made and making sure the union and the groups trust one another to fight for their demands on all fronts—during bargaining, during the legislative sessions (both at the state level and locally), and by pressuring the school board and other local officials.

On the fourth night of the strike, Jimenez and many other members of the coalition went to the Pacific Palisades home of Austin Beutner, the LA schools superintendent, bearing electric candles, protest signs, and a song: "The community is calling." When, predictably, Beutner failed to answer his door—or rather, the buzzer outside of the gate to his driveway—parent activists and students held a speak-out in his driveway.

"I found out that we had our nurse one day a week and I went to war!" one mother declared. "I have one biological child at that school and 588 adopted children at that school." Student Cheyenne McLaren spoke of her anger and frustration with the unequal conditions in the schools. She was a member of a group called Students Deserve—led by students, with parents and teachers like Jimenez as allies—that was inspired by the Black Lives Matter movement to fight racism in the schools. It was from them that the demand to end random searches came, and also the desire for more community schools. "We really have been inspired by Black Lives Matter and their framework of divesting and investing. Divesting from policing and from other things that police our schools and students and communities and investing in things that see our students as fully human and provide them what they need to really thrive," Jimenez said.

It was the fact that the community was with the teachers that led the district to give in rather than to dig in, hoping to break the union in a protracted strike. The UTLA strike was the first big battle of the post-*Janus* age, and as Jimenez pointed out, the administrators failed in all their attempts to divide and conquer—they were unable to divide the teachers with a two-tier health-care plan, unable to divide the public school teachers from charter school teachers, and unable to divide the teachers from their students.

Since the strike, Jimenez had felt the difference in the classroom. Her students were curious about the work that went into the strike, and began to apply its lessons to the history they had previously learned. It gave her an opportunity to try teaching history in a new way. "We were studying about strikes and the history of strikes right before we went on strike and then, when we came back, I had them do a little exercise where they were the historians, and they were writing a history of the strike that they just witnessed. They were really into it." Studying the movements of the 1960s and 1970s, her students asked her, "How did they get so many people? I don't get it—my mom doesn't even let me go out to the corner, how did these young people get involved?" That question is an invitation, she said, to ask them what has changed since then.

The students connect those historical struggles to the movements they see and participate in now. "The other day we were talking about the courage of Emmett Till's family to speak up and stand up for things even though they thought they might be killed. They asked me, 'Have you ever done anything where you felt scared? Where you felt like you were in danger?' I say, 'Yes, it is scary every day. But it is also scary not to do anything and not to fight to change things.' It was one of those moments, just a reminder that they see me as somebody who is obviously doing this work."

Those connections were especially valuable to her students in the middle of the Trump administration's crackdown on immigrants, during the coronavirus pandemic, and in the upswell of protest after the police killings of George Floyd and Breonna Taylor in 2020. For her, all of these issues were intertwined, and they all underlined the question of sanctuary at school.

When the schools shut down to prevent further spread of COVID-19, Jimenez's school managed to distribute a number of laptops to students, but, she noted, it was still incredibly difficult to translate classroom teaching to virtual learning. Any experimental projects were suddenly out the window. "It just kind of turned everything upside down," she said. And for teachers like her who were parents as well, there was an added layer of stress.

The power built with the strike meant that UTLA was able to quickly mobilize and get a side letter added to its contract that, Jimenez said, "really spoke to the needs of students and teachers, especially those of us who are multitasking at home with kids and family." Jimenez was working on special projects that spring, supporting interdisciplinary work, and helped other teachers pivot to using the pandemic as a teaching device, to combine social studies and history and science by teaching both the biology and history of pandemics.

But even so, the changes were difficult for teachers and students alike. "Many of our students are just struggling not just to log on, but to have enough food and have enough money," she said. "I work with a lot of newcomer students and a few have just stopped attending to online learning—they've started working. . . There really isn't another option because their family members or whoever was taking care of them lost their job or lost hours. The choice was, 'Am I going to do this online schoolwork or am I going to get to making some money?'"

Students Deserve had put forth demands around the coronavirus pandemic, ranging from universal passage (to eliminate the pressure of getting grades in a global crisis) to rent cancellation to the freeing of prisoners to stop the spread of the virus. And teachers, Jimenez said, had taken those demands into the classroom. "They're going through it one by one with students: 'Where is this demand coming from?' and looking at statistics around the virus in prisons, looking at how Black people are dying more, looking at other moments in history where questions of race and class were driving the way people were impacted."

This organizing between teachers and students, she said, had opened up space "to reimagine what is possible in terms of schooling." Because of the pandemic, all state-required tests were canceled. "Nobody misses them!" she laughed. But the questions were becoming sharper as the teachers and students looked toward the potential reopening of schools. "What do we want to be in place before we reopen? And, if we don't have those things, what are we willing to do?" The union eventually won an agreement with the district to maintain distance learning in the fall, rather than forcing teachers and students back into the classroom at risk of spreading the virus.[48]

It all made her think back to her first days as an educator, having to fight for the public schools' budget. "We were just not in the place—our union wasn't and the world wasn't and all unions were not in a place to fight back in the way that we are now," she said. But now, with a strong union and a strong coalition in the city, the teachers were preparing to use their power once again.

One point in that fight was likely to be over the police budget. Even before the protests began in May 2020, Black Lives Matter Los Angeles and other organizations had been pushing for a People's Budget that would cut police funding—54 percent of the city's discretionary budget had been set to go to the police department—and reinvest in public services. UTLA also backed a successful push to cut the budget for the school police—a separate department—by $25 million, or 35 percent.[49]

Jimenez took on some new roles after the strike. She's expanded on her work organizing with parents and students and her work in the community school, finding new ways to ensure that the demands of the entire community are met. She's now on the Community Schools Steering Committee, for example, a body that includes district staff, and even students, working to bring the promised thirty new community schools to fruition. She was also elected area chair for the union in the North Area, a position in which she was learning more about the union structures in order to keep building its strength.

Through all this work in the union and the community, it could be hard to remember to think about herself. But the strike had taught her something important, something that hit her on the very first morning on the picket line. "We get told so often that we are greedy and we only care about the money," she said. "But we are living in a really expensive city and it is getting more expensive all the time. It is not easy." On the line the first day, as police arrived to keep an eye on the strikers, the feeling brought tears to her eyes. Watching her colleagues in the rain, struggling but keeping their spirits up, dancing to "Proud Mary" from a portable speaker, drove it home for her.

She continued, welling up again. "I had this moment this week where it was like, 'Oh, I am also doing this for myself as a worker, as a working-class person, as a single mom. This is actually not that easy for me. I am not getting paid. I am actually also sacrificing.' It is okay to say, 'This is also for me.'"

CHAPTER 4

SERVICE WITH A SMILE

Retail

Aɴɴ Maʀɪᴇ Rᴇɪɴʜᴀʀᴛ ᴅɪᴅɴ'ᴛ ɪɴᴛᴇɴᴅ ᴛᴏ sᴘᴇɴᴅ ʜᴀʟꜰ ʜᴇʀ ʟɪꜰᴇ ᴡᴏʀᴋ-ing in retail. It just sort of happened that way.

"I have always worked. I have worked two and three jobs," she explained. She had left her position in medical billing right before her first child was born, and hadn't quite figured out what was next. A few months after her son's birth, she stopped by a Toys "R" Us store and saw a "Now Hiring" sign. They hired her on the spot for the holidays. That was 1988.

"I had no aspirations of being a permanent cashier or working in retail. It was definitely not on my bucket list," she said with a laugh. "The make-up of a part-timer today is either you are a mom, you are a student, or you are working a second job." But she liked the idea of getting back to work, in part because she didn't want to buy her husband a Christmas present with his money. "I always had my own money," she said.

Reinhart is from Long Island, and you can hear it in her voice even though she's been in North Carolina for years now; she is warm and motherly but with a mischievous twinkle in her eyes when she's telling a funny story. She'd assumed her stint at Toys "R" Us would be over after the holidays, but instead the store started training her in customer service and how to keep track of the money. The pay wasn't great, and retail could be stressful, but the company always gave her some flexibility in her schedule so she had time to be with her family. "Those will be my dying words, 'They always worked with me,'" she laughed. "That was when it was more of the company that Charles Lazarus created, that family type of atmosphere."

The flexibility allowed her to stay through her second pregnancy, when she briefly considered leaving for good. When both of her children were in school, she gave in to her managers and coworkers and took the full-time position her managers offered her, moving into a supervisor's role. It came along with a new benefit: health insurance. Her husband worked in a small business with his brother, and insurance had been costing them thousands each year. The insurance from her job—and the continued flexibility—made it worth her while to stay. "Back then, Toys 'R' Us was very good to all of us. I was a Cub Scout leader. I was a mom on the football team. It let me be the mom that I wanted to be."

That's not to say it was a perfect job, not at all. The company might have allowed her time off for some of her kids' activities, but she still worked long hours. "I think that nobody realizes all the sacrifices that are made by the people that work in retail. They sacrifice their families," she said. "Almost the entire month of December, I didn't see my husband. He got up early for work. I would come home and he would be sleeping. Then, he would leave for work and I would be sleeping." Her husband once suggested it was time for her to find a "real" job, which frustrated her. "I was like, 'You think I am not busting my ass every day at work? This is a real job.'"

And then, of course, there were the customers. Some of them were lovely, but others could be unbelievably nasty. Sometimes the customers abused her—"I have been called every name in the book"—and other times she had to intervene as a supervisor when they bullied her colleagues. Reinhart brushed her brown bob off her forehead to show me the scar from a Green Power Ranger toy that a customer had thrown in her face. The customer, she said, had brought the same toy back over and over again, taking advantage of the company's return policy. "Finally, my boss was like, 'Listen, she can't come in here every week with this. She is showing no receipt, no box. We aren't doing this anymore for her.'" So Reinhart had to tell the woman they wouldn't take the toy back. "I am a good schmoozer, that is why it took me by surprise. She took it and she threw it at me!" She recalled touching her forehead and feeling blood.

Another incident that stuck with her had happened to one of her colleagues, and she'd had to intervene. A woman came in wanting to return something—again, clearly used—and the employee at the customer service counter politely told her that the store could not accept the item back. The customer, as Reinhart watched, "started berating her and insulting her." The customer turned to her daughter, "who was maybe seven or eight," and said, "This is why you get an education, so you don't end up like her," Reinhart recalled. "I turned around and said, 'What did you just say?'" The worker was in tears, and Reinhart told the customer to leave. "It was just an 'A-ha!' moment for me, like, everyone does view people who work in retail as worthless."

Another horror story involved Reinhart's daughter-in-law, who also worked in customer service at the store. "[One] lady was so mad at her, she took her daughter's wet panties off and threw them at my daughter-in-law," Reinhart said. Her eyes welled up as she recalled her daughter-in-law's scream when the wet underwear hit her.

Retail might have given her a thick skin, and she might have prided herself on her ability to manage difficult people, but these memories clearly still stung. "That is another thing with retail. If you are good at a job—no matter how crappy that job is—they won't take you out of it," she said. "Some days you go home feeling depleted." And the worst part was that after customers behaved horribly, management would often give in to keep them happy. "Not only are you insulted and berated by customers, you felt it double for your store manager to come out and give that customer what they wanted anyway."

The idea that retail was not a "real job" was echoed constantly by her customers. "The word 'stupid' comes out so much that I truly believe they think we are all uneducated," Reinhart continued. "I went to college. Half my cashiers are all in college right now. How dare you?" But in the changing economy, she pointed out, retail work was far from just a job for teenagers. For her, it had been a career that paid her as much as the factory jobs that had built the American middle class—though with no union and with that modern innovation, a 401(k), rather than a pension. "Most of the people my age—I am sixty—grew up with stay-at-home moms," she said. Now, women make up most of the workforce in retail and service, and many of them are moms like her, supporting a family.

After nearly ten years at the big Toys "R" Us store in Huntington, Long Island, Reinhart transferred to a new Babies "R" Us store. The holidays were calmer, without the mad rush every year at the toy store, and she was able to spend more time with her kids. "I came home and my house was decorated right after Thanksgiving. All those years, I didn't get to enjoy the holidays. My kids were like eight, nine, ten years old, and they appreciated it more, too."

As her sons grew up, Reinhart and her husband began to consider moving south, following her sister and brother, who were already in North Carolina. She once again questioned whether she wanted to stay at Toys "R" Us, but since the company had nearly eight hundred stores, she could move and have a job already lined up—and keep the salary she was making in New York. She also had noticed that in her years at Toys "R" Us, retail had begun to change: all the ads she saw were for part-time jobs with no benefits. So she moved to Durham, North Carolina, and became store supervisor at a Babies "R" Us by the Southpoint Mall. The baby registries, in particular, made the job worth it—she enjoyed sitting down with new parents and helping them pick things out. Years later, at a different job, she ran into a former customer, who remembered her immediately. "She says, 'You did my whole registry with me. You sold me my furniture.'" It was moments like that that made her actually like the work.

It was sometime around her move that Reinhart first heard mention of Bain Capital's involvement with Toys "R" Us, though, as it was explained to the employees, Bain was investing money in the company to help it expand the baby stores into superstores. She didn't think too much of it at first. As a human resources representative, she said, she used to go to job fairs and talk up the company. "I would say things like, 'It is a financially stable company. Toys "R" Us has been around forever.'"

Those words haunt her now. In 2005, Bain Capital, Kohlberg Kravis Roberts (KKR), and Vornado Realty Trust took over the company, and things began to change. Slowly at first—slowly enough that Reinhart was shocked when she was told her store was being closed. It was shuttered in April 2018, and the company was liquidated shortly thereafter. Private equity buys up firms that are wobbly through leveraged buyouts that put the debt used to buy them back on the company's balance sheets; if any more trouble hits a company, whether it be increased competition, in the case of Toys "R" Us, or, more recently, the global pandemic, things can unravel quickly. Once iconic brands like J. Crew and Neiman Marcus have fallen into bankruptcy in this way.[1]

What that meant for Reinhart was the loss of a job she'd had for twenty-nine years, with no severance. "It was almost my entire adult life," she said, shaking her head. "What was I thinking?" But the time she'd put in taught her to advocate for herself and for her colleagues, from those moments on the customer service desk to arguing, as HR, for higher wages. "I am most proud, probably, of my work then," she said.

"It did prepare me to fight the company."

IN 1892, THE WORKERS AT THE HOMESTEAD STEEL PLANT IN WESTERN Pennsylvania challenged their employers' demand for massive wage cuts. They were locked out, the lockout became a strike, and the employer called in the union-busting Pinkerton detectives. In the resulting battle, seven of those workers were killed. Today, the smokestacks that burned over those deaths still stand, but the rest of the plant is now a shopping mall, with the tagline, "Where tradition meets trend." Those factory grounds, where workers fought and died to uphold labor standards, now house retail jobs—the wages low, the turnover high, as if those old battles never happened.[2]

Retail salesclerk is the single largest job category in the United States and also a common occupation in much of Europe. Even with the rise of Internet sales, a pandemic, and headlines in recent years proclaiming a "retail apocalypse," retail remains a cornerstone of the economy and a way that millions of people put food on the table. Yet those jobs, in so many cases, are "bad" jobs, with low security, few benefits, erratic schedules, and virtually no opportunity for upward mobility.[3]

Retail jobs are not new, of course, and they have long retained many of the characteristics we still associate with them—they are dominated by women and part-timers, and they are taxing not just physically but mentally and emotionally, as workers often feel trapped between customers and managers. But as the economy shifted from a manufacturing focus to a focus on consumption, the manufacturing jobs—gendered masculine and built on a full-time schedule—were cut back. Retail rose to dominance in manufacturing's stead, and as it did, so did those feminine-gendered labor patterns. But the real difference between the retail jobs and the manufacturing jobs that were fading was the requirement of that "service with a smile." Retail workers, unlike manufacturing workers, have to appear to love their work.[4]

Retail was long considered a sideline, an add-on to the "real" economy, its workers less important or serious than those in factories. For a long time, retail stores were small businesses; up until the Great Depression in the United States, independently owned stores constituted 89 percent of retail establishments and did 70 percent of retail sales. "Mom-and-pop" stores were just that: family establishments that had maybe one or two outside employees. Mostly, the family did what was necessary, even the children.[5]

But capitalist production led to capitalist retail—the massive department store or the sprawling chain that replicated across the country, promising a familiar array of goods wherever the shopper went. And capitalist retail, with centralized management, meant salesclerk jobs. In the

United States, non-owner retail jobs exploded between 1880, when there were about 32,000 clerks, and 1930, when there were 2.3 million. The work varied with the stores—high-end clothing retail involved high-end personal service, with saleswomen patiently outfitting the shopper from head to toe. By contrast, "five-and-dime" stores served the growing working class, providing groceries, dry goods, and the occasional treat, with perhaps just a passing grin from the clerk. The jobs tended to be similar, though, in that they stretched over long hours for low pay.[6]

As retail stores expanded, the job of the clerk did, too. Hand-selling required a range of skills, from product knowledge to physical stamina (fifteen-hour workdays were not uncommon). It also called for the kind of patience and "people skills" needed to read a customer's mood as well as her budget, in order to suggest products that would appeal and upsell extras. Yet such skills were not considered as important as the ones that men in the factory or on the farm might have; the service economy, historian Bethany Moreton wrote, "capitalized on this broad social agreement that women weren't really workers, their skills not really skills." In other words, they capitalized on the same logic that applied to women's work in the home, paid or unpaid, as well as to child care and teaching.[7]

Shopping was also women's work, an extension of housework. Retail stores therefore were designed to appeal to women's sensibilities, whether they were upscale or downmarket. Retail employers staffed up with women workers, who the employers assumed innately had those sensibilities, and would be good at making the store feel homelike. Women, after all, were presumed to be naturally caring and sensitive to the needs and desires of others—and that made them better at selling to other women without overstepping boundaries.

Department stores, in particular, made skilled selling central to their business model. But they had to balance the need to develop the skills of their employees with the desire to keep labor costs down, profits high, and prices affordable. Hiring women, particularly young women, who were presumed to be pliant, helped. That those young women would presumably depart in relatively short order to get married and have families of their own had the benefit for the bosses of keeping turnover relatively high, so that workers never got too expensive or too demanding. And part-time scheduling went hand in hand with low wages: younger women were assumed to be dependent on parents, while married women, if they managed to hold on to a job at all in an era of intense prejudice against married women working, were assumed to be working for "pin money." Their real job was supposed to be homemaking.[8]

Sales jobs were, despite the relatively low pay, respectable work for young women who aspired to class mobility. The department store clerk was expected to model the merchandise she sold, and store discounts encouraged her to shop. This expectation of respectability also meant that sales jobs were largely for white women. Black women—and even Jewish women and immigrants—did not give off the impression of middle-classness needed for sales work. Yet the saleswoman also had to give a convincing performance of deference to her clients, even when they irritated her or reported her to management. Skilled salesclerks found innovative ways to carve out space where they, not the imposing (and usually male) managers or imperious shoppers, were the boss. They maintained their own coded language for talking about customers in front of them; they collaborated to help one another meet sales quotas; and they revenged themselves on coworkers who did not follow the rules. The workers also could make occasional alliances with shoppers who, particularly in the Progressive Era (before World War I and the Depression), took an interest in social reform.[9]

The work it takes to suppress one's true feelings, to maintain a calm smile and the appearance of enjoyment, in order to maintain the customer's mood is familiar to anyone who works with people. This work—which sociologist Arlie Russell Hochschild famously dubbed "emotional labor"—remains a major component of the retail salesperson's job and a key difference between it and factory work. If you're standing behind an automobile assembly line, it doesn't matter if you smile or frown, but your failure to emanate a pleasant mood on the sales floor can ruin your workday (particularly if you rely on commissions or tips). "Seeming to 'love the job' becomes part of the job," Hochschild wrote, "and actually trying to love it, and to enjoy the customers, helps the worker in this effort."[10]

Such labor is deeply gendered: women are made responsible for others' emotions off the clock, and that emotion management has become part of the job while punched in. Yet this distribution of emotional labor reflects the inequalities of the broader society. To manage your feelings in order to avoid imposing them on others is to place yourself in a subordinate position; to have to massage others' feelings all day long is to get used to swallowing your own emotions and needs. Skill in this field is a skill learned from a life without power; it should not be surprising, then, that such a skill is rarely seen as a skill by the powerful, who expect deference as their natural right.[11]

Even as women's emotional skills were undervalued, by paying women a wage at all, retail bosses provided some recognition that they contributed something important. The introduction of training programs and even vocational education in the early twentieth century upheld the idea that sales work was skilled work, yet the workers were also undermined by consistent low pay. Saleswomen earned between 42 and 63 percent of what men did in sales jobs—one shoe saleswoman complained to a labor investigator, "I don't get the salary the men clerks do, although this day I am six hundred sales ahead! Call this justice? But I have to grin and bear it, because I am so unfortunate as to be a woman." Unions, too, accepted the framework of what researchers Jonas Anshelm and Martin Hultman called "industrial breadwinner masculinity"—the breadwinner's job was what mattered, and it was those jobs that should be prioritized, while "women's work" was less important and less worthy of the unions' attention. The same ideology that promoted the family wage therefore undermined the wages of women. It contributed to the sense that retail work was dead-end, short-term work—and easy.[12]

Despite sometimes having to convince unions that they were worth the effort, retail workers fought for shorter hours, higher wages, and looser dress codes, but most of all for recognition that their jobs counted, that their work was also work. Inspired by the sit-down strikers at the General Motors plant in Flint, Michigan, Detroit Woolworth Five and Dime clerks—all of them young women—sat in and occupied their store for seven days in 1937 before winning nearly all their demands. The

Woolworth's was a four-story brick building, a shopping palace, historian Dana Frank wrote, "built for working-class people." The saleswomen at Woolworth's dished out candy and served food and sold a variety of low-priced goods for purchase by people who were slowly winning themselves disposable income and spare time in which to spend it. The saleswomen wanted these same things for themselves. They demanded union recognition, an eight-hour workday, overtime pay, discount lunches, free uniforms, seniority rights, hiring of new workers through the union, and a ten-cent raise per hour on their twenty-five-cent-an-hour wages.[13]

Striking Woolworth's was a shot across retail's bow; it was, Frank wrote, "like striking Walmart, the Gap, and McDonald's all at the same time." And the women did it with flair. They knew that the same charm that had gotten them hired in the first place would play well with reporters, and they performed for the cameras that turned up as well as for one another. They sang songs and danced and did one another's makeup and hair. Their working-class clientele supported them, as did other unions in the city; the musicians' union turned up to play for them. Strikers at a second Detroit store joined them days in; the Waiters and Waitresses Union threatened to take the strike national. Kresge's, a competing chain, gave its workers an immediate five-cent raise, and then on the seventh day Woolworth's gave in. Seeing the success in Detroit, retail workers around the country duplicated their efforts.[14]

Thus the period of rapid growth of chain stores was also a brief period of rapid victories for chain-store workers. The remaining opposition to chain stores—a hangover of the mom-and-pop days and a kind of littler-is-better populism that we still hear echoes of today in politicians' paeans to "small business"—ensured that there wasn't much sympathy in the Depression-era press for the titans of the retail industry. Particularly in the South, there was a belief that "socialism, atheism, chain stores, and companionate marriage" were linked in spelling doom for American culture, yet activists couldn't stop their growth. By the late 1940s, the Retail, Wholesale and Department Store Union (RWDSU) had ninety thousand members, and the Retail Clerks International Association (RCIA) nearly two hundred thousand. Yet even at their peak, retail unions only represented one in ten employees in the industry, and retail workers were left out of early minimum-wage laws.[15]

The anti-chain-store movement, somewhat perversely, helped one of the twentieth century's largest chains find early success. Walmart benefited from the down-home image cultivated by Sam Walton, its baseball-capped founder. Walton spun that image into a lasting perception that Walmart was a "family" company with local roots long after it had expanded beyond any possible family bounds. In the 2010s, longtime Walmart workers were still telling me fond stories of Sam. But the family, as we've discussed, is itself a style of work, and Walton understood how to capitalize on it. In order to appeal to the rural housewife as a customer, as well as to appropriate her labor as she moved into the waged workforce for the first time, Walmart had to *feel* like the family.[16]

Walmart was born in the rural Ozarks, in the northwestern corner of Arkansas, and there the company maintains its base to this day. From there, it grew, until, as historian Nelson Lichtenstein wrote, it controlled a swath of global trade roughly equal to that of the eighteenth-century Dutch East India Company. And in the time of its growth, the global economy was shifting from one driven by manufacturers to one driven by retailers. Woolworth's and the early mail-order houses—Sears and others—were able to use their size to exert some power over the manufacturers from whom they acquired goods to sell, but Walmart epitomized a larger change in the way the world did business.[17]

Though Walmart's major innovation was in distribution, its success in this particular corner of America, largely rural and scarred by Depression-era evictions, relied heavily on the women who worked in its early discount stores. Those women taught Walton what mattered to them: a sense of Christian service and a feeling that they were helping their community, which animated them more than their (low) wages did. Christian family values were infused into the company by its employees and trickled upward to influence the folksy identity that Walton was building into his brand. While part of the anti-chain-store panic was inflected with a gendered fear that "a nation of clerks" would be unmanly, Walmart's familial hierarchy restored order, with women doing the selling for the smiling male founder at the top.[18]

Walmart was also able to cut costs through its self-service model, where (mostly women) shoppers did much of the work themselves, finding branded products in neatly arranged aisles and only occasionally needing assistance from the sales staff. So even as Walmart advertised its quality service, it was in fact trying to cut down on the number of people it had to hire to provide that service. The company rewarded its employees for faster scanning at the checkout counter, giving out pins to cashiers who could scan five hundred items per hour. That scanning efficiency meant sore wrists, certainly, but more importantly, more data for Walmart's distribution system and just-in-time stocking practices. It also meant deskilling the workers and devaluing the very emotional labor it had learned to pay lip service to.[19]

In the 1960s, John F. Kennedy made a raise for retail clerks a campaign promise and got it enacted into law. That was despite the opposition of conservatives like Barry Goldwater, himself the scion of a department-store family, and Sam Walton, who viciously opposed the minimum-wage increase and demanded that his managers ensure the stores remained union-free. Walmart achieved that goal by maintaining a culture that emphasized the importance of service work, even if that acknowledgment came verbally (and on name tags reading "our people make the difference," a slogan reinstated in 2015 after Walmart workers began going on strike) rather than through pay increases. Walmart, and the other companies that followed its lead, worked to infuse a sense of belonging into its workers that would make up for low pay—and would make them better at projecting the aura of care that helped the company succeed.[20]

Walmart's spread across America and the world coincided with—but barely acknowledged—the feminist revolution, even as it relied heavily on the labor of women entering the workforce in droves. While middle-class women were going to work to find meaning, though, working-class women were going to work to find a paycheck, and the work they found was all too similar to the work they did in the home. Retail and food-service jobs didn't pay well, and managers often treated their workers abominably; in such an environment, the pains that Walmart took to at least acknowledge the efforts and care of its workers made it a better employer than many. And as it continued to grow, factories were shrinking, closing, or departing for lower-wage countries; Walmart (or its distribution centers) might soon be one of the few jobs in town. In this way, even as women moved into the workforce, more men moved into jobs that looked like women's work, where they, too, had to learn to do the emotional labor that, in women, was taken for granted. It wasn't the equality feminism had dreamed of: men and women both cobbling together a living from multiple low-paying jobs as the conditions of women's work became more and more widespread.[21]

The Walton family expanded its reach politically as well as economically. It invested in organizations like Students in Free Enterprise (SIFE), now known as Enactus, which sponsors programs at universities to teach students about the beauties of "free enterprise," otherwise known as capitalism. It poured money into small Christian colleges, from which it harvested management trainees loyal to the company and its professed values and willing to put in long hours. And through the Walton Family Foundation, it directed funds to "school choice," the euphemism for privately owned charter schools. According to the foundation's own documents, one in every four charter schools created in the United States has received Walton Family funds. Such an investment in education has ideological goals; it aims to reshape schools and what and how they teach. After all, with widely accessible education, but service industries dominating the economy, what we get is educated workers doing service jobs, and so the Waltons and others like them aimed to make sure those workers believed in the system under which they worked.[22]

Walmart has changed the American workplace: more and more of the jobs of the twenty-first century are made in its feminized, low-wage image, with no health insurance, volatile schedules, and high turnover. More than 70 percent of all jobs, by one count, created in the United States between 1973 and 1980 were in services and retail trades, creating a new "service proletariat" mostly made up of women and people of color. Walmart argues that its low prices make up for the low wages, raising the standard of living of working-class people by offering them cheap goods. It also argues that its workers like their work. Regardless, the company's impact has been such that, as Bethany Moreton argued, "the economic vision we call neoliberalism, Thatcherism, Reaganomics, or free-market fundamentalism could also claim the title of Wal-Martism."[23]

In the wake of Walmart, retail businesses had few options. Walmart's entry into a community often triggered a wave of closures among shops that couldn't compete with the chain's massive advantages. One study found that in the ten years after Walmart's arrival in Iowa, "the state lost 555 groceries, 298 hardware stores, 293 building supply stores, 158 women's apparel shops, 116 drugstores, and 153 shoe stores." As a whole, the retail sector was growing, becoming a larger part of the economy in the United States and Europe, but it was also segmenting, splitting into high-end and low-end and then further in an effort to appeal to different demographics. Few companies could compete with Walmart; those that did either imitated its business model with a slightly fancier gloss (Target) or improved upon it (Amazon). Other companies—like Toys "R" Us— applied it to their specific sector, coming to ruthless dominance. Self-service and the barcode scanner deskilled the formerly skilled sales jobs in department stores, clothing retail, and grocery stores. Higher-end retailers did invest to a degree in service, even while attempting to keep labor costs (wages) low. But they went counter to the overall trend toward concentration and standardization, organizations that could replicate with a largely interchangeable workforce.[24]

As this retail model spread, the recession of the 1970s hit, and then the administrations of Ronald Reagan, in the United States, and Margaret Thatcher, in the United Kingdom, slashed public services and public-sector jobs. Retailers that had been unionized or had upheld near-union wages and conditions felt the squeeze and began to slice away at labor costs. Workers got wage cuts and more part-time, no-benefits jobs. High turnover became a blessing for employers who wanted to shed their costliest workers—a shift from the decades of welfare capitalism that characterized even the earliest years of retail work. The shift to what sociologist Peter Ikeler called "contingent control" gave retail stores and other service employers a flexible workforce that can be hired and fired at need. Those workers, in other words, are unlikely to be around long enough to question managers' power. Ann Marie Reinhart's decades at one retailer, by the 2000s, was a rare experience.[25]

By 2013, less than 5 percent of American retail workers were members of unions, down from 11 percent in 1983. Younger workers can expect more than twenty job changes in a lifetime, nearly double the number of baby boomers. In lieu of providing unionized jobs with decent conditions, the new retail stores learned from Walmart to pay lip service to workers' wants and needs, to embrace "teamwork" while making sure workers didn't actually team up enough to organize. Such paternalism works best with workers who don't need to support a family on their wages—on young people, students, or women, as Reinhart noted, whose main job remains in the home. Something like one in three retail workers is a part-timer. It is easier for such workers to emphasize the positive parts of their jobs and shrug off the negatives; if it is, in the words of one young worker, "not my real job," but just a stopgap, there is less incentive for the workers to make demands. A "cool" supervisor or one who is "like family," snacks in the break room, those can make up for a lot if you never expected a family-sustaining wage in the first place. But it is still important to remember that two-thirds of the retail workforce is in fact over the age of twenty-five, and trending older. There are a whole lot of people working retail who are, in fact, supporting others.[26]

IN 2000, THE FIRST CRACK IN WALMART'S ARMOR CAME WITH THE FILING of a class-action sex discrimination lawsuit against the company. Women at the time made up 72 percent of Walmart's workforce but only 34 percent of its managers; they earned less than men at nearly every level of the company's hierarchy. The company's history of exploiting the service skills of women was still visible in the evidence in the *Wal-Mart Stores, Inc., v. Dukes* case: it had only added its first woman to the board in 1986, when then First Lady of Arkansas Hillary Clinton joined up. The suit landed in the wake of welfare reform, when women were being pushed into low-wage work, and it was decided (in Walmart's favor, on a technicality) in 2011, as the world struggled to climb out of the recession caused by the 2008 financial crisis. Women's work was holding together the economy, but it was still valued less than that of men. The contrast could be stark. One of the *Dukes* plaintiffs, for example, had discovered the pay discrepancy when she was accidentally handed her colleague's tax form—a glance at it revealed that the man, in his first year as an assistant manager, a job she'd been doing for five years, made $10,000 a year more than her. When she complained to upper management, she was told that her coworker "supports his wife and his two kids." Pregnant at the time, the woman realized how much Walmart's vaunted family values were worth. Betty Dukes, the lead plaintiff, told reporter Liza Featherstone that the company was like a bad boyfriend. "They tell you exactly what you want to hear. But then you fall out of love and feel you were basically played."[27]

Walmart has not been the only major retailer to face such criticisms. Target has been accused of race discrimination by the Equal Employment Opportunity Commission, and a class-action suit against grocery chain Lucky Stores resulted in a ruling for the plaintiffs in 1992. Home Depot, too, faced a class-action suit. An employee of Hobby Lobby—the same retailer that sued the US government to avoid paying for its employees' birth control with their health insurance—said she was fired for asking for time off due to pregnancy. When she attempted to sue the company, the case was dismissed because she had, unknowingly, signed away her right to do so in a binding arbitration agreement.[28]

Retail remains overwhelmingly gendered and racialized. Young workers of color tend to wind up in fast-food jobs, while white teens find jobs in higher-end retail. Those are the jobs more likely to be concentrated in whiter, wealthier areas that are harder to reach by public transit. Thus young people, in particular, tend to get jobs based not on economic need but on access. If they do make it into retail, workers of color are more likely to end up in the stockroom than on the sales floor. One study found that 70 percent of Black and Latinx retail workers make less than fifteen dollars per hour, compared to 58 percent of white retail workers. And another study found that transgender people faced a 42 percent rate of discrimination just in attempting to get a retail job.[29]

Increased competition even for retail work means that employees often have to jump through hoops to get the decent jobs—and small, independent retailers are no better than the chains. A New York bookshop made one college student take a quiz on authors, and then recite her favorite passage from a novel—all for a minimum-wage job. A London toy store had prospective employees make up songs and demonstrate selling skill by choosing a random product from the store and making up a play about it. Some companies weed out workers who need a job by ensuring long wait times during the screening process, leaving them with workers driven less by economic necessity than by the desire for a specific position. Presumably, they'll be more loyal.[30]

There are "aesthetic labor" requirements for higher-end stores, which expect employees to embody their brands and use their products, modeling the goods the way early saleswomen did. These norms particularly affect women, who are expected to put forward a certain image of beauty; the cost of the products women are expected to use creates something known as the "grooming gap," as writer and organizer Mindy Isser explained. The gap creates, as Isser wrote, a "pay cut catch-22: If women don't conform, they are paid less; if they do conform, they're expected to use those higher wages on beauty products and grooming regimens." These requirements cut into women's time as well as their budgets, yet forgoing them might mean forgoing the job. Buying and wearing the products they sell is yet another way that retail employees demonstrate their dedication to their jobs. "Sometimes I feel like all the money I earn goes back to the company," one young worker said. Their pay, after all, remains low, and then some of them find that their dedication to the brand is used against them. "You're just in it for the discounts," they are told, another way of telling them their work isn't work after all.[31]

High-end stores do not, in fact, necessarily provide higher-end jobs. Researchers found that high-road retailers that tout their excellent service rarely couple that with high-road labor conditions. In 2017, I spoke with Bloomingdale's workers Betty Lloyd and Kathy Houser, members of Retail, Wholesale and Department Store Union (RWDSU) Local 3 and on the verge of a strike. They were in the aristocracy of retail workers, serving wealthy customers in a flagship New York City store, yet their commissions had dried up, their incomes had shrunk, and their conditions had worsened. Internet sales had eaten into their take-home, as Lloyd explained: "You give them your product knowledge. You show them what you have that is in their needs. You fit them, size them, give them the color. You tell them how great they look. You hear the customer say, 'Thank you very much, Betty, for your service, but I am going to go home and order this online.'" Small boutiques are no better. As writer Aaron Braun pointed out, they trade on workers' desire for a more authentic workplace the same way they do on customers' desire for a more personalized shopping experience. "While these jobs promise a work environment void of the monotony and corporatism usually associated with working-class jobs," he wrote, "they often simply deliver precarious work and a more personalized form of exploitation."[32]

There is, too, the overwhelming suspicion with which retailers have always treated their workers. "Service shopping" or "secret shopping" dates back to the early 1900s, when department stores would send undercover shoppers in to report back on their saleswomen's behavior. Being patted down when one leaves the store is a common occurrence for retail workers. "Loss Prevention" is an obsession of most retailers: at Walmart it dovetailed with the company's anti-union obsession, and the company created a sort of internal police department that monitored workers for pilfering or for protesting too much. New technology makes such surveillance easier—the scanning devices handed to workers to track merchandise also tracks the workers, who have to plug in their information to start the device. Japanese workers have been subjected to a "smile scanner" that gauges how well they project happiness on the job—an automated test of emotional labor. The video cameras that are now common in stores not only pick up shoplifters, but can also tell whether employees are smiling.[33]

The schedule, though, is the biggest complaint among retail workers, and technology plays a role there as well. Retailers attempt to match staffing levels to sales flow, but that is always a guessing game. Scheduling software allows an algorithm to calculate the likelihood of a busy day based on a host of data points, from weather reports to the previous year's sales on that day, and to assign workers based on the results. That means workers' schedules are always changing and may vary wildly from week to week, with preference given to those whose availability is "open," and who do not admit to any other demands on their time, such as school responsibilities or child care. With schedules so in flux, it is easy for managers to use hours to reward favorites, or as punishment for slipups, real or imagined. The dreaded "clopening," where workers close a store late at night only to have to turn around and open it the next morning on just a couple hours of sleep, has made its way into popular consciousness. On-call shifts have expanded, too—one 2014 study in California found that one-quarter of retail workers had to be on call to work that same day. Women remain more likely than men to work part time, whether or not they want to—something like half of part-time retail workers would prefer to be full time.[34]

These conditions are broadly true across the world in postindustrial nations. In the United Kingdom, the zero-hours contract is common—though a work contract at all might sound dreamy to US at-will employees, a zero-hours contract gives the worker no guarantee of any hours at all. As of 2017, over nine hundred thousand workers were on such contracts. In the book *Where Bad Jobs Are Better*, researchers Françoise Carré and Chris Tilly studied retail work in Denmark, France, Germany, the Netherlands, the United Kingdom, and the United States and concluded that while conditions varied by country, "in general, retail jobs have gotten worse across all six countries over the past two decades," with women and young people overrepresented, and lower-than-average wages. German workers, who had better training, got their schedules six months in advance, and had union protections, nevertheless were increasingly in "mini-jobs" with lower pay and fewer benefits. French cashiers got to sit down on the job, and stores closed earlier in the day and on Sundays, yet French retail workers too were tracked for their scanning speed. In Mexico, Walmart is unionized, but the workers complained of excessive unpaid overtime.[35]

Even without the union protections that workers in other countries enjoy, retail workers in the United States have managed to push back some of their worst conditions. On the heels of voting for the highest minimum wage in the United States—$15.20 an hour—and paid sick time, Emeryville, California, a tiny town in the Bay Area clotted with retail stores, voted in a fair workweek ordinance in October 2016. The ordinance required large retailers to give their employees their schedules at least two weeks in advance, and required an extra hour of pay for every time the employer changed that schedule—meaning workers would get paid if they were sent home early or called in from an off day. It also required employers to offer hours to existing employees before hiring new workers. The ordinance came from demands made by workers who organized with the Retail Action Project in New York and in Emeryville with the Alliance of Californians for Community Empowerment (ACCE). Those groups realized that simply raising wages wasn't enough. "You needed to also tackle the means by which they get those hours so that workers have more of a say and more of a voice and more control over the schedules and hours that they get," said Anya Svanoe, an ACCE organizer.[36]

Of course, every gain for retail workers has come amid howls of protest from the employers, who argued that raising retail wages will accelerate what's come to be known as the "retail apocalypse." Stores are closing, the Internet is now where people do their shopping, and entire brands are closing up shop. The result is that people like Ann Marie Reinhart are forced to restructure their lives. To keep up with changing demands, stores lay off workers or cut back hours, often worsening their already-existing problems, according to Richard Granger, organizing director at the United Food and Commercial Workers (UFCW) union Local 23 in Western Pennsylvania. "Our fear is that if people are spending less time and money in a brick-and-mortar location, that if they then also start to experience less customer service, less attention because a corporation makes a staffing decision, that creates a vicious cycle that drives consumers to look for other options," Granger said. There is also the push to automate jobs: the self-scanner is now common in grocery stores and some other retail outlets in the United States and the United Kingdom, but thus far it has had a relatively modest impact on job loss.[37]

The apocalypse was sometimes overstated. Sociologist Stephanie Luce explained that brick-and-mortar retail and even customer service remained popular. "Shopping isn't just buying; it is also an activity. Tourism, for example, involves lots of looking in stores." The Bureau of Labor Statistics projects only a slight decline in the industry over the next decade. While e-commerce has grown relatively rapidly, it still makes up a small portion of total retail sales and only employs a small percentage of total retail workers.[38]

But e-commerce has also expanded the role of the distribution center. Central to Walmart's business model, and now to Amazon's, the distribution hub is a place for goods to move rather than to be held, and jobs in it are infamously miserable. Yet in some ways the jobs are similar to those in the retail stores: the handheld scanner, the shelves of goods, the pressure to go faster. But instead of the emotional labor of smiling at customers, the "pickers" in the warehouse face the grinding boredom of long hours alone, without even music to keep them company. Emily Guendelsberger, a journalist who took an Amazon "fulfillment center" job and wrote about it in her book *On the Clock*, encountered a coworker one night dressed as Santa Claus for a pre-Christmas shift. He was, she wrote, a professional—well, a volunteer—Santa in his time outside of the warehouse, but Santa-ing didn't pay the bills. Santa encouraged her to feel "blessed" to be "healthy enough to work here." But the shift toward more distribution center work is unlikely to leave anyone feeling blessed—or fulfilled.[39]

It might be easier to differentiate oneself from the warehouse work, though, than it is from the enforced smile of the retail shop floor. Arlie Russell Hochschild noted that the risk of overidentifying with the job was the dreaded "burnout," now a buzzword of sorts. Burnout, associated, in particular, with the millennial generation, in the case of retail workers, could be the exhaustion that comes from convincing oneself over and over again that low-wage work is fun and fulfilling, even if not deserving of higher wages.[40]

And now even emotional labor, rarely recognized as requiring skill in the first place, is undergoing its own process of deskilling. Big-box stores like Walmart and Target give workers scripts to follow when they interact with customers, foreclosing their own ability to make decisions, and secret shoppers might also check to see how closely workers follow such a script. Such deskilling itself seems once again to point toward full automation, but in the moment, it's just another tactic of control.[41]

The coronavirus pandemic accelerated many of the trends already existing in retail. With the shift to online ordering as shelter-in-place orders spread across the globe, some companies, such as J. Crew, slid into bankruptcy, while some e-retailers—particularly Amazon—profited wildly. Companies laid off workers, particularly part-timers, as they tried to save money for eventual reopening. Big-box stores like Walmart and Target remained open, putting up safety shields for workers and providing in some cases short-term bonus pay for those who continued to show up. Workers, however, demanded more. The workers deemed "essential" during the pandemic, explained Travis Boothe, a pharmacy technician at Kroger in West Virginia, were retail workers like him, and the whole country was realizing "just how essential we are to the very foundations of this country's economy." Kroger, he noted, was doing "extremely well": "Profits are up, sales are up. They pretty much have a guarantee that those profits will continue throughout this crisis." But the company moved to take away the workers' $2-an-hour "hero pay" just two months into the crisis, and the workers (and some customers) were angry. Telling them that they were essential, that they were heroes, one minute and then taking away their hazard pay the next didn't sit well with them, and that anger lent fuel to the protests that erupted across the nation in late May 2020.[42]

⁂

WHEN ANN MARIE REINHART FIRST HEARD THAT TOYS "R" US WAS GO-ing bankrupt, she said, "I think it was the seven stages of grief. I think we all went through them. It was mostly denial at first."

The announcement came in September 2017. At first the company said it would keep operating as usual; then, Reinhart said, they were told that over one hundred stores were closing, including the superstore where she worked in North Carolina. She tried to keep up her hopes, though, telling herself, "I had seen them close stores before." Since the leveraged buyout—one of a stack of finance terms Reinhart and her coworkers would learn in the ensuing years—"the whole mentality changed." Before, Toys "R" Us had a family atmosphere, she said—she recalled the founder, Charles Lazarus, arriving at her store for an unexpected visit one time, in jeans and a plaid shirt. The store, she said, "was his baby." Lazarus, she noted, died just as the company went into liquidation, in March 2018.[43]

Reinhart had researched Bain Capital during the 2012 presidential race. Mitt Romney (now senator from Utah) was running, and he had been one of the firm's founders. She always read up on the candidates before making her choice, and Bain's business model struck her as predatory well before she had any idea how much it would affect her life. So when her manager mentioned Bain's involvement as they changed her Babies "R" Us to a superstore, she said, "It was like, 'Ding! Ding! Ding!' I said to him, 'Do you know what Bain Capital does to companies? Do you know anything about Bain Capital?'" He defended it to her at the time, but during the liquidation, she said, he messaged her to apologize for not listening to her. "He was with the company maybe ten years, but they sucked thirty years out of me," she said.

The Toys "R" Us workers weren't the only ones poring over the news to find out what would happen to their jobs, their health insurance, and their retirement plans. The organization now known as United for Respect was looking to expand its organizing among retail workers. United for Respect had begun as Organization United for Respect at Walmart, or OUR Walmart, as a project of the UFCW to organize Walmart workers around the country. It used social media to build a broad-based group of workers who might never win a union election at any one store, but who could take action at many locations at once, coming together to apply pressure to the company's leadership to improve working conditions. The organization's founders had always thought of their work around Walmart as a way to affect the retail sector as a whole—as goes Walmart, so goes the low-wage job. But what was happening at Toys "R" Us seemed to them to be another piece of the retail story—the "retail apocalypse" wasn't just because of the Internet, but because finance capital had gotten involved and was attempting to wring every possible dollar out of retail firms before dropping them.

Toys "R" Us workers, like Walmart workers, had deeply identified with the company. They felt betrayed by the liquidation, and had felt the erosion of their working conditions as private equity turned up the heat. And they were organizing themselves. One of Reinhart's coworkers told her about a Facebook group called the Dead Giraffe Society, but at first, she said, she wasn't interested. When she took a look at it, she saw people sharing memories and pictures, mourning and remembering good times.

The society was also a space for a lot of anger, and the United for Respect organizers dove in, hoping to help. But how do you organize workers at a chain that is closing? Strikes don't work—you can't shut down business to make demands if the business itself is closing down. Still, the workers were eager to figure out a way to fight. People would say to Reinhart, "It's just a job," she said, but "it is a job that I gave thirty years to, so I am willing to fight. We weren't treated well."

The stores weren't all closed yet when Reinhart's shut down, and lots of the workers on the Facebook page were nervous about making trouble. But Reinhart had had enough, and though the company had always warned workers about talking to reporters, when a request went out in the Dead Giraffe Society from United for Respect, asking if anyone would like to talk to a *BuzzFeed* reporter, she said she'd do it. "What are they going to do? They can't fire me, I don't have a job anymore." Her first media interview took an hour, and she said she "was very tearful. It was very, very raw."

The same organizer from United for Respect then wrote her to ask if she'd like to come to Washington, DC, and meet with Senator Bernie

Sanders of Vermont. She called her friend MJ, who had moved to Texas from New York and had also worked at Toys "R" Us. "She said, 'Are you sure?' I said, 'I've spoken to them on the phone twice. I have to trust my gut instinct.' She said, 'Tell her to call me.'" On the basis of Reinhart's gut, she and MJ went to DC with United for Respect. "My daughter-in-law was like, 'Are you crazy?! You are going to get on a plane with strangers. You don't know these people!' Lo and behold, it was the best decision we ever made."

There were only six of them at the meeting in May 2018, out of over thirty thousand workers losing their jobs. Reinhart was nervous—she'd never done anything like this before, and suddenly she was meeting a senator and making her first picket signs. "We didn't think anybody cared about our story," she said. "We made all these signs and I was like, 'Yes, but we are six people.' We went to Bain Capital. They have an office in DC. We came around the corner and all of a sudden these two buses unloaded onto the streets of Washington, DC, with signs and balloons, and they were all Walmart workers. This one lady, Donna, she said, 'We got you. We've got your back.' I looked at her tearing up like, 'Oh my god.' She hugged me and I will never forget that day."

It was the beginning of the campaign that would be called Rise Up Retail, which brought the Walmart workers to support the Toys "R" Us workers and showed the Toys "R" Us workers that it was okay to make trouble. The video that Sanders put on his YouTube channel helped, Reinhart said, and then, as more workers came together, the campaign built momentum and power. Other stores joined in as the private equity apocalypse spread. "It is just sad that there are so many of us now," Reinhart said.

She went from a nervous activist to volunteering to do civil disobedience. Lily Wang of United for Respect recalled Reinhart looking at her and saying, "We're not going to get severance, are we?" Wang said, "Probably not." But Reinhart and the others were committed to raising hell to make sure that at least the people who came after them wouldn't have to face what they had. Wang recalled, "They were like, 'We are not going to hold out the hope that we are going to get it. What we really want to do is to change the law so that no one has to go through this.'"

The stores were closing, but the workers had the offices of the private equity firms and pension meetings and the halls of Congress for targets, and they had the Internet. They held press conferences—the next one had seventy-five workers, from the original six—and marched on Wall Street. They learned to make their actions dramatic to draw press attention, and to hold them in stores as they closed, sharing videos online. They had, too, their personal conversations, as they learned more about how private equity companies operated and the ins and outs of what had happened to their company. They learned that executives were getting "stay bonuses" while the workers got nothing; that Bain and KKR and Vornado had made something like $470 million off destroying Toys "R" Us. "This has truly been an education and the more we find out, the madder we get," Reinhart said. "It just puts more fire in our belly to fight."[44]

"I think they kept me sane because it gave me an outlet to all of this anger and resentment that I had," Reinhart said. "Especially in that situation, you feel like you don't have a voice. I felt like they gave us all a voice who didn't have one." From the low point—when she found herself, without her Toys "R" Us health insurance, literally choosing between her own asthma medication and her husband's diabetes medication—she found her power. She's traveled back and forth several times; she's met Senator Elizabeth Warren of Massachusetts as well as Sanders. She was the named plaintiff in a class-action lawsuit asking for the bankruptcy court to take the workers' claims seriously in the process. She's spoken on a Senate panel before the Financial Reform Committee. "It was a surreal moment. Like, 'What am I doing sitting here in Washington, DC, speaking on finance reform?'" She pointed to New Jersey's new labor law requiring severance payments for mass layoffs as a success of the campaign.[45]

And then there was the settlement. KKR and Bain announced, in November 2018, a $20 million fund for the workers—less than the $75 million that Reinhart and her colleagues had asked for, but still a victory. It was a small check each—"I just got a check for $300 a week before Christmas. That was the last of the fund money," Reinhart told me in January 2020—but nonetheless the workers enjoyed spreading the news in the Dead Giraffe Society, which lives on. They won another $2 million in bankruptcy court, Reinhart said. "Nothing but good has come out of it for me."[46]

Not long ago, Reinhart was on the phone with a friend, who said to her, "You realize this is in the books now. You were the plaintiff." In that moment, she realized the significance of her fight. "There was power in numbers, for sure."

CHAPTER 5

SUFFER FOR THE CAUSE

Nonprofits

ASHLEY BRINK REMEMBERED VIVIDLY WHAT IT WAS LIKE IN HER KANsas high school when Dr. George Tiller was killed. The Wichita doctor was beloved in progressive and reproductive rights circles, but he was a target for anti-choice violence because he was one of the few doctors in the country who would provide abortions after twenty-four weeks of pregnancy—a difficult procedure only done in extreme cases, made more difficult by the stigma attached to it. When Tiller was shot (while serving as an usher in his hometown church), it was May 2009; Brink was on the verge of graduating. "I remember people in my class celebrating in the hallways and saying, 'Oh my gosh, finally! All these babies are going to be saved,'" she said. "I remember being like, 'How can you all say you are pro-life, but you are celebrating the murder of a man?'"[1]

At Wichita State University, Brink "found my people," as she described the pro-choice activists and the movement she joined. In 2013, she applied to be an intern at South Wind Women's Center, the health-care clinic that was reopening in the location of Tiller's former practice. "I started as an intern and I fell in love with the work," she said. "Never in a million years, had someone asked me, 'Where do you see yourself after you graduate college?' would I have ever said, 'an abortion clinic.' But everything about it, I was in love with. I was in love with the patient care. I was in love with my coworkers. I felt like I could be myself and say the things that I had always been thinking, but that people wouldn't agree with or that people would judge me for thinking."[2]

Brink speaks confidently, with a poise born of years doing difficult, emotionally challenging work. She has dodged protesters and soothed patients through the worst moments of their lives, and celebrated with them during the best. Reproductive health care was where she wanted to be, and she planned to spend the rest of her life doing it. Like so many workers in nonprofit organizations, she was devoted to the cause first, giving little thought to her compensation.

After three years at South Wind, Brink said, she and her partner were ready for a new challenge. They knew they didn't want to live in Kansas forever, so in the spring of 2016 they headed farther west, to Colorado, where Brink got a job with Planned Parenthood of the Rocky Mountains (PPRM). Moving was expensive, and the cost of living in Denver much higher than in Wichita—even more significantly, she took a pay cut, from $15.50 to $12.65 an hour, in taking the PPRM job. But the job was certainly an adventure; she was in a traveling position, hopping from clinic to clinic in Colorado and Wyoming to fill in as needed when clinics were short of health assistants. Every month, she explained, health-center managers would send requests for her when they lost a staffer or someone took leave or was out sick.

"Some days, I would drive to Colorado Springs, which is an hour and a half south of me. Sometimes I would drive to Steamboat Springs and stay a couple of days. I would fly or drive all over the state," she explained. "Frequently, I drove to Casper [Wyoming], when that clinic was still open, to provide coverage for a couple of days. There were times where I was flown to Durango and flown back to Denver in the same day. I would fly down in the morning, get a rental car, work all day, drive back to the airport, and fly back to Denver on the same day. That is a sixteen- or seventeen-hour day, at least. I could do it, but it was very emotionally draining." It occurred to her then that there might be a more efficient way for PPRM to solve staffing issues and improve retention, but she liked the work, so she kept going.

When in the clinics, she did a wide variety of tasks: checking patients in and verifying their insurance, counseling patients and providing education on sexual health and pregnancy—"very intimate counseling services," she noted—as well as taking part in medical procedures. Brink was trained to give injections, draw blood, and provide ultrasounds for patients; she assisted with insertions of intrauterine devices (IUDs) and abortion procedures. She scheduled patients, collected payment, and dispensed medication. The clinics, supported by donation as well as payment for health-care services, served low-income patients on Medicaid as well as those who had insurance. The days could be exhausting—some days, with a lot of walk-in patients or a crisis, there'd be no time for a break or for lunch, Brink said. "You felt like you just didn't have the time to calm your body so that you could go back out there and continue providing care."

As a traveling staffer, Brink's job was the same wherever she went, but, she said, "the frustrating part with that is often clinics are run a little bit differently." Every clinic's providers had things set up very specifically for the way they liked to work, she explained, but those specifics could vary widely from clinic to clinic. She had to remember where equipment was kept, which drawer to file patient charts in, at each different center, refreshing herself with each new arrival. Her travels also allowed her to get to know her coworkers at over twenty-four different clinics. "I loved that part of my job. But I always would tell my partner that I felt like I had to be a different person at work every day—I had to change my personality just a bit to fit in with the clinic I was going to be at," she said. "It wasn't a negative thing as much as it was just the nature of that position. It definitely wasn't for everyone. I just happened to be good at it."

Planned Parenthood's political arm is kept separate from the clinics, which are run by separate nonprofit organizations, like PPRM, that are affiliates of the Planned Parenthood Federation of America (PPFA). The clinics are not directly controlled by PPFA, but they bear the same name and mission, and many of the staffers, like Brink, have a background as reproductive justice activists and got involved in the clinical work as part of their devotion to the cause. Others, Brink said, took jobs at the clinic because they had been patients there. Some of the staffers were students planning to get medical degrees and become providers themselves. Some, like Brink, wanted to move up into management and make reproductive health care their careers; others just wanted a job they could feel good about, that helped them live their values. Many of them continued to get their own health care at the clinics—it was part of PPRM's benefits system. For nearly all of them, Brink said, a commitment to reproductive justice motivated their work.[3]

But working at PPRM also made the staffers a target for anti-choice protesters and politicians. It was a lesson that Brink had learned when she first became involved in reproductive justice work in high school; she was reminded of it when, in 2015, the Colorado Springs Planned Parenthood was the site of a mass shooting that left three dead and nine wounded. At some clinics, the staff and patients ran a gauntlet of shouting protesters in order to get inside. And for the staff, there were other stressors that shadowed each day of work. Brink spoke of a "heightened sense of security that you have to have every day when you are talking to patients." Planned Parenthood had been the target of several anti-choice "sting" videos alleging that the clinic was selling fetal body parts or otherwise perpetrating horrors, as part of an attempt to get the organization shut down. "You had to be cautious with what you said on the phone and who you said it to. The antis are always trying to get something out of you, and any of it can and will be twisted if you are being recorded," Brink said.[4]

The most important part of the job, she said, was the patients, and it was to them she felt her loyalty, even as her days ratcheted emotionally "from zero to sixty, and sixty to zero, back and forth." She would go from a patient worrying about a cancer diagnosis to a patient thrilled about a positive pregnancy test. While the positive appointments were exciting, she said, "it is emotionally exhausting because you are having to adjust. You are dealing with people's lives and it is not just like, 'Okay, here is my fifteen minutes with you. Let's move on.' These are people and we had to and wanted to treat them with the amount of respect that they deserved in the time that they were going to be there."

The staff had to put their own lives and their own problems on hold in order to provide the best care they could. "We can do it, but as a human you can only do it for so long," Brink said.

⁙

CHARITY IS A RELATIONSHIP OF POWER.

The history of charity, and of the development of what we now sometimes call the third sector—nonprofits, nongovernmental organizations (NGOs), or, in the United States, 501(c)(3)'s, referring to their tax-code designation—is the history of the powerful distracting from their power by "giving back" to the less fortunate. This relationship has created a trap for today's nonprofit workers, who enter a field hoping to do good while also making a living—one that has been shaped by the fact that for centuries it was performed by people who didn't need a wage. Like other caring fields, nonprofit work was structured as women's work—in this case work for wealthy women looking for something to do with their time. And that expectation continues to configure the work that people do in this sector— now a massive part of the workforce, about the same size as the entire manufacturing sector in the United States. "The charitable ethic is based on hierarchy, and dependency on the part of the recipient; it responds only to immediate material needs and relocates collective concerns into a realm of private benevolence," wrote Amy Schiller, a political scientist who studies philanthropy and has worked in the nonprofit sector. In other words, charity is necessarily asymmetrical and reproduces inequalities.[5]

The problems of today's nonprofit sector are outgrowths of this necessary inequality: nonprofits exist to try to mitigate the worst effects of an unequal distribution of wealth and power, yet they are funded with the leftovers of the very exploitation the nonprofits may be trying to combat. Nonprofit work then is also caring work, also service work, privatized, on the one hand, unlike public school teaching, but supposedly not in service of the profit motive. Nonprofits are not, despite their supposed lack of interest in profit, exceptions to the capitalist system but embedded in it, necessary to its continued existence.

But even before the rise of capitalism, charitable giving or philanthropy was an expression of inequality; the rich as far back as ancient Greece gave back by sponsoring public buildings, festivals, and even schools. Caring for the poor and the needy was less the focus of such giving than institution-building—the ancient version of today's wealthy donors stamping their names on theaters and sports stadiums. It was with the rise of Christianity that charity became specifically about giving to the destitute. And such giving provided the benefit not of a pretty building that could be used in life, but the expectation of rewards in the afterlife for the donor.[6]

This shift meant that the poor now had, in a way, use-value to their wealthier neighbors. Giving to them was a way to demonstrate one's own goodness and worthiness—one's deservingness, perhaps, of that unequal accumulation of wealth to begin with. The church, meanwhile, mostly mediated between the two, the donor handing over the money and the church doing the charitable works on their behalf. Giving to the poor was thus shaped the same way as the purchase of indulgences—a way to buy forgiveness for one's sins through good works, a one-way system sanctioned by the church. Such an attitude marked poor people as different from everyone else—they were either worthy objects of magnanimity or potential troublemakers, but either way, the have-nots were fundamentally different from the haves. And it wasn't only the church but also the state that began to take an interest in their behavior.[7]

The religious obligation to give to the poor in its own way encouraged begging, but if everyone was to take up begging, who would do the work? After all, the need for laboring hands required that people be enticed—or coerced—to work. That resulted in early regulations of poor people, including an act of the English Parliament in 1531 that registered poor people who were deemed actually unable to work, giving them legal permission to beg. Hospitals came into existence as extensions of the church's charitable function, places where the sick and destitute who had no other means of support (those without family to do the caring) could be looked after. Everyone else had to get a job or face brutal punishment.[8]

Such regulation was a sign that the poor were beginning to be seen as a potential problem, a force capable of unrest, of uprising. They had to be controlled, corralled into the workplace or the workhouse, under the watchful eye of their betters. The state would provide relief, but only under certain circumstances (mostly, as Frances Fox Piven and Richard Cloward noted in their classic *Regulating the Poor*, when the poor threatened to raise hell). And meanwhile, churches and private donors were expected to mop up around the edges, maintaining a more or less harmonious society.[9]

Charity has thus long been intertwined with the need to press workers into service and the accompanying suspicion of anyone who does not work. The Poor Relief Act of 1662 codified this relationship in England, setting up the poorhouse as the option for those who truly couldn't work and didn't have families to look after them; anyone else would be put to work. The relief system at this time was a shock absorber for early capitalism, managing the people who were displaced from an agricultural system and slowly integrating them into the new wage-labor system. "Relief arrangements," Piven and Cloward wrote, "deal with disorder, not simply by giving aid to the displaced poor, but by granting it on condition that they behave in certain ways and, most important, on condition that they work." Such relief could expand and contract, and it also required a new type of worker—those who managed the poor.[10]

Hospitals and universities had long existed as not-for-profit entities, recognized and taxed differently from other businesses, but the formalized, professionalized nonprofit sector, taking on the work of caring for society's less fortunate, arose in the nineteenth century alongside the spread of industrial capitalism. And it was, broadly, women's work. Middle-class women, considered "guardians of moral virtue" and not expected to earn a wage outside the home, expanded their circle of influence from the house-hold outward through the embrace of public service work—though that service work was mostly done through private institutions rather than the state. Some, guided by the church, went into missionary work; others did their moral reforming closer to home, in the burgeoning cities, where the working classes were often crowded into foul tenements, or, in the United States, within a growing movement to abolish slavery.[11]

Much of the work these women did was unpaid, voluntary labor that because they were women was not really seen as labor at all, and this ex-pectation has crept into the work of women like Ashley Brink in today's nonprofit sector. And yet it was very much work. Some of it could be done from the home, but most of it required them to go outside, to investigate the conditions they found so offensive, from those of enslaved people la-boring on plantations to the working conditions in factories to slum hous-ing to prisons. Women reformers spoke at meetings, gathered signatures on petitions, taught one another, and challenged the ideas of men—and such work, though inspired by their gendered roles, taught many of them to think about their own social position. The early feminist movement drew many of its leaders from the abolitionist ranks. Susan B. Anthony and others turned their attention to the limits placed on their own move-ment as they fought to break the chains of others.[12]

In this movement, though, we can see some of the contradictions that remain in today's nonprofits. Through their abolitionist commitments, white women were able to gain some level of power for themselves, power that was not necessarily shared with Black women who had experienced slavery personally. These women were able to do abolitionist work because they did not need to work for money, because their husbands or fathers had enough of it to allow them to take up the unpaid work of the move-ment. White women like Anthony and Elizabeth Cady Stanton turned from abolitionism to making the case for women's rights in explicitly rac-ist language; they believed that their education levels qualified them for the vote and to speak for others. They were thus, despite their opposition to one oppressive system, as Angela Davis pointed out, reliant on the in-equalities of another one—industrial capitalism. They would work around the edges, perhaps demanding better housing for the poor or supporting a shorter workday for women in factories, but their investment in the system as it existed meant they often ignored the realities of exploitation.[13]

The spread of higher education—and in particular, the opening of a limited number of colleges to women—created a generation of would-be workers primed for charity work. Large numbers of women who attained college degrees remained single, and those who did not go into teaching searched for other ways to have influence in the world. In Saidiya Hartman's words, "slum reform provided a remedy for the idleness of the privileged, a channel for the intelligence and ambition of college-educated women, and an exit from the marriage plot and the father's house." The women's club movement disguised women's work as socializing; Black women's clubs in particular organized to work in their own communities, demanding better public services. Yet the social Darwinism popular in this era was also reshaping attitudes toward charity work: still entangled with the work ethic, charity was to be given only in forms that would enable those best fitted to succeed to pull themselves up by those famed bootstraps. This form of charity wound up being more labor intensive than simply distributing money. Women worked as "friendly visitors," going into the homes of charity recipients to teach them how to live better and to make sure they weren't wasting what they were given or behaving immorally.[14]

But there was another model even during this period that did more to break down barriers created by capitalism. The settlement house movement encouraged would-be do-gooders to live and work in the houses alongside the poor people they served. In doing so, they built friendships across the boundaries of class, and they learned that poverty was not, in fact, a matter of individual failing, but a result of inequalities that could be challenged collectively. This was at least the start of a political understanding of women's caring work, and the settlement house women often took to political agitation as a result. Jane Addams, who established and lived in the Hull House settlement in Chicago, understood it both as a way to give women useful work to do and a way to provide not just the basics of life but language lessons, art and handicraft education, and even entertainment for those who would otherwise be trapped in slums. The women—though men, too, worked in the houses—saw themselves as "social housekeepers."[15]

The settlement houses sought to give their residents alternatives to working in the factory system. Some of the skills taught in the houses, like the production of handicrafts, aimed to offer another way to make a living, and they also learned from the arts and crafts that immigrant workers had themselves brought from their countries of origin. The handicrafts would not provide most residents with a sustainable living, though, and often wound up as just another way to impress upon the residents the value of hard work. Some women, such as Ellen Gates Starr, who sought in handicrafts a form of work that she could do out of love, realized that it was not enough for poor women to make crafts that would adorn the homes of the wealthy. Starr became an agitator for changes to the industrial system and was arrested on a picket line with striking waitresses—jeopardizing, as historian Eileen Boris noted, contributions from wealthy donors to Hull House, where she lived.[16]

Starr was not the only hell-raiser to come out of the settlement house movement. Florence Kelley used Hull House as a base for her organizing around demands for shorter working hours and the prohibition of child labor. Eventually, she became the director of the National Consumers League (NCL), which aimed to use the buying power of women to influence working conditions for the women who in factories made and in retail shops sold the things that they bought. The NCL's influence extended to presenting evidence before the Supreme Court that overwork was harmful to the health of women workers. The Women's Trade Union League (WTUL) also counted settlement house women among its ranks, alongside socialists and women unionists. While the upper- and middle-class women gave money and lent their names and status to the struggle, wage-earning women organized on the shop floor and led strikes.[17]

"Social housekeeping" pushed at the limits of what was permissible for elite women. Addams and others cleverly worked within the image of wife and mother while carving out space for women to do real work, political and caring and teaching work. But, historian Alice Kessler-Harris wrote, "the only remaining question was whether they could be paid for their work without losing status." Some women thus began to agitate for professional status for the social service work they were already doing, fighting for education, training, and scientific rationales for change. The Progressive Era saw the opening of new fields for women, who became factory inspectors, visiting nurses, and the like, serving in roles that were outgrowths of the old "friendly visitor" role. The training required for these jobs meant that women won access to expanded higher education, including medical and law schools. As long as the women's desire for education was "rooted in virtue and not in ambition," as Kessler-Harris wrote, they could even go to business school.[18]

Just as arguments about moral virtue justified women's entrance into the professions, gifts to charity justified the massive Gilded Age accumulation of wealth into the hands of a few. Titans of industry like Andrew Carnegie created giant foundations for their charitable giving with their names prominently attached. Corporate leaders advocated "welfare capitalism," as we saw in department stores, to alleviate the worst conditions of their workers and to encourage them to aspire to upward mobility rather than class power.

As businesses consolidated and grew, reformers cast their eyes on the supposed inefficiencies of charities, organizing them in order to ensure the maximum effectiveness of their giving—and for "maximum effectiveness," read "giving only to those who we can be absolutely certain deserve help." "Scientific charity" involved gathering extensive data on the poor, but it also entailed educating them about hygiene, as if their problem was that they didn't know they ought to bathe, rather than that the only homes they could afford had little space in which to do so. Such education, in the United States, aimed to "Americanize" new immigrants, assuming that rising out of poverty would be easier for those who fitted a certain image of hard-working whiteness.[19]

The modern charitable foundation, the tax-exempt vehicle for the wealthy to funnel their money to a variety of causes, developed in this period. Schiller pointed to a key change in 1936, when US law began to allow corporations as well as individuals to take charitable tax deductions, although the matrix of laws that allow for tax-exempt giving dates back to the 1890s, and it continues to evolve today (notably in the Trump tax break package of 2017). Through these tax laws, the state has always been deeply intertwined with NGO and nonprofit work, subsidizing their privatized provision of social services. The foundation allowed the wealthy to extend their influence beyond their corporate domain; they were, they felt, by virtue of being extremely rich, best suited to decide how others should live their lives. This control extended to the people who actually did the charitable work that foundation dollars paid for—women might be doing the work on the ground, but it was wealthy men who assumed decision-making power over the way it would be done.[20]

Modern social work grew from but was a step away from the "friendly visitor" role, where middle-class women worked to discipline the poor. In turn, the professionalization of some of this caring work allowed some women to make money at the social roles they'd long been pushed into. The gendered and racialized division of labor still held, though—white men would be the titans of industry who made the money, the elected officials who would decide what to do with public funds, and the managers who decided how caring workers would be allowed to do their jobs.[21]

With the coming of the Great Depression, private charities could no longer care for all the needy. The crisis of capitalism ensured that tinkering around the edges would not be enough—to prevent the system's total collapse, the state had to step in and give direct relief, create jobs, and pay for care. The modern welfare state was taking shape, and while private charities still had plenty to do, the Depression's severity cut through the long-held attitude that poverty was the poor's own fault. Instead, the poor were marching, demanding that the government step in. The Depression also turned the great wealth accumulated by the Carnegies and other "robber barons" of the Gilded Age into less of a badge of honor and more of a target: progressive taxation and spending, not charitable giving, was the order of the day.[22]

The nonprofit sector, of course, didn't go away. Its influence shrank during the Depression and World War II, when the state did what private charity couldn't, but after the war, when women were pushed out of the industrial workplaces they'd stepped into in crisis times, the better-off among them turned to volunteering and political work, and the big foundations (such as the Ford Foundation, founded in 1936) began to flex their muscles abroad as well as at home, working in tandem with the state as the Cold War developed. The desires of foundation heads to tamp down social unrest in the years after the wars—particularly in the 1960s, and particularly in the civil rights moment—sometimes clashed with the genuine wishes of lower-level nonprofit workers, who could find themselves squeezed between their political goals and the threat of lost funding. This pattern continues today.[23]

PLANNED PARENTHOOD HAD ITS ROOTS IN THE FEMINIST MOVEMENT OF the early twentieth century. Margaret Sanger founded the United States' first birth control clinic in Brownsville, Brooklyn, in 1916, and was arrested for it shortly after. Charged with obscenity, Sanger spent time in jail and her clinic was closed, but after her release she began to travel the country as a public speaker, advocating for family planning. Her early organizations were backed by the same kinds of wealthy do-gooders that supported other philanthropic ventures. She also courted the support of those interested in eugenics, a fact that has made her legacy complicated for the organization to claim. The two organizations Sanger founded merged legally in 1942 to become the Planned Parenthood Federation of America, the name chosen because "birth control" was too radical and anti-family for some. Sanger herself bitterly opposed the name, writing, in 1956, "If I told or wrote you that the name Planned Parenthood would be the end of the movement, it was and has proven true. The movement was then a fighting, forward, no fooling movement, battling for the freedom of the poorest parents and for women's biological freedom and development."[24]

As the organization had grown, Sanger felt it had left its original ideals behind to conciliate potential supporters. It was, after all, reliant on private funding to keep its clinics open. In the 1960s as the feminist movement and the Great Society moved forward, they brought public support for its health clinics, but the organization itself became a lightning rod—a fact that would affect the working conditions of women like Ashley Brink.

Historian Jill Lepore wrote, "The fury over Planned Parenthood is two political passions—opposition to abortion and opposition to government programs for the poor—acting as one."[25]

The 1960s were a boom time for foundations. As their number multiplied, the US government moved to regulate them, to ensure that they were actually vehicles for delivering needed funds to organizations doing charitable work rather than solely tax shelters for the well-off to maintain control over their fortunes. These regulations in turn spawned the growth of legal nonprofits, with many existing organizations now incorporating as such, the better to receive foundation largesse. But such funding came with strings attached. Scholar Robert L. Allen traced the way the Ford Foundation's strategic donations to civil rights organizations, such as the Congress of Racial Equality (CORE), shaped their direction. He found that as they came to rely on the foundations, the organizations began to back away from criticisms of capitalism and to start calling for Black people's further integration into it. Black Power would be turned toward the goal of enabling Black capitalism.[26]

The proliferation of issues to care about in the 1960s—from racial justice to environmental degradation to ending the Vietnam War to nuclear nonproliferation—came from what was at first a more unified movement. Yet the New Left was easily splintered into single-issue nonprofits. As young college radicals grew into boomers running the family business, noted organizer and researcher Eric Tang, they took up respectable means of pressing for progressive ends. That often meant nonprofit work—giving money, taking up party politics, or, for those with real money, setting up their own foundations.[27]

Foundations weren't the only source of funding for nonprofits doing community work in the 1960s and 1970s. President Lyndon Johnson's Great Society, following on the heels of the New Deal, aimed to carry out a "War on Poverty" by many different means, and one of them was distributing government money directly to nonprofit groups, including Planned Parenthood. The money even came with requirements that the poor participate in the War on Poverty. That requirement placed money in the hands of organizations to hire workers from the communities they served, jobs directly with municipal governments but also with activist groups newly flush with funding—and for a while, at least, some of those groups used that money to make trouble. As noted in Chapter 1, this stream of funding supporting welfare rights organizing around this time made it possible to hire activists rather than middle-class caseworkers. This brought a change from personalizing the problems of the poor back toward the social roots of the problem. In the case of welfare rights, the root of the problem was that women's work in the home was not recognized as work.[28]

The tension between the professionalized do-gooders—those closer to the donors in class and ethnic background—and the people who were struggling was not only a problem in the United States. In 1982, when the English Collective of Prostitutes occupied the Church of the Holy Cross in London, demanding an end to police violence and aiming to preserve the community legal services they had created, the group's initial victory turned sour in the aftermath, when the sex workers' direct action was written out of the story. Selma James, spokesperson for the group at the time, wrote that the action was seen as "an invitation to careerists to professionalize and depoliticize the legal and other services prostitute women had created as campaigning tools." A report that came out afterward made no mention of the occupation; legal services created by the sex workers would be dismantled and a new, professional service created. "What we are witnessing before our very eyes is the process whereby women's struggle is hidden from history and transformed into an industry, jobs for the girls," James wrote. Elsewhere, she commented, "Every time we build a movement a few people get jobs, and those who get the jobs claim that this was the objective of the movement, this was the change."[29]

As charitable or NGO work began to be considered real work, worthy of a wage or indeed a salary, the old split was reformulated. Better-off, educated white women now had careers, the careers that feminism had demanded for them, but they still were not allowed to have much power at work—at least not power over men. In the nonprofit sector, they could retain their old social role in a new format, using caring work as a way to have power, even if it was mostly over other women.

As the Great Society of the 1960s gave way to the crisis of the 1970s and the neoliberal era, cuts to publicly funded social services meant that NGOs expanded greatly, filling their old role of softening the blows of capitalism's changes and caring for those who fell through its (many) cracks. In 1953, about fifty thousand organizations had nonprofit status in the United States; by 1978, that number had multiplied nearly sixfold. In the words of geographer Ruth Wilson Gilmore, nonprofits grew under the assumption that "where the market failed, the voluntary, non-profit sector can pick up any stray pieces." They began to act as a "shadow state," picking up the slack from the cutbacks to the expanded welfare state, and their sheer numbers (along with the numbers of foundations that fund them) skyrocketed. Today, the nonprofit sector employs the third-largest workforce in the United States.[30]

The growth of foundations has multiplied their political power, and the cutbacks to the state have included the parts of it that should be overseeing these tax-exempt vehicles. Nicholas Lemann wrote in *The Atlantic* in 1997, "The shift in power from government to foundations makes the exercise of that power less visible. . . . The main policy questions about them—How, exactly, should their economic and political activities be restricted in return for their tax-exempt status? Does the tax exemption still make sense?—go unasked."[31]

But the people who worked in nonprofits still, by and large, aimed to do good. Many of them even aspired to shift the distribution of wealth, even if they were restricted in their ability to criticize its accumulation. Nonprofits have been a way for activists to sustain and support their work; they have allowed for movements to find ways to fund themselves. And it is those workers, those activists themselves, who have leveled a critique of the "nonprofit industrial complex" (NPIC), who can help us understand the limitations of the form. In *The Revolution Will Not Be Funded*, an anthology from the INCITE! Network of feminists of color against violence, a variety of authors who worked in and studied nonprofits examined this complex and its effects on movement work. They came to no unitary conclusion: nonprofits were neither all good nor all bad. Rather, they argued for understanding the intertwined relationships between governments, donors, foundations, and social service and social justice groups—an understanding that also includes an analysis of the working conditions within those organizations.[32]

The long-standing tension, for nonprofits and for those who work in them, between service provision—alleviating suffering—and fighting for political change continued apace through the 1980s and 1990s, as the cutbacks to the public sector left more suffering people in need of care. This has only been exacerbated by the crises of 2008 and then 2020. Service provision is often easier to fund, as it fits into the old model of charity; saying "we want money to help marginalized people organize and gain power" is a dicier proposition when it must be made to those who already hoard power. The tension at the heart of nonprofits remains that they are funded by the proceeds of an inherently unequal capitalist system, yet this system requires—indeed cannot exist without—humans who must be fed, housed, clothed, and cared for. In doing that caring work, nonprofits grease the wheels of that system; if they aim to stop its rolling, they may have to turn from work that allows the system to reproduce itself. This presents a difficult choice when that work is necessary for people to survive.[33]

There is also a tension built directly into the nonprofit model, whereby organizations that accept the nonprofit or charity structure are restricted in what kind of political work they can do. In the United States, for example, nonprofits are forbidden to campaign for parties or candidates, and in practice the restrictions influence political activity well beyond what is legally restrained. In the United Kingdom, a 2014 law further restricted what charities (and trade unions) can do and say about politics in an election year; ahead of 2017's general election, more than fifty charities sent a letter demanding reform of the legislation, known as the Lobbying Act, and saying they were "weighed down by an unreasonable and unfair law which restricts our ability to contribute fully to a democratic society." Such restrictions leave NGOs dancing carefully around their political statements and action.[34]

Nonprofits also wind up competing with one another for funding, which in turn requires workers to spend their time marketing their successes—whether or not they truly achieved their objectives—to the funders, much the same way that for-profit companies market their products to consumers. But the "consumers" of nonprofits' services are, in this model, the funders rather than the people being served. Nonprofits wind up structured like little corporations, with workers under a kind of pressure to produce that mimics the pressure of the assembly line. Nonprofit staff, Ruth Wilson Gilmore wrote, "who often have a great understanding of the scale and scope of both individual clients and the needs of society at large—become in their everyday practice technocrats through imposed specialization." The legal structure of the nonprofit limits its ability to do "political" work. Moreover, Gilmore noted, progressive funders, in particular, want their money to go to programs rather than to core operations. The right, meanwhile, she wrote, spends freely on ideas. As a result, people like Ashley Brink work long, grueling schedules to make up for the work that should be done by a much larger workforce.[35]

Indeed, in the era of capitalist realism, charity itself became a business model. Perhaps the most famous example of this was Project (RED), U2 singer Bono's branded clothing and tchotchke line that raised money for AIDS research. (RED), Bono and his colleagues insisted, was not a charity but "hard commerce," a thing the pop star incredibly likened to "punk rock." The model has proliferated, making giving into something one can consume—buying a T-shirt or a pair of shoes makes one into an "activist" in this model, the work of caring shrinking down to the price of purchase. Nonprofit workers often feel they are treated the same way, bought and traded by funders like this week's trendy item. The obsession with data commodifies their projects into "deliverables" to be handed back to funders as proof their money was well spent, and funders often shift gears in search of the next hot item, leaving established groups high and dry.[36]

This short-termist outlook tends to create high turnover. Nonprofits are sometimes forced to close their doors for lack of funds before they've had a chance to figure out what works. That's what happened to the organization Amara H. Pérez worked in, Sisters in Portland Impacting Real Issues Together (SPIRIT). The organization was just over three years old when it was shuttered. Pérez wrote that as SPIRIT got off the ground, most of the advice they received was not on how to effectively organize in their community, but rather how to raise funds. The work they did in the community, she wrote, was very different from the work of sustaining the organization. The staff had to move back and forth between the two, juggling two different sets of skills. The "business culture" imposed by funders' demands, wrote Pérez, preempted the real work of the organization even as it demanded to see results. And the work of reflecting on what works and what does not was not considered work at all. The whole system required staff to work longer and harder, giving more of themselves, tending toward burnout.[37]

Burnout is complained of by a wide variety of workers, but it varies from sector to sector. In retail, it might be the struggle to paste on a smile for yet another eight-hour shift; with nonprofit workers and others committed to a cause, it's a bit different. The World Health Organization characterizes burnout as "feelings of energy depletion or exhaustion; increased mental distance from one's job, or feelings of negativism or cynicism related to one's job; and reduced professional efficacy." Such a definition, of course, assumes that one had a mental connection to one's job and positive feelings about it to begin with; only the "exhaustion" part applies equally to all workers. Burnout, in other words, is a problem of the age of the labor of love, and it's no surprise that it is often discussed in the context of nonprofit or political workers. These workers are expected, like Ashley Brink was, to give their lives over to the work because they believe in the cause; but it becomes harder and harder to believe in the cause when the cause is the thing mistreating you.[38]

Yet nonprofits resist improving working conditions. When the US Labor Department under President Barack Obama moved to raise the overtime threshold, meaning more employees would get overtime pay, several major nonprofits put out statements claiming that paying more overtime would put them out of business. Pitting their staff against the people they serve, nonprofit managers argued that if more money went to salaries, services would have to be cut. And the salaries are quite low to begin with: one 2014 study found that over 40 percent of nonprofit employees in New England, one of the most expensive areas of the United States, made less than $28,000 a year, well below the national median wage. One observer noted, "Too often, I have seen the passion for social change turned into a weapon against the very people who do much—if not most—of the hard work, and put in most of the hours." Studies have found that nonprofits in the United States and Canada have higher rates of turnover than the overall labor market—a sign that workers are pressured to work long and hard and see little escape from that routine, other than leaving for a new job or perhaps a new sector. The organizations blame tight budgets and tight-fisted funders, but it is also true that nonprofit culture prioritizes "doing more with less."[39]

The reality of funders' influence is illustrated in one oft-retold story. When setting up his Open Society Foundation, billionaire George Soros allegedly got angry with others in the room and pounded his fist on the table, saying, "This is my money. We will do it my way." Then, the story goes, a voice piped up from a junior staffer: "Excuse me, Mr. Soros, roughly half the money in this foundation is not yours but the public's—if you hadn't placed your money in this institute, half of it would be in the US Treasury." Whether or not the story actually happened, it illustrates how the wealthy exert control over the money that keeps society going, and the reason they can exert that control is that there are rules written into the tax code that allow them to do so. They retain control even over the money they're giving away. In order to avoid that trap, some grassroots groups have turned to fundraising models that draw money from the communities they serve, arguing that it is to those people, not the rich, that they should be accountable.[40]

Long-standing structures of inequality mean that wealthy funders are more likely to be white men, and that organizations staffed by and serving people of color have to struggle for funding. As noted above, the funds that do flow to these communities tend to go to NGOs that have a moderating influence, or that provide services, rather than to those that advocate or organize. The problem extends beyond the low wages, though the low wages ensure that it is easier for people who do not need the money to take the jobs (and people of color are more likely to need the money). But when well-off white people dominate the nonprofit jobs, it just perpetuates the age-old assumption that the poor need to be uplifted and taught to imitate the lives of well-off white people. Black women, who might have a different idea of how to improve the lives of the poor—by tackling structural racism, say, or challenging the way wealth is accumulated in the first place—are seen as troublemakers. And when funding cuts come—as they inevitably will, especially in difficult times, such as the coronavirus-induced recession—they fall hardest on organizations led by and serving people of color. Often, wrote Vanessa Daniel, founder and director of the Groundswell Fund, in the *New York Times*, philanthropists "gentrify" social change work. They start out by "noticing the success of strategies innovated by women of color," she said, "but instead of funding them at the source, they are writing checks so that larger, white-led nonprofits can replicate their work." Daniel, whose foundation does make grants to organizations led by women and transgender people of color, noted that "it's far easier for a young affluent white man who has studied poverty at Harvard to land a $1 million grant with a concept pitch than it is for a 40-something black woman with a decades-long record of wins in the impoverished community where she works to get a grant for $20,000."[41]

In movement moments like the one that began in the spring and summer of 2020, as the cries of "Black Lives Matter" rang once again from streets around the world, the question of who gets funded to do the work is particularly important. An incredible outpouring of support—donations in small amounts, $5 and $10 and $20—flowed into bail funds and grassroots organizations like Reclaim the Block and the Minnesota Freedom Fund in Minneapolis, organizations that had been working for years. But the experience of organizations in the wake of the previous uprising in Ferguson, Missouri, was instructive; as Princeton professor Keeanga-Yamahtta Taylor wrote, donors came to Black organizations not out of solidarity, but because they were "trying to connect the inherent progressive character of social movements to their 'brand.'" The scramble for dollars—particularly as they began to dry up—noted Taylor, left organizers competing with one another for scarce funds. "With more resources came more authority because of the ways it elevated the profile, presence, and voices of some," Taylor wrote. "This dynamic eventually cut into the kind of unity in purpose necessary to confront the challenge of stopping police abuse and murder." Those most able to get funding were often those who spoke the language of incremental change, not the words of rebellion echoing in the streets.[42]

It is not an accident that the people most likely to get nonprofit funding look a lot like those most likely to get funding for a tech startup. The people making the funding decisions, after all, come from the wealthiest parts of society, and these days, it's tech and finance billionaires doing a lot of the investing or donating—with the same mindset applied to both. This kind of results-oriented consumerism among funders leads to intense pressure on the workers to produce results that make their work look like a good "deal" for the donor class, even if that "deal" is a Band-Aid on a gaping wound.[43]

NGOs spill out across the rest of the world the same way they do across the advanced capitalist nations, bringing do-gooders and their model of change to developing countries. If philanthropy serves as a form of political power within a country, allowing the wealthy to shape public policy with the directed flow of their dollars, it also works as such when it is directed outside of national borders. The model of the middle classes dictating to the poor how they should behave maps, Silvia Federici noted, onto the "new international division of labor," where the poor countries do the production for consumption in the rich ones. Thus, women from the wealthier countries become the supervisors of women in the poor ones, integrating them into global capitalism through NGOs and aid as well as the workplace. The movements for change that already exist in the Global South are circumvented by the tastes and priorities of the wealthy in other nations.[44]

If the donors are a specific class of people expecting the organizations they fund to fit a certain idea of what "works," what do the workers think? The expectation to work long hours for little money isn't just coming from the top—the culture of "movement" work also tends toward self-sacrifice. The assumption that "activists" are a different type of person, more committed than the rest of the world, replicates the old division between the volunteer service worker and those whom they served. The professionalization of the nonprofit sector has now made it more accept-able a workplace for men, but it has also made it relentlessly middle class. The influx of men has added a new inflection to the tradition of feminine self-sacrifice already embedded into the history of the NGO sector: the "cowboy mentality" that comes from political and labor organizing, that values the toughest work, the biggest commitment, as a mark of dedi-cation to the cause. Work-life balance is something that these workers choose to give up, missing the way that their choices quickly become job requirements—something that only shows up later, when they want to take time off. Both gendered tendencies produce burnout, and those who do burn out are judged as insufficiently committed or insufficiently radi-cal. Those who have moved up in the organization through such a style of work then impose it on others.[45]

This culture of sacrifice, whether swaggering or self-abnegating, leads workers to stay past closing time—in the room with a client, on the phone with a funder—or up late at night planning a program at home. Yasmin Nair, cofounder of the radical queer editorial collective Against Equality, wrote of the way nonprofit workers were expected to share personal stories and reveal vulnerabilities, all in the name of love: "We were not only ex-pected to love our work—and what that meant for those whose work was unpaid or underpaid was quite unclear—but to love each other, to believe that we were all in the struggle together." Some of this work may be no-ticed, appreciated, seen as heroic; some of it is likely ignored (who does the cleaning up, who sets up the folding chairs for meetings—who, indeed, reminds people to clock out and go home early when they're tired?), but all of it is the reproductive work that allows not only the organization but capitalist society to go on ticking.[46]

Nonprofit workers are used to being pitted against their clients when they make demands for themselves; like teachers and health-care work-ers, if they ask for higher wages or organize or threaten to go on strike, they are accused of being insufficiently caring, of neglecting their jobs. If they get too close to their clients, however, they are accused of being unprofessional—a suspicion leveled particularly at nonprofit workers who come from similar backgrounds to those they serve. This double bind manages in either case to differentiate the worker from the client. It is true that nonprofits are underfunded, and that they hesitate to spend money on overhead—which includes base salaries for staff as well as training and equipment and decent office space—but it is not fair to expect that the workers will be the ones who pick up the slack. One's willingness to go above and beyond is read as passion for the work, but this modus operandi leads to people justifying the exploitation of those passionate workers.[47]

At the last count, there were some 12.3 million workers in nonprofits in the United States, which amounts to over 10 percent of total private-sector employment. At the same time, there were over 800,000 people working in the charity sector in the United Kingdom. This is a massive workforce, and though some of these staffers are well-educated professionals bearing graduate degrees in "nonprofit management" or something similar, most of them are workers lower on the rungs who got into the work because they believe in it. Many of them are laboring under something like the conditions Ashley Brink described. "The working conditions of nonprofit workers, whether in direct service, community organizing, health care, or education, represent the value of that service and advocacy work," wrote Chicago organizer Ramsin Canon at *Jacobin*. "When they are exploited, overworked, and when turnover is high, the implication is that the value of that work is low." It is not surprising, then, that many of those workers have turned to unionizing to protect themselves and improve their conditions.[48]

But when nonprofit workers try to organize, they run into the contradictions of their position. Bosses who preach equality and dedication to the cause are suddenly fierce opponents of the union. The New York–based organization StoryCorps, inspired by the work of labor advocate and journalist Studs Terkel, fought its employees' union drive tooth and nail. The organization's founder and president, Dave Isay—author of a book titled *Callings: The Purpose and Passion of Work*—sent staff an email arguing that a union at StoryCorps would "build walls, harden divisions, create a more regimented and formal workplace, and foster an increasingly adversarial culture." The union resorted to picketing outside StoryCorps' annual fundraiser, part of their more than two-year process of winning their union election and bargaining a first contract. "We thought, like many progressive organizations, they would understand that the same values we communicate through our work we would ask for in-house," Story-Corps worker Justin Williams said.[49]

StoryCorps was far from the only organization with such a story. The National Center for Transgender Equality saw the majority of its workers leave in the midst of a similar dispute. They filed an unfair labor practice charge with the National Labor Relations Board (NLRB), saying that the staff had, in effect, been forced out after they announced their intention to join the Nonprofit Professional Employees Union (NPEU). "Ironically, organizing a union and negotiating a contract that prohibits discrimination based on gender identity is the only way for transgender workers to have explicit legal protections in the workplace in over half the country," the union noted. Southern Poverty Law Center workers, too, pushed for a union and were met with resistance from management. The center's administrators hired a prominent union-busting law firm to represent them and drew criticism for their heavy-handed response, particularly in the wake of the departure of the cofounder and president of the organization over allegations of sexual harassment, racial discrimination, and other mistreatment of staff. The NPEU has seen an uptick in nonprofit organizing, more than doubling its number of bargaining units in a year, and it is not the only union that represents nonprofit workers. In the United Kingdom, the Independent Workers Union of Great Britain (IWGB) launched a charity workers branch in early 2020, promising to organize not only around working conditions, but around the political direction of the sector.[50]

When the coronavirus pandemic hit in 2020, the NGO double bind was ratcheted up. More people needed services, and more people wanted to organize, but the accompanying recession meant that funding for the nonprofit sector was likely to dry up. The virus, said Kayla Blado, president of NPEU, "created an added uncertainty about what the workplace will look like if/when we return to normal, and if management will have had to lay off workers by then." Nonprofit workers who had already been looking to unionize were motivated to do so quickly in order to have an influence over the future of their work.

"In a sixteen-day span in mid-April, the Nonprofit Professional Employees Union announced seven new units had asked for recognition from management," Blado explained, and they were, at the time of this writing, talking to "hundreds of other nonprofit workers who are in the early stages of organizing a union." Many of NPEU's members, Blado noted, are carrying heavy student debt. They graduated into the recession, and they have uncertain access to health care and housing.[51]

The pandemic, IWGB's charity branch wrote in a statement, "has both highlighted and exacerbated existing issues and inequalities within the charity sector." In particular, the union noted, charities led by Black people and other people of color are facing dramatic losses of funding. Organizations took advantage of the government's furlough program: "We have had reports of furloughed staff being pressured to 'volunteer,' despite this breaking the conditions of the Job Retention Scheme, alongside employers using the 'training' exception as a loophole for staff to continue working whilst furloughed."[52]

To rephrase Canon's statement and to borrow a formulation from the Chicago Teachers Union, the conditions in which nonprofit employees work are also the conditions in which their clients or members receive services and support. Overworked, burned-out workers are not simply extra-passionate: they are exploited. The system allows rich philanthropists to reap the tax benefits of their charitable giving while maintaining control over their fortunes. But nonprofits are so deeply embedded in the capitalist system that even grassroots donors—such as the hundreds of thousands who gave to Planned Parenthood after the 2016 election of Donald Trump—can feel a sense of entitlement. Backlash ensued on social media when the Minnesota Freedom Fund—previously a tiny organization—could not spend all of the $30 million in donations it received after the uprising in Minnesota immediately. The impulse to demand deliverables had spread from big philanthropy through to the rest of us.[53]

This kind of short-termism, whether from wealthy donors or Twitter backlash, is antithetical to actually making real changes—racism or even cash bail will not be eliminated in a matter of weeks. Such grassroots donations could point the way to a better model for making movement work sustainable, for allowing organizers to be accountable to the community rather than to the same people already controlling so much of our world. They could help those organizers move past the stasis in which they so often exist, mopping up around the edges of capitalism's never-ending crises, and toward a more lasting change, a different equilibrium. As Ruth Wilson Gilmore wrote, "the purpose of the work is to gain liberation, not to guarantee the organization's longevity."[54]

ASHLEY BRINK'S MOTHER HAD LONG BEEN A UNION MEMBER; OTHER members of her family, too, had union jobs. So when a fellow health-center staffer at Planned Parenthood of the Rocky Mountains (PPRM) asked her if she'd be interested in unionizing, she was immediately on board. "What is the harm in unionizing? It only helps workers," she said.

The pay cut she'd taken in order to take the job was on her mind, but the thing that really ramped up their union campaign was the announcement, in May 2017, that PPRM was going to close several clinics in the region, including the only Wyoming health center. The decision was financial, they were told—the clinics weren't getting reimbursed enough from insurance and Medicaid to stay in operation. To Brink, who had spent time in all of the clinics slated for closure and knew their staffers and their patients, this decision was upsetting. "No one from health centers were brought in on these decisions. We weren't consulted, we weren't asked, we were just told this is what is happening and these are the decisions that had been made."

Yet it was the health-center workers who had to answer the questions from panicked patients wondering where they'd go for their care. Brink said, "I had patients crying in rooms because they were like, 'I don't know where I am going to go. I can't afford insurance and you are the most affordable place for me to go.'" That experience led workers to get serious about their union drive; they'd been in contact with Service Employees International Union (SEIU) Local 105 for a while, and the organizers helped them prepare for what they could expect once their union drive went public. Cecile Richards, then the long-serving president of national Planned Parenthood, had been an organizer for SEIU in her younger days, a fact that the health-center workers liked to cite when they were signing coworkers up to union cards. But it wasn't Richards the burgeoning union had to negotiate with—it was the leadership at their regional affiliate. And that leadership hired a law firm, Fisher Phillips, that on its website trumpets its services in "union avoidance."[55]

Brink was surprised at the intensity of the anti-union campaign from her bosses. They held captive audience meetings—a common anti-union tactic, where part of the workday is carved out for all staff to attend a lecture on the potential downsides of a union. At PPRM, Brink noted, that meant holding time where patients wouldn't be scheduled in order to have the meetings. "They were claiming that there would be pay freezes because it takes so long to bargain to get pay changes, that it was going to negatively impact our relationships with our managers, that it was going to negatively affect patient care," she said. But Brink felt the union would improve patient care, because the workers would no longer be burned out, exhausted, and worried about how to pay the bills. "For an organization that claims to be feminist and states that they take on reproductive justice values, to also have staff that can't afford to pay their bills or take care of their families . . . that is very hypocritical and frustrating. Those are not my values. So it is hard to say, 'Yes, I am proud of Planned Parenthood.'"

Brink and her coworkers weren't the only ones having trouble at various Planned Parenthood affiliates at that time. Employees from around the country told the *New York Times* in 2018 that they'd been discriminated against when they got pregnant: they were denied leave or doctor-recommended breaks, or pushed out after they gave birth. Others said they had not been hired when they disclosed their pregnancies. The organization did not, as a rule, provide parental leave, though there were exceptions. (It told the *Times* it would conduct "a review to determine the cost of providing paid maternity leave to nearly 12,000 employees nationwide," but in 2019, employees at state affiliates were still petitioning for family leave.) The same *Times* story noted that a dozen lawsuits had been filed against the organization since 2013. Employees in those suits, according to the *Times*, accused managers of "denying workers rest periods, lunch breaks or overtime pay, or retaliating against them for taking medical leave." Planned Parenthood's Seattle regional director told the paper that providing medical leave could require her to close clinics; meanwhile, a Colorado employee had turned to GoFundMe to raise money to cover her bills after having a baby because she was on unpaid leave. Out of fifty-six Planned Parenthood affiliates, only five were unionized when Brink and her colleagues began their union drive. A nurse practitioner told reporters of the struggles she faced when she was part of a union campaign at Planned Parenthood of Central North Carolina: "There's so much focus on the mission and the cause and people become, like at many nonprofits, very vulnerable to being manipulated into lower pay and less benefits for the cause."[56]

The organization's pleas of poverty frustrated employees and observers during the union drive because donations to Planned Parenthood had skyrocketed following the election of Donald Trump, as did donations to other liberal-identified nonprofits, such as the American Civil Liberties Union. One calculation said that Planned Parenthood's donations had gone up 1,000 percent after the election; according to the *Times*, the organization brought in $1.5 billion in fiscal year 2016. Brink noted that after the 2015 shooting in Colorado Springs, donations had increased specifically to PPRM. And then there was the money spent on the anti-union campaign: the workers were getting anti-union mailers sent to them at home. Anti-union lawyers don't come cheap.[57]

Brink was in a unique position during the union drive. As a traveling employee, she was able to talk to many more of her colleagues than the average health-center staffer. But that additional work made her life even more exhausting, she said: "I can honestly say that there was a solid six to eight months that I cried every day on my way home in my car. Trying to unionize is also a job in and of itself. It was all of the emotional pieces of my job, and then another job, plus travel time." Because, of course, during the union drive, she was still doing the rest of her job, as were all her coworkers (aside from the time they spent in those anti-union meetings, which took away from their work time). It frustrated her that hourly staff, like her, were being "nickel and dimed": they were sent home early if the clinic was slow; if budgeting was tight, their hours might be cut back. "That was always hurtful, this idea that we were disposable. Just like, 'Oh, well, you all can just go home.'"

Like the North Carolina practitioner, Brink felt that the assumption was that the clinic workers were doing their work out of dedication to the cause, not because it was their job for which they were paid. "This comes up in every nonprofit," she noted. "If your mission, your values are feminist-driven, then you cannot use not paying your staff as an excuse. That is how it often felt, that the respect and dignity and the reproductive justice framework was only afforded to patients and everyone else, but not to staff. We had to give that to them, so we had to take it from us."

The union vote came at the end of 2017. "The day that the vote was counted, Planned Parenthood gave what they called a holiday bonus to everyone, which was interestingly timed," Brink laughed. The staffers voted 72 to 57 in favor of the union, and Brink was excited. Heading into 2018, with the union battle, she thought, behind them, she was elected to the bargaining team and looked forward to negotiating the union's first contract. And then they found out that PPRM had appealed their vote to the National Labor Relations Board. "Before we got the union, they were claiming, 'We are a family. We don't need a union. We have an open-door policy. We listen to each other. We don't need some outside person to come represent us and help make decisions for us. We can just talk about it together,'" she said. Then, when the employees voted for the union, the organization argued that the election had been unfair to staffers in New Mexico and Nevada, because only fourteen of PPRM's twenty-four clinics—the Colorado clinics—had been included in the bargaining unit. The appeal, Brink said, was the moment she realized how hard PPRM was willing to fight their union. "This is not family. You want to say that we are a family, this isn't how family treats each other."[58]

The appeal was a slap in the face, too, because by then the NLRB was dominated by Trump appointees, who were busily paring back union rights and also, presumably, opposed to the mission of Planned Parenthood.

The dispute brought about more publicity, a national story. Thirty-seven Democratic members of the Colorado state legislature signed a pledge of support for the PPRM union and called on PPRM management "to recognize and respect the vote of their employees to form a union, and . . . immediately withdraw their appeal at the NLRB." The lawmakers who delivered the pledge told reporters, "We find it surprising and troubling that when frontline employees have made the choice to sit at the table when pay, working conditions, safety and customer satisfaction are discussed Planned Parenthood of the Rocky Mountains leadership would fail to respect that choice."[59]

That April, the initial decision from the NLRB panel took PPRM management's side. It was hard at times, Brink said, to keep staff interested in fighting for the union as the case dragged on. Many people just wanted it to be over—a feeling that anti-union consultants count on. But the union-busting just made Brink more determined. "It often felt like we were having the finger pointed at us, that we were the reason why donations had been pulled, we were the reason why they were negatively impacted in the media about this union fight. 'No. You did that to yourself.'" The attitude of "How dare you challenge us?" from leadership, she said, made her angry. "How dare we expect to have a decent workplace?" she asked. "Well, how dare they not pay us a living wage? How dare they not listen to us when we have concerns about our working conditions?"[60]

Finally, she said, Planned Parenthood and SEIU came to an agreement and the organization dropped its opposition to the union. The workers at the ten other health centers that made up PPRM would have the opportunity to vote to join the union, but either way, the fourteen centers that made up the original bargaining unit got their union. "I think the decision came in August," Brink said. "I left in September. I was like, 'Cool, we got our union! I cannot work here anymore.'" The comments that had been made to her—people who had told her they didn't believe she deserved a living wage, or that she was "too progressive" for PPRM and needed to get "perspective"—left her uncomfortable at work. She believed that she'd never be promoted because she had been outspoken about the union. "My dedication to our patients and to reproductive health and rights work was questioned," she said. "But I am doing this because I care about you. I am doing this *because* we can do better and we should do better."[61]

The union got its contract in 2019. The ten Nevada and New Mexico clinics also voted to join the union. And Brink moved on to a management position at another reproductive health organization. At her new job, though, she found some of the same old problems. "This is happening in reproductive health and rights organizations all over the country," she said. Part of the reason she felt it was coming to light now was a generational shift. Not only are younger people coming up with more student debt and economic instability, but they are also coming up with a different set of political values. "A lot of us get into this work because we have been impacted by some unjust issue or policy, and to get to these organizations and just feel like we've been duped, essentially," Brink said. "Economic justice is not a separate issue from reproductive justice. Labor rights are just as much in line with reproductive justice values and feminist values."[62]

Planned Parenthood workers at affiliates across the country continued to organize after Brink left—particularly, in 2020, against the backdrop of COVID-19 and Black Lives Matter. In Texas, around twenty staffers were laid off in April 2020, and they suspected it was retaliation for their union drive. The workers had raised issues around the lack of personal protective equipment and paid sick leave. "There's this big disconnect between the people managing us and the work that is being done on the ground," Ella Nonni, one of those workers, told reporters. In New York, meanwhile, as protests roiled the country, Planned Parenthood staff rose up and ousted the CEO of the affiliate, Laura McQuade, describing "issues of systemic racism, pay inequity, and lack of upward mobility for Black staff." The employees noted that while clinic staff were furloughed, McQuade kept her six-figure salary, and they offered an alternative view for the organization that echoed Brink's goals: "We . . . envision a Planned Parenthood where all our staff, in particular our Black and other staff of color, are honored for their expertise and included in the decision making process."[63]

For now, Brink has left reproductive health work, though she's heading to graduate school and hopes eventually to return to the field—it is still, after all this, where her heart lies. But she continued to wonder if she'd be able to do so. "They argue, 'Well, you don't do this work for the money. You do it because you care about it.' It is like, 'Well . . . Both? Why can't I have both?'"

PART TWO

ENJOY WHAT YOU DO!

CHAPTER 6

MY STUDIO IS THE WORLD

Art

WITH LATE AFTERNOON SUN STREAMING IN THE WINDOWS OF THE print studio at Crawford College of Art and Design in Cork, Ireland, Kate O'Shea flooded a massive screen for printing with bright spring green paint. She was artist in residence at the college, which brought no paycheck but provided access to some nice facilities. She leaned into the printing press, laying down the eye-popping green on top of a dark purple print, the words on the screen cutting different directions across bold shapes, handwriting, and type. The colors blended like the faded rainbow that was her hair as she bent into the print and then lifted the screen to see how the colors looked side by side.

She was in fact layering new ink over old for this new project, as she does with many of her prints, playing with patterns and colors and words to make new works, new art. The older prints beneath the green were from an exhibition she staged, along with her collaborator Eve Olney, in an abandoned bank building in Cork. "All the work is about layering lots of ideas and practices and theories," she explained. "How I make sense of all the other work is through the process of printing. Every exhibition builds on the last exhibition. So, I basically print over whatever is left. It is all the one work."

O'Shea uses different printing processes to make her works, including monoprint, industrial laser-cut stencils, and the screen at the college. That day, she was printing over old work on heavy paper and on newsprint, on folded and jumbled pieces and on brand-new white sheets, testing ideas against one another. Another artist came into the studio while I was there, making his own prints, and then left again; a studio attendant helped O'Shea set up the press. "In terms of the fine arts—which are printmaking, sculpture, and painting—sculpture and painting can be very much the lone artist, but printmaking can never be," O'Shea commented. When not at Crawford, she works at Cork Printmakers, a collective space where she keeps a cubby and a drawer of work that she'd picked through that day, deciding which pieces to layer new paint over. "There are printmakers in every city," she said. "There is Limerick Printmakers, New York, Philadelphia, everywhere." On a recent trip to the United States she wound up driving seven hours to use a print shop in Pittsburgh and back again to Hamilton, New York, where she was staying. "That is why I love printmaking, because there is such a community."

O'Shea's art has always been about connecting with people. Originally, she went to school to be an architect, since, she laughed, "I was like, 'I can't be an artist because that is not a real job and it is not socially acceptable.'" Architecture seemed like a creative field that could allow her to make a living, but, she said wryly, "Luckily I got a huge depression because of it and dropped out. If I didn't get really sick, I wouldn't have dropped out because I would have been too stubborn. I would have kept going." The depression, she said, made her rethink everything in her life.

She went home to Kerry, where she'd grown up, to heal. "Slowly, I got into cooking. The one thing I could do would be to cook a recipe a day." That cooking practice led her to turn an old cottage on her father's land into a little café, and having the ability to support herself, she said, helped her get better.

What that whole experience taught her, she said, was that she needed to find a way to make a living making art. And the tanking economy perversely helped: "I feel it is easier to choose to be an artist now because around me, most people are struggling to get to what they want to do and doing the in-between job to get there and it is all quite precarious." Choosing to be an artist hasn't made her much more precarious than any number of talented people she knows who are working shit jobs in order to get by.

Being an artist in Ireland has its advantages. Unlike in the United States, where an art degree can cost you hundreds of thousands of dollars, in Ireland O'Shea was able to study for free. "There is no way that I could have justified becoming an artist if it involved the kind of money it involves in America," she said. Also, though arts funding per capita isn't as high in Ireland as in some European countries, there are grants available for Irish artists, another way that she and other artists are able to at times pay the bills. And then, of course, there's the welfare state; even in its pared-back current shape, it's available as a last resort when she really can't make ends meet.

O'Shea used her café as a way to make space available for her community, a practice that has become part of her art and organizing work. "I got into the idea of food as a community-based, social project," she said. She returned to school for a one-year course, still not sure she could make it as an artist, but that year convinced her that she could and should do it. When she discovered printmaking in art school, it felt akin to her work in the café, a different way to control the means of production. She made art prints, printed little political 'zines, and then published a book, bringing her activist work to her art, and did a master's degree researching printmaking as a space for solidarity. As part of that research she studied everything from the Paris Commune to the radical print shops of the movements of the 1960s to present-day movements. "When I started printmaking, I was just making really colorful architectural work about the inside of my head," she laughed. "I didn't discover political printmaking until my third year."

Printmaking and the café experience, and, in a way, her architecture background, all came together in the bank exhibition in Cork, where her art hung on the walls and she curated not just visual exhibits but events and dinners. When we visited the bank, workmen were pulling down the remnants of the exhibit, and O'Shea was able to grab a few more pieces of her prints as well as a box of political pamphlets, which had been left in the library they'd built in the old bank vault.

"Galleries by their history and nature are super elitist," she explained. "Because my practice is about building alternative worlds and alternative ways of seeing things and reimagining space, then if you are just doing that in a contemporary regular gallery you are not doing what you are saying. Turning a space like a bank or a church, taking something and totally reimagining the space, is just as important as the work that you are showing."

It's not that she's opposed to galleries, or to what people often call, with implied capitalization, the Art World. It's that her art is about bringing people in who might feel excluded from those spaces. At the same time, she said, "If I get an opportunity to exhibit in some big art gallery, I am going to do it. I am always trying to figure out a way of surviving financially." Finding a way to survive and to make the work that matters to her requires a combination of selling art, applying for grants and residencies, and collaborations. She's taken part in group shows with other printmakers, including an exhibition in Liberty Hall, a Dublin union hall with a storied history, and done solo shows in cafés and small galleries. And she tries, she said, to make sure each exhibition is more than just an exhibition, that the space has food and drink and is a place where people can connect with one another as well as come to purchase art to adorn their walls.

The coronavirus pandemic scrambled but did not halt most of O'Shea's projects. In early June 2020 she was working as a producer for another artist, Marie Brett, for a project looking at the cholera pandemic in Ireland in 1832. The prints she was making at Crawford the day I visited, in January 2020, were the beginning of something else, for a project at A4 Sounds in Dublin called "We Only Want the Earth," which had been postponed, but not canceled, due to the pandemic. She had to postpone, too, an artist's residency in Dublin that she'd been looking forward to, but the pandemic gave her the opportunity to use the support of the residency to host conversations online. She'd been looking forward to the retreat time, but in a way the lockdown—which she spent with family in Kerry—also allowed her time to nurture herself as an artist, letting her make things without immediately worrying about having to sell them. She also appreciated the way the lockdown let her spend more time talking to people far and wide, and apply those conversations to her art. "I think I am literally the opposite of the lone artist in the studio," O'Shea said. "My studio is the world."

LOVE HAS BEEN WOMEN'S WORK FOR MOST OF HISTORY; EQUALLY, FOR most of history, we have presumed that the artist is a man. That lone artist in the studio, splattering paint everywhere, unwilling to leave even to eat, compelled by his genius to work or die trying, is a myth that many still believe in, unaware that it, too, is a product of history and a particular culture's image of itself.

The image of the male genius has been with us a long time, as celebrated as the wife in the home is unsung. Not only that: the genius is defined almost literally as the opposite of the woman in the home. Megan Garber at *The Atlantic*, pulling the etymology of the word "genius" from the *Oxford English Dictionary*, found that one of the derivations of the word was "male spirit of a family," as well as "personification of a person's natural appetites, spirit or personality of an emperor regarded as an object of worship, spirit of a place, spirit of a corporation, (in literature) talent, inspiration, person endowed with talent, also demon or spiritual being in general." That's why, Garber noted, the women are often airbrushed out of the story of the genius. Women are muses (or the wives who clean up the mess) in this narrative; rarely do they get to be artists themselves.[1]

This is also why we have a hard time thinking of what the genius does as *work*. Look at all those words: spirit, demon, spiritual being, object of worship. "Natural appetites" aside, most of them are ethereal, implying something a little bit magical. As Garber wrote, "a fealty to genius is its own kind of faith: in transcendence, in exceptionalism, in the fact that gods, still, can walk among us. And genius, itself, is its own kind of infrastructure. We have organized our art around its potential; we have organized our economy around its promise." That faith in genius has slipped into many places we never expected to find it: breathless paeans to it dot the tech press and sports journalism as much as art-world publications. It convinces us that there is something that some people just *have* that the rest of us can't, no matter how hard we work. It elides the real skills that some have worked for, and it often, in fact, allows some to take credit for other people's work.[2]

This elision of skills, of the labor that creative workers have put in, is the flip side of the elision of caring labor into an innate quality of femininity. In both cases we are led to assume that people are born with a tendency toward a certain type of work, a belief that along the way teaches us that work itself is natural. Just as the assumptions made about women's unpaid housework spilled into other types of work, from teaching to retail, our ideas about artists have colored our reactions to the work of programmers, scholars, and even, in a way, athletes. The romantic attachment of the artist to his work is the counterpart of the familial love women are supposed to have for caring work, and these two halves together make up the labor-of-love narrative that shapes our perception of work today.

This occurs with artists because there does seem to be something magical about works of art that have lasted for decades or even centuries: the piece that strikes to the heart, the beautiful and the profound. Why do some people feel the need to create art? "They had the time and the means by which to do so" seems like an incomplete explanation, though the drive to create things for pure enjoyment is perhaps one of the most deeply human things we do. Even a Marxist art critic like John Berger, well attuned to the ways society's inequalities made it possible for some to make great art and others not to, wrote of the "mystery" of art—"and by mystery," he wrote, "I mean the power of a work of art to affect the heart." Lewis Hyde argued that art was a form of gift, unsuited to the capitalist economy, because the artist was "gifted" with talent and therefore made a gift of his art to the world.[3]

Be that as it may, art can and very much does exist under capitalism, and for many people it is a job of one form or another. For some of them it is a side gig, for others it pays nothing at all. Some teach art, some sell it, some criticize it, and many assist in the making of it but never see their names on a gallery wall. Artists may work to delight the soul, as Hyde wrote, but their work is nevertheless material, existing because someone took substances—paints, clay, stone, film, even their own bodies—and turned them, as Berger wrote, into "'artistic' material" and created a work of art.[4]

If the term "genius" has spiritual roots, so does "creative." As cultural critic Raymond Williams noted, these words developed in tandem, with "creative" at first a term for something not done by man, but by God. The shift to apply the word to art made by humans maintained the sense that, as literature scholar John Patrick Leary wrote, building on Williams, "creativity was a work of imagination, rather than production, of artistry rather than labor." This split between art and work continues to mystify the work that goes into making art.[5]

But the early arts were themselves a form of worship or magic-making, and it is not easy to separate this aura from today's arts even when they're held in "ego-seums" that double as tax shelters for the world's richest. Religious paintings on cave walls or carvings in temples were offerings to the gods first before they were there to be admired by humans. Only later did art become something done for the enjoyment of mere mortals, and later still did it become something that could be reproduced and shared broadly.[6]

Our modern idea of the artist as someone special, gifted, and outside of the normal bounds of society was born in Europe during the Renaissance. It was at that time that the wealthy began in earnest to invest some of their vast fortunes into art, and the artist began to have a unique reputation—after all, wealthy merchants wanted to ensure that they hired the best to paint their families and their possessions. Oil paintings were, Berger wrote, "a celebration of private property." They were, of course, also a form of private property themselves. For the artist, though, they were a *job*.[7]

The ability of artists to trade on their individual reputations rather than the reputation of a guild was a result of a society that began to emphasize the individual, that was hierarchical and structured around the idea that inequality was natural. Still, most artists were painting portraits and the like to make a living, not because the spirit had suddenly struck them to depict the richest man in town or his prize cow. The emergence of great works of art from this period is in a way in spite of the format that many of the artists worked in, yet the desire of the wealthy patrons of the arts to collect the best art possible helped to create our idea of the genius creator driven by something both bigger and more ephemeral than money.[8]

The tension between artist-as-worker and artist-as-visionary is rarely visible in the art itself, but sometimes you can see it if you squint. Berger pointed to the paintings of the regents and regentesses of an almshouse for old men, done by Frans Hals in the winter of 1664, when Hals himself was an old pauper. Did the relationship of power that the governors held over Hals shape how he painted them, in their matching austere black? The fact that so few acknowledge this dimension of the work of art, Berger wrote, is mystification.[9]

With the slow decline of patronage, particularly in the wake of the French Revolution, and with the development of industrial capitalism, the market grew for art as a commodity, a store of value in itself. Before the Revolution, French artists needed credentials; afterward, more people could attempt to become artists and sell their work. Such a flood of new workers meant a need for new institutions, and this expansion, art critic Ben Davis wrote, "gave birth to bohemian society and the modern art movement, symbolically inaugurated by the 'Salon des Refuses' of 1863, when a number of important artists rejected by the salon demanded to be heard on their own."[10]

The Industrial Revolution's impact on art lay not just in the rise of a new bourgeois class with disposable money to spend buying decorations; it also, strangely, helped to shape the notion that art is opposed to work.

As mass production spread, the unique art object gained value precisely because it was not produced by machines. As the work of craftsmen declined in favor of the factory, the artist became separated still further from the artisan. Art, a term that had simply meant "skill" at one point, became a term for what we now think of as the fine arts, and indeed, to be contrasted to skilled labor as something that could not, in fact, be taught. An artist was thus a special kind of person. Like caring work, art work was something outside of and contrasted to capitalist production—but while the carer presumably works out of love for those cared for, the artist has a romance *with the work*. No longer did art need religious value; it was now a higher good in itself.[11]

But all of this hype for the value of art being stronger than its value as a commodity doesn't change the fact that artists, too, have to eat. The "starving artist" cannot in fact live on air, and we should remember that all the great works we're aware of came to us because the artist had some means of subsistence. Most artists are not able to make "pure" art that only satisfies their souls; most of them, like Frans Hals, have had to compromise with the demands of the market. The idealization of the artist as a mystical being served, as Williams wrote, not to solve the problem but merely to soften our realization of it. Artists may have resisted the turning of their art into a product for the wealthy to purchase, but capitalism is not so easy to escape.[12]

The romantic image of bohemian artists living on whatever they could scrape together, carousing and painting and dancing and free-loving their way through life and the occasional radical political action, has its roots in the reality of artists in the 1800s cobbling together a living and a community. It is an image of people who reject the concept of "work" as we know it. Yet that romantic image reinforces the idea of artists as gifted individuals, whose needs and desires are set apart from the rest of the world. Artists might be "dangerous," their art potentially subversive, but bohemian chic made an excellent site for "slumming" by those who wanted a taste—just a taste—of radicalism with their arts purchases.[13]

Some critics of capitalism, meanwhile, looked to reunite art with labor in order to make work itself more enjoyable. John Ruskin and William

Morris, though from different political perspectives, both, in historian Eileen Boris's words, "defined art as man's expression of his joy in labor and lamented the fact that modern civilization had robbed work of pleasure." To Ruskin and Morris, art was anything crafted by hand to be beautiful as well as useful; although the movement that sprang up in their wake often fell short of their goals (particularly of Morris's revolutionary socialism), it sought to break down the wall between art and work, creating pleasant spaces in which to craft beautiful things. Morris argued that to really return pleasure to work, capitalism would have to be replaced, but that creative work could be a way to combat alienation. In practice, however, the arts and crafts movement, organized through groups like the Art Workers' Guild in the late 1800s and early 1900s, celebrated handicrafts for their own sake, and often its attempts to reorganize the workplace to be less miserable simply rearranged the workplace to better suit its managers. The beautiful goods it produced mostly went to adorn the homes of the new middle class—"playthings for the wealthy," as one critic described them.[14]

Another group of artists with revolutionary aspirations also identified as workers and even attempted to organize as workers. Inspired less by Morris than by Marx and their own revolution at home, the Mexican muralists—Diego Rivera, David Alfaro Siqueiros, José Clemente Orozco, and others—called for a publicly funded art for public display, an art that would represent the people of Mexico, the workers and the colonized, an art that would be worthy of the revolutionary country they hoped to build. While the Mexican Revolution fell short of expectations, the artists drew on their experiences as rebel students and revolutionary fighters to build a political argument for their art. In 1922, the muralists formed the Revolutionary Union of Technical Workers, Painters, and Sculptors and wrote a manifesto pledging their membership to the Communist International and their support to collective art projects that would pay workers equally. They experimented with modern materials for making art (including automobile paint and industrial spray guns), published a radical journal, *El Machete*, and became involved in the broader Mexican labor movement. However, their art, too, was in the main purchased and commissioned by the wealthy, not the working class. Siqueiros argued, as had Morris before him, that real, pure art could only exist in a radically changed society; his revolutionary activities were therefore a way of "fighting for pure art."[15]

The Mexican muralists inspired artists around the world, but particularly across the border in the United States, where during the Great Depression artists and public officials alike sought to create, through relief programs, a more democratic public art. Through the programs of the New Deal, particularly the Federal Art Project (FAP), part of the larger Works Progress Administration, artists were hired and paid as workers, leveling the playing field for art creation for the first time. They were paid to make art in community spaces, where it could be seen by many more people than previously had access. Work was the subject, too, of much of the art, from photographs by Lewis Hine capturing factory workers in luminous black and white to Stuart Davis's brightly colored abstracted workplaces. Artist and organizer Ralph Pearson argued that the printmaker should see themselves as "a workman among workers," writing, "He prints his etchings, lithographs or woodblocks with hands which know ink and the rollers and wheels of his press. He works. He produces. He lives."[16]

Artists had to fight to be included in the relief program, arguing that the economic collapse had put them out of work as surely as anyone else, and challenging long-standing ideas of the artist as existing outside of the wage-labor system. The FAP put the focus not on the product but on the production of art; it stressed getting artists working, not their end result. That gave artists with a broad range of political views and styles of work an opportunity to experiment, to push boundaries, without needing to satisfy rich patrons. Artists organized, too, in the Communist Party's John Reed Club and its offshoot, the Unemployed Artists' Group, which then became, after its successful push for federal arts funding, the Artists' Union. The union was not a union in name only; it bargained with and demonstrated against the FAP's leadership and eventually joined the Congress of Industrial Organizations (CIO), the more militant of the two national labor federations. Not everyone approved of such organization, of course—one art critic wrote that unions were antithetical to art: "The very nature that leads him to be an artist makes him intensely individualistic.

To such men the very thought of unionization is distasteful. They are not the same as coal miners." But to many of the artists, the union made perfect sense, and aligned them with the vast numbers of Americans relying on some form or other of Depression-era relief.[17]

While the FAP treated artists as workers, it did not treat all workers equally. The jobs for technical workers, gallery assistants, and fine artists were all supported, though not paid the same. In one important respect, though, the project did treat workers equally: Black artists were given the same wage as white ones, though they sometimes had to fight for their chosen subject matter (their own communities). In the end, the US government spent over $35 million on the arts between 1933 and 1943, resulting in tens of thousands of murals, sculptures, paintings, prints, posters, and photographs. Gordon Parks, Stuart Davis, and Dorothea Lange were among those who got work from the art programs, as were future art stars such as Lee Krasner and Jackson Pollock. In addition, the government poured money into community art centers, which not only displayed art but held lectures and classes so that everyday people could make art rather than simply consume it. The New Deal, in art historian A. Joan Saab's words, provided a "redistribution of artistic opportunity."[18]

The programs were attacked from two directions (though mostly by the same people): that they produced bad art and that they funded Communists. The former charge was almost by design impossible to counter—it has been dragged out over and over again in the years following the Depression to decry government spending on the arts, with those who make this claim cherry-picking mediocre or offensive pieces in order to denounce any investment at all. The project almost certainly funded plenty of art that any number of people might consider "bad," and yet the production of bad art is on some level necessary if a society values art at all. The latter claim might have been true on some level—certainly the Communist Party's agitation had helped bring about the arts project, and the Soviet Union certainly subsidized artists and their training and production. But for the New Dealers who backed and supported the project, the aim was the maintenance and expansion of an American art. When World War II began, the artists were conscripted like anyone else into the war effort, becoming employees of the WPA War Services Subdivision, where they produced posters and works that aestheticized the war. With the war's end, American artists became a symbol of the ability of capitalism (glossed as "freedom") to produce great works. New York benefited from the destruction of European creative centers, becoming the world's art capital.[19]

The image of the lone artist, the uniquely brilliant individual differentiating himself from the crowd, served American Cold War interests. Jackson Pollock was the ideal American artist of the postwar period, splattering his id onto the canvas, incomprehensible to all but those smart enough to understand his special genius. Pollock's abstract works were contrasted with Soviet realism and held up as the epitome of freedom; state-subsidized art, even though it had helped make Pollock's career possible, was criticized as too limiting, too strict to produce great works.[20]

Artists continued to rely on a variety of direct and indirect subsidies in order to produce, though. The postwar welfare state in Europe, in particular, brought decent living conditions, the dole, and state-funded arts education that still produce artists like Kate O'Shea, even in their currently pared-back state. And art continued to present a more attractive working option than fitting oneself into the postwar work routine, whether it be the factory or the proverbial gray flannel suit. The 1960s brought the beginnings of what French sociologists Luc Boltanski and Eve Chiapello called the "artistic critique" of capitalism: that it was capitalist work discipline, not the collectivism of the Soviet Union, that produced endless dull drudgery and conformity. Workers began to demand more from life than a nine-to-five job.[21]

In this moment of upheaval, artists once again turned to organizing as workers. In late 1960s New York, rebellion was everywhere, and the New Left's critique of capitalism left space for artists to imagine themselves as workers whose labor was also significant—and potentially dangerous—to capitalism. In trying to find the levers they could push to dissociate from and destroy the system, a number of famed artists came together as the Art Workers' Coalition (AWC). They challenged the idea of art as commodity, organized to make demands on museums and other art institutions, and produced defiantly political works and minimalist creations fabricated by hired workers. They fought and challenged each other and ultimately the AWC fell apart, shattered in part by issues of sexism and racism.[22]

The artists of the Coalition did not all agree on what it meant, even, to be an art worker. Art historian Julia Bryan-Wilson noted that some "asserted that their practices were governed by the power differentials (and exploitation) inherent to the rules of employment within the capitalist West. For others, the recognition that art was work . . . was a move of empowerment rather than degradation; work signified serious, valuable effort." They argued, too, over their target. Unlike the Artists' Union of the New Deal era or the state-funded artists of socialist and social-democratic countries (Dutch and Danish artists, for example, had unions), New York artists lacked a central employer. This, though, did not mean that their art was not work, or that they lacked common antagonists: they wound up, many times, targeting museums. They demanded representation for Black and Latinx artists; challenged museums to pay artists and speculated on possible wage systems; and claimed rights over how their art was displayed, even after it had been purchased. In all these ways they challenged their alienation as workers. They also demanded "free days" at museums so that a broader public could see their work—perhaps their most successful legacy.[23]

The Coalition also left behind the seeds of a unionization movement among museum staffers, one that has reappeared in recent years alongside other rebellions from laborers of love. Some AWC members had been museum staffers before their art careers stabilized; the Coalition argued that curation and other support roles were also important art work, and so supported the move in 1971 by the staff at the Museum of Modern Art (MoMA, perhaps the AWC's readiest target) to form the Professional and Administrative Staff Association, the first union of art museum workers in the country. The museum did not concede easily to the union, and the workers struck for two weeks that year to preserve their win.[24]

As the Art Workers were rebelling, though, the modern art world was coming into its own. Artists enjoyed new levels of prestige (which the AWC used to gain attention for its actions and demands). The National

Endowment for the Arts was formed and made grants to artists, including members of the Coalition. While nothing like the levels of state funding outside of the United States, the grants were still a source of income for many artists. But although there was something of an art boom, a 1970 report noted that still, only one in ten painters or sculptors actually supported themselves with their art work. "Almost nobody could pay rent from art," Lucy Lippard of the AWC said. A few stars became famous and sold works for fabulous sums; the rest of the field looked on longingly from their part-time jobs and crumbling apartments. Art stars became mini-industries in themselves, hiring workers themselves in order to produce works of art. How could such artists be in solidarity with the working class?[25]

At the same time that the AWC was raising hell in New York, Italian artists were inspired by radical movements of the time, *operaismo* (workerism) and *autonomia*, which understood the fight against capitalism as extending outside of the workplace and into all facets of society, the "social factory." While the Wages for Housework movement used this understanding to formulate its demands around women's unpaid work in the home, artists aligned with the movements rejected art institutions and instead made art in public that aimed to disrupt business as usual. While factory workers revolted, artists looked for ways to participate in what seemed at the time to be a revolutionary moment.[26]

But the revolution of the 1960s and 1970s never quite coalesced, though radical artists like Kate O'Shea have never stopped trying to find ways to make art outside of the market. State officials and capital recognized the potential of artists and the artistic critique, allied with worker rebellions, to disturb the consensus that allowed capitalism to proceed uninterrupted, and under neoliberalism we see where this has ended: fetishizing the individual artist while cutting off all the legs of the state supports (or even the benign neglect) that had made her possible in the first place. The welfare state and publicly funded arts education were stripped away, housing costs were jacked up in the cities once celebrated for their arts culture, and that art culture itself turned into a tourist commodity. Tourists flock to Broadway to see the 839,258,256th replaying of *Cats* or the latest Harry Potter spinoff, while experimental theater dies. They go to the art museum to gawk at the famous paintings, while avoiding the outer boroughs where the working artists have been pushed.

The artist then became the ideal worker for the neoliberal age just as neoliberalism made it harder and harder to succeed as an artist. Today's worker must be "a creative figure, a person of intuition, invention, contacts, chance encounters, someone who is always on the move, passing from one project to the next, one world to another," in Boltanski and Chiapello's words, in order to succeed. Stability, never a hallmark of the artist's condition, disintegrated under the guise of improving work, of concession to the artistic critique. Work would be exciting, fulfilling, creative, a place for self-expression, but you had to give up knowing where your next check was coming from. If the work itself is its own reward, it is much easier for the boss to tell workers to shut up and look grateful.[27]

Into the crueler world of neoliberalism crashed the AIDS crisis, devastating New York's arts community in the 1980s. The activist group ACT UP had an artists' wing, Gran Fury, that produced propaganda for wildly dramatic direct actions, and artists affected by the virus, who lost friends and lovers or were dying themselves, produced haunting artworks forcing their audience to confront the realities of the disease. They challenged the brutal conservative regimes of Ronald Reagan and Margaret Thatcher to *see* their suffering. And yet conservatives tended to use the works of gay artists as reasons to attack what little arts funding there was. Art in these cases was political work, as it had been in the 1930s and the 1960s, but now it was drained of hope and laden with grim determination.[28]

Even as the AIDS crisis laid bare the realities of a political-economic system uninterested in the realities of artists' lives, the neoliberal era, with its stripped-down public services and go-go markets, was creating new levels of art star and new arguments to justify its own existence. The term "creative class" entered our vocabulary as an argument, as filmmaker and author Astra Taylor wrote, "that individual ingenuity can fill the void left by declining institutions." Capitalism has taken the members of the so-called creative class, in the terms of its most famous advocate, Richard Florida, from outsider status, as "bizarre mavericks operating at the bohemian fringe," and placed them "at the very heart of the process of innovation and economic growth." In Florida's framework, the Protestant work ethic has now fused with the "bohemian ethic," and the bohemians suddenly had the power; it was no longer necessary for workers to struggle over control of the means of production, because those means were all in their heads anyway. It's another gloss on the artistic critique, synthesized into the revitalized, sprawling capitalism of the 1990s and 2000s. Who needs public funding when creativity is an engine of economic growth itself?[29]

⁂

THE ART MARKET OF THE NEOLIBERAL AGE MIGHT AS WELL HAVE BEEN designed purely in opposition to the demands of radical art workers of the past century. Art buyers hold art because of its value; its uniqueness points to their own brilliance as consumers, and acquiring it is a way for them to acquire some of the sheen of the artist on themselves. Art is perhaps the ultimate fetishized commodity, where the work that went into creating it is almost entirely mystified, forgotten, wiped away. It appeared as if by magic, as if buyers conjured it with their dollars, blessed by the sanctifica-tion of an art world that makes it clear that it is art, and art worth owning. The existence of the artist is only there as justification—this famed artist made this, therefore it is art.

Attempts to peer into the art-production process were hard to find as I worked on this book; coming up dry on this research again and again convinced me that I was heading in the right direction. The process of making art is too rarely studied and described *as work*. But sociologist Howard Becker, in his classic *Art Worlds*, did dig into the process of cre-ating art: not just the inspiration of the lone artist but the supporting cast that makes it possible.[30]

An art world, in Becker's term, is not singular but rather "the network of people whose cooperative activity, organized via their joint knowledge of conventional means of doing things, produces the kind of art works the art world is noted for." Art worlds are made up of the various workers who do the funding, producing, distributing, displaying, criticizing, observing, and, yes, purchasing of art as well as educating artists. The size of these supporting casts varies, but art production and circulation nevertheless depend on a broad network of workers even as those workers' participation is mystified.[31]

Conceptual artist Kerry Guinan drew attention to the breadth of art worlds with an exhibition that included a collaboration with factory workers in the Dominican Republic, who manufactured the canvases commonly bought at art stores in Ireland, where she lived. "The factory workers each signed a blank canvas and shipped it over to Ireland and I exhibited them," she explained. "This work was questioning the labor that is behind everything that we produce, even dematerialized conceptual art like the type that I do." For Guinan, her work "is always revealing power relations in a very experiential way to myself and to everyone involved in it."[32]

Art worlds are always stretching, bending, changing, and even dying. Would-be artists compete for the privilege to be considered such; there is often an oversupply of workers for the art work considered creative. The creative work, after all, is the part worth loving, and the part that grants special status. To be eligible for inclusion in the systems that ensure an artist can pay the bills—can be represented by a gallery, apply for public or foundation grants, get hired for commissions, sell their works or reproductions thereof—one must be granted the status of artist in the first place, a status conferred by institutions, from art schools to galleries to museums. Even now, few artists make their living solely by producing works of art; indeed, many of them pay the bills working in different parts of the art world, like the museum workers who were themselves artists, or art teachers producing works on the side.[33]

In an uncertain system, where artists must please someone in order to get their work funded (either up front, with a grant, or on the back end by selling the product), there will be limits on what they can do, on how radical a message they can send. In this sense, though independent artists are freer than wage laborers, they are still embedded in a system of power hierarchies structured by capitalism. They may not have a boss, but, unless they are wealthy themselves, they nonetheless have to appeal to others to support their work. Ben Davis argued that artists are quintessentially middle class, having some power and autonomy at work, and some status, but not freed from the pressures of working for a living. And like others in the middle class, they have been sold the idea that not having a boss is liberation. This position, as the workers of the Art Workers' Coalition discovered, limits artists' ability to organize for better conditions. Upon whom are their demands to be made?[34]

It is not surprising that artists are often loath to think of themselves as workers. Work, after all, sucks. Yet this vision of art work as somehow outside of the economy means that we know very little about the working conditions of actually-existing artists. Are they broke, are they struggling, how do they pay the bills, what do they contribute to the economy, could the state do more to help? Surveys have been done by activist organizations like Working Artists in the Greater Economy (W.A.G.E.), which released a 2012 study of around one thousand New York artists, which found that the majority did not receive any compensation for their participation in shows in museums or nonprofits. A 2014 UK survey found that "71% of artists had received no fee at all for exhibiting in arts council–funded galleries, and 63% had been forced to turn down exhibitions because they could not afford to carry the costs themselves." In 2018, US researchers found that the median income of the artists they surveyed was between $20,000 and $30,000 a year, with 21 percent pulling in $10,000 or less. Meanwhile, the audience for museums and galleries is (perhaps unsurprisingly) older, whiter, and richer than the rest of the population, on average, and that audience is shrinking. At the same time, the art market—with time out for a dip around the global financial crisis—is bigger than ever, generating well over $700 billion a year.[35]

State support for the arts varies in the industrialized West, from the tiny trickle of funds disbursed in the United States to more robust programs across Europe, with the amounts spent, unsurprisingly, higher in social democratic countries where the public sector as a whole is larger. In 2010, Ivo Josipović, a composer who was then president of Croatia, argued, "When regulating the position of artists in the society, one shouldn't have Mozart, Rembrandt, Beethoven, Balzac or some other genius in mind, but a human that chooses art as his profession because he has his internal motives to be a genius. The system should give opportunity to an artist to be independent, to express his talent in the way he finds the best, and in the same time secure a decent life for him and his family." In Denmark and some other countries, there are trade unions for artists; in these places they are more likely to receive state funding and therefore to have a target for their organizing efforts. Mexican artists are able to pay taxes with art work; the government displays the work in offices or public museums.[36]

But working-class people remain underrepresented in the arts. One US survey from 2014 found that artists and other "creative workers" were more likely to come from middle-income homes even as they make something like 35 percent less than their comfortable parents did. A 2018 UK study noted that in addition to the very real barriers of money, artists also face a series of gatekeepers who remain attached to the idea of art as a meritocracy—gatekeepers who tend to come from more comfortable backgrounds themselves, making it easier for them to wave away the difficulties that artists of color with less (or no) family support face just getting to enter that meritocratic contest.[37]

In all of this inequality reigns; in fact, it grows. A handful of superstars' success does not, in fact, trickle down; more art school graduates are pumped out each year than will ever make a living making art. Filmmaker and writer Hito Steyerl noted that the perception of the art world is that it is sponsored by the wealthy, but that in fact, "throughout history it has been artists and artworkers, more than any other actors, who have subsidized art production." It is the artists, still, who have made art valuable, and so often that is because they have done their work out of love, and in fact have done plenty of other work in order to be able to support their art. Sociologist Andrew Ross called this "sacrificial labor," a way that one gives up certain facets of stability in order to pursue work that is seen as meaningful—more meaningful, perhaps, even than personal relationships. (This notion echoes, of course, the conditions of the nonprofit worker.) Artists, after all, must love their work above all other things. One particularly ludicrous 2018 study used medical imaging technology, scanning the brains of self-identified "creatives," in an attempt to prove that sacrifice was simply hardwired into artists' brains.[38]

Hardwired or not, in order to continue this cycle, it is necessary to have a few superstars visibly raking in the money, and it is necessary to continue to depict art as an end in itself. In the space between these two joys—the anticipated thrill of success, and the pleasure of the art-making itself—most artists get lost.

There are, of course, paths to art-making that don't truck (mostly) with the Art World. Graffiti and street art, Davis argued, are essentially reactions to neoliberalism—reflections of the decline of the industrial core of so many cities, leaving fertile space for painting, on the one hand, and of gentrification, on the other, as advertising thrusts itself into every facet of urban life. Like the subway breakdancers who can turn an average commute into a moment of magic, graffiti typically isn't recognized as "art," because of where it takes place and its position outside of the law—although galleries have begun to embrace street artists, too, welcoming them inside the shifting boundaries of art worlds.[39]

So-called "outsider" artists, who make their work disconnected from any art world and often even from the kind of community that shapes something like graffiti, demonstrate a few of these contradictions. Untrained, perhaps intensely isolated, religious, or mentally ill artists who appear to have made their work simply to please themselves, these artists are often laughed at until someone qualified pronounces their work "art." Yet art critic Angella d'Avignon noted, "The art world needs outsiders more than they need the art world." The narrative around these artists suits art's image of itself, where brilliance is not a thing to be worked for but simply to be achieved—even if "outsider" artists put in quite a lot of work on their creations. The story of Vivian Maier, a nanny by trade whose massive oeuvre of hauntingly beautiful street photographs was found at an auction after her death, echoes this trope—she appeared to have taken her photos purely for the love of them, never attempting to show them in public. In a way, the "outsider" or "naïve" artist is the ideal artist: working on their own with no hope or even desire for payment or acknowledgment, with no study and no one teaching them skills, they produce something surprisingly brilliant for no one's edification but their own. Yet Maier proved so confounding to the man who "discovered" her that he made a documentary about "finding" her—when confronted with someone who appears to actually have done her work for love, despite all our cultural programming, we have a hard time comprehending her.[40]

It has been the support workers of the art world of late who have stood up to demand recognition as workers. Art museum staff picked up the example set by the MoMA workers in the 1970s and have been joining unions. Workers at the New Museum in New York helped set off this wave, challenging the museum's management to live up to its progressive reputation and recognize the workers' organization. Their campaign began in 2018 with the support of the MoMA workers and UAW Local 2110, to which the MoMA union belongs; in reaction, the museum hired an anti-union law firm. The crackdown backfired, though. Told that "unions are for coal miners" (perhaps a conscious echo of that critic of the Artists' Union), the workers nevertheless overwhelmingly voted for the union. Workers at the Marciano Art Foundation in Los Angeles were less successful; when they made their union drive public, the private museum simply shut its doors, firing them all. "I think that arts labor is really viewed as the sort of privileged sector of labor that, you know, people who are working in the arts often have college degrees or postgraduate degrees, and that somehow this is not our main source of income or is not our livelihood or is in some way that we are not serious workers," Izzy Johnson, one of the Marciano workers, told reporters. But the wave continued, with a spreadsheet circulating online in 2019, on which art institution workers anonymously shared their salary information, creating a broad picture of a low-paying industry and giving workers more fuel for organizing.[41]

During the coronavirus pandemic of 2020, art workers faced a swath of new challenges. In a world suddenly divided into "essential" and "nonessential" work, artists topped a poll asking respondents to rank the least (and most) essential jobs. Museum workers faced furloughs and layoffs; yet, as Bryan Cook, a member of the new union at the Guggenheim Museum in New York, noted, art is also one of the things that people want "on the other side of this," a thing that gives people "something to live for." Workers at the Philadelphia Museum of Art (PMA), who had begun organizing around the salary spreadsheet, went public with their union drive in the middle of the pandemic. "Now, more than ever, when things are so uncertain," said Sarah Shaw, a museum educator at the PMA, "this is the time when we need the power of collective bargaining, and to have a voice in these incredibly important decisions that are being made." In August, 89 percent of the workers voted for the union amid layoffs.[42]

It can still be difficult for artists themselves to conceive of their problems as collective issues, rather than individual ones. Artists, suggests artist and designer Bill Mazza, tend to be more antiauthoritarian than explicitly political. It's an alignment that suits the lone artist, whose instinct, often, is to make art about it—perhaps to make the problem visible, but often to stop short of offering a solution or taking collective action.[43]

Art and parenting, in this way, are oddly similar. One of a series of writers who tackled the question of art and mothering, Heather Abel, gestured to a photo of the sculptor Ruth Asawa taken by Imogen Cunningham, of Asawa making art while her children played. "This photo served as a challenge: if I really cared about my kids, I'd create art only while watching them," Abel wrote. "It was only much later that I realized Imogen Cunningham had posed her photo. That tableau must have lasted only as long as the flick of a camera lens, and then the baby was wet and crying, and the older children jabbed each other with wire." The challenge of finding time and space to make art is here contrasted with the everyday work of parenting, but still, ultimately, portrayed as a personal problem rather than a social one.[44]

Some of the more successful art-world organizing has indeed used artistic interventions to make political change. The Guerrilla Girls challenged the art world's sexism through their costumed performances and creative posters, taking the problem Abel described and turning it around, demanding inclusion into museums and galleries. If artists' work is not supported, if artists must find a way to self-sustain, then women, who remain responsible for so much caring labor, will find the odds of breaking into the mythic meritocracy stacked against them. "The majority of people who work in the arts will identify themselves as liberal to left-wing, often radically left-wing. This is going from the poorest artists to the highest paid curators in institutions," artist Kerry Guinan argued. "But, if this is the case that we are a field in which everyone is all left-wing values, then why are we all agreed that the art world is a piece of capitalist shit that is relying on private capital that exploits its workers, that exploits artists, relies on unpaid labor?" Guinan continued, "This, to me, is living proof that art cannot change the world and that is why we need to organize. Artists need to realize how little power we all actually really have and how power needs to be built. It doesn't come naturally and it is not a divine gift you get by being an artist."[45]

The reality is that today's successful artist is more likely a cottage industry held up by support workers who are made invisible just as women in the home have long been invisible. Damien Hirst is one such example: his massive success led novelist and journalist Hari Kunzru to describe him as "art that *is* the market—a series of gestures that are made wholly or primarily to capture and embody financial value, and only secondarily have any other function or virtue." Hirst's diamond-encrusted human skull was sold for $100 million. *ARTnews* described his business thus: "He has a company, Other Criteria, that licenses his imagery, creates products, and sells them on the Web. In addition to Hirst's own prints, editions, books, posters, and T-shirts, the company markets the wares of other artists. And this is just one piece of an umbrella corporation, Science Ltd., that oversees Hirst's vast studios, 120 employees, and other business interests." These artists aren't middle class: they are capitalists, employing workers to produce commodities for them that they can sell at (often a stupendous) profit.[46]

Jeff Koons, meanwhile, laid off a chunk of his assistants at his "round-the-clock studio" after rumors surfaced that they were considering unionizing. "I was in this room when I got to the studio and there are no windows and I was working a night shift," said Lucia Love of the *Art and Labor* podcast, who did a stint in Koons's "Factory." "For the time that I was there, I never saw sunlight, really. It was very brightly fluorescent lit. It was incredibly painful because the thing we had to do was like mix 200 minutely different colors. Then, there were these mass firings all the time where they wanted to demoralize you, but they were also like, 'Well, we just finished a show. We can't justify keeping everybody hired.'"[47]

Assistants are nothing new to art, of course, and some of them may even be paid well and treated fairly, and possibly one day launched into their own individual careers. But their names remain missing from the gallery wall, whether they are paint-mixers in Koons's "factory" or industrial workers making the likes of Richard Serra's massive metal *Torqued Ellipses* (though at least the description at Dia: Beacon, where those ellipses are housed, does mention them, if not by name). Kara Walker's gargantuan *Sugar Sphinx*, displayed in Brooklyn's soon-to-be-renovated Domino Sugar factory, was "built from Walker's sketches by a team of nearly 20 fabricators, the 3-D sculpting and milling firm Digital Atelier, and Sculpture House Casting," according to *New York* magazine; later in the article, Walker's assistants appear like ghosts in a throwaway sentence, unnamed, but briefly, at least, acknowledged. Kehinde Wiley's art, author and painter Molly Crabapple pointed out, is now painted by assistants in his Chinese studio; he told *New York* in 2012, "I don't want you to know every aspect of where my hand starts and ends, or how many layers go underneath the skin, or how I got that glow to happen," he says. "It's the secret sauce! Get out of my kitchen!" Crabapple responded, "I am happy that his work exists. It is beautiful. I just don't like the myth that he is the one who is painting it. Why can't we have movie credits for art? Because there is a lot of work that you cannot do yourself. You just need a credits list. That is all. And fair payment."[48]

Even as these "superartists" become household names, visual artists struggle with the devaluation of their work that the Internet has made possible. If mechanical reproduction, as Walter Benjamin famously pointed out, created problems for art, the problems of lightning-fast digital distribution have multiplied them. Astra Taylor wrote, "New-media thinkers believe social production and amateurism transcend the old problem of alienated labor by allowing us to work for love, not money, but in fact the unremunerated future they anticipate will only deepen a split that many desperately desire to reconcile." A wonderful efflorescence of amateur creativity has been brought on by the Internet, the argument goes, and why should we care if any of those people get paid when they appear not to? Yet Taylor pointed out, drawing on her own experiences as a filmmaker, that art production is expensive, and just because her films can now be seen on the Internet (potentially for free or on a streaming service for a fraction of the cost of a movie ticket) doesn't mean they have become free to produce. "Due to technological shifts," she wrote, "all manner of creative works have effectively become open access, and now we need to fund them."[49]

The Internet can be a way for artists to make money, too. Crabapple noted that selling prints of her work online and taking commissions made art sustainable for her in a way that a more traditional art career would not have. "Basically, you are expected to front all of the money and fund yourself to produce a show. That show sits in a room for a month and then, if that show sells, you get good money. But, if that show doesn't, you are just out a year's work and that is not sustainable for me." But tech companies would rather not share the wealth with those who use their platforms to create. The example of Vine, a short video service that briefly brought stardom to a handful of Internet personalities—and extra dollars to its parent company, Twitter—is instructive. When a handful of Vine creators with millions of followers demanded that the company pay them for their creations, it instead pulled the plug on the platform. Writer Malcolm Harris noted, "The important lesson from the story is that platforms would rather disappear entirely than start collectively bargaining with talent."[50]

Whether Vine creators are "artists" is beyond the reach of this book; the point is that the celebration of amateur creativity, of work done out of love, is often the velvet glove over an iron fist that will crack down quickly on any resistance. In November 2019, I attended a talk in an art gallery in London about the "future of work." During the question-and-answer session, two different artists referred to their abusive relationship with the art world. Young people work very hard to be accepted to exclusive art schools, noted OK Fox of the *Art and Labor* podcast; at the same time, they are drawn to those schools in many cases because they were misfits, or disillusioned by the vision of the capitalist workplace on offer. Those same young people go on to work incredibly hard for years in the hope of maybe becoming a professional artist one day, both Fox and Lucia Love said, shaping their lives around this desire only to find out that the art world doesn't love them back. Those art schools, noted longtime arts industry worker Natasha Bunten, often turn out graduates with no idea how to make a career in their field, how to gain funding, or where there might be jobs that would pay. Artists are still likely to be held to the fringes, despite Richard Florida's cheery framework: the flipside of the Koons Factory is the hollowed-out industrial spaces that artists claim for themselves. After the 2016 fire at Ghost Ship, an artists' collective in an old warehouse in rapidly gentrifying Oakland, California, which killed thirty-six people, Alexander Billet and Adam Turl of *Red Wedge Magazine* wrote, "America hates its artists. America hates its young working-class people." The victims of the fire, they argued, "are victims of an art and music economy that doesn't work for the majority of artists and musicians. They are dead because art has become financialized. They are dead because gentrification is taking away our right to the city—and pushing artists and young workers to the margins—especially (but not only) artists of color."[51]

Creativity in all these ways has been turned from a basic human quality, one that anyone is capable of expressing, to a private preserve, enclosed behind the boundaries of its own world. The narrative that artists will create solely for the love of it—a fact that might be true if all humans had the stability and the free time and resources with which to do so—is used to justify a variety of exploitative practices rather than to call for an opening up of art worlds to all. Yet despite it all, art remains both essential and the deepest of pleasures. As Alison Stine wrote at Talk Poverty: "When I feel like I have nothing, I can give my son the gift of creativity, the gift of imagination, the gift of spending a happy hour painting cardboard on the porch."[52]

We will not make the world friendlier for artists by denying that their work is work, however, even as we should—and do—acknowledge the joy of creating. Rather, art workers will have to do that, as Kerry Guinan said, by organizing. Natasha Bunten cofounded the Cultural Workers Education Center in New York City because her years working in the world of fine arts had left her frustrated with the exploitation that surrounded her. The granddaughter of an artist who seeded a modest foundation to support art and craft workers, Bunten went to art school as an undergraduate and then as a graduate student at New York University; she did unpaid internships before landing a job at the Guggenheim and moving to consulting. "What happened for me personally was that it became clear that the work that I needed to do was about people in my own community and people with whom I have class solidarity," Bunten said. That led her to researching the issue of labor in the art world, and looking at unionization practices in other industries in which she saw similarities.

Inspired by the work of organizing campaigns in other parts of the service industry—home care workers, domestic workers, and food-service workers, in particular—she began to ask how the art world could learn from these strategies. "One of the big glaring voids that I kept butting my head up against was this issue of how we talk about the art world as this insular thing," she said. "When you start to look at the way in which an artist in their studio is functionally an isolated worker that is producing something that then goes into the market, their isolation is not dissimilar from the isolation of a home health-care worker." The art world also intertwines with public education and the broader nonprofit industrial complex, yet, Bunten said, it is still treated as unique. She and her colleagues launched the Cultural Workers Education Center in 2019 to begin to make space for education and organizing for art workers, and they were thrilled with the response—in particular, the interest in discussions about organizing. Bunten said, "For us the answer has always been the collective. These systemic issues can't be addressed by targeting one person, by acting as an individual. They can only be addressed when we start to understand our collective needs and our collective rights and to demand those rights alongside our peers."

It was late January 2020 when I crisscrossed Ireland with Kate O'Shea, hopping trains and buses from Dublin to Limerick to Cork and back again to meet a collection of the artists with whom she works. In Dublin, we had breakfast and tea with Marie Brett, an installation artist who, like O'Shea, specializes in creating spaces where people can interact, and for whom O'Shea was project-managing an upcoming installation. From there we caught a night bus to Limerick to stay with Kerry Guinan and meet one of O'Shea's printmaking mentors as well as Ciaran Nash, an artist who had collaborated with Guinan and others to make an alternative currency to celebrate the anniversary of the Limerick Soviet (a time in 1919 when the workers of Limerick turned a general strike into a takeover of the city). From there we went to O'Shea's home of Cork, to meet Eve Olney and to visit the bank where O'Shea and Olney had built their installation, titled *Spare Room*.

The space, which was an iteration of Olney's practice as Art Architecture Activism, was designed to be open to the public—not just for the appreciation of art, but to be a social and political space where people came together for workshops. These ranged, O'Shea said, "from the banking process to feminist economics to printmaking."

They took over the vacant TSB Bank on Main Street, near the city center, "to pinpoint at least one building and show this could be used to multiple purposes and it is practically a crime that it is not being used," Olney explained. But once the project began, it snowballed beyond their expectations. It turned into thirteen exhibitions from artists as well as social organizations, including the Cork Women's Travellers Network and the Movement of Asylum Seekers in Ireland. There were twenty-six workshops, and in between those O'Shea pulled together her "People's Kitchen" to feed the people who came in. They hosted a radical library in the bank's old vault. But the point, they stressed, was to create new organizations that would last beyond the period of the exhibition.

Figuring out how her print work fitted in with the work of creating the spaces was at one point a challenge for O'Shea, but the bank project helped her to understand how the art could "create a space visually that can hold activism," she explained. The art served to make the space accessible, to draw interest from people who might never attend a radical political meeting, to get people in a space with others with whom they might never have spoken on the street. "My work is people, in a way. It is whoever is in the space at that moment [and] is creating whatever part of the revolution they are creating."[53]

For O'Shea, and the artist community to which she belongs, organizing is a part of their arts practice. Yet she is quite aware of the way that art trends can veer toward or away from a particular kind of political art. It is what keeps her doing different types of work, from the prints to publishing to the spaces and the People's Kitchen. And it is also what keeps her and her community aware of the need for political organizing that goes beyond political art.

Kerry Guinan, whose art is often in fact *about* labor, nevertheless said, "Ultimately, I don't think it's possible to interrupt or go outside capitalism through art. I do think it's possible through organizing." Her art is about, she said, "trying to test very particular aesthetic techniques and, I suppose, test the boundaries of the artistic encounter. Whereas organizing is a completely different field altogether and it has limits in itself."

The organizing that O'Shea and Olney and Guinan do has a range of impacts—from the small-scale, organizing with other artists to improve their working conditions—which does in its way open up space for funding for more political art work—to the long-term aim of challenging the capitalist system. "One of the reasons why I want to start an artists' union, it's not even so much as fighting for better positions for ourselves. I just don't think that the arts will be truly accessible until we create better working conditions for those that are in it," Guinan explained. "I don't think working-class people and marginalized communities will ever be as represented as we want them to be in the arts if we don't fight to change the field so that it is not so precarious and it's not so underpaid and doesn't rely so much on unpaid work." The art world's typical solution, of finding a few artists from diverse backgrounds to uplift, she noted, is still "an art solution to a structural problem."

Guinan launched the artists' union as part of yet another collective art project. In Dublin, the A4 Sounds art space—a gallery, workspace, and community—was hosting a yearlong series of exhibitions and events around the theme "We Only Want the Earth," a line from Irish socialist and trade union leader James Connolly. Guinan used the moment to start a concrete campaign with a winnable goal for collective action. "We are not going to go looking for millions more in arts money, because we won't achieve that in a month," Guinan said. "But if someone has an invoice that hasn't been paid, we might collectively decide to approach the gallery or whoever it is and win that battle for them. What I want is for members of the artistic community to go away feeling what winning feels like and, also, how hard it is, how hard it is to even win a small battle, because that will make you realize how little power we actually have right now." The artists' union also held a campaign around arts funding from the government during the coronavirus lockdown.

I suggested to O'Shea that, in a way, all of these collaborations and mutual support projects were themselves the beginnings of such a union. When I told the A4 Sounds crew about Natasha Bunten's workers' center, they reacted by saying, "Wow, that's kind of what we are. An art workers' center."

A4, too, began from collective exhibitions and grew into a collective artists' space, where politically minded artists in wildly expensive Dublin can work. "This year is the first year that we had a funded program. In the past we have been doing things like the residency on a shoestring which basically meant we could give in-kind stuff to artists so they can use the space," explained Donal Holland, one of A4's founders. That program became "We Only Want the Earth." Consulting artists like O'Shea and Guinan would serve as mentors for less established artists, giving them access to material supports rather than just gesturing at an acknowledgment. The virus closed the studios down for a while, but the programming was going ahead as Dublin reopened.

"I just love connecting all these things," O'Shea said. "With 'We Only Want the Earth,' I have a small part, which is exciting because I am then part of a bigger team, and I will be working with the Movement of Asylum Seekers in Ireland." They would be creating an award for someone seeking refuge in Ireland. The whole idea behind "We Only Want the Earth," O'Shea said, is "a redistribution of wealth," taking arts funding that A4 gets and using it to support marginalized artists. "It is all about building the movement of the artists—it is like slowly working and building an army. We joke about that now. When we meet someone we are like, 'They would be good for the army.'"

CHAPTER 7

HOPING FOR WORK
Interns

Camille Marcoux's first experience as an unpaid intern was while she was studying for her bachelor's degree at L'Université du Québec à Montréal (UQAM). She was preparing for law school, but as an undergraduate, she interned at a nonprofit community organization one day a week for a whole year, while a full-time student.

The internship, like those done by so many students (and graduates) in Quebec and around the world, was unpaid. "The organization basically runs on interns during the school year," she explained, as for many students an internship was mandatory before graduation. Then, during law school, she was required to do another internship for six months. That time, she got lucky—she got paid. But that wasn't a requirement. "Obviously, the kind of law that you went into had an influence on whether you were going to get paid, but the obligation to pay or not is the same for everyone. Even if you worked for the biggest firm in the city, you could work for free."

She had to apply for her internship just as one would a job, but, she noted, since the internships were mandatory, if students were not accepted at the workplaces of their choice, "it could happen that you were forced to work somewhere."

The variety of internship experiences struck her, early on, as unfair. "The different internships have different value. The people that were doing internships in corporate law—and obviously it was more men—during the summer, got paid and got more academic credit for that internship. While I was doing one day a week during a whole year, I couldn't get paid and I had less credit at the end of the year." The way this was weighted in practice meant these men could graduate faster with more cash in hand; student protests changed the weighting practices a little bit, but pay rates (or lack thereof) remained the same.

Marcoux and a growing number of other interns also noticed that internships were required in certain disciplines and not in others. While more fields were demanding students complete internships, fields like education, social work, and nursing—fields dominated by women—led the way. Meanwhile, in engineering and other male-dominated disciplines, internships were paid and protected by labor law. "The labor law, for it to apply, you have to have a wage," Marcoux, now a labor lawyer, explained. "What is in the labor law regarding internships is that when the internship is mandatory in your curriculum, the labor law does not apply to you, so the employer is not forced to give you a wage. But when you get a wage, you are an employee." When you don't get a wage, you are not an employee—and that means that protections against abuses on the job—against sexual harassment, for example—don't apply, either. Unpaid workers could thus be doubly or triply exploited.

Professional organizations had some sway over the internship process, which was the reason that engineering interns were paid, she explained. "They actually said to the schools, 'We are not going to recognize the internships that are done if they are not paid.' In those conditions, the labor law applied to those types of students because they were automatically paid during their internship."

During her undergraduate internship, Marcoux said, the interns often felt they'd been thrown in at the deep end, expected to know how to do the job from the beginning. There was little oversight or training as they learned through doing—the opposite of the on-the-job education internships are billed as. Marcoux worked for a community organization providing a variety of services: "We gave consultations about social services, about tenants' rights, but also about financial aid. Sometimes it was very sensitive information, a very delicate situation, and it was very difficult to just work without any discussion with our colleagues, with our boss, about how we were supposed to do that work."

The interns were kept out of staff meetings, she explained, which could create or exacerbate messy situations. "Sometimes people had very difficult experiences with certain service users and we didn't have any space to discuss it, either with the school or with our internship environment." They worked alongside paid staff, and were expected to do much of the same work, but the interns did not have the same power.

There was little help to be had from the university. "The school, they don't have any idea what we do during our internship. For them it is a complete mystery," she laughed. And yet, because the internship was required for her degree, she received a grade from the university for the experience. "It is still a little bit difficult to understand how they can actually grade us because they don't understand what we do," she said. Even though her direct supervisor at the nonprofit provided an evaluation to the university, she didn't think that gave the university enough insight to grade her, let alone provide a constructive evaluation or any real oversight of her working conditions. This, too, was a common complaint among the interns.

As the internship programs expanded, they became more demanding, requiring more hours of the students, longer commitments, and more sacrifice in order to do the unpaid work. Even lower-level students, at Quebec's CEGEPs (institutions that provide pre-university education for university-bound students as well as technical programs for those learning skilled trades), are required to do internships. Students in programs from cosmetology to nursing to administration are doing longer internships, despite the fact, as Marcoux pointed out, that their degrees do not usually lead to particularly high-paying jobs. "This shows that it is a very classist issue, because we are expected to do free work during our training," she said, "but it is not going to lead us to a more valued job and something with good work conditions that are going to help us pay back our loans."

The expansion of unpaid internships in the public and nonprofit sector in Quebec, Marcoux said, has helped to make up for years of budget cuts to the government—budget cuts that students have fought against over and over again. As nonprofits expand into doing work that the state used to do, the work of volunteers, and now interns, helps keep those organizations afloat—and making those internships mandatory provides a steady stream of cheap or free labor. The nonprofit sector in Canada, as in the United States, has expanded greatly in recent decades, and relies on the dedication of workers who often take pay cuts out of a commitment to the cause—or, in the case of the interns, take no pay at all.[1]

"Very early on during our education, we learned to help to compensate for the budget cuts," Marcoux explained. "We are learning what is expected of us, and then we go into our workplace and we see our colleagues and they are all doing free labor. A lot of them are working extra hours that they are not getting paid for because they are all working with vulnerable populations and you cannot just say, 'Now it is time to go home. Goodbye.'"

She added, "I feel like they are training us for exploitation."

WHAT IS AN INTERN?

Unlike most of the workers in this book, the intern is not defined by the kind of work she does, but by her status in the workplace. She can be a law student, like Camille Marcoux, on her way to a middle-class profession but laboring in a community organization one day a week. She could be an assistant on a film set, fetching coffee and checking lists in hopes of breaking into the industry. She could be a young journalist, as your humble author was, fact-checking pieces by big names she's long idolized and eagerly pitching pieces to the editors who occasionally breeze by her cubicle. She could be an Ivy League student putting in time at an investment bank, or she could even be serving cotton candy at Disney World or assembling iPhones at Foxconn's massive factories.[2]

She might be paid, but probably isn't.

Interns are not technically workers at all. Instead, they are assumed to be students first, learning on the job and making their way toward eventual (and eventually, perhaps, lucrative) careers. One researcher defined an internship as "any experience of the world of work from which a student can learn about a career," which is both vague and as specific as it is possible to be.[3]

What really defines the intern, after all, is hope. Communications scholars Kathleen Kuehn and Thomas F. Corrigan coined the term "hope labor" to apply to "un- or under-compensated work carried out in the present, often for experience or exposure, in the hope that future employment opportunities may follow." Hope labor is a snake eating its own tail, and the intern is the hope laborer *par excellence*. Working for free in order to one day get one of those jobs that are worth loving, the intern is the vehicle by which the conditions of contingency and subordination that are common to low-wage service work creep into an increasing number of salaried fields. Justified by the meritocratic myth that the best interns will get jobs, the internship actually drives down wages by introducing a new wage floor—free—into the system, allowing companies to substitute interns for entry-level workers. The interns replace the very employees they hope to be.[4]

Hope labor, and the internship, is a problem of power. The intern is the least powerful person in the room; interns are there to do what is asked of them in such a way that it inconveniences no one while drawing the positive attention that might lead to the ultimate prize: a real job offer. The internship turns a job into something to be lusted after, dreamed of, all while justifying today's grunt work as "paying one's dues," "networking," and "making connections"—the key to getting an opportunity to work in the brave neoliberal economy. The idea, of course, is that it will be different once you get the coveted job. Once you get a real job, the story goes, you'll get not just pay but respect and equal treatment; you will no longer have to scrape and hustle. Yet what the internship really does, often, is give the intern a glimpse of the messiness and ugliness of the real world of work, particularly the lack of control that they will have over their conditions—and that lack of control often continues even when wages are introduced. The internship, in other words, naturalizes lousy—and gendered—working conditions. As Kuehn and Corrigan wrote, "we lack agency, so we hope."[5]

Flexibility is the primary trait demanded of interns, and it is the main condition of their work. Interns must learn on the job but have demonstrable skills; they must be willing to do whatever is asked and do it with a smile. No matter which industries they are in, they are in the position of service workers, having to smile and say, "Yes, whatever you need," to whoever asks. The connections made on the job are the most important thing to interns, as those connections might build a network for future employment. Thus the actual work they do is secondary. But, as the internship has spread into more and more parts of the working world, more and more workers in turn have job experiences that are more like internships. Flexible, temporary work has spread; employers have less responsibility for their employees; and the employees are more concerned with making connections with which to jump to the next, insecure, position. The internship, and the casualization of the workforce more generally, requires the would-be worker to demonstrate love just to get a job in the first place.[6]

Many writers trace the history of the intern back to the apprentice of old, and specifically to the apprentices within the guild system. Apprenticeship, a tradition by which practitioners of a craft were to pass on their trade, dates back centuries, perhaps all the way back to the Code of Hammurabi. Apprentices were to learn by doing, getting hands-on practice at a craft they could expect to spend the rest of their lives performing. But before the idea of "art" was separated from skilled crafts, craftspeople handed down what they knew in a process quite different from today's internships.[7]

The apprenticeship of the precapitalist guild years was intensive; apprentices spent years learning their trade at the master's side, often becoming, in a way, a part of the family. The master was obligated to provide room and board, clothing, and other such things in lieu of parents. Wrote sociologist Alexandre Frenette, "Apprentices were expected to obey their master much as they would a parent, providing valuable labour as well as loyalty and child-like love." Beyond simply a trade, the master was to pass on invaluable life advice and morality, and to have a lasting relationship based in a contract. Formalized in 1563 in England with the Statute of Artificers, the apprenticeship system had set rules for the obligations of master to apprentice as well as apprentice to master, and a set period of time (seven years). But that doesn't mean the system wasn't varied and rife with abuses.[8]

Adam Smith was a notable critic of apprenticeships, considering them a restriction on the freedom of workers. He argued for a wage for the apprentice rather than payment in lodging and meals, writing that "the sweets of labour consist altogether in the recompense of labour." And indeed, the system declined as the Industrial Revolution spread and wage labor became common. In the colonies, at first British law held sway and governed apprenticeships, but the fledgling country had a few factors that mitigated against the growth of a strong guild system. The myth of American independence was strong, but so was the promise of supposedly unsettled land, open for those who would rather try to make their own way than stay put and learn from a master. (As long as they didn't mind displacing Native people from it.) Apprentices often skipped out on their indentures and lit out for the frontier. And so the rise of chattel slavery solved the problem of workers who could escape work; it helped level the playing field among white workers while condemning kidnapped African people to the undesirable labor.[9]

In Canada, too, apprentices voted with their feet and left their positions. In Montreal, where centuries later interns would hit the streets on strike, the turning point was in the early 1800s, when the flight of the apprentices, combined with the growth of larger-scale manufacturing and the shift to cash wages, led to a precipitous decline in the system. The spread of public education and higher education, too, contributed to the decline of the individualized apprenticeship, and preparation for the workforce—if any was necessary—shifted form.[10]

As reformers fought to ban child labor, and the family wage became common, reform movements instilled new ideas about young people and learning. Adolescence, they argued, was a special time of life, set aside from childhood or adulthood, and young people's work should be a sideline, a summer or after-school job, something to be managed around their real work of getting an education. The apprenticeship system continued for some skilled trades, and continues to this day, but it was no longer the prevalent form of job training.[11]

In 1861, the Land Grant Act was instituted in the United States to fund colleges for more practical education, in fields like agriculture and trades. The cooperative system (which persists in a few colleges today) was also created as a way for students to alternate classroom education with practical learning on the job, to formalize training in fields such as architecture. These programs, too, in some ways shaped our modern-day internships.[12]

But the "internship" as such was actually born in the medical field. According to Ross Perlin, author of *Intern Nation*, young medical students were "interned (in the sense of confined)" within the walls of a hospital, "enduring a year or two of purgatory before entering the profession." Before the 1900s, doctors, too, undertook apprenticeships, but as the profession formalized, young doctors began to go through a more standardized learning process, from medical school to internships, where they could get hands-on experience while remaining under the supervision of more practiced physicians. The American Medical Association's Council on Medical Education recommended a yearlong internship after medical school in 1904; by 1914, the vast majority of medical students were interning. Critics, Perlin noted, "were soon accusing hospitals (as many still do today) of squeezing exhausting, cheap labor from young medical graduates."[13]

The medical internship expanded into what we now know as the "residency," an extended period of years, and one that still denotes lengthy working hours, "scut work," and little power on the job. American medical interns and residents, some of whom are members of the Service Employees International Union's Committee of Interns and Residents, have fought to reduce their workweek to eighty hours and to trim back twenty-eight-hour shifts to a mere sixteen. Yet the interns, in particular, still face arguments that what they are doing isn't really work but part of their education. They also hear the familiar argument that their demands for shorter hours or rest breaks shortchange patients, that they should put their needs on the back burner to care for those in their charge—despite studies that have repeatedly shown the deleterious effects of long hours on a physician's quality of work. Although medical interns and residents are paid, their salaries are a fraction of what a full-fledged doctor makes— they're closer in pay to the hospital's cleaners than to the attending physicians. (The United States' privatized health-care system is uniquely demanding of residents; in Europe, residents work closer to forty-eight hours.) There's plenty of hope labor in this part of a doctor's career, as they rationalize "paying their dues" while walking past the doctors' luxury cars in the parking lot on their way to another sixteen-hour shift.[14]

The internship began to trickle into other fields by the 1920s, with university professors advocating the practice and professional journals in a variety of fields, such as accounting and the burgeoning marketing industry, calling for students to take it up. White-collar professions seized on the internship as a badge of class status, to be differentiated from the apprenticeship, which was for manual workers. But it was in politics where the internship really took off. Programs were launched by city and state governments in the 1930s to bring ambitious young people in to learn about public service. For several years during the New Deal era, the National Institute of Public Affairs—a nonpartisan, nongovernmental organization—ran a yearlong, unpaid internship program (eventually taken over by the Civil Service Commission) designed to bring new talent into civil service.[15]

The model of unpaid on-the-job learning made a certain kind of sense in politics, where the spirit of public service was supposed to draw people into the work. In practice, though, requiring unpaid work meant that only young people with a certain level of access and income could take advantage of the opportunity. After World War II, the US Congress changed shape significantly, with lawmakers hiring a growing number of staffers— and alongside them, the pools of interns who still today do much of the work on Capitol Hill. By the 1950s internship programs had spread across the country, but there was much variety among them: some were paid, some unpaid, lengths of time and coordination with educational institutions differed, and of course there was much disparity in the quality of the work carried out by the interns. In other words, the conditions under which today's interns work, where it's often a roll of the dice whether would-be learners find themselves scrubbing shelves and fetching coffee or collaborating closely with prestigious staffers, was coming into shape.[16]

At about this time, the US Supreme Court handed down a ruling that would shape the future of interns for decades to come. *Walling vs. Portland Terminal Co.*, a 1947 case, established guidelines under which trainees could be considered exempt from legal protections for workers (including, notably, a minimum wage), guidelines that held for many years. The original case focused on railyard workers who undertook a two-week training program provided by the Portland Terminal Company. "In such a context, creating an exemption [under the Fair Labor Standards Act] for trainees must have seemed like a reasonable proposition: a way of encouraging firms to provide vocational training for future employees without having to pay them like regular employees," Perlin noted. The decision laid out the criteria under which an employee could be considered a trainee and therefore ineligible for labor protections: the work had to be a practical training program, where the trainees benefited from the experience and did not replace any regular employees; the trainees could not be guaranteed a job after their training, and should not expect wages; and perhaps most importantly, the training could not "expedite the company business," and could in fact actually get in the way of it. It is this last factor that has remained contentious over the years as competing administrations have changed their interpretation of this ruling to apply to interns. How far outside the normal run of business must training be in order to count as training and not simply unpaid work?[17]

Internships continued to spread during the 1960s and 1970s, starting when Lyndon Johnson's War on Poverty pumped money into work-based learning programs, and young, politically involved people sought opportunities to put their values to work. Congress reorganized yet again, expanding the range of subcommittees and staffers, attracting a new wave of nonprofits, lobbyists, and others seeking to influence policy—and stocking up on ambitious, cheap young interns. The rate of college attendance was rising, and as the idealistic 1960s faded into the recession 1970s, young grads were looking for toeholds anywhere they could find them. Internships were a new way to differentiate oneself from the masses. The number of university-backed internship programs rose from two hundred in 1970 to one thousand in 1983.[18]

But it was in the 1990s that the modern internship really took off, and it was also in the 1990s that the pushback against the spread of unpaid internships began. Architecture students, organizing with the American Institute of Architecture Students, began to protest the prevalence of unpaid internships in their field—one already known for its grueling educational programs. The organization lobbied other groups to condemn the practice too and managed to change the culture in the field in favor of paying interns. Unpaid interns also sued a prominent public relations firm after the company had gone so far as to explicitly bill its clients for the hours worked by employees it wasn't paying. The students won $31,520 in back wages.[19]

But none of that stopped the spread of the unpaid internship. As the modern work ethic shifted and a job went from being a mere necessity—the main pleasure of which, as Adam Smith wrote, was the money—to something billed as the source of all fulfillment in life, it began to make a strange kind of sense that one had to *earn* one's job. In fields like journalism, as the internship became more common, the likelihood that it would be paid did not—one study found that in 1976, 57 percent of TV and 81 percent of radio interns got paid at least something; by 1991, those numbers were down to 21 percent and 32 percent, respectively. The hollowing out of the middle of the job market that came with the disappearance of unionized industrial labor (to outsourcing or automation) meant that higher education, and, increasingly, personal connections, were necessary to compete for a smaller pool of better-compensated work with better conditions. And the stick to the carrot of the "dream job" was the also-expanding low-wage service economy all around. Internships like those at Disney World, where low-paid college students work twelve-hour shifts in a variety of service positions, from serving popcorn and cotton candy to cleaning up vomit on roller coasters, show the overlap. The difference between a Disney internship and a regular job is a Disney line on a résumé for one, and job security and decent pay for the other (most of the full-time Disney workers are represented by a union). To Disney, having a two-tier workforce is worth something like $20 million a year in savings.[20]

Even when not literally serving food, interns remain subservient. Anyone who's ever prepared coffee, scooped ice cream, or waited at a blank desk in a cubicle for someone to notice their unpaid presence knows the emotional labor of appearing grateful while doing the worst jobs. The internship advanced alongside other forms of contingent work, and alongside the idea that trading in security for enjoyable work was a deal worth making. Hope labor, everywhere you look.

Interns are emblematic of what economist and author Guy Standing called "the precariat," a class of workers that he argued are identifiable by their lack of security. The precariat, he wrote, does not map "neatly onto high-status professional or middle-status craft occupations." Rather, it is a term for a set of working conditions that are becoming more and more common as the number of workers who have long-term security at work declines. Similar to the concept of hope labor is what Standing named "work-for-labor," or the work that it is necessary to do in order to get paying work. In addition to forward-looking hope labor, work-for-labor includes "networking outside office hours, commuting or reading company or organisational reports 'at home,' 'in the evening' or 'over the weekend.'" The internship is only one kind of work-for-labor, but it prepares the worker for a thousand other ways to go above and beyond.[21]

Somewhere between 50 and 75 percent of four-year college students do at least one internship, according to researchers, though the lack of good data continues to be a problem. It is also true that those interns are often balancing unpaid work, schoolwork, and a paid job—something like half of all undergraduate students have paid work that averages twenty-five hours a week. And despite the myths, lower-income students are actually more likely to have the unpaid variety of internship, while higher-income students tend to have the kinds of personal networks that get them access to the best internships, too. One's major in school is also a factor—as Camille Marcoux explained, for engineering and computer science students, in male-dominated fields that supposedly require more technical skill, internships are more likely to be paid. Education, the social sciences, and the arts are much less likely to have paid internships, and more likely to be filled with women.[22]

This brings out the factor that would motivate Marcoux and her fellow interns to get organized. Internships are extremely gendered. As Miya Tokumitsu wrote, "internships, insofar as they demand meekness, complicity, ceaseless demonstrations of gratefulness, and work for free or for very little pay, put workers in a feminized position, which, historically, has been one of disadvantage." The intern is, as Malcolm Harris pointed out in *Kids These Days*, the inverse of what people mostly imagine the working class to be—the stereotypical midcentury worker of a million nostalgic fantasies is a hard-hatted man, probably white. The unpaid intern is likely a smiling, retiring young woman, eternally grateful just for the opportunity to show up.[23]

When one is expected to perform gratitude every day on the job, it makes summoning the mindset necessary to organize for change that much harder. And so of course interns are the opposite of factory workers in one other way: they are extremely unlikely to have unions. Unions, after all, built power by making trouble, by refusing to work unless their demands were met. But when you're already expecting to give away your services for free, how much harder is it to get to the point where you'll raise a little hell to get your way?

Women have always been the largest part of the contingent labor force. Part-time work itself was a gendered concept, designed for women like the shop clerks and retail workers of the nineteenth and early twentieth centuries, who supposedly took jobs to earn "pin money" rather than because they needed a real job. As more women moved into the workforce, the conditions long expected to accompany "women's work" spread to more and more workers, and the internship is a key hinge point where those conditions enter workplaces that, formerly, were associated with a sheen of masculine prestige and privilege.[24]

And the internship these days is more likely to be, as it was for Marcoux and her colleagues, mandatory, or at least highly encouraged. Universities serve as clearinghouses and recruitment spaces for unpaid positions;

career centers steer students toward plum positions, and more and more majors require at least one internship in order to graduate. Some colleges even offer financial aid for unpaid interns, explicitly subsidizing the companies that take on their students. Meanwhile, students who do unpaid internships for college credit are often paying the university for the credits, literally paying in order to work. Internships, explained one professor who has researched the subject, are "a very cheap way to provide credits . . . cynically, a budget balance" for the universities that require or encourage them. In this way, the internship is connected to the corporatization of the university, which we'll discuss in more depth in the following chapter.[25]

As Camille Marcoux explained, because, in many places, unpaid interns are not considered employees under the law, they often fall into a legal black hole when it comes to various workplace abuses. Discrimination, sexual harassment? If you aren't an employee, say goodbye to what little legal protection you might have to sue. When Bridget O'Connor was doing an unpaid internship at Rockland Psychiatric Center in New York, one of the doctors referred to her as "Miss Sexual Harassment." The doctor also made other sexual comments, and other women who worked at the facility made similar reports of his conduct. Yet when O'Connor sued, her case was thrown out in court because she wasn't an employee: federal law didn't cover interns unless they received, according to a spokesperson for the US Equal Employment Opportunity Commission, "significant remuneration."[26]

Some states, and Washington, DC, have imposed laws protecting interns at least against sexual harassment or discrimination; nevertheless, there is a bitter irony to the fact that interns receive such protections automatically if they are paid, leaving the unpaid even easier to exploit. But perhaps it is understandable that policymakers have not been quick to act in interns' best interests: after all, many of their offices still run on unpaid internships. The offices of members of Congress and of the UK Parliament are filled with unpaid interns. Access to some of the most powerful people in the world is predicated, then, on free work, meaning that a class divide not only separates well-compensated politicians from their constituents, but a buffer zone of well-off interns stands between those constituents and their issues getting a hearing. When Alexandria Ocasio-Cortez, the socialist member of Congress from Queens and the Bronx, took her seat in 2019, she set shockwaves in motion by announcing that she would pay interns $15 an hour—90 percent of House members paid their interns nothing. Ocasio-Cortez pointed out the "rich irony" that people questioned how she would pay for the interns, but would then "grow awfully quiet when called out on their expectation that part-time workers magically invent money to work for free." In a video message later, she and other progressive lawmakers proclaimed, "Experience doesn't pay the bills!"[27]

Nonprofit organizations, filled with the same righteous rhetoric about public service, are also rife with unpaid interns as well as other kinds of volunteer labor. So is Silicon Valley, where public-service language is often used to inflate the moral value of startups, but the accepted motivation for working for less now is that it will pay off later—what sociologist Gina Neff called "venture labor," a kind of bet placed that hard work now will pay dividends in the future, much like a venture capitalist might pour money into that same startup. Venture laborers see such work as an investment in their future; as Malcolm Harris put it, "human capital is the present value of a person's future earnings, or a person's imagined price at sale, if you could buy and sell free laborers—minus upkeep." In such an environment, the unpaid intern fits right in, hoping that their time, too, will be an investment that pays off. When times were flush, Silicon Valley paid interns and fêted them lavishly, but when the rough times hit, the interns were the first to go.[28]

The coronavirus pandemic, too, meant that internship programs were slashed, particularly the summer programs that would-be workers at media companies, nonprofits, and congressional offices, among other fields, rely on to get a leg up. A survey of more than four hundred companies found that something like 80 percent of them were changing their programs or cutting them entirely. If internships these days offer "a chance to look at an environment rather than as a chance to learn the job," what are they worth when one can no longer be in the workplace?[29]

The real ground zero for unpaid internships—and for the publicity around them, as well as the highest-profile battles for justice—is in the arts and media industries, where competition is fierce and the sheen of glamour hangs around the top jobs, where hope labor has always been the name of the game. The art world is filled with unpaid internships, though in 2019 the Board of Trustees of the Association of Art Museum Directors issued a resolution calling for museums to pay their interns. One study found that 86 percent of UK arts internships were unpaid, and most of them were located in London, where the cost of doing an internship—in terms of expected rent and cost of living—ran at least £1,100 a month.[30]

Working for free in the rarefied worlds of art and media, surrounded by multimillionaires, is bad enough. But as if to underline the inequality that runs through these industries, the phenomenon of the "internship auction" burst on the scene. The proceeds ostensibly went to charity, and the internships—which ranged from fashion house Versace to a "blogging internship" at the *Huffington Post* (now *HuffPost*)—were in notoriously hard-to-crack industries. Beyond the still-rare auction, or the "internpreneurs" making money selling advice to would-be interns, there was also the University of Dreams, a private company that sold internships. At first, as Ross Perlin explained, the companies that received interns ponied up the cash. But after the recession, the University of Dreams realized that getting the interns (or more likely, their well-off parents) to pay was a better business model, as was marketing "destination internships." "Part of the appeal for young people is precisely that they are treated as customers, at least at first, rather than prospective employees," Perlin wrote. And who wouldn't prefer to be a customer, who can ask to speak to a manager if something goes wrong, rather than an eternally meek and grateful intern?[31]

With such gatekeeping in the way, it's no wonder that the culture industries, in particular, but also the world of work in general, are increasingly stratified, and that upward mobility has stalled. Research in the United Kingdom found that internships "operate as part of an informal economy in which securing an internship all too often depends on who you know and not on what you know." Paying interns, the researchers concluded, would help, but on its own would not be enough. And the results of such an economy were stark: in journalism, for example, fewer than 10 percent of new workers came from working-class backgrounds.

For people of color, who tend to have less family money to fall back on—median wealth for white households in the United States is around twelve times higher than it is for Black families—the internship is a barrier that keeps too many fields disproportionately white. Such inequality shapes the kinds of stories that get told, the sources reporters find worth interviewing, the subjects they care about. Similar statistics in the culture industries mean that pop culture is increasingly made by and for the middle and upper classes. Some programs exist to recruit interns of more diverse backgrounds—and pay them—but they are a drop in the bucket.[32]

Internships might be an American innovation, but they have rapidly spread around the world. Chinese law students, like Marcoux in Canada, are mandated to do an internship; meanwhile, interns also work on the assembly lines of China's factories. Britain thrives on internships, many of which are unpaid, in numbers that have spiked since the 2008 financial crisis. Indeed, the financial crisis was pivotal to the spread of precarious work and internships, and the coronavirus recession may prove to be the same: older workers trying to get back to work after recession-related layoffs in the 2010s found themselves interning—"paid in hugs," like one forty-seven-year-old profiled by National Public Radio during her internship at the Red Cross—and competing with younger people for a shrinking pool of full-time jobs. A 2016 survey found that less than half of the unpaid interns got job offers, and nearly one-third of the paid interns didn't, either.[33]

Not all interns have it as bad as the North Carolina zoo intern killed by an escaped lion, whose family told reporters she died "following her passion" on her fourth unpaid internship. Nevertheless, the interns have begun to rebel. Amalia Illgner, for example, announced, in the pages of *The Guardian*, that she was suing over her "dream internship" at UK magazine *Monocle*. She wrote of her 5:30 a.m. morning shifts, and interns dispatched "as human FedEx boxes," including one sent to Milan to hand-deliver magazines to *Monocle*'s editor. "So Monocle, since you're listening, I have taken the first step in legal proceedings to claim my unpaid wages," Illgner wrote. In another example, Diana Wang sued over what was her seventh unpaid internship, also in journalism, at *Harper's Bazaar*, alleging that Hearst (*Bazaar*'s parent company) had violated federal and state labor laws by having her work for free for up to fifty-five hours a week, including nights until 10 p.m., and shuttle pricey fashions around New York for free.[34]

The internship lawsuit heard around the world, though, or at least around the media, was the *Black Swan* case. Eric Glatt was an unpaid intern on the set of Darren Aronofsky's film, relegated to the accounting department because of his background in finance (Glatt was forty at the time, looking to switch to a second career in film), when he realized that what he was doing wasn't a learning experience. Instead, he was merely substituting for a worker the production company would otherwise have had to pay. Glatt's lawsuit was launched in the midst of Occupy Wall Street, where downwardly mobile college graduates made up a large swath of the protesters, and unpaid internships (and student debt) were common complaints. In that political context, in 2013, a judge ruled that Glatt and another intern should have been paid; in 2015, however, an appeals court tossed out the ruling.[35]

To get ahead of the lawsuits, some media companies began to announce that they'd pay their interns. At other media companies, interns began to organize. *The Nation* magazine (where I did an internship in 2009) first agreed to pay interns, and then to raise their wage to $15 an hour, after the interns banded together to demand wages. In France, interns struck against labor law reforms and won a modest wage, and protests against precarity in Germany centered on unpaid interns. Yet the unpaid internship persists: in the United States, in 2018, the Trump administration's Labor Department issued guidelines easing companies' path to hiring unpaid interns, lowering the bar by which the "primary beneficiary" of an internship could be judged to be the intern, rather than the company receiving the free work.[36]

And it was in Quebec, where the energy from the movements of 2011 spilled over into a massive student strike in 2012, that the interns really got organized. The announcement in 2012 that the government planned to hike tuition by 75 percent brought university students, already members of student unions, into the streets. They became further radicalized by the government's attempts to crack down on protest. For months, the streets of Montreal rang with the sound of pots and pans banged with wooden spoons and thousands sported the movement's symbol, a little red square of felt, the *carré rouge* (symbolizing being *carrément dans le rouge*, or "squarely in the red"). After the students succeeded in pushing back their tuition hike, many went on to careers, leaving the movement behind. But another group of students began wondering how to build upon what had been started.[37]

⁂

SWATHED IN COATS, SCARVES, HATS, AND HOODS AGAINST THE QUEBEC cold in the winter of 2019, tens of thousands of interns took to the streets bearing signs in French and English, decrying unpaid internships. "It's not complicated, all labour deserves a fair wage," "L'exploitation n'est pas une vocation" (Exploitation is not a vocation), and "Ne soyons pas invisibles, femmes devant!" (No longer invisible, women rise!) were just a few of the signs they bore. One demonstration, titled "J-F better have my money," for Jean-François Roberge, the minister of education and higher education in Quebec, saw the interns surging down the streets of Montreal; in the smaller city of Gatineau, they marched behind a sign that read, "Pas de salaire, pas de stagiaire" (No salary, no interns). Interns struck as well in Rimouski, Sherbrooke, Saint-Jérôme, and Quebec City.

Camille Marcoux and Chloe Cabral were among the crowds in Montreal, on strike against the internships that were required for their degrees. Their demands were simple: they wanted a wage, and they wanted to be recognized under labor law like any other worker.

The strikes were organized by the Comités unitaires sur le travail étudiant (Student Work Unitary Committees), known by their acronym CUTEs. A network of autonomous student organizations, they aimed to counteract some of the top-down structures of the 2012 student strikes, and therefore applied an explicitly feminist lens to their organizing as well as to their analysis of internships. Inspired by the Wages for Housework movement, they began organizing in 2016 around the idea that school work, too, was a form of reproductive labor. Unpaid internships, then, were a natural target, particularly since they were most common in fields where women predominated. The CUTEs were given a boost by the victory of psychology interns in Quebec in 2016, who won a financial compensation package for their doctorate-level internships, though it came in a lump sum rather than a wage.[38]

The interns struck first in November 2017; thousands more struck in February 2018, and again for International Women's Day, as Women's Strikers organized around the world. Fifty-five thousand interns went on strike in the fall of 2018, and in the spring of 2019, more than thirty-five thousand. The interns in one action gathered to read aloud the letters or emails they'd received from supervisors encouraging them to cross the picket line and report for their unpaid jobs, dramatizing the expectations they faced on the job. And in 2019, they added a new tactic: staging roving picket lines at internship locations, creating an "internship tour" to make sure the companies knew of the interns' demands. Previously, student strikes had mostly been located at the universities and CEGEPs, where strikers would go from class to class calling their colleagues out to join the action. But the picket lines were "a good way for us to engage with the colleagues in front of the schools," Marcoux explained, "so the intern didn't have all the responsibility to explain to all of the colleagues in the school why she was on strike and what the impacts were." In some of the internship locations—particularly in the schools, where teachers were heavily unionized and preparing for their own negotiations, but also in hospitals and nonprofits—it was a challenge to the waged workers: Which side were they on?[39]

"It was very visible during all the intern strikes that none of the workplaces, none of the internship workplaces, could afford to lose one intern," Marcoux continued. "It was a major, major impact."

Marcoux recalled her first CUTE organizing meeting, which took place in a dark, close basement room. "It was very intimate," she laughed. There had been one strike already by that time, in 2017, and friends of hers had reached out to her for her labor law knowledge, as some people within the movement were pushing for a more legalistic approach. She wrote an article about the legal implications for the CUTEs magazine, and met more interns, drawing further into the movement. "What was really cool was that at the end of the meeting, we did a dispatch of the tasks and most of the people there had something to do. You felt included, but also it was known that at the next meeting, everybody was going to speak and was going to participate in the meeting because everybody had to do follow-ups. It was very engaging."

To Marcoux and Cabral, the meetings, led by women, were a different, exciting experience—women were speaking loudly, expressing emotions and frustration, but also in control. "It was women who actually made suggestions to go on strike, who defended the proposition, the motions to go on strike. The people who ran the meetings, took the notes, who really put themselves on the line were women who struggled with internships," Marcoux said. "We were directly implicated in the cause. We were not speaking for anybody else."

Everything in their movement, she explained, had to be invented from the ground up. It had never been done before—something like a cross between a traditional workplace strike and a student strike, targeting both the university and the worksite. Interns were often the only ones in their position on the job, as they were surrounded by paid superiors, so striking could be intimidating. And the interns faced possible repercussions not just from their workplaces but also from their universities.

But when the strikers hit the streets, they suddenly became a visible force. People would get involved during the strike days, Marcoux said, and then continue to organize with the CUTEs in the interim periods. And the organizers, used to being compliant, people-pleasing interns, had to get comfortable with suddenly speaking out in front of crowds, with making demands, with raising some hell.

In the autumn of 2018, the interns went on strike for a full week, and the struggle deepened. "A lot of students got very angry with their workplace," Marcoux said. "Some of them had got expelled from their internship for doing the strike." As interns saw the consequences of striking, they felt a new fear that hadn't been there before. At first, Marcoux said, the universities had been unprepared for the strikes. But by 2018 they had strategies for containing the unrest.

Another challenge was that the student strikes in 2012 had been around an issue that affected all students—tuition increases across the province. By contrast, the very gendered nature of the unpaid internships meant that only some students had a reason to take risks. The same ideology that the CUTEs criticized, the one that said women's work should be done for love, not money, was common among some of their colleagues, and students hesitated to get involved if they did not themselves have to do unpaid labor.

Turnover, though, was perhaps the biggest problem for the movement. Marcoux and others graduated and moved into the (paid) workplace, and new students meanwhile came in. But to Marcoux, the CUTEs had given her and others a lens through which to understand all of their work, and she saw potential for the movement to grow beyond interns. "I think a lot of us are actually thinking about our workplace and to start organizing on the same terms and the same perspective as a women's movement, against free labor," she said. "We have discussed this between different activists, that the next step is trying to take the same analysis and the same way that we organize and trying to implement that in our different workplaces and keeping in touch so that we can continue to evolve."

The analysis the interns in the CUTEs brought to their work, in other words, could be applied to much of the work of the laborers of love. They questioned why certain jobs were well paid while others were undervalued, and they challenged the rules of behavior that taught young workers, most of them women, to be meek and retiring and always ready to serve. They also challenged the definition of what was work and what was not, and the gendered distinctions of whose work mattered, in a way that inspired them to keep going, keep questioning. Marcoux and some of the other interns launched an online magazine, *Ouvrage*, to continue the political debate they had begun in the CUTEs and to lay groundwork for further organizing.

As for results, J-F himself, Education Minister Roberge, said in 2018 that the then-new provincial government would move to address the intern problem. Interns were granted bursaries or stipends, Marcoux said, rather than a wage. "After a year, the main comment I have heard was that it took time to receive the money that was promised. The amount is split in half, and the second half is only given if you pass the internship, so people still needed to get indebted before they would receive the money." The lack of a real wage meant the interns were still not covered under labor law. "They want to reinforce the separation between your education and your work so that the internship is not full work, it is really something you do when you are in training," said Marcoux. "They want it to be more supervised, but they still want it to be something separate from the labor law that we know right now."[40]

The COVID-19 pandemic, she said, "amplified the hypocrisy of school administrations who severely punished interns for striking their internship." Some of those interns had been forced to retake a full year of school to complete the internship, but when some of them had to miss interning time because the pandemic closed many of the businesses, she explained, "the non-completion of their internship was not deemed to compromise their professionalism or ability to start working." When their free labor was not as necessary to the businesses, in other words, the internship was deemed unnecessary, making it clear that completing the internship was not, in fact, an essential part of their education.

Still, she noted, despite the fact that the government's response was not what the movement demanded, it was a step up from nothing. "It is always going to be a big thing after a strike, like, 'What is a win and what is a loss?' but we didn't have anything to lose. We all worked for free."

CHAPTER 8

PROLETARIAN PROFESSIONALS

Academia

KATHERINE WILSON HAS AN INTENSE GAZE; WHEN YOU FIND OUT SHE'S spent much of her life in and around the theater, it comes as no surprise.

Sitting in her small, spare office at Fordham University's Manhattan campus, just steps from Lincoln Center, she explained to me that soon she would have to give up the space. She's not a full-time professor but an adjunct, which means that she's paid by the class, not a full-fledged university employee. That gig doesn't come with permanent office privileges.

"Open an old encyclopedia and it says, 'Academic' or 'Professor.' What does that look like?" she asked. "It looks like an office lined with bookshelves, supplies, paper—nowadays, their own printer so they can print twenty-five copies if they need to or something. It has the desk surface.

This is what academic work is. Suddenly, they are expecting over 50 percent of their teaching faculty to work as if that is not how this labor was designed. For some reason, we can all work out of our cellphone or we can all work out of a satchel and we can do our grading on the subway."

And the subway is where she spends no small amount of her time. Besides Fordham's Manhattan campus, she also goes to its main campus in the Bronx, and then there's the class she teaches at Hunter College of the City University of New York (CUNY), also in Manhattan but on the other side of town. She's taught at other schools, too—in every borough of New York City except for Staten Island, and in New Jersey and on Long Island as well. Given that travel schedule, necessary just to cobble together a living, she'd have to grade on the train even if one of those jobs did give her a proper office. "Sometimes it was LaGuardia, which is in Queens, out to Brooklyn College on the same day," she said. Another time, it was Hunter up to Fordham in the Bronx, shifting from the mostly working-class city kids at the CUNY schools to Fordham students who lean more well off—and whiter—sporting Fordham gear and spending their weekends at sports games.

This has been her life since 2002 or 2003, when she returned to academia. It took her a minute to recall all the different places she'd taught since then, in multiple departments. For an adjunct to teach in multiple schools isn't rare, particularly in New York, where there are so many universities from which to choose. But, Wilson noted, "I teach three unrelated classes in three distinct departments. That is not so common." Much of her bread and butter has been composition courses, a core requirement nearly anywhere, but the semester we were discussing also had her teaching Arabic cinema in translation and a course she designed that she described as the anthropology of fashion. Fridays were her rough day, with her first class at Fordham at 8:30 a.m., and then another class later in the day, and then a double session on Saturday. "The point for the adjunct life is you take what you can get," she said.

The grading, course preparation, and any other work she needs to do happens at home. Where a full-time professor would be paid a salary that was expected to cover teaching, course preparation, and advising students, plus their own continuing research and publishing, adjuncts are paid by the class. That pay structure leaves Wilson falling well short of what a full professor would make even with three different jobs, and on top of that she still has to cover more of her own supplies. "A lot about the pay structure and the resources is designed as if we appear in class and God had given us all our materials for that lesson," she said. "It just emerged from nowhere."

Wilson grew up with a single father who was an English professor at CUNY, and he encouraged her and her twin sister to follow their dreams. "It was not the right spirit for the age, for the post-Reagan society I was living in," she said. She studied philosophy as an undergraduate, and then, like many a liberal arts grad, spent a bit of time figuring things out—time further complicated by a chronic illness. "I was groping toward art," she said. Landing in Boston, she "fell into theater quite accidentally. I never took a class. It wasn't on my horizon." The theater she did was politically radical and experimental but humorous, something she described as the "feminist granddaughter of Brecht."

Such theater, of course, didn't lend itself to a stable income. Alternative theater is rarely celebrated at the time of its creation, Wilson noted. What the theater world celebrates from times past, it mostly ignores in the present. After about a decade of doing work that didn't make money, she decided to pursue a master of fine arts (MFA), hoping it would lead to something more stable than the ad hoc jobs she was pulling together. That was 2003, and it was then that she began teaching, but the MFA didn't satisfy her.

"I realized in the MFA that what I was, was an intellectual, and theater had been my vehicle," she said. But the theater world no longer felt comfortable to her. "The university looked like a haven." Much of her social circle and even her family consisted of academics—besides her father, her sister had gone straight through school to a PhD and become a (twice) tenured professor.

Hoping for a career in academia, she enrolled at CUNY's Graduate Center. But, she said, the program didn't really prepare her for the academic job market she'd be turned loose into. Some of that was timing, of course—while she was working on her PhD, the 2007 economic crisis hit—but the field had been changing for a while. "We would start to get these emails saying, 'Alt Academic,' like 'Market yourself, brand yourself for an alternative academic career!' 'Oh, you can try nonprofits!' and it was very frustrating for me because anything they named, and then some, I had done that before," she said. "I came in saying, 'This is certainly the best fit in contemporary United States society for me.' To have all that discourse of 'Branding yourself, get your website, and be something besides what we have been educating you to be' was very, very demoralizing and painful."

Despite the struggles, she said, "I loved being in the classroom. It was challenging, but I like teaching a lot." She's never taught anything related to her dissertation, though—a study of the way a play script moves in the world—and only twice taught in theater departments. Her focus was Arabic theater in translation: she laughed, "I thought that after September 11, that theater departments would snatch up Arabic. Right." Her varied background gives her more options for departments in which to work, but the variation becomes just one more thing to juggle, one more gear to shift between classes. Between schools, her students vary: at the CUNY schools, she's often teaching them "how to be a student," while the Fordham students approach her very differently: "It is more litigious. A lot of them run to authorities here. An adjunct lives in terror of the student evaluations." Because, of course, bad evaluations could mean not being asked back. This is the kind of thing, she noted, that also leads to grade inflation: to many adjuncts, there are more incentives to make students happy than to grade accurately—though, she said, "I try to hold out and I think I pay the price for it."

Besides the different student bodies and the departments, there are also small yet frustrating differences from school to school. "Everything now is privatized," she explained. "For a grading system, it is not an internal university program. It is a rented program and they all have their own little names. You have to learn those programs." She has multiple email addresses, too, one for each of the different schools. Two or three of those a semester add up. "Mentally it is very challenging, and I think for most of us, our instincts would be to blame ourselves. For example, I will be in University A and I need to enter into the system and I will type the password for University B and I say, 'Oh, Kate, you are so stupid.'" The universities continue to shift costs onto the faculty and students, nickel and diming them for little things like photocopies. "Everything just multiplies about the bureaucracy," she said. "It is too much bouncing around. I think it is very much characteristic of postmodern life—fragmented, scattered, not coherent. And all of that amounts to—obviously—exhaustion. With no sick days."

Then there are the little slights of the obvious two-tier nature of the system. Department chairs who have tenure come off as oblivious to the conditions of the people who work under them. Teaching, of course, is hard work whatever you're paid, but it's frustrating to hear complaints from senior faculty when the adjuncts constantly have to "do more with less." For Wilson, it's an issue that is even closer to home: her partner is tenured faculty at Fordham. Yet that experience has also made it clearer to her that the distinction between tenure track and adjunct track is an accident of timing. "If anything, it has sort of helped me think, 'Yes, I would at least deserve to be on the pathway,'" she explained. "I think if I weren't so close maybe I would slide into that paranoia of, 'Oh, I must not be good enough or smart enough.'"

When the COVID-19 pandemic hit New York, all the uncertainty was magnified. "Fordham faculty were hurtled into 'remote' teaching and the school closed. CUNY followed, after wavering uncertainty, a week or so later, though my own spring class had been canceled so I wasn't personally affected," Wilson explained. "Those who straddled jobs at different schools had to juggle the different policies and technical parameters of that shift." How to teach, she said, was left up to faculty members; she opted for the virtual classroom, while others used recorded lectures or just posted assignments online. For adjuncts, too, there was the question of technology. "Obviously with our low salaries we're not likely to have state-of-the-art, top-of-the-line equipment. In my case, my mouse died, and I prayed my anemic Wi-Fi would endure the session of every class." And then there was the added burden of emotional labor as she tried to help students navigate the crisis—something, she said, that likely fell harder on women, whether adjunct or otherwise. Tenure-line faculty faced the same issues, but, she noted, "their exertions earn a livable wage, and greater inclusion in university processes."

The question of reopening was painful, too. As schools discussed a "hybrid" system for the fall semester—and as the different universities where she worked tossed around different plans—the adjuncts were left feeling powerless. The idea of going back to in-person teaching in a pandemic was, naturally, unnerving, but the loss of the classroom stung because Wilson put a lot of effort into making her time with students meaningful. When we sat down in her office, before the pandemic, she'd just come from her Arabic cinema class, where her students were making animations. Their engagement and pleasure in the material was fulfilling for her, too. "Most of the time," she had told me, "I leave that class happy. I have that."

⣿

THE WRITER AND PROFESSOR STANLEY ARONOWITZ ONCE CALLED ACAdemia "the last good job in America." At its best, the academic workplace allows the professoriat a great deal of autonomy at work, the ability to pursue projects that intrigue and inspire them with single-minded focus and little need to compromise. Historical precedent gives them a great deal of involvement in university governance, and their work has long been seen as more of a vocation than simply a job. In this way, though the teaching part of the job is not actually all that different from teaching a grade-school class, the image of the academic has much in common with the image of the artist as lone genius, though perhaps swathed in tweed in a corner office stuffed with books rather than a paint-splattered garret studio.[1]

Higher education has a long history as a tiered, hierarchical structure: after all, it's there in the name. Higher education was, from imperial China to the pre-Columbian Americas, a way to train the upper castes of society first and foremost. Only later did it develop into a place for the kind of intellectual pursuits Katherine Wilson was looking for:

independent scholarly work, with knowledge production more or less for its own sake seen as a social good.[2]

Even when higher education became a place for experimentation and debate, it was still restricted to society's elites. From India, where Hindu and Buddhist centers of learning also taught arts, mathematics, astronomy, and more, to ancient Greece, Plato's Academy, and later the Musaeum of Alexandria, where students came from far away to study, the ruling classes were able to pursue knowledge largely because someone else did all the work. Han dynasty China's imperial academy admitted students based on skills, providing some form of social mobility, but this was far from mass public higher education.[3]

The university as such was born in Italy in the eleventh and twelfth centuries, an offshoot of the guild system and existing religious education. It taught what were known as the seven liberal arts ("arts" in the original meaning of skills): grammar, rhetoric, and dialectic, along with music, arithmetic, geometry, and astronomy. In Paris and Bologna, centers of learning expanded and drew students from across Europe. The university developed at the intersection of Christian, Muslim, and Jewish influences, where the resurgence of classical Greek was made possible through translations back from the Arabic, where it had been preserved.[4]

Still, these universities existed to train the elites, and the intellectual curiosity of the academics was limited by the rules of the church and the state. Some who pressed too far into church terrain were even burnt as heretics. It is not surprising, then, that the academics organized into guilds—in part as a response to the way students also organized themselves, and occasionally raised hell, causing riots that in turn caused scholars to migrate to new towns to set up new universities. The students were roughly equivalent to a guild apprentice in the hierarchy; those who had passed through one level of schooling were equal to journeymen or bachelors (hence "bachelor's degree"), and those who had studied all the arts became masters. But power struggles continued, between city and university, master and student, church and university, state and university—power struggles that shaped the university as a space of contention.[5]

Fights between church and state also shaped the early universities: Oxford was opened in twelfth-century England after students returned home from France, driven by a spat between Henry II and the pope. The University of Naples, meanwhile, was founded as a public institution, perhaps the first secular university, though virtually all institutions taught religion as part of their curriculum. The Protestant Reformation hit the universities hard, and the 1600s generally were a low point in attendance and production. Most of the scientific discoveries of the period were made outside of the university's bounds, in the new (and mostly amateur) academies of science. There was even a lull in student riots.[6]

The French Revolution's leveling of French institutions also helped to revive the university as a center of learning—the new government nationalized universities and fired church-backed teachers, with the intent of creating a new state-run system. That system, like many of the plans of the revolutionaries, didn't quite come to pass, yet it helped clear space for the development of the modern university. The reforms of Wilhelm von Humboldt, who as part of his work in the Prussian Ministry of the Interior revamped the country's education system, enshrined in the University of Berlin the model that bears his name. The Humboldtian university combines research and teaching, expecting each professor to produce knowledge rather than simply passing it on. With this ideal was born the concept of academic freedom—freedom to learn and to teach. The mission of academe, to pursue truth, was supposed to set the university and its workers apart from the masses.[7]

By the late eighteenth century there were over 140 universities across Europe, and more and more of them were constructed upon this model. The beginnings of the research journal could be spotted, as academics began to publish their work for broader sharing across the community of scholars. Academic freedom of a sort was guaranteed, and some protection from interference instituted, though it did not, notably, extend to protection for political expression. Professors began to specialize in one subject, and to combine their teaching with specialized research as well; this began as a way to save money, in Scottish and German universities, and then scholars began to make names for themselves—including some we still know of, like political economist Adam Smith. Access to higher education expanded, becoming available to a growing middle class as industrial capitalism developed, and this meant more jobs for professors.[8]

The first universities in what would become the United States were elite institutions, religious in nature, but the United States' real contribution to higher education was the state university system. Beginning in North Carolina and Georgia in the 1780s, the state-funded institution helped to make higher education accessible to a broader swath of the country. City College of New York, now the CUNY system in which Katherine Wilson adjuncts, was founded in 1847 to educate, tuition-free, the children of the modest classes. Then the Morrill Act of 1862 created the "land grant" universities, paid for through the sale of public land granted to the states to fund "Colleges for the Benefit of Agriculture and the Mechanic Arts." The sixty-nine schools funded through this act include the Massachusetts Institute of Technology, Cornell University, and the University of Wisconsin at Madison. (This was land, it's important to note, that was seized from Indigenous nations and sold at a profit—a reminder once again that the new universities were never intended for everyone to access.) The American-style research university was a new kind of institution, better funded than universities had been and producing work, particularly in the fields of science and technology, that became a draw for scholars from around the world. Privately funded institutions and state-backed ones competed for students and research accolades. By the 1920s, the proportion of students in higher education in the States was five times higher than in Europe. Of course, those schools were still racially segregated—separate was certainly not equal—and women made up a much smaller proportion of the student body than men.[9]

Higher education was slowly becoming a path to upward mobility for a small but growing fraction of the working class. The post–World War II period brought more and more students into colleges and universities, across Europe and particularly in the United States, thanks to the act commonly known as the GI Bill, which provided military veterans with college funding. But despite the bill's facially race-neutral language, in practice Black veterans were excluded, often formally rejected or forced into vocational programs rather than universities. Historically Black colleges and universities (HBCUs), which would have happily taken on more students and where Black faculty were welcomed, were underfunded and could not accommodate all of the would-be attendees, leaving many more out in the cold.[10]

The Cold War brought new funding into universities as the United States and the Soviet Union competed for scientific (and thus military) superiority. States and the federal government both committed substantial funds to higher education, including student loans and direct university subsidies, and most students attended public institutions. But as the university expanded and became less elite, its professors began to lose status. Institutions and the students in them were ranked in terms of prestige, and that prestige would largely define working conditions. Still, upward mobility through the university into what Barbara and John Ehrenreich dubbed the "professional-managerial class" (PMC), was a fact of twentieth-century life, and more and more people wanted in.[11]

The PMC, according to the Ehrenreichs, consisted of those service and management professionals whose jobs required some schooling and gave them some degree of power, usually over those further down the class ladder than themselves, and who retained some degree of autonomy on the job. Teachers, doctors, journalists, social workers, and of course college professors were part of the class. As opposed to those in the "managerial" part of the PMC, the professionals mostly considered themselves outside of the battle for profits and saw their work as having intrinsic social value. "Educational work," the Ehrenreichs wrote, "was highly labor intensive, and there was no obvious way, at the time, to automate or streamline student-teacher interaction and make universities a profitable undertaking." Perhaps because of their status as a temporary respite from profit-seeking, universities began to be a home for dissent and rebellion, as well as agitation for the university itself to open up further to those long excluded.[12]

Faculty fought for tenure protections, in particular, to preserve their job security and academic freedom. Despite the caricature—like that lobbed at public school teachers—of tenure as a protection for "lazy" professors, tenure protections, much lampooned in the years of right-wing budget-cutting and culture-war mania, allow a modicum of independent thought in the university. Through the 1950s, Stanley Aronowitz wrote, most faculty existed on year-to-year contracts, keeping them toeing the line. The American Association of University Professors (AAUP) agitated for tenure not to protect the radicals but to make everyone's job more secure; nonetheless, tenure has always been particularly valuable to academia's rebels. "Well into the 1960s, for example, the number of public Marxists, open gays, blacks, and women with secure mainstream academic jobs could be counted on ten fingers," Aronowitz archly noted. "The liberal Lionel Trilling was a year-to-year lecturer at Columbia for a decade, not only because he had been a radical but because he was a Jew. The not-so-hidden secret of English departments in the first half of the twentieth century was their genteel anti-Semitism." Yet tenure still did not protect the radicals from the pressures that the job itself placed on them, the conformity encouraged by academia's own traditions of peer review, and the hoops to be jumped through while on the tenure track itself.[13]

The AAUP's definition of academic freedom, so precious to the university professor, holds up professionalism—the judgment of one's peers, in essence—as the standard to which academics should be held. An expansion on the Humboldtian concept, dating back to 1940, the AAUP statement on the subject "maintains that a professor's research and teaching should be free from outside interference as long as he or she abides by the academy's professional standards of integrity, impartiality, and relevance," though as scholar Ellen Schrecker noted, those protections were less regularly applied to what a professor did off campus—meaning they could still be fired for political activities or speech. But theoretically at least, a professor was supposed to be free to teach and research what she liked, as long as she upheld her duties to the university—which meant committees, peer review, a variety of governance duties that professors complained about but nevertheless valued as signs that it was they who ran the university.[14]

The public university, accessible to broad swaths of the working classes, reached its heights in California and in New York, in the system where

Katherine Wilson still teaches. The CUNY system was considered the "proletariat's Harvard" in its heyday; children of immigrants with dreams of scholarship and middle-class life, those who didn't make it into the Ivies, moved through its halls. It was also, from 1969 onward, fully unionized, with faculty, graduate students, and staff all members of the Professional Staff Congress (PSC). The year after the union was founded, CUNY gave in to pressure from Black and Puerto Rican student organizers and formally opened up to all New York City high school graduates who wanted to attend. "By combining an open admissions policy with free tuition, CUNY broke new ground in democratizing access to higher education in the United States," wrote CUNY professors Ashley Dawson and Penny Lewis. "And in 1973, after voting to strike, CUNY faculty and staff won their first contract." The University of California system, too, was free; its Master Plan (enshrined in 1960) committed to educate anyone who wanted to be educated, though the burgeoning New Right took aim at this ideal nearly as soon as it was written into law. One of Ronald Reagan's campaign aides, as he ran for governor, laid out the stakes clearly: "We are in danger of producing an educated proletariat. That's dynamite! We have to be selective on who we allow to go through higher education."[15]

In 1975 the right was able to strike back against CUNY. New York City's fiscal crisis—one of the turning points of the decade—marked a shift away from funding public goods that were accessible to the working class and toward the neoliberal politics we now know today. As the infamous newspaper cover had it, President Gerald Ford had told the city to "Drop Dead," leaving New York to fill its budget holes however it could, meaning deep austerity for public services and a turn to "business-friendly" policies. CUNY tuition was one of the first things to be instituted—just a few brief years after it had truly been opened up to the working class. Bondholders had to be paid off; students, meanwhile, would start taking out loans of their own, or more likely, for many of them, skip higher education altogether. The faculty union fought to keep its protections but could not stave off the institution of tuition, nor stop the firing of hundreds of young professors, only recently brought on to handle the expansion.[16]

In a way the Reagan aide was right: the rebellions of the 1960s and early 1970s, which had helped to create the open admissions period of CUNY's history, and had shaken up many other college campuses as well, had in part emanated from a newly educated stratum of society no longer content to simply move into professional-status jobs. Their idea of changing the world was different from that of the Progressive Era reformers: they wanted revolution and they wanted it now. Angela Davis became one of the early targets of the counterrevolution when Reagan sought to have her fired from her position at the University of California Los Angeles. Davis had a PhD and a stellar record, but was a Communist and associated with the Black Panthers, and Reagan was able to chase her out, academic freedom be damned. The university had been a target of the McCarthy-era witch hunts, but by the 1970s it had become easier to strip it of funds than to try to get individual professors fired one by one. Reaganism was tested out on the Cal system, as Aaron Bady and Mike Konczal wrote at *Dissent:* "The first 'bums' he threw off welfare were California university students."[17]

Margaret Thatcher too took aim at British professors. In what one researcher called "one of the most dramatic systemic changes in the terms of academic appointments," in 1988 the Thatcher government eliminated tenure for university faculty. Ostensibly, this was to reduce distinctions between the traditional—and traditionally prestigious—universities and newer institutions, and to introduce "accountability" for faculty, which, as it does for other teaching staff, tends to mean "making them easier to fire." The argument was the same as it is everywhere that the elimination of job security is debated: that "deadwood" tenured faculty who weren't up to internationally competitive standards should be cleared away to save money. An otherwise Thatcher-supporting professor from the London School of Economics argued to reporters at the time that eliminating tenure would "make British universities into something very second rate," and that the reforms would direct money to profitable programs while hacking away at the liberal arts. It was not the last time that refrain would be heard.[18]

The right had taken the analysis of the professional-managerial class from leftists like the Ehrenreichs and twisted it to useful form in order to attack the university. The right in the United States railed against, the Ehrenreichs wrote, "a caricature of this notion of a 'new class,' proposing that college-educated professionals—especially lawyers, professors, journalists, and artists—make up a power-hungry 'liberal elite' bent on imposing its version of socialism on everyone else." That the people doing the excoriating were, in fact, members of this class themselves was perhaps lost on them, but it is a reminder that just because one wants to call a group of vaguely similar people one opposes a "class" doesn't make it so. Classes, we recall, are composed, and as neoliberalism hit, the PMC was beginning, in fact, to be decomposed.[19]

While the managerial side of the PMC was doing better than ever—executive pay headed back upward in the late 1970s and kept going up—the professions were undergoing a very different process, one in which job security and pay rates were falling, and their treasured autonomy disappearing. Academia was at the very heart of this transformation. After all, education was the very thing that made one into a member of the PMC in the first place, as Barbara Ehrenreich noted, which made the university a central location of these changes as it trained the doctors, lawyers, social workers, and professors of the future. The academic profession itself, like many others, was becoming polarized into a handful of stars at the top and a vast academic proletariat at the bottom, made up of people like Katherine Wilson, cobbling together a living if they could, and feeling a sense of shame at not having achieved the career they'd aimed for. The middle class—a better term than "PMC"—as Ehrenreich wrote in *Fear of Falling*, was still "located well below the ultimate elite of wealth and power." Further, she wrote, "Its only 'capital' is knowledge and skill, or at least the credentials imputing skill and knowledge. And unlike real capital, these cannot be hoarded against hard times." A PhD might have been a symbol of so-called human capital, but its value could not be guaranteed.[20]

Just as the vaunted "knowledge economy" was making headlines, in other words, the labor of knowledge workers was being devalued and deskilled. Doctors became more likely to work for large institutions, lawyers in massive firms or to work in-house at corporations. We started to hear more about "stress" and mental health on the job than physical injury. Until the aftermath of World War II, the term "stress" was rarely used to describe something that happened to humans; researchers, though, began to apply the term to the wear and tear on the human body caused by, among other things, psychological strain on the job. By the 2000s, it had overtaken physical ailments as a cause of absence from work. Like "burnout," we can understand this concept as a side effect of the cracks in the labor-of-love myth. Fewer of us may be getting physically injured on the job, but more of us are struggling with the emotional toll of work.[21]

Professional workers were becoming subject to the controls of capital, and yet, as more and more people made it through higher education, the demand for credentials only grew. More and more universities were opened across the world, and the percentages of school-age cohorts attending them exploded, from under 10 percent in 1960 to around 50 percent in many countries by the twenty-first century. Something like 3.5 million professors taught over 80 million students worldwide by 2000. Yet their working conditions were, in many ways, getting worse.[22]

For one thing, even as access appeared to be expanding, a degree was also becoming more expensive. The cost of a degree in the United States spiked between 1987 and 2007, from less than $3,000 a year for public universities, and less than $7,000 at private ones, to nearly $13,000 a year for public and nearly $35,000 for private. Since then, and in the wake of the global financial crisis and austerity, those numbers have ballooned again—by nearly 25 percent. In the United Kingdom, university fees were reintroduced in 1998, and have expanded since. Yet that money was not going to pay more qualified professors better salaries; instead, teaching faculty were facing cuts. Complaints of lower quality at the universities were used as justification for public budget cuts, firing professors, and raising tuition. Universities competed for a few prestigious faculty members, offering not just excellent pay but lowered teaching loads, an ability to focus on research, and the opportunity to mentor graduate students who might enhance their own reputations. Meanwhile, that teaching load being removed from the fancier professors fell on the shoulders of those same graduate students, adjuncts, or junior professors scrambling for the tenure track. The resulting competition meant that research requirements were going up even as fewer people were given the kinds of job supports that would allow them to do that research.[23]

The Humboldtian ideal of the university professor has always been a combination of two related but distinct forms of work: part of it in front of a classroom, part of it hidden away in the lab or the office with a stack of books. To Aronowitz, who enjoyed both of these parts of the job, the two parts were complementary. "I am one of a shrinking minority of the professoriat who have what may be the last good job in America," he wrote. "Except for the requirement that I teach or preside at one or two classes and seminars a week and direct at least five dissertations at a time, I pretty much control my paid work time. . . . I work hard but it's mostly self-directed. I don't experience 'leisure' as time out of work because the lines are blurred." He described "writing days" where he composed articles and read and worked on longer book projects, fundraising time, and student-advising time and exams for grad students. Academic labor, he noted, bled, for professors like him, into everything; anything he read might make it into the classroom or into a piece of writing. For Aronowitz, teaching was a genuine pleasure; for many others, it's simply a distraction from the research they'd prefer to be doing. One might be a good teacher and a brilliant lab scientist; it's certainly possible, but nothing about the one suggests, necessarily, the other.[24]

The splintering of the academic workforce into tiers suggests that these two parts of the job have in fact come apart. The adjuncts and the full-time faculty, noted part-time lecturer and union activist Amy Higer, from Rutgers University, have a symbiotic relationship: full-time professors often don't want to be in the classroom. "Some of them like teaching, but I would say most of them don't. And it's a research institution; that's fine. I love to teach. This is what I wanted to do with my PhD." The problem was not the split workload, to her, as much as it was the devaluation of the part of the work that she did—the feminine-gendered work of teaching. Adjuncts are paid per class for their teaching and given no support at all for their research. For Katherine Wilson, research was something she'd hoped to do, and she found herself stymied by the demands of adjunct work. She agreed with Higer that the research part was often seen as the higher-level part of the job, teaching the lesser.[25]

The "last good job in America" (or in England, or France) is now reserved for a few: all over the world, academics face the increase of part-time positions and the loss of autonomy and power. Increasing enrollment has not come along with increased full-time staffing, and salaries have stagnated as class sizes have increased. While European universities still offer more security than many US institutions, the situation of part-time faculty in the Americas (Latin America, too, has a long history of so-called taxicab professors, part-timers with little attachment to their institutions) is a bellwether for the rest of the world. By 1999, an estimated one-fifth to one-half of European countries' academic staff were "nonpermanent." In the United States between 1975 and 2003, according to the AAUP, "full-time tenured and tenure-track faculty members fell from 57 percent of the nation's teaching staffs to 35 percent, with an actual loss of some two thousand tenured positions." Professors don't always have to be laid off; attrition does a lot of the work as tenured professors retire, and their jobs are filled in by temporary staff. Meanwhile, much of the expansion of college access has been at community colleges, where even if tenure exists, the job is nothing like that of a professor at a top-tier research university.[26]

And that more prestigious research part of the job is increasingly commodified. In 1980, the US Congress passed the Bayh-Dole Act, which allowed universities to generate funds from licensing intellectual property and the sale of research. Universities like Columbia—which made it policy almost immediately that the school had rights to faculty inventions, though they generously granted them royalties—generate hundreds of millions of dollars from their professors' intellectual work. Outside funding for research also has an effect: drug companies subsidize research at universities that they then get to patent. Research funds are scarcer in general, and often tied to specific outcomes—which may incentivize tweaking of results. Graduate students, paid far less than professors, do much of the actual work of laboratory research. And sometimes sponsors demand such secrecy that researchers cannot always publish what they've discovered—it's all swept up into the company, rather than the tenure file. Even in the humanities, corporate donations wound up shaping policy; sponsorship of "chairs" meant influence over which professors got to sit in them. The fears of that British professor in 1988 were well founded, as funds pumped into the sciences are often drained away from the humanities, creating yet another form of tiering in the workplace.[27]

All of these changes crept in under the mantle of "accountability," to use Margaret Thatcher's words. Accountability meant stripping away the traditional faculty governance in favor of external boards and executives who come in from other parts of the business world or from government. As it happened to public school teachers, and indeed, to the autoworkers at Lordstown, so it did in the university: demands for reform and accountability to the community or the workers themselves were turned into excuses to impose "flexibility" on the workforce. The protest movements of the 1960s, led by radical students demanding control over curricula and challenging the power structures of the university, were turned, in the hands of the right, into letting "the market" decide what should be taught, while challenging the usefulness of education for its own sake. Thus, Aronowitz wrote, "neoliberalism entered the academy through the backdoor of student protest."[28]

Globalization has in one way brought the university back to its roots. Medieval European professors taught in Latin, and faculty and students crossed borders freely in pursuit of education; now a global labor market for academic work has opened up, and students regularly study outside of their countries of origin. The European Union has instituted regulations requiring comparability of degrees, and some American schools, including New York University (NYU), have campuses littered across the world. This phenomenon has created an international job market for academic workers, such that conditions in one place wind up linked to conditions elsewhere.[29]

In academia, as in many other professional fields, the tradition of a period of apprenticeship dates back to the medieval guilds. In the modern university, PhD students teach and grade and research while they earn their degrees, doing the work that allows full professors to focus on their own projects; indeed, grad students do some of the research that goes out with the professor's name on it. This hierarchy is justified as paying one's dues, but it also, importantly, functions to maintain quality control. Not just anyone can be a professor; one must have done research judged to count by one's peers, passed through hurdles set by accomplished mentors, smiled through the long hours, and pretended to be cheerful while eating ramen noodles, all this hope labor performed in what used to be more than a hope of a career. Passing through the set of qualifications to a good job at the end was, for a time, a ritual that one could more or less count on. Nowadays, this isn't true.[30]

Graduate students who are funded receive a stipend, and in return, they do plenty of teaching and grading as well as their own research. Yet university administrators will argue, if those graduate students try to unionize, that they are not really working at all—that their funding is not a wage, but a grant to subsidize their education. Their labor is not really labor, but a privilege. Sociologist Erin Hatton called this double bind— applied not only to graduate students but also to student athletes (as well as to prisoner laborers and workfare recipients after welfare reform)—"status coercion," because their status as something other than workers allows their supervisors extra punitive power. "The education, degree conferral, and future employment of science graduate students are in the hands of the faculty advisors for whom they labor," she wrote. "Such advisors can dismiss them from the PhD program as well as delay their graduation because they have become productive workers in the lab." This kind of coercion links the working conditions of graduate students to other precarious workers—to retail workers and domestic workers as well as interns—as it primes them to accept undervalued and insecure work in the future. And like welfare-to-work programs, graduate programs mobilize both moralistic language about hard work and a labor-of-love rhetoric that denies certain work is work at all by denying that what workers are paid is indeed a wage.[31]

To Aronowitz and others, the "last good job in America" could be a guidepost for all: shorter working hours and more autonomy could be key demands to improve others' working conditions. Instead, though, the opposite has happened in the twenty years since he wrote about it: the academic workplace has become more like the rest of the service sector. For those who had that last good job, as it was with other parts of the PMC, it had been, for a while, easy to ignore the struggles of those outside the university, those with fewer credentials, doing manual labor, perhaps, or caring work. Even on campus, tenured faculty could be prone to ignoring the conditions of those serving the food or keeping the lecture halls clean; off campus, the tradition of seeing the university as a location apart meant that too few professors realized that the downward trajectory of other knowledge work was connected to their own. The university's culture of individualism—particularly the intense focus on individual research, created in part by the endless pressure to produce and publish such research—mitigated against academics' collective action for a while. But as the conditions of academic workers began more and more to resemble those of those other workers, academic workers began to reach for the tool of the working class: labor unions.[32]

Union density was in decline across the United States by the 1990s, but two hundred thousand or so faculty and staff at universities were still union members. Graduate students organized in large numbers, challenging the idea that their work was not work. They were aware of their importance in the institution, the amount of work that, if they refused to do it, would simply not be done. The corporatization of the university, by requiring graduate students to produce useful research, had hastened their realization that they, too, were necessary workers. By 2000 there were more than thirty graduate assistants' unions with contracts across the country. Most of that unionization came at public institutions, though; private institutions have had a different war to fight. The National Labor Relations Board, with its Yeshiva University decision in 1980, ruled that faculty at private universities were management and therefore ineligible for union protections. Looking over the arguments for faculty governance of the university, the board decided to take professors at their word, despite the trimming away of those privileges and duties as the tenure track declined.[33]

When NYU's graduate student union, the Graduate Student Organizing Committee / United Auto Workers (GSOC-UAW) Local 2110, struck in 2005, it made visible several of the many fault lines of academic labor. The strike dragged on for seven months before being broken by the university through a process of intimidation, media battering, firings, and more. GSOC had been the first union to win a contract at a private university in the wake of the 2000 NLRB decision that graduate assistants were workers, and the university management was determined not to have a second contract. And the board had changed by then—in 2004, with a majority of new conservative appointees, it reversed itself and said that private universities had no right to union recognition. Even at the time, NYU was a popular and relatively newly prestigious university, an emblem of the corporate or neoliberal turn in the academy, with high demand for applications and students who graduated with the highest debt load in the country. It also had one of the highest percentages of courses taught by non-tenure-track staff, including the striking grad students. Its president at the time had made an argument for the role of the university as anchoring a new key sector of the economy: he called it "ICE" (intellectual, cultural, and educational) as a complement to New York's famed FIRE sector (finance, insurance, and real estate), from which the university drew most of its trustees. He had thus concretized the argument that the university was key to the new "knowledge" economy, melding it with the "creative class" even as he tried to worsen working conditions for those knowledge producers.[34]

There was a core group of some 220 tenured and tenure-track faculty who supported the strike, even moving classes off campus so as not to cross the grads' picket lines. In the midst of the strike, the union managed to win another majority vote among graduate students, reiterating that it had wide support even if the university wouldn't recognize it and some of the grad students (particularly international students) had been bullied into returning to work. Protests by undergraduates and union activists, including the president of the AFL-CIO at the time, John Sweeney, supported the graduates, but in the end, the university held out and broke the strike. The union did not give up, though, and eventually, in 2014, after protracted battles and a new union vote, it won another contract.[35]

The question of what higher education is for is intimately tied up with the questions of the conditions of its work. If higher education is to be, as the students of the 1960s demanded, open to all, a place to explore and to learn and to challenge, that means it should be taught by faculty who are supported and encouraged in their own learning, who are challenging and exploring themselves. If, however, the university is simply a machine for producing credentials, with degrees like commodities to be purchased by students shopping in the market, then it is harder and harder to argue for the necessity of faculty who have time and resources to develop their own minds. What political theorist James Cairns called "Austerity U" is, he wrote, about "teaching disentitlement," not only to students, but also to faculty.[36]

Perhaps the best example of the simultaneous deskilling and deprofessionalization of higher education and its corporate takeover is the for-profit college. In her book *Lower Ed*, sociologist Tressie McMillan Cottom dissected the for-profit college industry, pointing out the ways in which it is a logical outgrowth of both the "education gospel" and the neoliberal turn. When demand expanded for education in the 1960s, she noted, public universities expanded. But now, with public funding on the decline, and the stagnant economy making a new credential more appealing, for-profits have stepped into the gap. As for work at the for-profits, recruitment is more of a focus than teaching, and forget about research. The courses remain the same, but the faculty are constantly changing: they are even more temporary than the adjuncts at more traditional institutions.[37]

In 2013, the Ehrenreichs revisited the professional-managerial class and found it much decomposed. In a report titled "Death of a Yuppie Dream: The Rise and Fall of the Professional-Managerial Class," they documented the "devastating decline" of many of the professions they'd originally tracked. "In this setting," they wrote, "we have to ask whether the notion of a 'professional-managerial class,' with its own distinct aspirations and class interests, still makes any sense, if it did in the first place." The replacement of tenure-track professors by low-wage adjuncts and the increasing concentration of control at the top of the university were high on their list of changes in the class's expected privileges. The cost of college itself was also part of the problem—it was increasingly untenable for the PMC to reproduce itself, with the price of a degree spiking nearly eight times faster than wages were rising. By 2020, a degree was 1,410.83 percent more expensive than it had been when the Ehrenreichs first coined the term PMC. Those who can, therefore, jump ship from academia into "direct service to capital," becoming analysts for finance or working exclusively for the wealthy. Those who can't wind up as adjuncts, in the service industry, or sometimes both. In a 2019 interview, Barbara Ehrenreich explained, "I would say that what happened to the blue-collar working class with deindustrialization is now happening with the PMC—except for the top managerial end of it." In other words, instead of a professional-managerial class, you have management—and everyone else.[38]

Years after her fight with Ronald Reagan for her academic post, Angela Davis suggested, as the Ehrenreichs did, that academics had to answer for their own elitism. The solution to the problems of academic labor, and particularly for Black women in the academy, she wrote, would come not simply from defending their individual rights to exist there, but through collective struggle—a struggle that should include university workers from the cafeteria and cleaning staffs to the professors. "I include workers because it would be a mark of our having reproduced the very elitism which excluded and continues to exclude so many of us if we assumed that there is only one group of Black women whose names are worth defending in the academy," Davis wrote. In the United Kingdom, meanwhile, lecturer and social theorist Mark Fisher noted that teaching itself was becoming a service industry, with teachers required to treat students as customers rather than encouraging them to challenge themselves. "Those working in the education system who still want to induce students into the complicated enjoyments that can be derived from going beyond the pleasure principle, from encountering something difficult, something that runs counter to one's received assumptions, find themselves in an embattled minority," he lamented. Once the United Kingdom's vibrant art school culture allowed the working classes to create; now education was being restratified, restructured along lines dictated in a report that was overseen by a former British Petroleum executive: the 2009 "Browne Report," commissioned by a Labour government but released under the Conservative–Liberal Democrat coalition. It recommended the series of changes, including huge tuition hikes, that would spur a massive student protest movement in 2010.[39]

The proletarianization of big chunks of the PMC makes them dangerous even as it strips away their power. As Nixon and Reagan and their advisers once worried about an educated working class, so today's politicians face uprisings of what journalist Paul Mason called "the graduates with no future." In response, they have cracked down further on the university. In Britain the student movement of 2010 was a response to student fee hikes and broader austerity and laid the groundwork for the left turn of the Labour Party. In Wisconsin, where Governor Scott Walker all but eliminated tenure and public-sector collective bargaining in 2011, faculty, and particularly graduate students, led the protests and the occupation of the statehouse that ensued. (Politicians also pursued access to faculty emails, in a breach of both academic freedom and privacy that seems both small and telling.) In Quebec, student protests against tuition hikes brought down the provincial government after weeks of strikes. As long as academia provides some top-tier positions to aspire to, hope labor may keep some graduate students and non-tenure-track faculty scrambling along, cobbling together a living and eking out research. But for how long?[40]

Even tenured faculty are feeling the crunch, the pressure to do more. As one professor wrote, "We live a day-to-day illusion that we don't have a boss. We have only 'self-imposed' deadlines. Everything we do is our choice." After her physical collapse due to overwork, she tabulated what she had been doing regularly: "In the fall semester, I taught two graduate courses. My department has three programs, and I was running one of them, with its 10 faculty members and about 50 master's and doctoral students. I served on two committees, one in the department and another at the college level. I completed six manuscript reviews for leading journals, serving as a deputy editor on one of them. I had four doctoral and two master's advisees and served on 15 graduate committees—providing feedback and writing letters of recommendation. Last fall I wrote close to 40 such letters. Add to that the steady stream of emails I must read and respond to every day." Her job description said that 60 percent of her time should be spent on research, but where were the extra hours in the day to come from? Faculty of color, particularly women of color, do even more of this "invisible work" of "making the academy a better place," everything from serving on diversity committees to extra mentoring for students of color. Such invisible work eats up their time and hinders, rather than helps, their chances at promotion up the ladder. And then there's yet another form of labor expected of faculty in the digital age—becoming a social media star. McMillan Cottom noted that, like these other forms of extra work in the academy, such a burden falls hardest on Black women.[41]

In higher education organizing, it is common for adjuncts or others to note their educational attainments as they draw comparisons to "other" low-wage workers. The implication can often be that perhaps low wages are fine for some, but those who have jumped through the university's hoops are entitled to the middle-class trappings to which they'd aspired. This can be an insidious argument, although, as theorist and occasional adjunct herself Yasmin Nair reminded us, "we might seize this opportunity to reconfigure the terms of academic success to signify a system that allows everyone opportunities to do the work they desire, without holding ourselves up to mythical standards of class empowerment." Nair called it "class shock," and we might note it as a symptom of the decomposition of the PMC, of downward mobility, or at least thwarted upward mobility. That sense of middle-class scarcity can lead at all levels to wanting to pull the ladder up behind you, whether that be the tenured professor ignoring the struggles of the adjunct down the hall, or the graduate student breaking the strike, or the adjuncts themselves casting aspersions on "those" workers.[42]

The coronavirus pandemic, as Katherine Wilson noted, sent universities scrambling. In many cases, the workers wound up pitted against each other as budget cuts loomed, particularly at public institutions. Because, as usual, the crisis did not hit all workers, or all departments, equally. Graduate students worried that their funding would disappear, that the research they could not do from home would be irreparably damaged. Adjuncts, whose contracts are renewed semester by semester, held their breath. But in some cases, the workers took Angela Davis's advice and tried to unite up and down the university, with tenured faculty standing up for service jobs. At Rutgers in New Jersey, the campus unions joined in a coalition twenty thousand workers strong, fighting to hold onto jobs for temporary faculty and maintenance workers alike, with the best-off volunteering to take furloughs to save the money for the most vulnerable. The coalition, said faculty member and historian Donna Murch, was giving the workers "a way to fight something that often feels abstract, which is this politics of corporatization, privatization, de-unionization, with real people that you know and that you see in regular meetings."[43]

Fighting for the university in a moment of crisis would take more than just convincing arguments. Adam Kotsko argued that this moment was an opportunity to reestablish faculty governance and potentially bring back "the last good job in America"—but, he noted, "that can't happen as long as we allow cost-cutting administrators to divide us into a privileged minority of tenured and tenure-track faculty and a disposable majority of contingent faculty and graduate students." Fully inclusive unions and coalitions—like the one at Rutgers—were necessary, and a reminder that "the answer is not persuasion, but power."[44]

The ideal academic workplace is often one that comes about not by following the rules, but by resisting them. Philosopher Amia Srinivasan found a vision of the university that she wanted to see during a 2019 strike. Part of the University and College Union and a professor at Oxford, Srinivasan was on strike for eight days with colleagues from sixty institutions across the United Kingdom. At issue, she wrote, were "pensions but also pay cuts, casualization, overwork and the gender and racial pay gap." Claire English, an associate lecturer at Queen Mary University of London, was one of those casualized workers, on a year-by-year contract, and to her, the strike helped break through the shame many of them felt at not having permanent positions. "It's been an amazing experience to be on the picket line, to find that there are so many other people in the same position as me and all of us being jerked around in terms of our pay, getting paid a month late, not getting our contracts until well after we've started teaching, . . . being told that we'll have five hours of seminars and then student numbers change and you only get three." Despite the exhaustion and the constant paring away of hard-won conditions, Srinivasan wrote, academic labor "contains a spirit of vocation and reciprocity" that is why people still aspire to it. Yet, she noted, "when people insist that the university is simply a place of love, and not also a place of work, they offer cover to exploitation—of staff, of students, and of the ideals of the university itself. . . . Those who insist that striking lecturers do not love their students fail to see that love can still be work, and that the picket can be a classroom."[45]

KATHERINE WILSON HAD BEEN AN ACTIVIST ON MANY FRONTS FOR MOST of her life, but labor hadn't really been one of them. She'd been a feminist and an activist for LGBT rights. She'd been part of Palestine and Latin American solidarity movements, and much of her theater work had been in collectives, where putting in time and sweat equity mattered and the ethos, she said, was "do what needs to be done." But at CUNY, the union felt distant from her; it included everyone from tenured faculty on down, and she never felt particularly drawn to it. That changed at Fordham, though.

Sitting in her office, she was wearing a maroon sweater to which she'd hand-applied varsity-letterman style letters, reading "FFU" across the back. FFU stands for Fordham Faculty United, the name of the union that includes adjuncts like Wilson as well as non-tenure-track lecturers, who were contingent as well but a step up from the adjuncts—"They get health benefits and they teach four courses a semester, whereas we are capped at two."

Getting involved in the union at Fordham was very different from the kind of "sitting and talking or screaming in the streets" that had made up her prior activism. She said, "It was fascinating to me. Like, 'Oh, we can't just scream our top ideals. We have to actually come in here and think of how this would work.'"

The organizing process began at Fordham with a handful of adjuncts, but initially they had a hard time getting a union to work with them. Wilson wasn't involved early on, but after the group connected with the Service Employees International Union's new Faculty Forward campaign, focusing on precisely their kind of precarious faculty, she was drawn in. Eventually, through a combination of public pressure from students and tenure-track faculty and actions by the adjuncts, they got the university to agree to allow a union election. The instructors voted 16 to 1 to unionize with SEIU Local 200.[46]

It was 2018 when bargaining began, and Wilson found the process engrossing. Their union representative held open negotiating sessions, so anyone could come and watch bargaining unfold. "I felt that I learned from every single session I attended," she said. "Every now and then we might say something, but it was mainly observing. But [our representative] would consult us and occasionally we would vote on something, like, 'Would we be willing to strike?' or 'Did we want to fight for health insurance or higher pre-course wages?'" Only later did she realize that the speed and success of the Fordham process had been inspirational to other schools. The contract they won included wage raises from 67 percent to 90 percent for adjuncts over its three-year duration; that would bring most of them to between $7,000 and $8,000 per class by the contract's end. Full-time lecturers would reach a minimum salary of $64,000 by the third year of the contract, an increase of roughly $14,000 a year for the lowest paid. They won just-cause protections, meaning they couldn't be fired without a reason given, as well as some professional development funding and paid professional leave for full-timers.[47]

When they held their first election for union officers, Wilson found herself recruited to be cochair alongside French lecturer Josh Jordan, and they went on to work closely together on both big-picture and day-to-day issues. The process had taught her a lot about the campus: adjuncts tended to be isolated from one another as well as from other tiers of faculty in the stratified system. "I had to learn who my brothers and sisters were, so to speak," she said. That involved getting to know the different campuses and schools, and learning that the social-work adjuncts "were paid a pittance" compared to her and others in the humanities, even though the adjuncts in the humanities were in turn paid little compared to those at the business school. Fordham had wanted to have the adjuncts and the lecturers in different bargaining units, but the contingent faculty stuck together, Wilson said, and made sure that while the contracts had different details, they "tied them together": "We hinged the calculus that determines our salaries so that if one goes up, the other one goes up. You are not going to divide and conquer."

Professional development funds were huge for Wilson. "Since 2002, I have been presenting at conferences, [and] I have never gotten a dime from a school for that," she said. "CUNY has it, but it is stringent about who qualifies for it." Of course, she laughed, now that she's a union officer, that takes up a lot of her time outside the classroom and she has less time for conferences. But the prospect of funding means a recognition that adjuncts and lecturers, too, are scholars doing research as well as teaching. They also won a level of security against last-minute canceled classes: the university has to tell them by a certain time whether they'll be teaching, and if they cancel a class, they still get paid a fraction of the salary. (The scheduling fights are reminiscent of those among retail and service workers, and were no doubt aided by SEIU's experience organizing other parts of the service sector.) Finally, they have the right to union representation at every step of their process. "That forces them to recognize us, that we are working people, that we have pasts and futures," said Wilson.

Implementing the contract has taught her about what needs to be improved next time. From the limitations on professional development funds to the impossibility of office hours without office space, she's realized more and more what it would actually take to make adjuncts equal to the rest of the faculty. In their first year on the job, she said, she and Jordan were expected to be the "pretty face" of the union, to do things like going to Central Labor Council meetings, meeting with administrators, and connecting with other unionists across the city. But instead they've been involved in the nuts and bolts of implementation. "I just said last week to Josh, 'Our real work starts now. A year and a half in, this is when we are finally turning to our real work.'"

Academia, she noted, often draws people who bought into the ideal of the lone intellectual: "We worked solo. We did a dissertation solo. We did the loneliest five years, eight years, whatever. . . . And now, you are throwing us together and saying, 'Oh, yeah, you will work together fine.'" She was one of the few involved in the union's leadership with activist experience, and even then, she hadn't been involved with many formal organizations. Within the contingent faculty, she noted, titles didn't determine rank, but there were in practice differences in whether one got involved with the union. Many universities justify hiring part-time adjuncts by arguing that they are working professionals in their field who supplement that work with teaching, and sometimes that's even true. The "moonlighters," Wilson said, were harder to sign up and get interested in the union than those like her and her cochair, who had gone through the PhD process and had looked forward to traditional academic careers.

Although there are union stewards on each campus, it can still be a challenge to get faculty involvement. Old-style union tips for organizing, Wilson noted, don't work for contingent faculty. There is little shared space, and schedules vary wildly. "We don't have a clique. We don't have anything. We have to invent the watercooler," she said. "That is about the structure of what they do with us and spatially . . . we sometimes don't share anything. The fact that you have to invent it is very, very different from what [happens in] a factory or hospital, where the organization already wants them to be a well-oiled cadre, and now if you can bend that cadre toward a union, you have terrific strength. Science is not solitary, but science doesn't get very involved. For those of us in humanities and social sciences, the nature of our work is very, very isolated."

The way the university has changed shaped Wilson's experience beyond just the nature of her own job, she said. She had let go of the desire for that window office with the bookshelves, the dedicated workspace. But what still got to her was how the students came in anxious and stressed, and how that led to less risk-taking, less learning, and more playing it safe to get the grade that would get them the credential. "It is chores you do to get the grade. I find it so alienated from working with knowledge and working with literature and working with writing," she said. "Also, arts are about adding—I don't mean beauty in the sense of pretty flowers, but about adding a kind of beauty and recognizing pleasure. That is quantified and that is commodified and commercialized, but in my mind—obviously—is not about price."

That kind of pricelessness, she said, connects to the dignity that adjuncts are fighting for. "It is not just about the pay. I don't put poetry on par with housing and food, but it is not far behind," she said. "Bare existence, bare subsistence, bare life, that is not our vision of humanity, and particularly for academics, we've immersed ourselves in the fruits of human creation and civilization. It is a painful oxymoron that then our daily lives and subsistence had become close to abject."

The union itself served to break up their isolation and provide something beyond that bare life. "We have monthly happy hours down the avenue. The social is a little slower, but we are trying to start to build those," Wilson said. "I would like to organize—in Fordham—adjuncts who straddle schools and start to build that." But it takes work to build a union that isn't just seen by most of the faculty as a service provider. "We get members approaching us like, 'Do this for me,' or 'Provide me this service.'" Contingent faculty still hang on to the hope that their gig will be short term; even if they want the protections of the union, Wilson said, they don't want to invest too deeply in it. There was still a sense of shame that made the adjuncts less inclined to identify with their role; no one, Wilson noted, said with a sense of pride that they were an adjunct. They had this in common with other parts of the precarious workforce: a need to break through the disappointment and decide that the way to change things was to improve the adjunct job, not just to keep hope-laboring toward escape from it.

She understood this feeling. "I did give up looking," she said. "After this contract it will be, 'So, do I continue this or don't I?' I don't know. Is this happy or content or how miserable and undignified is this?" Fifty-seven, she noted, would be a difficult age at which to be considering another change from work she trained for and is good at, but it is also the reality she faced.

"There is no question that the only time I have felt dignified working in a university was the activist work in the union here. That is the most dignified relationship I have had. My own work as an adjunct, I can't think of a semester or a month where I would say, 'That felt dignified,'" she said. "That is what most political struggles have been fighting for, in addition to the material gains and substantial rights." The five, ten, sometimes twenty hours a week of unpaid work for the union was the thing that mattered most to her. "People say, 'Why do you do it?' That is my answer. This is where the dignity comes from."

CHAPTER 9

PLAYBOR OF LOVE
Technology

VIDEO-GAME PROGRAMMERS LEARN TO CELEBRATE "CRUNCH" FROM THE get-go. Like many of his peers, Kevin Agwaze went to a specialized school that taught coding for games, rather than a traditional university. Such schools normalize a brutal workweek, treating high dropout rates as a badge of honor, and instilling the idea that the games industry is a shark tank where only the strong survive. While in his native Germany, he noted, "Uni is free," the program he attended, a two-year course, costs around €25,000 (about US$29,000). Such programs can cost even more in the United States, where a specialized education might run $100,000.

The schools, Agwaze and other programmers explained to me in a London pub, pump out "eight gazillion" games developer grads, for whom there are not necessarily enough good jobs. By the time they graduate, programmers expect to work long hours to prove themselves, and for those hours to stretch even longer when deadlines loom. To Agwaze, it seemed to be worth it to work in a field about which he was passionate. "I knew it was going to be bad for me," he said with a lopsided grin. "I thought, 'I am young, my body is going to be fine. I can do it for a while. I can handle bad conditions.'"

He wanted to work in what they call triple-A games—the video-game equivalent of a blockbuster film, with a big budget and production teams that span multiple countries and studios. He applied for jobs all over and wound up in the United Kingdom at a company called Studio Gobo. The company, which bills itself as "a family of graphics geeks and artistic misfits," offers "AAA console game development services for a global client base." What that means, Agwaze explained, is that they work on specific parts of bigger properties for major studios. "We have all the creative freedom but none of the risk, like if Ubisoft [a French video-game company] is going to cancel [a] game, they will still pay us," he said. He's pretty happy at his job, all things considered.[1]

His day-to-day work schedule depends to a degree on other programmers working in offices that might be several time zones away. There's no time clock to punch, no overtime pay; he comes in to work around 10:00 a.m., he said, and leaves most days around 7:00 or even 8:00 p.m. The late evenings are in part, he explained, because he's working with developers in Montreal, who don't arrive at work until after he's had his lunch. "I come into the office, read all the emails about stuff that happened after I left, when they were still working," he said. There is, he joked, a 50/50 chance that the thing he's supposed to be working on will be broken in some way when he arrives and he'll have to wait for Montreal to be online to fix it; if it isn't broken, he can do some work before they're up.

The seemingly inefficient process is common across the industry, he explained. In part, that's because so many different people work on different parts of big games that it would be impossible to have them all in one office, or even, it seems, one company. There is also the desire for what he called "acculturation" benefits—making sure that games are accessible and interesting to audiences in a variety of locations rather than being so culturally specific to one that players in a different market won't want it. "If you have people with different backgrounds working on a game," he said, rather than employing "the same Bay Area American people" each time, "it might just end up being a better game."

There is also the question of costs—some of the programming is outsourced to countries like India, where the wages are lower and the working conditions less regulated. "Somebody working in India and somebody working in Sweden can have completely different working conditions," he noted, "even though they are working at the same company on the same game and the same project, maybe even the same feature."

The grueling hours lead to high turnover at the jobs in the industry, even more so than the programming schools. It's a workload, Agwaze and the others said, designed for young men without families or caring responsibilities, who can dedicate their entire lives to the job. And indeed, the demographics of the industry bear this out: recent surveys of the United Kingdom's games workforce found that the vast majority were young men. Only 14 percent were women, and as for workers of color, like Agwaze, in 2015 they made up a dismal 4 percent. In the United States, meanwhile, a 2019 study found that only 19 percent of the workforce was female, while a slightly better 32 percent identified as something other than white. When the appeal of working on games no longer trumps the desire to have a life outside of work, programmers leave and go into a different industry. Their skills might have been honed to make blockbuster games, but the same code that makes up the backbone of *Red Dead Redemption* can also be used to make the latest financial technology app, for more money and shorter hours. "It's just a different planet," Agwaze said.[2]

That turnover itself makes the industry less efficient than it could be: rather than trying to retain experienced workers, companies bring in more young workers like Agwaze to make up the difference. Meanwhile, senior positions sometimes go unfilled for months. It becomes a circular problem: hours stretch longer and longer as junior developers scramble to fix bugs; they get tired of the struggle and quit; and then a new person with even less practice is plugged into their spot. And the companies' idea of how to make the job more sustainable is to put in a Ping-Pong table and give out free food. Agwaze laughed, "Let's put a bed in there! Sleepover! Put in showers!" Studio Gobo's website promotes "Gobo Friday Lunch," with "Freshly cooked (free!) food by our in house chef, the only rule is you're not allowed to sit next to the people you did last week. It's an opportunity to relax and hang out as a team and some of our best ideas have emerged over a warm home-cooked meal."

But, of course, it's not home-cooked. Instead, it blurs the distinction between home and work. "I have time periods where, like, I sleep for two or three hours," Agwaze said. "I'm just going home to bed and waking up and going back again. I don't remember what happened. I just remember going to bed and being in the office again." Coworkers become close friends, late shifts can take on a party atmosphere, and the feeling that everyone is part of something important often prevails. Studio Gobo's website again: "Fun is at the heart of what we do. We know that if we want to make fun games, we also have to have fun making games."

Yet that fun atmosphere itself is designed to entrap workers into staying longer daily, even without direct pressure from the boss. "I had a senior employee tell me, 'Kevin, I notice that you stay long hours a lot and I think it has a bad impact on the whole team, because if you stay longer, everybody else wonders, "Do I need to stay longer?" It puts pressure on your team. Even if you want to do that, that might negatively affect everybody else.'" At the time, Agwaze said, he shrugged it off. The individual pressures—the need to build one's CV—mitigated against collective concern. "I remember being like, 'Ah, whatever. I am fine. I am doing good.'"

Agwaze's experience was rare, though, he noted—most employers applied the opposite pressures. Crunch was endemic to the industry: over half of the workers questioned in one survey said they'd worked "at least 50 percent more hours during crunch than the standard work week of 40 hours." The issue came to the fore in 2004 with a public "open letter" from the spouse of a developer at Electronic Arts (EA), complaining of her partner's eighty-five-hour crunch weeks. Two class-action lawsuits followed, alleging unpaid overtime. Both were settled out of court, but the practice continued up to 2020. And it's not clear the practice is even worth it for employers. "Crunch," Agwaze noted, "produces bad games, a lot of average games, and some good games. Just because you crunch doesn't mean that the game is going to be any good at all."[3]

Beyond their expected loyalty to their own CV, the programmers were encouraged to consider themselves part of the family, and to work hard to pull their weight within it, even if, as Agwaze said with a sardonic laugh, "Maybe I crossed the country to start this job and I was fired in my first week after they told me I had now entered the family." While this had never happened to him, it wasn't an uncommon experience in the industry.

Some managers in the industry are starting to realize that they need to figure out better ways to retain experienced developers than trying to make the office feel less office-like. But the culture of the industry remains mired in the idea that putting in long hours is a mark of quality and dedication, rather than burnout and inefficiency. "They can't even imagine it as a bad thing," Agwaze said. "This is how it is. How can anybody believe this to be bad or wrong? This is how we need to do it."

With the arrival of COVID-19 in Britain, Agwaze joined the masses suddenly working from home. For him, that meant an even further blurring of the lines between time on and time off the job. At first, he said, he was told he needed to keep going to the office, but when the government announced its recommendations, he was allowed to stay home. He did some rearranging in his flat: when a roommate moved out, he was able to take over their room for a workspace, and he was able to borrow a computer with a bigger monitor on which to work. "I wake up, go to the other room to the PC. Then, I work for a long while. Then, at some point, I stop working. It might be after eight hours or slightly more or slightly less. I used to pretty rigorously take an hour of lunch break at 1 p.m. sharp with other people from work, but now I'm like, 'Did I eat anything today? No, I didn't. I should probably eat. What's the time? Oh, it's 2 p.m.'"

And after all the time that he spends dedicating himself to making games, he said, he doesn't really play them that much anymore. He laughed, "I don't have time. I sneak one in every now and then."

PROGRAMMING, A FIELD CURRENTLY DOMINATED BY YOUNG MEN, WAS invented by a woman. Ada Lovelace was the daughter of Romantic poet

Lord Byron, but her mother steered her into mathematics, "as if that were an antidote to being poetic." Lovelace was inspired by mechanical weaving looms to design a program for Charles Babbage's "Analytical Engine," an early idea of a computer. Her insight was that the computer could be used not just to calculate complex equations but to handle music, graphics, words, anything that could be reduced to a code—perhaps even games. Her paper on the subject, now considered the first computer program, was published in a journal in 1843, years before anything resembling a computer had actually been built.[4]

These days, the tech industry—as the shorthand would have it, leaving aside the question of just what is considered "technology"—is fawned over as the main driver of innovation in the world's major capitalist economies. Programmers are lionized in the press, their long hours held up as proof of romantic commitment to the work rather than inefficient work processes, their skills envisioned as something between God-given talent and Weberian hard work and grit. Those skilled workers are seen as geniuses the way artists used to be, gifted with superior abilities in a field inherently creative and specialized. Tech jobs are described as dream jobs, where the most skilled workers are wooed with high salaries, great benefits, stock options, and fun workplaces where you can bring your dog, get a massage, play games, and, of course, enjoy the work itself—and all of this leads to more and more work. The obsession with "innovation" is actually less than a century old, but the concept is often used to obscure the way skills become gendered and racialized, associated with a certain image of a certain kind of worker, and how that perception is reproduced along with our attitudes toward work.[5]

Programming was not always illustrious work, and computers were not always fancy machines. "Computer" was a job title for humans, often women, hired to crunch numbers on mechanical calculators at high volumes. Women did so in the United States during World War II, when men were being sent to the front lines and the first computing machines were being developed. The Electronic Numerical Integrator and Computer (ENIAC) was designed to replace those human computers, but its ability to perform calculations relied on human hands manually moving cables and flipping switches. At the time, the programming of the computer was considered routine work, and men were in short supply, so the University of Pennsylvania, where the ENIAC was born, recruited women with math experience to work on the machine.

In 1945, the first six women learned to be computer programmers: Jean Jennings, Marlyn Wescoff, Ruth Lichterman, Betty Snyder, Frances Bilas, and Kay McNulty. The women flirted with soldiers, argued about politics, and calculated differential equations to make the complicated machine work, learning its inner workings as well as any of the male engineers who'd designed and built the thing. The ENIAC—a massive, eighty-by-eight-foot mass of vacuum tubes, cables, and thousands of switches—"was a son of a bitch to program," Jennings later commented.[6]

The women knew their work was difficult, skilled labor, but the male engineers still considered the programming to be closer to clerical work—women's work, in other words—than the hardware side. Yet it was the women who stayed up late into the night, "crunching," to make sure the ENIAC was working for its first demonstration—to which they were not invited. "People never recognized, they never acted as though we knew what we were doing," Jennings said.[7]

After the war's end, the women who had been pressed into wartime service were encouraged to return home, free up jobs for men, and start families. Yet the women who worked on the ENIAC had a special skill set that made them harder to replace. "We were like fighter pilots," McNulty said. Instead, they stayed on and worked to design computers for nonmilitary uses, working alongside mathematics professor and navy reservist Grace Hopper. "Women are 'naturals' at computer programming," Hopper told a reporter in 1967. Yet even then, as software work gained prestige, the men were taking it over.[8]

Male programmers deliberately sought to shift the image of the field. Men, after all, wouldn't want to go into a field seen as women's work. To add cachet to the work, they created professional associations, heightened educational requirements, and even instituted personality tests that identified programmers as having "disinterest in people" and disliking "activities involving close personal interaction." People skills, like those taken advantage of in the classroom or the retail store, were for women, and apparently just got in the way of programming, a collective task being re-envisioned for solitary nerds. As Astra Taylor and Joanne McNeil wrote, the notion of the computer hacker "as an antisocial, misunderstood genius—and almost invariably a dude—emerged from these recruitment efforts." Changing the gender profile of programming, Taylor and McNeil wrote, also had the effect of boosting its class status. Rather than work learned by doing, programming was now the purview of rarefied graduate programs at the few research universities able to afford computers of their own.[9]

By the time the US Department of Defense bankrolled the project that would eventually become the Internet, computing was so thoroughly masculinized that there were no women involved. Instead, the Advanced Research Projects Agency Network (ARPANET) would be, in the words of Katie Hafner and Matthew Lyon, *Where Wizards Stay Up Late.* The men who built the network—funded by the DOD's Advanced Research Projects Agency (ARPA) in order to link computer labs up around the country to share research—were "geniuses" whose commitment to their work involved a lot of one-upmanship about who could work longer hours.[10]

ARPA's Information Processing Techniques Office was funding cutting-edge research that the private sector, and even the universities, might otherwise have shied away from throughout the 1960s. Created in reaction to the USSR's launch of the Sputnik 1 satellite, ARPA reflected the fear that the United States was falling behind. It was this same fear that led to an increase in the education budget and expanded public schooling, but it funded plenty of research that didn't have clear military applications. One of those projects was ARPANET.[11]

Making computers communicate required all sorts of new technologies. At the time, most computers didn't speak the same language. In Hafner and Lyon's words, "Software programs were one-of-a-kind, like original works of art." The innovations that would make the ARPANET, and then the Internet, possible were the result of a collective process between dozens of programmers and graduate students on multiple continents. Despite the tendency to ascribe progress to the unique genius of each of these men, researchers in different countries came up with similar ideas at nearly the same time.[12]

These computer whizzes were building on one another's breakthroughs, and the ARPANET would help them integrate their collective knowledge more deeply. In the obsession with the individual genius, we miss the real story, assuming that works of brilliance are the result of singular minds rather than collaboration—a notion that just happens to mitigate against the idea of organizing. "If you are not careful, you can con yourself into believing that you did the most important part," programmer Carl Baran said. "But the reality is that each contribution has to follow onto previous work. Everything is tied to everything else."[13]

The fetish for the tech innovator who dropped out of college may have begun, too, with the creation of the ARPANET. Bolt, Beranek and Newman, the firm given the contract to make the network a reality, was known for hiring dropouts from the Massachusetts Institute of Technology (MIT) in its hometown of Cambridge. Dropouts were smart enough to get into MIT, but without the degree, they cost less to hire. In just a few short years, the field had gone from instituting degree requirements as a class and gender barrier to entry to preferring those who cheerily tossed those requirements aside—and not long after that, to the legend of the Stanford or MIT dropout who created a company in his garage.[14]

There were a lot of sixteen-hour days, a lot of late nights and missed dinners, and a lot of sleeping at the desk for the programmers involved in creating the network—as well as for the graduate students who, at the various receiving sites for the ARPANET-connected computers, did much of the work of getting computers to talk to one another. They hammered out protocols, shared resources, and came up with the very first email programs collaboratively, sharing information with one another and hashing out disputes informally. The early Internet took the shape of the men who made it—it was anarchic, a place for sleepless computer nerds to express themselves, and argue for hours, whether it was about their ideas for the network or their political convictions (Defense Department money or no Defense Department money). They even figured out how to make games for it—a stripped-down version of the tabletop game *Dungeons and Dragons*, called *Adventure*, for example, was built by one of the Bolt, Beranek and Newman coders and spread widely across the Net.[15]

Video games were the perfect sideline for workers expected to be chained to their desks late into the night in a field where one's sleeplessness itself was a status symbol. If the programmers played with the network as much as they did hard work on it, that was just another way that they expanded its capabilities and kept themselves interested in the work they were doing. Later theorists named this *playbor*, simultaneously work and play, unforced yet productive. Adventure gaming blurred the lines between work and play just as the lines between work and home were being blurred by all those long nights at the office. That the network could be used for fun made the labor that went into making it seem even more worthwhile.[16]

Early video-game companies capitalized on these same ideas. As Jamie Woodcock wrote in *Marx at the Arcade*, "companies like Atari promised 'play-as-work' as an alternative to the restrictive conditions of industrial or office-based Fordism." The 1970s were, after all, the decade in which the rebellion against the Fordist factory was slowly synthesized into the neoliberal workplace. Forming a union was out. Instead, little forms of disobedience, like playing video games on the office computer, would come in and be absorbed into the workflow in the tech industry itself. Atari, which at this time developed early home consoles for playing video games on personal televisions, was the first company to prove that games could be big business. And as the computer business boomed, the tension between work and play, between fun and profits, only continued to grow.[17]

Programmers had been given a huge amount of freedom in the early days of the ARPANET. Coder Severo Ornstein from Bolt, Beranek and Newman had even turned up to a meeting at the Pentagon wearing an anti–Vietnam War button. But as the private sector began to get into the act (and woo away many of the academics and public employees who had been instrumental to the project), the question of how much power individual workers could be allowed to have was occurring to managers. Far from the purview of a handful of unique "wizards" and "geniuses," the daily workings of what was now a rapidly growing "tech" industry required a lot of work from a lot of skilled but interchangeable laborers. And those laborers had to be prevented from organizing.[18]

Silicon Valley eclipsed Cambridge as the tech hub for many reasons, but one of them was that the nonunion atmosphere allowed companies to maintain their cherished "flexibility." While Massachusetts had a long-established union culture, California was the wide-open frontier. Nevertheless, the 1970s and 1980s saw some attempts to unionize at tech companies from Atari to Intel, stories mostly written out of the history of tech as the industry grew.[19]

By this time, computers and games were becoming more firmly entrenched as toys for boys (or men who'd never stopped being boys). Women's participation in computer science programs fell from nearly 40 percent in the 1980s to below 20 percent at present, as personal computers, mostly good for gaming early on, were marketed to little boys, cementing further the idea that it was men who would be the new programmers. Pop culture picked up on this trend, making heroes of white male computer geeks. Anyone who didn't have a personal computer fell behind when it came to computer skills, erecting a class barrier to go with the gender barrier. Schools tended to accept, and companies tended to hire, people who looked like their idea of a "computer person," which was, according to science and technology researcher Janet Abbate, "probably a teenage boy that was in the computer club in high school." The assumption remained that computers, like art, were something one had to have a natural talent for; women were good at community and caring for others, and men were good at things that required an isolated, antisocial genius. The split between the two kinds of laborers of love solidified, keeping them from seeing that they both had similar struggles over long hours, capricious management, and a lack of control over the products of their work. That these gender roles were socially created stereotypes, not innate characteristics, seems not to have occurred to any of these supposedly brilliant men.[20]

The dot-com boom of the 1990s saw personal computers become ubiquitous, big profits reaped, and then the first big bust, as overvalued companies, inflated with venture capitalists' cash, deflated or popped. The

Clinton administration largely built on the privatization and deregulation of the Reagan-Bush years, but gave them a veneer of cool, and the dotcoms epitomized this trend. During this period, sociologist Andrew Ross was studying the workers of New York's "Silicon Alley" to understand these new workplace trends, which he dubbed "no-collar." In the brave New Economy, workers embraced a certain antiauthoritarian perspective, trading in the old status markers of power suits and briefcases for hoodies and T-shirts. The workers adopted the work styles of the bohemian artist, bringing their expectations of creative labor to their new jobs in tech. They also brought a willingness to work in lousier environments in return for deferred financial gain (stock options, in many cases) as long as the work itself was stimulating, creative, "work you just couldn't help doing." Ross dubbed this phenomenon the "industrialization of bohemia."[21]

These workplaces were designed to incorporate the "playbor" of techies, whose tendency to color outside the lines otherwise might have become more obvious resistance. Let the coder wear his "RESIST" button to the Pentagon, let the developers play games on their work machines, then they'll be happier to do their work. These "digital artisans," as Ross called them, were made to feel that they had a level of control over the machines. But unlike the original artisans, whose tools were theirs to control, the tech workers were still laboring for a big employer pocketing the profits. After all, the original Luddites didn't break machines because they opposed technology, but because the technology was designed to deskill them and make them obsolete. The fun-loving tech workplace, already beginning to be stocked with foosball tables and other games to play, made the programmers feel secure that they were powerful and could never be replaced. Yet companies were already increasing their workplace surveillance, and in many cases already trying to figure out ways to break up tasks and cut into the creative freedom of the programmers.[22]

These workspaces, researcher Julian Siravo pointed out, take their cues from the spaces that techies themselves created. "Hackerspaces" took inspiration from the 1960s and 1970s protest movements' tendency to take over public or private buildings for their own use; the emerging computer culture adapted this practice from student radicals and *autonomia* and began to create its own spaces in the 1970s and 1980s. Groups like the Chaos Computer Club in Germany established regular in-person meetings, which were imitated elsewhere. The spaces continued to pop up all over the world: communal, nonhierarchical locations in which members do a variety of programming and physical construction. Before the Internet, hackerspaces were necessary to share information and skills; after the Internet, they became places in which members are, Siravo wrote, "questioning radically the ways in which we currently live, work and learn," taking a William Morris–like interest in challenging the divisions in capitalist production. But that freedom is something different in a space that people have designed for themselves in which to explore and create; in trying to replicate those spaces in a for-profit company, the big tech corporations have co-opted this exuberance.[23]

The boundaries between work and leisure thus blurred even more in the new tech companies, bringing more of the things workers might have done in their spare time into the workplace. The growth of the Internet helped blur these lines even for workers outside of the tech industry, who were now expected to check email at home, or who might play a game or write a personal blog on company time—and, particularly with the growth of social media, sometimes face workplace consequences for things they did in their free time and documented online.[24]

The lines blurred in another way, too: users' online behavior, from the items they searched for on Google to their interactions during online multiplayer video games, created value for the tech companies. "Users made Google a more intuitive product. Users made Google," Joanne McNeil pointed out. But that didn't mean users owned Google. How was their labor—the labor of producing data, of producing a "user experience" that necessitates other users to be meaningful—to be calculated?[25]

The values of the early Internet—openness, sharing, collaboration— meant something different on a privatized Web where profit was the name of the game. As the cliché goes, "if you're not paying for it, then you're the product," but users on today's Internet are something more than just the product—they're more like a self-checkout counter where the thing they're scanning and paying for is themselves. The users are being sold to advertisers, but they are also providing the labor that makes these companies profitable—labor that is unpaid, and indeed invisible as labor. Facebook and Twitter would be worth nothing without the people who use them—and the fact that millions do is the reason why these platforms are hard to give up. Yet thinking of those users—ourselves—as workers would require us to understand the "social" part of social media as requiring valuable skills as well, something that tech companies resolutely refuse to do. And, of course, it's in their interest not to—if they had to pay for the value we create for them, those tech billionaires wouldn't be billionaires.[26]

THE CREATIVE WORK OF THE TECHIES, THEIR MUCH-VAUNTED "INNOVA-tion," is the thing that is celebrated in these flexible, toy-filled workplaces, but this emphasis belies the fact that most programming work is, frankly, boring. It's grueling, repetitive, requiring focus and patience—and often plenty of cutting and pasting or working from pre-prepared kits. Yet the myth of the tech genius obscures much of this labor. Think of how many of Apple's fantastic devices, for example, are attributed to the singular brilliance of Steve Jobs, who couldn't write a line of code, rather than the legion of engineers who did the real work. These tech prodigies were justified by such hype in hiring little clones of themselves, in never questioning how it was that everyone who was a genius was also white and male, never asking why the number of women who left tech jobs was double the number of men.[27]

The reality is that the work—like most creative work, ruthlessly romanticized—is a slog. A *New York Times* story on Amazon's work culture featured employees who'd been told that when they "hit the wall," the solution was to climb it. They spoke of emails arriving in the middle of the night, and followed by angry text messages if they did not answer immediately. The staff faced an annual cull of those who purportedly couldn't cut it. Employees "tried to reconcile the sometimes-punishing aspects of their workplace with what many called its thrilling power to create," but the exhausting pace made them feel more like athletes than artists. Employees frequently cried at their desks, trapped in something bearing an uncanny resemblance to the ups and downs of an abusive relationship.[28]

At Facebook, things were a little bit different—at least according to Kate Losse, who detailed her experience as one of the company's early nontechnical employees in her memoir, *The Boy Kings*. But the sense of awe at the power in her hands was the same, at least before Losse's eventual disillusionment and break with Facebook and its founder, Mark Zuckerberg. The work that Losse did—customer service work—was devalued from the very start by Zuckerberg, who fetishized hackers and Ivy Leaguers who he imagined were crafted in his own image. "Move fast and break things," was his motto, and moving fast and breaking things were things that boys did. Losse nevertheless worked her way in, figuring, "You can't run a successful company with boys alone."[29]

Losse befriended the "hacker boys," including one particular teenager who was hired after he hacked Facebook itself. She joined them on trips to a Lake Tahoe house that Zuckerberg rented for his employees, as well as to Las Vegas and the Coachella festival. She even convinced Zuckerberg to splurge on a pool house where his employees could move in—the ultimate home office. When Zuckerberg offered to subsidize housing for anyone who moved within a mile of the office, Losse did that, too—even though, as a customer service worker, she at first was excluded from the perk. "It wasn't enough to work [at Facebook], you had to devote as much of your life to it as possible," she wrote. To that end, the engineers' floor at Facebook HQ was littered with toys—puzzles, games, Legos, scooters. New toys showed up constantly to keep the boy kings amused while they worked late. "Looking like you are playing, even when you are working, was a key part of the aesthetic, a way for Facebook to differentiate itself from the companies it wants to divert young employees from and a way to make everything seem, always, like a game," she wrote. But even at the many parties, the coders had their laptops along and managed to get work done.[30]

In fact, they loved their work so much that they created new features and new projects without even being asked, and sometimes explicitly without permission. Facebook Video was one such project: it was done after-hours (if there were after-hours at Facebook) as an experiment—at least until Zuckerberg decided to publicly announce it, to much acclaim. At that point, the programmers who'd begun it as a lark worked to the point of collapse to make sure it would launch on time. "It was like my body wouldn't ever work again," one of them told Losse.[31]

The coders who were breaking their bodies were at least lavished with perks and praise. Meanwhile, customer care was women's work: low paid, undervalued, not really considered work at all. At Twitter, for example, complaints from users about relentless abuse on the platform have been met with a steadfast refusal to hire support staff. Startup founders, Losse wrote elsewhere, have often relied on friends or girlfriends to do any work that required emotional labor. Silicon Valley later outsourced it to other countries, such as the Philippines, or even to refugee camps in Gaza, where the disturbing work of purging social networks of violence, porn, and anything else that might prove offensive to users was done for a fraction of what US wages would be. One article estimated the number of such workers at over one hundred thousand. Astra Taylor called the process Fauxtomation, whereby actual humans perform jobs that most people probably assume are done by algorithm. It is the secret of Silicon Valley, nodded to by Amazon with its Mechanical Turk service—the Mechanical Turk was a gadget created centuries before the computer to, purportedly, play chess. Inside the Turk was a human making the decisions. Now Amazon's "Turkers," many of them inside the United States, do repetitive "microtasks" for pennies, but the myth of the genius programmer helps to mystify the work still being done by human hands and human minds.[32]

The Silicon Valley workplace, created in the image of the boy king, seemed almost designed to erase the caring labor discussed in earlier chapters. No family, no friends, and no responsibilities outside of the office; within the office, all their needs are catered to, and toys are provided to make them feel eternally nineteen. (Facebook and Apple even offer egg-freezing to their employees, offering up a tech fix to the problem of work versus family, at least for a while, so that women, too, can abide by the "no families outside the workplace" rule.) It's no wonder that the apps designed by all these man-children have been, collectively, dubbed "the Internet of 'Stuff Your Mom Won't Do for You Anymore.'" Need laundry done, dinner delivered, your house cleaned? There's an app for that, and the app's founders have no doubt been breathlessly hailed as technical geniuses, even though their real innovation is finding new ways to skirt labor laws. The result has been the gig economy—a patchwork of short-term non-jobs performed by nonemployees who are barely getting by.[33]

Whether they be app-distributed gigs or jobs in Amazon's warehouses, or even programming jobs themselves, the tech industry's solution for the continuing need for humans to do deeply un-fun work has been "gamification." Gamification is almost the antithesis of "playbor"—a way to pretend that the same old backbreaking manual work is "fun," a game you can win. To make the work of packing boxes at Prime speeds less like, well, hard work, Amazon has introduced video games to the distribution center floor. The games have titles like "PicksInSpace" and "Dragon Duel," and the employees can play alone or against one another—the latter bit designed to up the competition factor and perhaps encourage faster picking. One gamification expert explained that the games might "give a bump to workers' happiness," but can also be used to ratchet up productivity goals: "It's like boiling a frog. It may be imperceptible to the user." Uber has used gamification as well; so have call centers. And it's being applied both in learn-to-code contexts and in the actual workplaces of software developers. Turn work into a game! What could be more fun? The problem, as artist and author Molly Crabapple acidly predicted years ago, is that "the prize is what used to be called your salary."[34]

The gamifiers are on to something—people hate drudgery, and no one expects to enjoy packing boxes or lifting them for an eight- or ten-hour shift. But it's not being plugged into a game that makes work enjoyable or not. It's autonomy that people value, and that is precisely what is being pitched with all those toys on the Facebook shop floor. "We trust you to get your work done," the toys and perks imply. "You can decide how and when you do it and how and when you have fun." With the feeling of autonomy comes the feeling that long work hours are a choice; they become a status symbol rather than a sign of unfreedom. As Miya

Tokumitsu wrote, in *Do What You Love*, "The promise of worker autonomy is embedded in the 'you' of DWYL."[35]

But surveillance is as rampant in the tech industry as it is elsewhere. As early as the 1990s, Andrew Ross found that tech companies routinely monitored their workers. It shouldn't be a surprise that companies like Facebook, who make their profits off extracting data, might want to keep an eye on their employees, or that the fallen WeWork, a real estate company that leased coworking spaces yet sold itself to investors as the techiest of tech companies, harvested a wellspring of data from the people who worked—and might have lived—in its buildings. WeWork pitched itself as "creat[ing] a world where people work to make a life, not just a living," selling a version of the dream tech-industry workplace to the masses of freelancers on their own in the neoliberal economy. And the more time those workers spend at the office, the more data that can be extracted. Sleep pods, rare whiskies, steak dinners, and all the toys are designed to enclose the worker in the workplace, just as the social networks enclose users—they offer free tools that the user then feels unable to give up.[36]

The company provides everything, in other words, that the tech worker needs to reproduce himself (and the worker is always assumed to be a HIM-self), leaving him free to focus solely on work. In this way, it fills the role less of his mother than his wife. The tendency of companies like Facebook to hire those boy kings means that the company is often shepherding them from youth to adulthood, filling that gap, perhaps, between mother and marriage. As video-game programmer Karn Bianco told me, when it comes time for slightly older workers to consider having a family of their own, they must create distance from the company and its desire to be all things to them.

And while, for now, programmers are lavished with benefits and treated as irreplaceable, the capitalists of tech are also betting that their status won't last. The plethora of "learn-to-code" boot camps are designed not as altruistic ways to get the working class into high-demand jobs (even the ones that promise to teach girls to code to counteract decades of industry sexism), but to drive down the cost of labor. Programming might be destined not to be a prestige field for wizards and boy kings, but rather, as Clive Thompson of *Wired* wrote, "the next big blue-collar job." Some of the boot camps are out-and-out scams, like one that promises to pay you to learn—and then takes a cut of your salary for the next two years. But all of them will have the effect of making coders more common, and thus making the work less rarefied—and less well remunerated.[37]

Mark Zuckerberg also has a plan to bring in lots of short-term workers from overseas. His immigration nonprofit, FWD.us, was created to lobby for immigration reform. That sounded nice in the age of Trump, but Zuckerberg's main concern was increasing the number of H1-B guest-worker visas for skilled workers. H1-B workers are tethered to a particular job; if they quit or get fired, they have to leave the country, which makes them spectacularly compliant as well as cheaper to hire.[38]

All of this means that tech workers might have more in common with the industrial workers of midcentury than they might think. Silicon Valley touts itself as the "New Economy," but it still relies on products that have to be built somewhere, and the tactics of offering perks on the job don't work quite as well on them. Elon Musk promised free frozen yogurt and a roller coaster to disgruntled employees at his Fremont, California, Tesla car factory—but the workers were complaining of injuries on the job because of the pace of production, and they didn't want frozen yogurt to soothe their pains. They wanted a union.[39]

Yet the hype for Silicon Valley continues, and ambitious programmers don't want to just be labor, anyway—they want to be startup founders, the next Zuckerbergs themselves. Peter Thiel, the PayPal billionaire and Trump buddy, advises would-be founders to "run your startup like a cult." Cult devotees, of course, will work their fingers to the bone out of love, not for money. Not many people consciously want to join a cult, but as Losse pointed out, there's another name for a group that inspires love and commitment and unpaid labor, and it's one that tech bosses cheerily invoke: the family. As Kevin Agwaze said, though, families don't lay you off once a year.[40]

Better by far to be your own boss, and start your own startup, even though startup founders themselves are reliant on the bigger boss—the venture capitalist. Author Corey Pein recalled asking a VC if startup founders were capital or labor. His "cheerfully cynical" reply was this: "For every Zuckerberg there's one hundred guys who basically got fired from their startups. They aren't capital. They're labor." The wannabe Zuckerbergs are their own kind of gig worker, scrambling individually to make a buck, just on a grander scale.[41]

Rather than leave to become startup founders, some tech employees have instead taken a page from the Tesla factory workers, or indeed, from the workers who serve them those catered lunches: they're organizing. The Tech Workers Coalition (TWC) began with an engineer and a cafeteria worker turned organizer who challenged a few of the shibboleths of Big Tech—namely, the idea that different kinds of workers have no interests in common, and the assumption that the programmers have more in common with the Zuckerbergs of the world than they do with the working class. It built slowly for a while, and then, after Trump's election in 2016, a burst of action drew many new recruits, both to the TWC and to Tech Solidarity, a group begun to help tech workers find ways to act on their anger. The first actions of many tech workers were to challenge their companies not to work with Trump. IBM employees petitioned their CEO, Ginni Rometty, asking that IBM not work with the Trump administration as it had with Nazi Germany and apartheid South Africa. Nearly three thousand workers at a variety of companies, including Amazon, Facebook, and Google, signed a "Never Again" pledge promising they would not work on projects that would aid the Trump administration in collecting data on immigrants or racialized groups. Amazon workers demanded the company not provide facial-recognition software to law enforcement; Microsoft employees called on the company to stop offering its cloud services to Immigration and Customs Enforcement (ICE).[42]

The first real tech-worker union drive, though, came at a smaller company, Lanetix. The problems began with the firing of an outspoken programmer. Coworkers described her as a stellar employee but said her questioning of company decisions had gotten her sacked "out of the blue." If she could be fired like that, the others began to worry for their own jobs, and decided to unionize with the NewsGuild. "As soon as they started to compare notes, they realized that each manager was just trying to *individualize* the complaints that everybody had," engineer Björn West-ergard explained. But after sending a letter to management requesting rec-ognition of their union, they were summarily fired. All fourteen of them. The story spread through the industry, and they filed a complaint with the National Labor Relations Board—retaliation for forming a union is illegal. Before the NLRB hearings could proceed, Lanetix settled with the fired workers, paying out a total of $775,000 to them. One of the former workers called it "a landmark win for tech workers."[43]

Which brings us to Google, a company that—with its mini-golf and climbing walls and free food—is a dream job for many. That is, for those who get the coveted full-time-hire white badge. For others, who come into Google only as temps, there is the red badge, and interns get green. The inequality rumbling through Google, as with Lanetix, wasn't limited to a few malcontents, and it spilled over in 2018. There was another petition, this time over Project Maven, an artificial intelligence program that was to be used with military drones, and some workers quit in protest before Google gave in. But it was sexual harassment that got the workers to orga-nize as workers.[44]

There had been rumblings before at Google. A wage discrimination investigation by the US Department of Labor "found systemic compensa-tion disparities against women pretty much across the entire workforce," according to DOL regional director Janette Wipper. The anger sparked by the investigation was fanned by the distribution of a memo written by a Google employee, James Damore, who insinuated that the gender gap in tech labor was due to inherent differences between men and women. But the Google walkout—by tens of thousands of employees across multiple countries—came after the *New York Times* published a report of wide-spread sexual harassment and impunity for perpetrators at the company. The $90 million golden parachute given to one executive, who was forced out after he was accused of sexual assault, was too much.[45]

The walkout took place at 11:10 a.m. in every time zone, rippling across the world (and Twitter) in an impossible-to-ignore wave. The orga-nizers gave credit to the women who'd organized in the fast-food industry through the Fight for $15, as well as to the #MeToo movement, which began online after Hollywood mogul Harvey Weinstein was accused of numerous instances of sexual assault. "A company is nothing without its workers," the Google organizers wrote. "From the moment we start at Google we're told that we aren't just employees; we're owners. Every person who walked out today is an owner, and the owners say: Time's up."[46]

That organizing was followed by demands, in the summer of 2020, that Google end its contracts with police departments. Tech workers joined in solidarity with protesters across the country, calling for defunding and abolishing policing after a Minneapolis officer killed George Floyd. A letter signed by more than 1,600 Google employees read, in part, "Why help the institutions responsible for the knee on George Floyd's neck to be more effective organizationally?" Amazon programmers, meanwhile, had been organizing to support the company's warehouse workers, protesting their dangerous working conditions during the COVID-19 pandemic. In both cases, the tech workers were taking their lead from those on the front lines.[47]

Suddenly the tech industry no longer seemed so impenetrable. After all, these behemoth companies operate with a relatively tiny workforce. Google's parent company only broke the hundred-thousand-employee mark in 2019, and Facebook had a little under forty-five thousand employees at the end of 2019. This means big profits, as Moira Weigel noted in *The Guardian*, but it also means that individual workers still have quite a lot of power, and it doesn't take many of them to shut things down. If workers could organize at Google, one of the world's most powerful corporations, and pull off a massive collective action that spanned continents, what else is possible?[48]

THE FIRST STRIKE IN THE VIDEO-GAME INDUSTRY WAS CALLED BY VOICE actors. Members of one of the old Hollywood unions, the Screen Actors Guild–American Federation of Television and Radio Artists (SAG-AFTRA), struck against eleven of the biggest games companies for just over a year. They were calling for residuals and royalties to be paid to voice actors, like those film actors enjoy, and though they did not win those demands, they did win raises and proved that games companies could be brought to the table to negotiate with a part of their workforce.[49]

To Kevin Agwaze, at the time, the victory seemed far off from the work he was doing. There was a sense from the developers, he said, that they were the ones doing the real work of making the games, and the voice actors just showed up and talked—a sense that echoed the companies' treatment of the actors. He'd been in the United Kingdom for just a few months at the time and remembered thinking, "Yeah, it's bad but that is just how it is." He thought he'd be able to adjust, to work his way up the ladder. But the discontent was bubbling up around the industry.

It boiled over at the 2018 Game Developers Conference in San Francisco. A panel was scheduled for the conference titled "Union Now? Pros, Cons, and Consequences of Unionization for Game Devs." The people putting together the panel, Agwaze explained, were closer to management than the rank-and-file developers, and a group of developers who were talking union began to organize around the panel to get pro-union workers to attend and ask questions. What had begun as a Facebook group, and then a chat on the Discord service, became a campaign that now had a name, an official website, flyers, and a goal: Game Workers Unite (GWU).[50]

After the panel, Agwaze said, the discussion of organizing snowballed. People joined the Discord chat, and then began to start local chapters where they lived. The conference was based in the Bay Area, but as workers in a massive international industry, the developers knew they had to take advantage of their reach on the Internet to start chapters on the ground where they worked. They talked about crunch, but they also talked about sexual harassment and discrimination. And discrimination was something that particularly drove Agwaze to get involved. "A bunch of these problems, they just get progressively worse if you are a person of color and LGBTQIA person," he said. "They become factors compounding an already shitty environment." His actual work experience has been fine, though the long hours persist, but, he recalled, "in school, they asked us for a current figure in the industry, in your field, that you look up to, relate to. I couldn't name a single Black person in games." He remained, at the time we spoke, the only person of color at his company, and for him the union was a way to speak up for marginalized people in the industry.

Most of the games workers had no experience with unions; the industry's age skew mitigates against that, but it is also true that young workers are driving a recent uptick in unionization in many industries. The workers have also needed to be creative about organizing. The UK group moved from the Discord chat into offline spaces, and then into forming an actual trade union for games workers, one of the first in the world. Agwaze is treasurer. After talking with a variety of different unions, the games workers became a branch of the Independent Workers Union of Great Britain (IWGB). A relatively new union begun in 2012, IWGB represents mainly low-paid immigrant workers in fields that had been long nonunion: cleaning workers, security guards, and gig economy workers like Deliveroo bike couriers and Uber drivers. It was both a strange and a perfect fit, explained Game Workers Unite's Marijam Didžgalvytė.

The games workers in many ways, obviously, are better off than many of the workers who are already part of IWGB, but they bring a militancy that can be infectious, and the union holds social events to bring members together in a solidarity that reaches beyond the picket lines. The games workers' social media reach is a help for the other workers as well. And social media helps the union reach a key audience: video-game consumers, who are notably vocal when they dislike a game, but could be marshaled, too, to support the games workers. A recent campaign to "Fire Bobby Kotick," the CEO of Activision-Blizzard, who received a multimillion-dollar bonus after laying off eight hundred employees, drew plenty of attention from gamers and the games press. Laying off workers while juicing stock prices with buybacks and raising investors' dividends is a fairly common practice in today's economy, but the campaign aimed to make the human cost of such practices visible to gamers. Didžgalvytė said, "I think the players are beginning to understand that the people creating their games are suffering."[51]

The GWU-UK union was helped by the United Kingdom's labor laws, which do not require the union to win a collective bargaining election in a particular workplace in order for workers to be able to join. Other workers in other countries have different challenges, but the demands of the UK union, voted on by the membership, are largely the same as the demands elsewhere. They include improving diversity and inclusion at all levels; informing workers of their rights and supporting those abused, harassed, or in need of representation; securing a steady and fair wage for all workers; and, of course, putting an end to excessive and unpaid overtime. "We try to avoid the term 'crunch' because it sounds so funky," Agwaze explained. "'It's crunchy! It is cool!' No, it is excessive unpaid overtime."[52]

Because of the developers' relative power in the industry, they have been able to put forward demands on behalf of less powerful workers. Issues like zero hours contracts—work contracts, in the United Kingdom, where contracts are common, that do not promise workers any hours or give them a regular schedule—are still pervasive in the lower levels of the industry, particularly for workers doing quality assurance (QA) testing. Some QA workers, Agwaze said, even get paid per bug found in a game. "This incentivizes the wrong thing," he noted, and it also means that someone could spend hours poring over a game, find nothing wrong, and make no money. GWU's concern even extends to professional game players in "e-sports" leagues—which tend to be owned by the companies that produce the games. A company, Agwaze explained, can just wipe an entire league out of existence if it no longer wants to pay for it. And the workers wanted, too, to make demands on behalf of the people who did the work to produce game consoles in the first place, from mining rare minerals in the Congo to assembling the products in factories, often in China.

There is still a tendency in the industry, which affects workers' desire to organize, to pretend that it is apolitical. "We make great art, we don't make politics," is how Agwaze summed up this argument. Yet the games, he pointed out, are inherently political, from war games (discreetly funded by the military) to superhero games, like a Spider-Man game that featured Spider-Man using police-operated surveillance towers to track down criminals. "How can this not be a political statement?" he asked. Online gaming culture had a track record of toxic culture, particularly the right-wing "Gamergate" movement, and that kind of culture rubbed off on the workplace. Games companies, in the wake of the 2020 racial justice protests, rushed to put out statements saying Black Lives Matter, but they rarely, Agwaze said, acknowledged the conditions they created inside their companies.[53]

One of those companies, Ustwo, billed itself as a "fampany," an awkward portmanteau of "family" and "company." It proclaimed its commitment to diversity and inclusion, but when it fired Austin Kelmore, GWU-UK's chair, its internal emails criticized him for spending time on "diversity schemes and working practices," and for being a "self-appointed bastion of change." One email, shared in *The Guardian*, proclaimed, "The studio runs as a collective 'we' rather than leadership v employees," but also said that Kelmore had put "leadership . . . on the spot." (The company spokesperson told *The Guardian* that Kelmore was leaving for reasons unconnected to his union activity.) GWU-UK fought for Kelmore, but even before the pandemic, such processes took time; after the pandemic, they were backed up even more.[54]

Agwaze's time organizing with GWU-UK had taught him that companies were often less efficient and practical than he'd expected. "They're more of a chaotic evil," he laughed. Few of them were aware of the labor laws, or of how their actions would be perceived. Then, as with the Black Lives Matter protests, they scrambled to try to win some goodwill through largely symbolic actions, like donating money to racial justice organizations.[55]

Still, all of this reflects the start of a change in the industry, signaled by the rise in political awareness within and about games. Members of the UK Parliament have even formed an all-party group to look into the gaming industry, though Agwaze noted that GWU-UK's invitation to speak to the group had been delayed as a result of Brexit and the general election in December 2019, and then because of the COVID-19 pandemic. Still, it marked a change from the assumption most people had, he said, that "it's fine, because it is video games. It must be fun, even in its working conditions."

With the pandemic, Agwaze said, some of the union's usual means of gaining new members—in-person meetings and speaking engagements—had to be scrapped, and the 2020 Game Developers Conference, where they'd planned a panel, was postponed. New members were finding them anyway, however, because of immediate problems on the job. "They are more like, 'Oh, shit is on fire right now! I need to find some union assistance!'" he said. Workers at some companies were being furloughed, but being asked to keep working without being paid. Others were being told they had to go to the office despite the lockdown. And then there was the immigration question. The games industry, Agwaze noted, depended on immigrant labor—he himself was an EU migrant living in the United Kingdom, a status that could be disrupted by Brexit and, under Prime Minister Boris Johnson, the government's intention to crack down on migrants. The pandemic exacerbated these problems: workers who lost jobs were unsure about their visa status, and with the backlog at both the Home Office and employment tribunals, there was a lot of uncertainty among workers that brought them to the union for help.

All of this meant progress—and more challenges—for Agwaze and the union. The workers at games companies, and in the broader tech industry, were finally starting to understand themselves not as lucky to have a dream job, but as workers who are producing something of value for companies that rake in profits. After all, as Agwaze noted, "for the one and a half years we've been around now, we've been the fastest-growing branch of the IWGB. We're the fastest-growing sector that they've ever had." The union is a crucial step toward changing power in that industry and claiming more of it for themselves.

CHAPTER 10

IT'S ALL FUN AND GAMES

Sports

MEGHAN DUGGAN DRIVES HARD TO THE FRONT OF THE NET AND HAS A lightning-quick wrist shot; she's often the player who picks up the rebound and sends it home. She's what they call a "power forward," using her strength as well as speed to push through opponents and clear ice space to score, and she uses that same strength defensively. She's a team player, lauded by her coaches for her leadership ability. Teammates and fans call her "Captain America."[1]

The USA Hockey captain has three Olympic medals (one gold, two silver) and several trophy cases' worth of honors in international play, college play, and across two fledgling professional leagues. She's been skating since age three, graduating from pushing a milk crate across the ice to a hockey stick and puck not long after. In her hometown of Danvers, Massachusetts, she explained, youth hockey was a big deal. It was natural that she would follow her older brother into the sport.

At first it barely occurred to her to care that she was the only girl playing with the boys. "I was a wicked tomboy when I was a kid," she said. "I never really thought it was different or weird and my parents supported that, as did my teammates." It was only when she was a little older that she realized that her idols had all been male athletes—specifically when she saw, in 1998, women playing Olympic ice hockey for the first time. Team USA beat Canada for that first gold, and Duggan said, "It was the first time I had seen elite women playing hockey. I didn't even know that they existed." Those women went on a media tour after the Games, and she got to meet Gretchen Ulion, who'd scored the very first goal in that gold-medal game. "I got to put her medal around my neck and take a picture and put her jersey on. That is the moment I would say changed my life. I became committed to the dream of captaining Team USA to a gold medal, really, from that young age."

She's since reconnected with Ulion and taken a new photo that includes her own three medals as well. But there were thousands of hours of ice time to be logged in between those moments. Duggan broke her goal down into smaller goals: she'd have to join a girls' team, and then play college hockey at the Division I level. Competitive girls' hockey was still a rare thing to find; her best chance was to get into and attend a private high school where there were teams to join. She was able to do that thanks to her family's support, and was recruited from there to play collegiate hockey at the University of Wisconsin.

"Even now, when I go speak in schools, the number one thing that student athletes want to hear about is 'How do you juggle it? How do you maintain it all?'" Duggan competed in Division I hockey while working on a biology degree and then wound up joining the national team while still in college, adding to her jam-packed schedule. "It took a little bit of trial and error to figure out how it worked. My freshman year, I struggled a little bit with the balance of intense elite-level Division I athletics, playing for a team that was trying to win a national championship, and new demands of school, and there is no hand-holding in college. I went to a school with forty thousand undergrads, so they don't even care if you show up in class," she laughed. "I always prided myself on being a great student and there is something to be said about balancing your social life to an extent, and having friends and doing things that make you happy outside of hockey and school as well."

Duggan had been invited to her first USA Hockey training camp in December 2006, and she made the national team that next spring. "There had been a few other girls in my position. We had grown up together through prep-school hockey and college hockey. A few of us made the national team for the first time together," she said. "It was my first time playing with the big girls and putting on that US jersey. I can picture what the locker room looked like and the feelings that I felt. To this day, every time I put that jersey on, I always take a moment and take a deep breath. It is a really special thing that you can't take for granted." In sports, she noted, injuries and aging mean that you aren't assured another shot. The only guarantee is that you won't have it forever. But she also takes that moment to appreciate all the work she's put in to get there.

They may not have held her hand at the university, Duggan noted, but there were resources available there that she and the rest of the women's team would miss after graduating. "I played at a Big 10 school that valued its athletics. We won a lot of national championships and they put a lot of resources into us," she said. "But upon graduation you are pretty much thrown to the wolves. The pro leagues that had existed and do exist are nowhere near offering what the collegiate experience was like." Once out of the university, she had to find her own ice time in order to keep in shape, and sometimes practiced at 11:00 at night to fit skating in around a full-time job to pay the bills. The pace was grueling, and there was nothing like the support she'd had from the coaches and trainers that the university paid for. "You are on a bus trip back from Buffalo to Boston at three or four o'clock in the morning. How is your body going to recover from that?"

The women have nothing that compares to the men's National Hockey League (NHL) in terms of resources, audience, and most importantly, pay scale. The Canadian Women's Hockey League (CWHL) didn't begin paying players at all until the 2017–2018 season, its eleventh. And those pay rates would range from just $2,000 to $10,000 (Canadian dollars) for the season. The American National Women's Hockey League (NWHL) had launched in 2015 to much fanfare, announcing that it would pay a decent rate, but those salaries ranged from $10,000 to $25,000, still nothing like the men's league, where even the lowest-paid players make high six figures. Duggan knew going in that it wasn't going to be like the NHL, that it would be a grind. She knew women were still in a fight to be taken seriously as professional athletes, and that carving out an audience for women's pro hockey would take time and more work. She knew what it was like to spend hours each day training, on the ice and off it, in the gym, working to build muscle and speed and endurance. In her senior year, she'd won the college game's highest honor, the Patty Kazmaier Award, granted annually to the top player in the National Collegiate Athletic Association (NCAA). That was 2011. She figured she could make it all work.[2]

But to commit to the game after university required an additional level of effort from the players—it meant Duggan had a commitment to fight for the sport as a whole. It meant doing media appearances (when the teams bothered to promote themselves) and talking to fans no matter how tired she was. It meant finding a job to pay the bills, since pro hockey and USA Hockey didn't do that. For most of her time on the US team, the athletes were paid a meager stipend, not enough to live on and certainly not enough to cover the costs of training, and only in the months leading up to the Olympics. The CWHL didn't pay at all when she started there, and when she joined the NWHL, Duggan, one of the league's highest paid and most marketable stars, made just $22,500 for that first season.

In order to fund her playing career, Duggan found a position coaching hockey at Clarkson University in upstate New York. That was while she was playing for the CWHL's Boston Blades. She would spend all week at her coaching job—finding her own training time—then coach their games on the weekend and drive all night to her own game on Sunday, then drive back the same night in order to be at her desk on Monday. Her wife, also a hockey player (for the USA's archrival Canadian team) supported her through it, as did friends, coworkers, and teammates who understood her commitment. But the travel was exhausting, and in 2018 she left the coaching job in order to focus on training.[3]

Within a decade of graduating from the University of Wisconsin, she'd won a title with her CWHL team, a second Olympic silver (the first came while she was still playing college hockey), three international titles, and then the gold in 2018. By then, she'd made playing her full-time focus, and was part of an ongoing fight for recognition for the sport. In that time, too, participation in women's hockey had grown by 34 percent, with over eighty thousand women and girls playing the game by the 2018–2019 season.[4]

The juggling act was more than exhausting—it was a constant reminder that women's hockey didn't get the respect it deserved, even as Duggan and her teammates proved their commitment and skill time and again. "When I think back to that time now," she said, "I am like, 'Oh my gosh. How did I even do that?'"

⚏

SPORTS, LIKE ART, IS A NEAR UNIVERSAL HUMAN HABIT THAT HAS BEEN commodified and turned into a multibillion-dollar industry. It is also a lens through which we can see what—and who—we value as a society. Sports tell us much about whose bodies and lives we think matter.

We still refer to "playing" a sport, though the earliest organized sports were more likely drawn from training for battle than from play. These roots are obvious for boxing and wrestling, as well as for fencing and the hurling of various objects; they are perhaps less so for gymnastics, but still related to the need for physical fitness for war. Other sports come from means of transportation—boating, ice skating, skiing, and long-distance running. Team sports might date back to China, where the sport called "football" by most of the world and "soccer" in the United States was born perhaps two thousand years ago, though it was formalized in England. The ancient Greeks brought us the Olympics, where athletes competed in javelin and discus, footraces and horse-drawn chariot races, wrestling and more.[5]

Many of the sports we have professionalized had their debut between the eighteenth and twentieth centuries. Cricket dates back a little earlier, as does rugby, modified from a Roman game. Monks invented something like tennis in the eleventh century in France. Native people in the Americas played precursors of lacrosse, ritualized games that had a spiritual purpose as well as physical; the colonizers tried to eradicate the games before co-opting them. Golf was invented in Scotland, where it was banned in 1457, along with soccer, when the Scots needed to defend themselves against English invasion. Field hockey and similar games date back centuries, and the Mi'kmaq people of what is now known as Nova Scotia played something we now recognize as ice hockey. But it was the late nineteenth century when sports began to be codified and shaped into competitive leagues, and when the Olympics were revived and turned into an international athletic competition. According to Mark Perryman, author of *Why the Olympics Aren't Good for Us, and How They Can Be*, the Olympics at that time was "an event for patricians, immersed in the cult of the gentleman-amateur." Those without the means to train, to travel, and to compete without being paid were left out entirely.[6]

Those first modern Olympic Games, in 1896, were held in Athens but founded by a Frenchman. The committee banned women (though one snuck in and ran the marathon anyway), and treated Black athletes as lesser. Countries under the yoke of imperialism competed under the banners of the colonizers. Still, the Games were held with a lofty goal in mind: international cooperation and peace. The Olympic Charter of 1894 included the idea of an "Olympic village," where all the athletes would live alongside one another; the founders hoped that if they could interact peacefully for a couple of weeks, they'd be less likely to go to war later. (Unfortunately, those patrician founders seem to have forgotten who declares wars in the first place, and their aims for world peace spectacularly failed.)[7]

These twin ideas—sports as play, and sports as war—continue to shape our experience of sports to this day. Yet despite their history of entanglement in political wrangling, too many people still have a hard time understanding sports as political, and when athletes remind us that they are so—as Colin Kaepernick did when he took a knee to protest state violence against Black people—they are told to "shut up and play." Sports as what they have become today—a workplace for the players and team staff, and a multibillion-dollar industry that has made a small number of people incredibly rich, and provided a playground for those even richer to exert power—proves even harder to take seriously. After all, it's just a game, right?

Yet sports have been intertwined with global capitalism since those early attempts at professionalization. Despite the gloss of "amateurism," those early Olympics were connected to trade fairs and "commercial exhibitions"; international trade was flourishing, and friendly competition seemed to be another way to make a little money putting on a spectacle. But in the Victorian era, sports were mostly deemed a waste of time and energy that could be better spent working, for men, and looking decorative while laced into a corset, for women. Those who had leisure time at all were supposed to look elsewhere for entertainments, and those who worked physically grueling jobs all day had little energy for sports when they left work (though the shorter hours movement would slowly change that). The sports that the working class did participate in were considered uncouth by those who thought of themselves as their betters— entertainments like cockfighting or dogfighting or bare-knuckled boxing too brutal to bear. But that opinion began to change with the turn of the century, as social reformers decided sports could be a means of uplift for the workers.[8]

Sports, in the minds of the reformers, could teach the working class the value of healthy competition. Such exertions could improve their work ethic, give them a sense of self-discipline, and hone their bodies, the better to work longer. President Theodore Roosevelt, a devotee of all sorts of physical activity himself, argued, "Virile, masterful qualities alone can maintain and defend this very civilization. There is no better way [to develop this] than by encouraging the sports which develop such qualities as courage, resolution, and endurance. No people has ever yet done great and lasting work if its physical type was infirm and weak." Sports made men out of, presumably, boys. So capital turned to funding organizations through which (some) workers could let out their energies in sporting activities, either through external institutions like the YMCA or directly creating teams for their own employees. Professional teams like the Green Bay Packers reflect this history in their names.[9]

As sports became professionalized, there was money and fame for the grabbing for ambitious working-class athletes. It was a risk, of course, but when the alternatives were other forms of back-breaking work, why not see if boxing or football or baseball could buy you a ticket off the assembly line? The ideal of hard work as a path to upward mobility wasn't going to be true if you stayed at your day job; maybe, just maybe, it could pay off if you put that work into mastering a sport instead. Star boxers, such as Jack Johnson, the first Black world heavyweight champion, way back in 1908, or jockeys, like Isaac Murphy, who rode racehorses to fame and fortune in the late 1800s (until Black riders were quietly pushed out of the sport), provided something to aspire to that was beyond a lifetime of drudgery.[10]

The Communist Party's Lester Rodney understood the potential of sports to reach people politically. As sportswriter Dave Zirin wrote, Rodney believed in "covering sports in a way they had never been covered before—with an eye on their social impact." He campaigned for baseball to integrate in the 1930s, covered the famous fight between Joe Louis and Hitler's Aryan hero Max Schmeling, and got union workers engaged in the fight against racism by using sports as a mechanism to explain power and fairness.[11]

Sports spread alongside the growth of the mass media, particularly radio. More people could listen in to a game or a boxing match than could possibly attend it personally; radio, moreover, was a thing that one could listen to at work. World War II was played out on many battlegrounds, but one of them was a propaganda war. Hitler's Germany took advantage of the new technologies to broadcast an image of Aryan superiority to the world. For "Brown Bomber" Joe Louis to knock out a white German champ, for Jesse Owens to win four gold medals at Hitler's very own Berlin Olympics (where the modern torch relay was invented), was to undermine this idea of racial purity and to remind those watching that Black athletes had been held back not by genetics, but by racism. Louis was both an exceptional star and a symbol of the wasted potential of so many others who'd never been given a chance in white supremacist societies. In this way sports both undermines and underlines the notion of individual genius that the artistic narrative has brought us.[12]

The work that celebrity Black athletes had to do, then, was doubled. Like Meghan Duggan, they often felt a responsibility not just to personally be their physical best or to be part of the team, but to carry a message beyond their sport to those who looked up to them. That responsibility fell most heavily on the backs of those who broke barriers, like Jackie Robinson, the first Black man to play Major League Baseball (MLB), who had to endure being spat upon, opponents throwing balls to injure him, and racist slurs shouted from the stands and whispered on the field, and, like any disciplined civil rights activist sitting in at a lunch counter, never show that it got to him. Robinson did twice the work of anyone else on that field and still managed to be one of the best.[13]

While professional sports grew, the United States also was home to a different kind of empire, built on the idea of "amateur" athletics. Like the Olympics, which celebrated amateurism in a way that echoed the values of its wealthy creators—who saw in sports a pastime for the comfortable, rather than a job deserving a wage—college sports would make some people rich while athletes labored unpaid. Following the logic of Teddy Roosevelt and others, the advocates of college sports, and particularly college football, saw sports as a way to toughen up elite students at the country's poshest schools. The first American football game was played in 1869 between Rutgers and Princeton. Other Ivies, including Yale and Harvard, soon took up the tradition. But college football players weren't aiming for a career in sports; even if they had wanted to, there wasn't a professional league at the time that would have allowed them to keep playing. Nor was it the goal of these programs: if you were attending Harvard, you were already pointed in the direction of an elite position.[14]

Of course, someone was making money from college sports right from the start. The first-ever paid college coach, at Harvard, made nearly twice what a (well-compensated) full professor at the university did. But the amateurism—a word derived directly from the Latin verb meaning

"to love"—of the athletes was never questioned, even as the sport sometimes destroyed their bodies. The term "student-athlete" was invented by
the founders of the National Collegiate Athletic Association in the 1950s
in order to deflect claims for workers' compensation—it was first used,
according to historian Taylor Branch, writing in *The Atlantic*, against the
widow of Ray Dennison, a college football player who died of a head injury sustained on the field. "Did his football scholarship make the fatal
collision a 'work-related' accident? Was he a school employee, like his
peers who worked part-time as teaching assistants and bookstore cashiers?
Or was he a fluke victim of extracurricular pursuits?" Branch wrote. In
1957, the Colorado Supreme Court ruled in the school's favor, saying that
Dennison's family was not eligible for benefits, because the college was
"not in the football business." Student-athletes, the court implied, were
playing a game for fun and for self-improvement, a narrative that comes
back to haunt today's players of professional and amateur ball alike.[15]

American football, then, was initially monetized and professionalized through the massive college sports complex, even if players weren't
deemed workers. Other sports, including soccer and hockey, developed
through international competition. The first recorded international soccer
match was between England and Scotland in 1872, and shortly after the
turn of the century the Fédération Internationale de Football Association
(FIFA) was founded, sparring over the right to control international competition with the International Olympic Committee. The first World Cup
was played in Uruguay in 1930. Ice hockey was Canada's national sport,
but the Canadians would play against European teams and learn from one
another, and the game was shaped, too, by the children and grandchildren
of enslaved Black people who had escaped the United States for Canada
and made the game their own. Without the kind of mass media spotlight
of other sports, hockey spread through contact between countries, even
during the Cold War, where it became a sporting battleground between
the Soviet bloc and the United States.[16]

Television brought sports to yet another level: the excitement of listening to a radio broadcast paled beside the ability to have the game in
your living room, to watch from the comfort of your couch. At first, sports

moguls tried to restrict broadcasts in order to keep selling tickets in the stands. But the rapid spread of television sets in the 1950s helped to up-end the pecking order of sports, particularly in the United States, where American football seemed made for TV in a way that other sports weren't. The National Football League became big business in part because of its TV-revenue-sharing model, and individual players could make extra money through sponsorships, commercials, and more.[17]

Most pro athletes, though, weren't getting rich in this period. "A typical athlete in 1967," Zirin noted, "worked in the off-season." Their lives were probably more like Meghan Duggan's than like today's highly paid athletes, as they slowly built an audience for their sport while picking up extra money with additional jobs. Many athletes spent years of their lives, from childhood onward, practicing, getting injured, and giving up other pursuits to put in unpaid hours, only to peak without ever seeing a dollar. Few became household names. It was this reality that drove athletes to unionize.[18]

Before the 1960s, pro athletes were accustomed to believing the story that they were incredibly lucky to get what they got. "This was because they were a workforce basically unschooled in working conditions," Marvin Miller of the MLB players' union told Zirin. "They had all undergone a bunch of brainwashing that being allowed to play Major League Baseball was a great favor. That they were the luckiest people in the world. They were accustomed never to think, 'This stinks. We need to change this.'"[19]

But the ferment of the 1960s gave force to the bargaining power of athletes, many of whom were Black and Latinx and had been politicized by the same forces that drove bus boycotts and lunch-counter sit-ins. The baseball players' union beat the team owners, lawsuits in basketball and baseball won free-agency rights for players that drove up salaries for all, and players won salary minimums for those who wouldn't command top dollar on the free-agent market. Without union solidarity, perhaps some of the superstars would have broken out and won major gains for themselves as individuals, but the sports world would have become even more stratified and lopsided than it currently is. And the players proved, in baseball and football, that they were willing to endure grueling strikes—during which they were painted as greedy man-children wanting to get rich for playing a game—in order to be treated fairly, to get a slice of what were rapidly becoming, in the 1960s and 1970s, mega-profits.[20]

The movements of the 1960s helped athletes and the rest of the world understand the relationship between the people playing the game and the people profiting from it. Whether it be the NCAA (making coaches, the league itself, and even the manufacturers of branded apparel rich, while the players didn't see a dime), or the owners of NFL teams, somebody was exercising power to make money off the efforts of the athletes. And the racialized nature of these relations made it extra clear to the players that the owners were not just kindly old men giving them a chance to escape poverty and get paid to play a game. The 1960s brought us John Carlos and Tommie Smith raising black-gloved fists in the Mexico City Olympics, a proud vision of Black power that drove officials mad. And most importantly, the decade brought us Muhammad Ali.[21]

Ali is perhaps the best argument for the belief that athletes are inherently gifted, carrying natural talent that none of the rest of us could ever hope for. He was simply faster than anyone at his weight class, and when age slowed him down, he turned out to have a near-superhuman ability to take a punch. Yet Ali made history not simply for the beauty of his performance, his graceful brutality, but for his mind and for his appreciation of his own value as a human, and as a Black man. He came to the sport and to public life with an understanding of the world that challenged everyone around him. Ali demanded respect—when opponent Floyd Patterson refused to call him by his chosen name, instead deliberately using Ali's birth name, Cassius Clay, in the press, Ali pulverized him, shouting all the while, "Come on, America! Come on, white America. . . . What's my name? Is my name Clay? What's my name, fool?"[22]

His refusal to go to war in Vietnam, for which he was stripped of his championship titles and sentenced to prison, was polarizing but prescient—Ali spoke up against the war in 1966, well before most Americans, when Johnson was still president and largely popular. He made international news and became a hero of a different kind even as he endured calumny in the United States. His stand took his best boxing years from him, when giving in would have been easy and expected. Ali's fight reminded everyone that athletes—and Black athletes, in particular—were thinking, breathing humans, not simply bodies to be traded around by their wealthy bosses.[23]

The stand of John Carlos and Tommie Smith on that podium is often remarked upon, but we hear less often about the organizing that went on behind the scenes to create that moment. Like Rosa Parks, Carlos and Smith are discussed as if their protest were spontaneous, but it was the result of athletes realizing that their labor power—and potentially the withholding of it—could be a powerful tool. The Olympic Project for Human Rights (OPHR) was formed by amateur Black athletes and at first aimed for a boycott of the 1968 Games. They demanded the removal of the US Olympic Committee's Avery Brundage, the restoration of Ali's title, and the banning of apartheid states South Africa and Rhodesia from the Games. When that campaign was unsuccessful—athletes were reluctant to give up their once-every-four-years chance at glory—they determined to find ways to make their protests heard, from the medal stand if possible. Many athletes spoke out, or wore black clothing, but none had the effect—or received the punishment—of Carlos and Smith, who were kicked out of the Olympic Village and stripped of their medals. "Those people should put all their millions of dollars together and make a factory that builds athlete-robots," Carlos said later. "Athletes are human beings. We have feelings too. How can you ask someone to live in the world, to exist in the world, and not have something to say about injustice?"[24]

Women, too, were agitating for inclusion in sports in the 1960s and 1970s. They had been playing some sports longer than others: although in the Victorian era all sorts of ridiculous theories were peddled about the damage that athletic activity could do to women's supposedly fragile bodies and minds, women still managed to take up some sports, such as bicycling and archery, without fear of their uteruses falling out. Later, industrial leagues for women popped up in the workplace, with women playing softball and basketball on their own teams. Avery Brundage—the same man the Black athletes were protesting in 1968—wanted to push women out of track and field at the Olympics entirely, but he failed.[25]

During World War II, with most able-bodied men overseas fighting, a few moguls got the idea for women's sports to fill in the gap. The All-American Girls Professional Baseball League, which lasted from 1943 to 1954, and was immortalized by the 1992 film *A League of Their Own*, put young working-class women on the diamond to entertain the home front. The women played hard, but were also expected to be feminine off the field—they were sent to charm school, given beauty advice, and admonished to behave and appear as "real All-American girl[s]" at all times. But like most working women, they were sent home not long after the war ended, even though they'd had some nine hundred thousand paying fans in 1948. As the men returned to the game, though, the women's sport declined, and the league disbanded, the women told to do their "real" job: managing their families. Sports, after all, were a man's pursuit. Women who did too much physical activity, moreover, have long faced accusations of being masculine—and worse. Josephine D'Angelo had been cut from the Girls League for her "butch" haircut, and "sex testing," everything from a nude parade to chromosome testing, at the Olympics began in 1968 and continues, in some form, today.[26]

The feminist agitation of the late 1960s and 1970s reached the sports world, often inspired by the activism of Black athletes. Most famously, in 1973 Billie Jean King demolished Bobby Riggs on the tennis court, making him eat his taunts and reminding everyone that women were not, in fact, weaker than men in any sense of the word. But King's fight wasn't over—she also became a union leader, helping to create the Women's Tennis Association that same year, and becoming its first president. She'd already called for a strike at the US Open unless the women's and men's prize packages were made equal—and won.[27]

The United States was forced to pay attention to women's sports with the passage of the Education Amendments Act of 1972, which included the famous Title IX. Title IX reads, "No person in the United States shall, on the basis of sex, be excluded from participation in, be denied the benefits of, or be subjected to discrimination under any education program or activity receiving Federal financial assistance." College sports, under the law, are an educational activity, meaning that women need to have access to sports programs. Anyone who has attended a school with a football program (Tulane, 1998) knows that "equal" is a stretch, but Title IX pushed schools into creating teams for women in such previously unfeminine sports as ice hockey, making Meghan Duggan's career possible, and laying the groundwork for the possibility of professional women's team-sports careers in soccer and basketball, as well as swelling international competition as other countries raced to catch up. Women even played American football in the short-lived National Women's Football League, turning what had been a joke into serious play.[28]

Women athletes crack into so many of our stereotypes of femininity. Women are supposed to diminish themselves in service of others, a trait that applies whether they're paid or unpaid domestic workers, teachers, or interns. Watching women compete in sports, watching them express themselves and want with fervor—How many articles have been written about Serena Williams's grunts on the tennis court, let alone her physicality?—is striking precisely because such expression, such desire, has been proscribed. Sports, like the arts, were presumed to be for men, to be the result of natural categories. Men are stronger, we hear; we have a hard time understanding women like Serena Williams, Meghan Duggan, and Megan Rapinoe. "Elite athletes have spent their entire lives articulating themselves through moving their bodies. To watch them want something is an exercise in watching desire become a visual, physical force," wrote journalist Autumn Whitefield-Madrano about the Women's World Cup, in words that have stuck with me. Women's bodies being used for something so far from what we are told they are for—for bearing and nursing and attracting others—hold power. And women athletes, more than men, are told that sports should be done for love, not money.[29]

As women were making strides in "amateur" sports, though, the very idea of amateurism was coming apart at the seams. It was the 1984 Olympics, Mark Perryman argued, that marked a turning point away from the celebration of athletics for their own sake and toward a high-gloss corporate-sponsored TV extravaganza studded with the most famous—and highest-paid—athletes in the world.[30]

From the NCAA to the Olympics, amateurism has often been a cover for exploitation. Commercial interests have long been part of popular sports. But the neoliberal era's shifts in capitalism and attendant ideological battles meant something new: every part of the game was privatized, branded, and sold as a shiny image, from corporate sponsorship to product placements to multimillion-dollar endorsement deals. And—as I have argued over the course of this book—pitching it to all of us as a new opportunity to find fulfillment on the job has wrought a change in the sports world as well. The 1984 Los Angeles Olympics gave President Ronald Reagan a chance to show off his vision of America—brought to you by McDonald's, the way cleared for it by mass arrests of young Black men in the name of cleaning up the city.[31]

But the dissolution of amateur participation in the Olympics was in fact demanded by athletes themselves. Seeing that other people made money on the games, they argued for their own share; more importantly, they argued that in the off-season, they should be allowed to get paid to play, whether that meant keeping prize money from competitions or getting sponsorships that helped pay the bills. As Meghan Duggan told me, keeping oneself in peak condition is not a thing you can do once every four years. It's a full-time job, and to be the best, they needed to be able to compete. With the demise of the major state-funded athletic programs of the Soviet bloc, privatization was the name of the game, and at least going pro gave the players a way to make a living that didn't require the faux purity of some imagined amateurism.[32]

The neoliberal era's expansion of the sports industry seems to both reflect and be reflected in its political conversations. Pro athletes are sponsored by companies ranging from Wheaties to Nike to Visa; politicians, meanwhile, use sporting metaphors for everything they possibly can. That sports are not, in fact, anything like real life doesn't seem to matter. They still demonstrate to us the values that our society has chosen to uplift. Competition is the lifeblood of capitalism, we are told, and therefore competitive sports are the best place to teach us how to operate in a dog-eat-dog world. Yet, as William Davies noted in *The Happiness Industry*, all this competition leads to depression, in athletes as well as in the broader society—studies found depression higher in participants in intensely competitive sports. Particularly, we might assume, when someone's entire future is riding on an ability to keep playing a sport. Because, of course, when a few can win—and win big, Michael Jordan or David Beckham–style—we have something to aspire to, but when we don't win, we're told it's our own fault.[33]

And who benefits from all this? The sports system as it is, after all, is as unequal as the rest of the world under capitalism. The attention given to athletes' massive salaries often obscures the fact that the team owners are an order of magnitude richer. They are billionaires like Paul Allen of Microsoft, who owned all or part of three professional teams before his death in 2018, or Stanley Kroenke, married to Ann Walton of Walmart fame, who owns the NFL's Los Angeles Rams, the NHL's Colorado Avalanche, the National Basketball Association's Denver Nuggets, the US pro soccer team Colorado Rapids, and the English Premier League's Arsenal team. There are enough of them that an article titled "The 20 Richest Billionaires Who Own Sports Teams, Ranked" can exist and make sense. The United Kingdom's Labour Party focused on this issue leading up to its 2019 election campaign, targeting Mike Ashley, owner of the Newcastle football team, and noting that the Sports Direct mogul had made his money as a low-wage employer, keeping workers in abysmal conditions. "It's a vehicle to support wider conversation about inequality in our country," said Callum Bell, a Labour Party organizer, of the campaign, which, as he put it, drew attention to "this billionaire who doesn't give a crap about this thing that millions of people love, that lack of control over something that we love."[34]

The inequality is fractal, getting bigger as it goes down. While Alex Rodriguez made over $300 million playing baseball, the Steinbrenner family, which owns the New York Yankees, is worth over $3 billion. But a minor league baseball player might make less than $8,000 for a season. And a college baseball player won't be paid at all. A lawsuit from a group of minor leaguers challenged this system, saying their pay rate violated minimum wage and hour standards; in 2019, an appeals court granted them expanded class-action status, but the case drags on. "If they can form a class and win against baseball, that could cause some major changes in how the league operated with regard to its minor leagues," wrote sports reporter Travis Waldron when the case first emerged.[35]

The inequality perhaps reaches its peak when one takes into account Major League Baseball's other farm system: its baseball "academies" in the Dominican Republic. For a fraction of what it costs to pay a minor leaguer or even invest in a youth baseball team in Los Angeles, teams can have their pick of hungry young would-be stars looking for a ticket to fame and fortune. And they don't have to obey the same labor laws that are already obscenely bent in their favor: they can sign young players at the age of sixteen, with less training, and certainly less education in the ways of the world, and those players don't get health-care and other benefits. "When I signed at 16, I didn't know what the fuck I was doing," Boston Red Sox superstar David Ortiz told a reporter, referring to his experience in the academies. It worked out for him, but for every David Ortiz there are hundreds who never get off the island.[36]

Meanwhile, the high-pressure culture also incentivizes players to maximize their earning potential by any means necessary—and that often includes performance-enhancing drugs of various kinds. "As sports have grown into a global Goliath, players have turned their bodies into chemistry sets," Dave Zirin wrote. Yet, as Zirin also noted, the use of steroids to improve strength dates back to 1889, when a French scientist began injecting himself with animal hormones in order to find a way "to increase the strength and mass of workers in the service of the industrial revolution." The owners and sponsors encouraged the steroid era in sports as well, advertising the oversized physiques of their athletes and cheering every Home Run Derby with dollar signs in their eyes, yet blaming the players for doing what seemed to make sense—because, it seemed, if they didn't, someone else would. Steroids then became a way for owners to try to break the MLB players' union, demanding that the players give in to invasive testing regimes that would allow employers to turn a blind eye when it suited them, and dump players "randomly" tested when they wanted to lose a pricey contract or a sudden cold streak.[37]

Steroids aren't the only health risk for athletes, or even the worst. Attention has increased in recent years to the horrific results of repeated head trauma, with research on the issue of chronic traumatic encephalopathy (CTE) highlighting its frequency in football and hockey players. A *New York Times* story on Derek Boogaard, a hockey player known more for fighting than scoring, detailed the personality changes his friends and teammates noticed before his death: "Those who went to New York noticed his memory lapses were growing worse. Boogaard joked about them, saying he had been hit on the head too many times. But they also came to worry about his darkening personality and impulsive behavior. His characteristic sweetness and easy manner, his endearing eagerness to please, had evaporated." Boogaard died of an overdose at twenty-eight, an age that would have been mid-career; the doctor who examined his brain was shocked by the amount of damage. "This is all going bad."[38]

For those who survive, life can just get worse. Lorraine Dixon, the wife of Rickey Dixon, a former NFL player diagnosed with a different neurodegenerative disease, amyotrophic lateral sclerosis (ALS), let reporters into her daily life. Dixon played six seasons in the NFL; the money was gone by the time he got sick, at forty-seven. The $1 billion settlement the NFL agreed to pay out over traumatic brain injuries meant some money for the Dixons, but not even enough for Lorraine to quit her job. So she cared for two children and her husband, who used a wheelchair, around her work schedule—the health insurance from her job was necessary to keep her husband's treatments up. Dixon and other NFL wives had organized on a Facebook group, supporting one another while they waited out the legal battles and the heartbreak of watching their husbands spiral down. "I look at Rickey laying in the hospital bed, [tracheotomy] in his throat, tube in his stomach, has lost 57% of his body weight, can't talk and can barely move and I think about the NFL and I ask Jesus to help me forgive them," Dixon wrote. "Money is truly the Root of all Evil."[39]

Even leaving aside the possibility of such injuries, the sports system has intensified its demands on the bodies of athletes. To reach the top level of a sport, as Meghan Duggan did, one must start as a child. The kind of "human capital" that children are increasingly pressed to build from a young age to turn toward the workplace, as Malcolm Harris wrote in *Kids These Days*, is especially visible in the bodies of young athletes. "Building muscle is a great way of thinking about human capital because it's so literal: work over time accumulates in the body." Such a process turns play into work far earlier than it probably should; children are being honed for future college scholarships and professional dreams before they're old enough to pick a major, drive a car, or sneak a beer.[40]

Yet the language of play and its universal benefits masks the work that young people do in the name of sports, and that runs straight through to the supposed amateurs of the NCAA. The Southeastern Conference, just one of several collegiate leagues, reached the billion-dollar mark in 2010. As Taylor Branch explained, "that money comes from a combination of ticket sales, concession sales, merchandise, licensing fees, and other sources—but the great bulk of it comes from television contracts." Tens of millions watch college sports; the biggest football schools bring in tens of millions of dollars in profits. In forty states, the highest-paid public employee is a public university's football coach. "For all the outrage, the real scandal is not that students are getting illegally paid or recruited, it's that two of the noble principles on which the NCAA justifies its existence—'amateurism' and the 'student-athlete'—are cynical hoaxes, legalistic confections propagated by the universities so they can exploit the skills and fame of young athletes," Branch wrote.[41]

The argument for collegiate sports rests on the idea that sports are part of a well-rounded education. It's the argument made by elite colleges in the nineteenth and early twentieth centuries; it can be found, in a different form, embedded in Title IX—that access to sports should be equal for all as an educational activity. But the reality of top-level sports, Branch wrote (football and basketball, mainly, but also hockey and soccer), is that athletes are expected to put their sport first and their education last. Special courses for athletes and resources to make it look like they're passing classes are a given, and scholarships are usually canceled if an athlete is cut from the team. At some schools, less than half of the student-athletes actually graduate with a degree, according to the league's own numbers. During the trial for a lawsuit filed by an instructor who didn't want to play along with grade inflation, the defense attorney for the university involved in the case, the University of Georgia, argued, referring to a hypothetical student-athlete, "We may not make a university student out of him, but if we can teach him to read and write, maybe he can work at the post office rather than as a garbage man when he gets through with his athletic career." Sounds like a lot of concern for education.[42]

Like graduate-student workers, college athletes make money for their schools, and like those workers, they are trapped in a kind of limbo status between "student" and "employee." That makes them vulnerable to the same kind of status coercion. Particularly for Black athletes, this peculiar status brings with it strange working conditions, at times reminiscent, in the workers' own words, of the plantation. A mix of paternalistic concern and scorn colors the way coaches and administrators talk about and to student athletes, wrote sociologist Erin Hatton. "In particular, they are said to need protection from two sources of possible corruption: their own poor choices and commercial exploitation." And yet coaches also made explicit threats to cut players' scholarships, or bench them—denying them playing time during which a pro scout might see them. One former football player told Hatton that when he played in the All-Star game, "I had a guy that evaluated me mentally as soon as I got there. Then, I walk in . . . , they tell me to strip down to my underwear. . . . I got guys checking body fat percentage on me, guys looking me up and down, [asking] my height, my weight. And, if you think about it, back in the 1800s when they had the slave trade . . . that was the same thing they did when they were auctioning people off."[43]

Lately, though, NCAA players have been challenging this status. Quarterback Kain Colter and a group of his Northwestern University football teammates pressed a case that they should be allowed to form a labor union. The regional director of the National Labor Relations Board ruled in their favor in 2014, based on "the enormous revenue and benefit that result from the efforts of the Northwestern football players and on the rigorous control that Wildcats coaches have over the lives of the scholarship athletes." (Northwestern had taken in $235 million from football between 2003 and 2012.) The NLRB director detailed the extensive control that coaches exerted over the players' lives, from social media restrictions to workout requirements to approval of living arrangements, and concluded that this level of control was the control an employer exerts over an employee, not a teacher over a student. But the full NLRB dismissed the athletes' petition the following year, in a narrow decision that nevertheless upheld the status quo.[44]

Lawsuits against the NCAA have had more success. A 2014 antitrust lawsuit argued that the NCAA "has unlawfully capped player compensation at the value of an athletic scholarship." The attorney in the case, Jeffrey Kessler, told reporters, "In no other business—and college sports is big business—would it ever be suggested that the people who are providing the essential services work for free. Only in big-time college sports is that line drawn." Other lawsuits have been filed and have even resulted in some damages being awarded. The NCAA, seeing the writing on the wall, loosened its rules preventing athletes from making money off their own images (yes, you read that right).[45]

As colleges began to reopen their athletic programs in the summer of 2020, bringing athletes back for practice during the COVID-19 pandemic, those athletes faced yet another disturbing trend: they were asked to sign waivers absolving their university of liability if they caught the virus. "More than 30 athletes at 14 college programs, at the very least," had tested positive in early June, wrote Ross Dellenger at *Sports Illustrated*, and those athletes had been asked to sign documents bearing "virtually the same message: here are the virus risks, here are the precautions the school is taking, here are what precautions you should take and here's why you can't sue us." The documents, Dellenger noted, do say athletes can't lose their scholarships for not signing—but they can't play until they do. It's just another risk those players are being asked to take with their health—again, while they aren't getting paid. This and other issues around the season led to a push, in August 2020, toward unionization. First, hundreds of players from one conference announced that they would not play unless their demands around health, safety, and racial justice were met. Then, players from across the NCAA's conferences joined a Twitter call for unionizing, following in the footsteps of Kain Colter and his teammates at Northwestern.[46]

The women of USA Soccer fought for years to challenge the idea that loving the game means they don't need—or deserve—equal pay. Long dominant on the international scene—thanks to Title IX—the American women had racked up a string of victories. At home, it had been a struggle to make professional play viable; the third professional league, the National Women's Soccer League, launched in 2013, was slowly expanding, but it still didn't pay most of its players a living wage (unless they were subsidized by their national federation). But the women of the national team were household names: Abby Wambach. Ali Krieger. Megan Rapinoe. Crystal Dunn. The US men's team couldn't make it past the World Cup quarterfinals; they failed to qualify entirely in 2018. Meanwhile, the women, when they won the Cup in 2015, pulled a TV audience of twenty million just in their home country. And so they organized, they sued, and they threatened a strike; they called for equal pay and equal conditions (no more playing on Astroturf when the men got fresh grass). They put their fame to use, winning gains in their 2017 bargaining agreement with USA Soccer, and they continued the push as they headed to the 2019 World Cup in France. Once again, they dominated. As Megan Rapinoe, her hair dyed purple, kicked in the first goal of the game, as the clock ticked down on their 2–0 victory, the stadium filled with cheers, and then, slowly, the din settled into one clear chant: "EQUAL PAY."[47]

Unquestionably, though, the biggest challenge to the powers that run the sports world in recent years has been Colin Kaepernick. Inspired by the protests rocking the United States over the deaths of young Black men at the hands of police officers, then San Francisco 49ers quarterback Kaepernick refused to stand for the national anthem at a preseason game in August 2016. He later switched his protest to taking a knee, and other athletes—including Rapinoe—followed his lead. Many were threatened, or benched, but Kaepernick had lit the fuse, and he was punished for it.

He opted out of his contract with the 49ers in 2017, choosing free agency, but no NFL team has signed him since. Kaepernick settled his lawsuit with the league—he'd argued the league had violated the terms of the union contract by colluding not to put him on a team—but still no one hired him, even after Nike signed him up to a massive endorsement deal. Kaepernick, like Muhammad Ali before him, sent a signal to the owners and to the world that they could not control him, and he has used his fame since then to give high-profile donations to social justice organizations and to hold "Know Your Rights" camps for young Black men in cities across the country. But Kaepernick said he wanted to keep playing, and the NFL still refused to let him.[48]

In spring 2020, the eruption of nationwide protests at a scale never before seen, after a Minneapolis police officer killed George Floyd, vindicated Kaepernick. NFL owners and coaches tripped over themselves scrambling to apologize, plastering their social media accounts with "Black Lives Matter" statements. Jim Harbaugh, Kaepernick's coach in San Francisco, said he was proud of the player (though he'd opposed the protest at the time) and called him a "hero," comparing him to Jackie Robinson and Ali. Commissioner Roger Goodell apologized for "not listening" to players, but did not specifically name Kaepernick, a move that director Spike Lee called "piss poor and plain bogus." Goodell said he would "welcome" Kaepernick's return to the game, but continued to say that was up to the teams; the teams professed interest, but none had committed as of September 2020.[49]

Kaepernick's protest laid the groundwork for, in August, an explosion in the world of professional sports. On August 26, the NBA's Milwaukee Bucks announced that they would not play their playoff game, citing the police shooting of Jacob Blake in Kenosha, Wisconsin, and the ongoing white supremacist violence. Their strike spread across the league, swiftly jumping to the WNBA, where the Washington Mystics came out for their game and knelt, backs to the camera, in white T-shirts rent by seven bullet wounds. Naomi Osaka of tennis skipped her semifinal match, and refusals to play halted games in baseball and soccer too. While the strike—reported, falsely, in the press as a "boycott," an indication of just how hard it remains for us to see sports as work—was short-lived, it was a powerful reminder of athletes' platform and ability to force the rest of us to take notice.[50]

Athletes like Kaepernick and Rapinoe have proved that they have a massive platform for discussions of workers' rights: Kaepernick's case against the NFL is at bottom a giant labor grievance. Running back Marshawn Lynch's refusal to perform at press conferences is a job action, work-to-rule, a way of showing up the boss by performing strictly along the lines of your job description and by doing so highlighting the ways in which you are expected to give up more of yourself to your job than that bit for which you're getting paid. These athletes are millionaires, savvy marketers all of them, who have turned their own images into a means not just to make money, but to send a signal to everyone who watches them: you can't silence us. We deserve respect, as humans, as people who will no longer be marginalized, as workers. You don't own us.[51]

⁂

MEGHAN DUGGAN AND HER USA HOCKEY TEAMMATES HAD BEEN talking about their working conditions for a while. During conversations on the bus or around the dinner table while on the road, they'd find common themes, things that didn't feel right to any of them. "When you're a young kid, you have the mentality of 'Keep your head down, keep your mouth shut, and work,'" Duggan said. "As a lot of us evolved in our careers, this was something that we were passionate about and that we devoted our lives to. We were pretty strong powerful women. We started talking about a lot of the different changes that we thought we could make and thought we could see in the program."

It was 2015 when they reached out to a legal team to support them. It was a long process, Duggan said, of researching, learning about their legal rights and what other teams in other sports had been able to do. They decided that what they wanted from USA Hockey was a four-year contract that would cover the Olympic cycle and their other international events, that would provide regular pay, disability insurance, and pregnancy benefits—everything, in other words, that full-time employees could expect at a decent, unionized job. They knew, though, that their power came from standing together, and that at some point they might have to refuse to work in order to make their point. "We knew that it could eventually get to the point where we would have to boycott a world championship," Duggan said. "That is our Stanley Cup, that is our end-all-be-all, that is what we train for all year long in a non-Olympic year."[52]

Over a year went by with no progress in their negotiations, though, and so they made their move. They announced publicly that without a contract, they would refuse to play in the 2017 International Ice Hockey Federation (IIHF) Women's World Championship. They were supported in their declaration by Carli Lloyd and other women's soccer stars, as well as by the men's hockey legend Mike Eruzione and others. The NWHL players promised not to play on a replacement team, refusing to undermine the players' solidarity. "I am just so proud of our team," Duggan said. "We were dead serious. We were willing to risk everything for it."

It was a moment for feminism—the Women's March had just gone off in January, marking what was likely the single largest demonstration to that point in US history, and it was followed by a Women's Strike on March 8, International Women's Day. The women's soccer team had been making demands for equal pay. And the hockey women made themselves part of it—making more news with their threatened strike than if the championships had gone off without a hitch, since, as they noted in their demands, the women's game was often very badly publicized. Their demands also included expanded programming for women's hockey. They were fighting, Duggan said, for the bigger picture, for all of the women who would come up after them. "I can't even tell you how many phone calls I made, but it felt like I called every single female hockey player in the entire country," she said. Her message, in asking them not to cross a picket line if it came to a work stoppage, was, "This is about all of us and this is what it means. I don't know what you're hearing or what you're reading, but from the horse's mouth, this is what's happening, this is what we're trying to change, and we are asking you to stand with us." The excitement those players might have felt at being called up to play in a championship, she said, couldn't be underestimated, yet USA Hockey was unable to pull together a replacement team to break the players' potential strike.[53]

The players got their contract. It included the maternity protections that Duggan has now availed herself of, as she gave birth to her and her wife's first child on February 29, 2020. It also included travel and insurance provisions that equal the men's national team and a $2,000-a-month stipend year-round for training. They got a pool of prize money to be split each year and bonuses for winning medals—which they promptly did. They also won a Women's High Performance Advisory Group within USA Hockey, to work to grow the women's game, modeled after a similar group within Canadian women's hockey. The argument Duggan had made to the younger women she called had been proved right: they had made gains for everyone who would come after them.[54]

But the women weren't done. They won the world championships when the boycott was called off, and they topped that off the next year with Olympic gold to go with Duggan's two silvers, beating Canada. The NHL started featuring some of the women stars at its All-Star game. Off the ice, though, the US and Canadian women were overcoming their rivalry to start planning something bigger. They wanted an international women's professional league with real money behind it. And they'd realized from their successful organizing that the way to get to one was to bring players together. Girls' hockey was growing—aided by their successful fight, certainly—and the women wanted something better than the barebones leagues they were playing in.[55]

The stakes grew higher when the CWHL abruptly shut down in the spring of 2019, leaving many players without work. And so the women went public with their new organization: the Professional Women's Hockey Players Association (PWHPA). "It is basically a movement of a lot of passionate players to try to create a better future for the sport, just like we have been trying to do all along," Duggan said. The PWHPA's statement said, "This is the moment we've been waiting for—our moment to come together and say we deserve more. It's time for a long-term viable professional league that will showcase the greatest product of women's professional hockey in the world." With 173 dues-paying members from the United States, Canada, and Europe, the association aimed to build a more sustainable base for the sport, and to press those interested in it to take action. Billie Jean King was one of their advisers.[56]

With the PWHPA, they once again decided to withhold their labor— this time from any existing professional league, which in this case meant the NWHL. Instead, they put together a tour; picked up sponsors, including Budweiser and Dunkin' Donuts; and traveled, playing games and scrimmages and holding community events to drum up support. Duggan, who was pregnant over the winter of 2019–2020, wasn't playing, but she remained deeply involved. "The tour games have been awesome, the support from fans and people who are invested," she said. "I'm not going to lie: it is still a grind. We are still not where we need to be. There is no woman in the PWHPA that is being paid anything this year to play professional women's hockey. In my opinion, things had to get worse before they get better." In perhaps their biggest victory, the NHL featured members of the PWHPA in a three-on-three exhibition game on All-Star Weekend in 2020. "I think to be on that stage was so special. With an All-Star Weekend you might introduce people that haven't really watched a lot of hockey before to the women's game, as well. I'm definitely thankful to the NHL for giving us that platform and that opportunity to continue to be visible and certainly hope for more growth and opportunity in those areas in the future," she said.

The PWHPA had to postpone part of its planned tour when the coronavirus outbreak began. First, three games in Japan, scheduled for late February against the Japanese national team, were canceled, and then more of the tour was canceled as well. However, the association announced plans to keep going into 2020–2021, basing players in "hub cities" where they could train, practice in front of audiences, and have dedicated support staff. Despite the pandemic, corporate sponsors for the association had indicated continued support. And despite the cancellation of the world championships for the year, players continued to train.[57]

When her former elementary school gym teacher came down with the virus, Duggan stepped up and recorded workout videos for the students. "I wanted to do everything that I could," she told reporters. "For whatever reason, I remember just as a middle schooler and elementary school kid, just connecting with her. She was someone who I looked up to athletically, because she was such a great athlete and I was an aspiring athlete at that age. She and others in my community have supported my Olympic journey, for really the last 20 years of my life."[58]

"It is a great time to be a female athlete right now. There is a lot of power and a lot of energy," Duggan said. That power and energy, despite the myriad roadblocks, kept her going off the ice. Memories, too, of the breakthroughs on the ice reminded her of the commitment she'd made to the sport. She recalled as particularly powerful the moment when the US team won the world championship, right after the threatened boycott. The massive, sold-out crowd on home ice in Michigan included, of course, the bosses they'd just been battling. "We were energized by everything we had been through prior to that. I remember Hilary Knight scored the game-winning goal in overtime and the way we celebrated and rejoiced with each other was extra-special that time," she said. "'See! We told you we were worth something!'"

CONCLUSION

WHAT IS LOVE?

> We want to call work what is work so that eventually
> we might rediscover what is love.
>
> —Silvia Federici[1]

WHAT WOULD YOU DO WITH YOUR TIME IF YOU DIDN'T HAVE TO WORK?
I love asking people this question. Sitting on a hill in Columbus,
Ohio, in 2012, I learned that a woman I knew as a political organizer
actually trained to be a dancer. When I went to Indianapolis and asked
the workers from the Carrier and Rexnord plants what they'd do if money
wasn't an object, one said he'd like to be a fishing guide. Another wanted
more time to spend with his family, thought maybe he'd start a small
business with his sons. But they always circled back around to the reality:
money *was* an issue. They *did* need to work. To spend too much time
thinking about what they'd do if the world was otherwise just seemed to
underscore the reality rather than provide an escape from it. Work was not
a choice.

Work has not brought us liberation, freedom, or even much joy. There are occasional pleasures to be had on the job, certainly—as a writer, I take pride in a well-turned sentence, and as a reporter, I thrill to a good interview. Even as a restaurant server I enjoyed the occasional chat with a regular customer. I am not arguing that we should strive to be miserable at work—quite the contrary, we should take any opportunity for happiness, pleasure, and connection that we get. I do believe, however, that our desire for happiness at work is one that has been constructed for us, and the world that constructed that desire is falling apart around us. As it does so, we suddenly have space to think about a different world, and what we might want once it is here.[2]

The workers you have met over the course of this book have all fought, in one way or another, to have their work recognized and valued *as work*. For them, it has mattered to be seen and understood as doing something not purely out of selfless (or for that matter selfish) love. They were not amateurs, hobbyists, or members of a "family." They might have chosen a field that required years of training and sacrifice, or they might have just filled out an application on a whim, but they all understood somewhere along the line that their choices were not limitless, that they could not just expect to be paid for whatever they wanted to do, that even within their labors of love, they were making money for someone else, and they were doing it to get by.

The labor-of-love myth is cracking under its own weight. For every worker that I included in this book, for every occupation, there were twenty or thirty more that I couldn't fit. Every conversation I had while in the process of writing seemed to involve someone suggesting an example that would belong in these pages. I spoke with actors, hairdressers, bartenders, therapists, social workers, museum staffers, lawyers, nurses, political organizers, elected officials, and other journalists who immediately offered up stories from their own lives that could have gone in this book.

The myth is cracking because work itself no longer works. It no longer pays what it used to: wages have stagnated for most working people since Reagan and Thatcher's time. The professions are suffering cutbacks, and a college degree no longer gets you a guaranteed middle-class job. The 2008 financial crisis shifted the neoliberal era into what sociologist Will Davies dubbed "punitive neoliberalism," with increasing punishments heaped on those who would not comply even as compliance became, under austerity, ever harder. Prisons are growing, social services shrinking, jobs that are halfway decent barely exist. The pandemic exposed the failures of the American health-care system and the brutality of "essential" work for those who had no choice but to keep going to their jobs despite the heightened danger. Those whom journalist Paul Mason famously called the "graduates with no future" are everywhere, and they are angry. Teachers across the United States began a strike wave in 2012 that shows no signs of stopping, with at least sixteen states having seen educators walk off the job demanding better conditions, and the pandemic only lending new urgency to their organizing. Art museum staffers and journalists have passed around collectively written Google documents comparing salaries and have used that information in their union drives. And protests have filled the streets from Greece to Chile to France to the United States, repeatedly demanding an end to the austerity measures that have heightened the crisis of work and broader social changes. Feminist rebellions challenge patriarchy on the job and in the home. Massive global uprisings followed the police killings of Breonna Taylor and George Floyd, pulling down and setting alight monuments to white supremacy and challenging the state's monopoly on violence. The promises made to a generation of hope laborers are being revealed for the lies they are.[3]

We cannot simply go back to a time before neoliberalism: the return to the Fordist bargain and to the factory is not a thing that anyone should be wishing for, even if it were possible to turn back the clock. That model of capitalism destroyed the planet in order to provide benefits for a relative few, and neoliberalism simply sped up the process. Capitalist hegemony is collapsing before our eyes. The positive ideals of freedom, choice, and fulfilling work are increasingly unsellable to a public that can see now the realities behind those pipe dreams. The exposure of capitalism's cruelty makes the command to love our jobs a brutal joke. We are, to steal a term from the feminist movement of the 1960s, having our consciousness raised. Capitalist realism has had a thousand growing cracks put in it since the 2008 financial crisis, and at any moment now it could shatter entirely.[4]

And all this breakdown is happening in a moment of deep ecological crisis. As Alyssa Battistoni, a fellow at Harvard's Center for the Environment, wrote, "to put it bluntly, we're confronted with the fact that human activity has transformed the entire planet in ways that are now threatening the way we inhabit it —some of us far more than others." We cannot, Battistoni pointed out, move forward "without tackling environmentalism's old stumbling blocks: consumption and jobs." Public-sector cutbacks increase private consumption, she wrote—personal cars rather than trains, private yards rather than public parks, bottled water if the tap water is bad—and our culture of work itself contributes to the problem. A 2019 report from UK think tank Autonomy posed the question, "Rather than discussing how to maximize economic performance (all too often a code for forcing the vast majority of the population to work long hours to the benefit of capital owners), the climate crisis forces us to change the conversation and raise the question: provided current levels of carbon intensity of our economies and current levels of productivity, how much work can we afford?" Massive reductions in working time are not only desirable, as work is increasingly miserable—they are necessary.[5]

THESE DAYS, FREE TIME IS A LUXURY THAT FEW CAN AFFORD. WE HAVE both done away with and strangely re-created the society of the ancient Greeks, where many of us are so busy with work that actually being informed members of society feels impossible, and political and social engagement are indulgences for the wealthy. We have turned into work the things that we might have done for pleasure, and then made even that relatively pleasant work accessible to only a few.

The Greeks built a democracy around the idea that work would be done by someone else, whether slaves, *banausoi*, or the laboring classes, who were denied rights to participate in the activities that constituted citizenship. Citizens' work was *praxis*, what Guy Standing described as "work done for its own sake, to strengthen personal relationships." It was the work of what we call social reproduction, of the creation of a public communal life. They valued this work but also differentiated it from true leisure time, which they valued for its own sake. Free time was necessary, as was learning and caring, in order to participate fully in society.[6]

We've been thinking about whether machines could do the work, a sort of automated laboring class, at least since George Orwell found his way to Wigan Pier, or perhaps since Marx's "Fragment on Machines." Could automation, rather than taking away working-class livelihood and identity, free us to do something else entirely? We hear "robots are coming for our jobs" as a threat, but in fact it could be a way to create more free time for all. It will depend on who creates, designs, and owns the robots, or the algorithms. But the obsession with technology misses the point: we are not locked in some John Henry–style competition, man vs. steam engine, to prove who is superior. Rather, we are all locked into a system of production in which we must work in order to survive, even as production needs fewer actual human hands than ever.[7]

Work does not love us back: that much we can, I hope, agree upon. A society where we must work the majority of our waking hours will never deliver us happiness, even if we are the lucky few who have jobs in which we do gain some joy. As Silvia Federici wrote, "nothing so effectively stifles our lives as the transformation into work of the activities and relations that satisfy our desires."[8]

Capitalist society has transformed work into love, and love, conversely, into work. Capital, Selma James wrote, takes "who we could be and limits us to who we are. It takes our time, which happens to be our life." But we are beginning to change our minds about our priorities, whether capital likes it or not. Surveys find more people rating "working hours are short, lots of free time" as a characteristic of a desirable job over time, while their desire for "important" work went down. This was true among the highly educated as well as the less educated, though the perception of each might differ—as Ray Malone (from Chapter 1) pointed out, a mother on Universal Credit wanting to take more time with her child would be stigmatized as lazy, while a well-off mother leaving a high-powered job to do so just wants "work-life balance" (though she might, too, face criticism for failing to "Lean In").[9]

But a side effect of all this love for work has been that talking about love between people has lost its importance. To talk of love is to risk being seen as unserious, particularly if you are a woman. Instead, our personal relationships are to be squeezed in around the edges, fitted into busy schedules, or sacrificed entirely to the demands of the workplace. Working-class women, in particular, are choosing to remain single even to raise children, finding that men's job-market problems make them poor bets for long-term partners. That this is a horrible calculation to have to make seems not to bother the powerful. (And too many people still assume that interpersonal relationships only matter if they are heterosexual couplings, leaving out a vast spectrum of ways that people form caring relationships.) The shreds of the neoliberal work ethic have turned our hearts into appointment books; the rhetoric of the factory, as cultural critic Laura Kipnis wrote in her polemic *Against Love*, has become "the default language of love." Love, for the working class in particular, is a complicated affair.[10]

It's not just romantic relationships that have suffered under neoliberalism. Friendship, too, is a casualty of the way our working lives are organized. A 2014 study found that one in ten people in the United Kingdom did not have a close friend; in a 2019 poll in the United States, one in five of the millennials surveyed reported being friendless. These studies reflected, a reporter noted, "long-term rising trends in loneliness." The extended lockdown period of the coronavirus pandemic only exacerbated feelings of isolation that so many already had. We might have Facebook friends, but do we have real ones? People have tried to blame the Internet for our collective loneliness, but in fact it comes alongside the change in our working lives, the decline of unions and other institutions that gave people a sense of shared purpose and direction beyond just the job. When I asked the union activists at the Rexnord plant what they'd miss when it closed down, they all mentioned their friends and the union. Not the work itself.[11]

The movement of young people into political organizations—the Democratic Socialists of America, perhaps, or the Labour Party or other new left formations—represents not just a political awakening but a desire for that connection and purpose. We spend so much time at work; there are dating apps to streamline the process of finding a mate (at least for a night). Yet for so many of us, the couple form and the job wind up bearing the weight of all of our hopes and dreams and needs for human contact, and they were never meant to bear that weight. We need human relationships that extend beyond the romantic or the transactional.[12]

Love as a concept has a long and complicated political history. It is, as Samhita Mukhopadhyay, executive editor at *Teen Vogue*, reminded us, "more than just a chemical or emotional feeling; it is a social and cultural force." It was also understood for a long time to be the opposite of work. Love was for the home, for the family, for the couple; the workplace was where you earned what you needed to sustain that love. Love was also presumed to be more important for women than for men; the home was women's sphere, the workplace men's.[13]

In reality those lines were always blurred; plenty of women always worked, for one thing, even from the very beginnings of industrial capitalism, and plenty of bosses wanted to extend their control into the home. Antonio Gramsci noted that "the new type of man demanded by the rationalisation of production and work cannot be developed until the sexual instinct has been suitably regulated and until it too has been rationalised." Industrialists, he argued, were constantly struggling to regulate the "animality" in humans, to bring the things that made us other than robots under stricter control, and that included introducing discipline into one's off-work romantic relationships. Henry Ford famously sent investigators into the homes of his workers to make sure they were upstanding, straight, and monogamous, and therefore deserving of higher wages.[14]

As the workplace has changed, our ideas about love have also changed. The feminist revolution known as the second wave notably demanded access to career-track work for women, seeing it not only as a path to financial independence, but to something more interesting to do with one's day than clean the house and feed the children. And love, as sociologist Andrew Cherlin has documented, has undergone a

transformation from married monogamy to something more open, flexible, and often, of course, not heterosexual at all. Yet the way we talk
about partnership—even the word "partner," increasingly popular as a
gender-neutral term, but also one oddly reminiscent of the workplace,
the boardroom, the law firm—still reflects the origins of the family as a
complementary institution to the job. When our relationships fall apart,
we still blame ourselves, rather than looking to all the social, institutional
pressures that made it nearly impossible to continue them. Love is still
just another form of alienated labor.[15]

⁛

WHAT IF IT WERE OTHERWISE?

It is, as Selma James wrote, a miracle that under patriarchy men and
women manage to tolerate each other at all, let alone live together and love
one another. Despite all of the roadblocks thrown up by the way we live
our lives today, we still try, and that is itself a beautiful thing. What if, as
James suggested, we tried to make a world that served that impulse rather
than profit? How, as Kathi Weeks asked, might we understand our obligations to those we love "outside of the currency of work"?[16]

The greatest pleasures of my life, the most meaningful memories, remain those of the times spent with people I love—commiserating about
breakups over a meal; laughing and crying together; dancing till our knees
and hips hurt and we no longer care how silly we look; sprawled on a
couch at four o'clock in the morning casually touching one another's skin
as we catch up on the past month's little victories and heartbreaks. When
political tragedy came, I curled up in someone's arms; when victories
happened, we cheered and cried some spare happy tears and I hugged a
woman I didn't even like that much (nor she me), because in that moment
what we had done was bigger than us.

When my father died and I was in a state of robotic shock, it was people who knew what that pain felt like who reached out to me and told me
that what I was feeling was all right, that it was more important than work
(and I was blessed with editors and the team at Type Media Center who
understood, too, that some things mean work stops). And it was a series of

small kindnesses I have tried to pay forward in the time since, when other friends lost loved ones.

I wrote much of this book recovering from that loss and then in what seemed to be a pattern of cracking further pieces off: heartbreak seemed to become a habit that I had gotten into, something I was getting good at. I learned to like how I looked with dark circles under my eyes, and who could tell if they were caused by lack of sleep due to love or to work? Could I?

Heartbreak felt like its own kind of exuberance. I was gloriously wasting time, losing sleep, not working. Taking time to grieve luxuriously is a pleasure I allowed myself too rarely and in fragments; mostly, I tried to work, but when I let the emotions take over, listened to the rattling in my chest, allowed the feelings to stop me from doing what I was doing, briefly, I felt alive again. In the vacantness of grief I placed more pain because I could not find pleasure.

And in the finishing of this book I am trying to settle a bet with myself, it seems. Trying to love things more than my work even as I stare down a deadline and imagine the published version in my hands. I dream of someone reading these words and feeling cracked open themselves. I dream of reaching past the walls that our careers put up between us and everyone else. I dream of connection. I write in order to connect, to drop breadcrumbs on a path that I hope brings us somewhere better. I write this conclusion and I think of the first person to whom I'll send it.

Work will never love us back. But other people will.

CONCURRENT POLITICAL AND ECOLOGICAL CRISES CAN SEEM OVERwhelming, impossible, but they have also done something else for us: they have created the possibility of imagining ourselves in a different world. If it was previously easier to imagine the end of the world than the end of capitalism, we have now glimpsed both, and must now begin to think up something new.

And the ways of relating to one another that bring us joy can also be key to creating the necessary change. Nadia Idle of the podcast *#ACFM* (the AC standing for Acid Communism or Acid Corbynism) said on an episode about urbanism, "I don't want to 'catch up for a coffee' with anyone anymore. . . . I'm not interested in this minute city neoliberal forced way of interacting with other people in some kind of transaction where you catch up with people you've not seen for like eight weeks because everything's so expensive and you don't have any time." What we need instead, she argued, was a way of living where we have space and time "to be able to relate to each other as human beings, which of course has revolutionary potential, which is why it's dangerous." Slowing down the rate of our connections, rather than collecting people like they're business cards or stamps, and making those connections deeper and more meaningful, luxuriating in them, is itself a step toward liberation.[17]

Instead of turning our desires to the objects we can buy with the proceeds from our endless work, what if we turned our desires back onto one another? Instead of, as Kipnis wrote, "routing desire into consumption," spending time with other people has potential to disrupt the entire economic system. The process of organizing, on the job and off it, is, after all, a process of connection. The first hesitant hello, the chat in the break room, the careful email from a non-work email address, are all ways of bridging the artificially created gaps between us to articulate a common interest, to gesture toward the power we can have together. A union is only meaningful if the workers in it believe and act like a union, if they are willing to take risks to have one another's backs, if they believe in the oldest of labor maxims: "An injury to one is an injury to all."[18]

We might still create beautiful things together in a world beyond work, as William Morris argued, but as gifts, presents, adornments that we took pleasure in the making of as well as the use and display of— things to be kept and treasured rather than tossed with the season. If we lingered over our human connections, we might find out what we have in common rather than what keeps us divided.[19]

I think of the freed Black women, formerly enslaved, that Tera Hunter described in *To 'Joy My Freedom*, "playfully constructing new identities that overturned notions of racial inferiority." Those women, though they worked and worked hard, also demanded space to make their freedom meaningful. "Black women were determined to make freedom mean the opportunity to find pleasure and relaxation with friends, family, and neighbors," Hunter wrote. They balanced the need to make a living against "needs for emotional sustenance, personal growth, and collective cultural expressions."[20]

Those cultural expressions—dance and song, pretty clothes—were ways to express something that had been brutally repressed for so long. And while they can be, and are, also work in this society, they meant something more, and still do, when they break through the dreariness of our routines. It is true that there is no outside to capitalism, but it is also true that there are moments in our lives where we can see, briefly, beyond it. Our desires, as Mark Fisher wrote, are still mostly nameless. "Our desire is for the future—for an escape from the impasses of the flatlands of capital's endless repetitions—and it comes from the future—from the very future in which new perceptions, desires, cognitions are once again possible." Those desires can be terrifying when everything about our current lives says they cannot be fulfilled. But they are also the ground from which we can grow something new.[21]

To reclaim that sense of exuberance, that space in which to find the connections that matter, we need something more than slight improvements in our individual workplaces or even massive overhauls of labor laws, though we need both of those things desperately. But beyond that, we need a politics of time. A political understanding that our lives are *ours* to do with what we will.[22]

Society will always make demands of us, and a world that we built to value the relationships we have with others would perhaps make even more of them. But it would be a world where we shouldered those burdens equitably, distributed the work—pleasant and less so—better, and had much, much more leisure time to spend as we like. It would be a world where taking care of one another was not a responsibility sloughed off on one part of the population or one gender, and it would be a world where we had plenty of time to take care of ourselves.[23]

In a capitalist society, the things we create are never really ours, neither to keep nor to share. Artists are the image society gives us of freedom, but capitalism has made art into a luxury that few can afford. The little bits of us, art critic Ben Davis noted, that manage to find expression, "our creative lives, like our love lives, bear the burden of representing the good part of our existence, of standing in for the richness of an unalienated world we lack; without the prospect of companionship or of creative fulfillment there's just the unending abyss of working for someone else in return for being able to survive another day to do it again." But with all that pulling on those bits they so easily tear. Our creativity, like our love, is not truly free.[24]

Creation, play, love: all these are human desires, perhaps even human needs, that have been enclosed, commodified, sold back to us. While we have to do our jobs for a living, it makes sense to make demands for better conditions; but alongside those demands we should always be making demands to reclaim our time. What would we be able to create without the constraints of making a living? As Marx wrote so long ago (and not that long ago at all), "The realm of freedom really begins only where labor determined by necessity and external expediency ends."[25]

Part of the joy is the risk.

This is what being alive is. It's your heart pounding in your chest because of a text, the up-and-down swing that you get from connection and then loneliness. The work itself only matters as a way to connect. All of the labors of love, stripped of the capitalist impulse to make money, fame, and power, are really at bottom attempts to connect to other people. They are attempts to be bigger and better than our lonely little selves—even the most solitary artist's creations are in a way a request to be seen, to be known. Stripped of the need to fight to survive, how much more connection could we create? How much more could we try to know each other?

ONE OF THE THINGS THAT THE MANY SOCIAL MOVEMENTS OF THE PAST decade or so have in common is a reclamation of public space in which to be with other people: the occupied squares of Spain and Greece; the occupied universities of the British student movement; Occupy Wall Street; Tahrir Square in Egypt; the protests of 2020, exuberantly reclaiming public space after months of lockdown to shout "Black lives matter!"

Those spaces were spaces of debate and of action, yes, but they were also spaces of care. The "food" and "comfort" committees at Occupy made sure not just that people's basic needs were met but that they felt good in the space. There was singing and dancing, a library for borrowing books, visiting lecturers to share their knowledge. Protest movements, Barbara Ehrenreich wrote in *Dancing in the Streets*, keep reinventing the spirit of carnival, of festivals of collective joy, and of overturning, for a while, the existing society's power relations: "The media often deride the carnival spirit of such protests, as if it were a self-indulgent distraction from the serious political point," she wrote. "But seasoned organizers know that gratification cannot be deferred until after 'the revolution.'"[26]

In the wake of Occupy, many turned toward electoral politics, getting "serious" about change. Yet even in the midst of that seriousness, the utopian space reappeared. The teachers' strikes that rippled across the United States after 2012 created anew the spaces of connection. In West Virginia, the teachers flooded together to the capitol, brandishing home-made signs and wearing matching red. The picket lines in Los Angeles and Chicago featured dance routines and new songs. University lecturers in Britain on strike create "the university we all want to exist: 'rampant collegiality, teaching on topics of importance with no bureaucratic overhead, staff-student solidarity, our children tagging along.'" The strike itself is a means of *reclaiming time from work*, a way to demonstrate the workers' importance by refusing labor and halting business as usual, but also a way to stake one's claim to one's time and one's creations. In the midst of the strike, utopia is briefly visible. And the mass strike, as Rosa Luxemburg wrote, has the potential to turn the world upside down.[27]

The protesters in 2020 brought masks and hand sanitizer, little acts of harm reduction for activists in a pandemic. They sang and danced and reclaimed zones free of police in Seattle and Minneapolis, where they organized to take care of one another, giving out food and medical supplies and allowing one another to relax in places where no one would stop them and demand to know what they were doing there. The Seattle protesters evoked the spirit of the Paris Commune, or indeed, of the Seattle General Strike of 1919, where the working classes ran the city in their own interest;

they built, in one protester's words, "a discussion space; a café space called 'the decolonial café.' A community garden, informational tents, and informational sessions with free literature, nightly film screenings and a band stand with nightly performances from different bands." In a protest during a respiratory pandemic, when the rallying cry had been another Black man's plea of "I can't breathe," the protests cleared space in which Black people could exhale. The protesters calling for the abolition of police and prisons, organizer Mariame Kaba wrote, "have a vision of a different society, built on cooperation instead of individualism, on mutual aid instead of self-preservation."[28]

These moments and spaces are insufficient, perhaps, to completely overhaul the system. Yet as Fisher wrote, the alternative visions that we create in these spaces "are not only 'political' in the narrow sense—they are also emotional." Fisher envisioned a politics that he called "Acid Communism," not because psychedelics, either, are going to make political change, but as a way of returning to the social liberation politics of the 1960s. They can help us create a politics of pleasure, of desire, of joy, of "a new humanity, a new seeing, a new thinking, a new loving: this is the promise of acid communism."[29]

Fisher wanted to meld the artistic critique and the social critique: to create a world of plenty (the "communism" part) for all. In the age of climate crisis it may seem impossible to imagine anything other than scarcity, but in the streets around the world the youth climate strikers have been showing us another way. They gather with their tight-knit teenage friends, drawing our memories to that time in our lives where we'd just begun to create our own little wolfpack of people outside our nuclear families, our gangs, whom we trusted with our scariest whispered secrets, and they turn their fears into ringing chants that shame the adults who have created this broken society. The student strikers know that another world is possible because they are creating it already. They are making it real every time they take back their time, every time they refuse to do the hope labor expected of them because the world that they are supposed to grow up into has failed them utterly.[30]

Imagining love alone as capable of change is idealism, it's true. I cherish a tote bag gifted to me by the Art + Feminism organization that reads, "We need love but we also need a fucking game plan." Or, in Angela Davis's more eloquent words, "Love alone is impotent, yet without it, no revolutionary process could ever be truly authentic." Solidarity is a process of love, blended with power and directed, as my colleague and dearest of friends Melissa Gira Grant and I once argued. The utopian spaces we create in our protests and our strikes may be temporary; solidarity doesn't mean you have to like every person you're fighting alongside. But in those moments where you stand shoulder to shoulder, you do love one another.[31]

Freeing love from work, then, is key to the struggle to remake the world. And people are already reclaiming spaces to experiment with what it means to love one another without the demands of capitalist work patterns. As Silvia Federici said, recalling Plato, "if only you could have an army of lovers, that army would be invincible." Love, she argued, is a power that takes us beyond ourselves. "It's the great anti-individuality, it's the great communizer." Capitalism must control our affections, our sexuality, our bodies in order to keep us separated from one another. The greatest trick it has been able to pull is to convince us that work is our greatest love.

IT IS VALENTINE'S DAY MORNING AND THE SUN IS SHINING THROUGH THE windows in this borrowed London apartment where I have come to finish this book, because the people I love most in the world are here, and they have helped me put the pieces of myself back together again. And because if there is one thing worth doing with our brief, flickering lives on this dying planet, it is loving other people, attempting to understand them across a space of difference that will always contain mystery no matter how well you think you know someone.

What I believe, and want you to believe, too, is that love is too big and beautiful and grand and messy and *human* a thing to be wasted on a temporary fact of life like work.

ACKNOWLEDGMENTS

JOURNALISM IS A PROCESS OF SYNTHESIS; I LEARN FROM EVERYONE I SPEAK with, and the things they say change how I think. This book is the product of thousands of conversations, thousands of pages of reading, and countless passing interactions. But it is first and foremost a product of the conversations I had with ten people: Ray Malone, Adela Seally, Rosa Jimenez, Ann Marie Reinhart, Ashley Brink, Kate O'Shea, Camille Marcoux, Katherine Wilson, Kevin Agwaze, and Meghan Duggan. Thanks to them, and many, many working people like them, for fighting to bring a little justice to the process of working.

Thanks to Katy O'Donnell, gem among editors and among friends. All writers should be so lucky to have their work in the hands of someone as sharp, generous, and insightful as Katy has been. She handled every crisis with grace and patience, and has made me a much better and more careful writer and thinker. If you thought this book was any good at all it's because Katy believed in it.

To Lydia Wills for shepherding this book towards its existence and to Sarah Burnes for stepping in: thank you for your encouragement and all your efforts on my behalf.

Laura Feuillebois, who's worked with me on basically every story I've reported and now two books: you are a wonder, and thanks for every word you've transcribed.

Everyone at Bold Type Books who worked on this project: Jocelynn Pedro, Jaime Leifer, Lindsay Fradkoff, Brynn Warriner, Clive Priddle, Miguel Cervantes, and Pete Garceau. (Also Kristina Fazzolaro, I miss you!)

And everyone at the Type Media Center: Taya Kitman, it is so good to get to do this work with you in my corner. Thanks to Roz Hunter, Annelise Whitley, Kristine Bruch, and the whole crew. Thanks to the Lannan Foundation and everyone there who's supported my ability to be a cranky labor reporter for half a decade now.

Evan Malmgren for a wonderfully precise fact-check. Truly, blessed are the fact-checkers, they will always save you from yourself.

The person who ran the @javelinarunning Twitter account for the laughs that got me across the finish line. Everyone who sent me cat and dog photos and silly memes on Twitter and Facebook when I asked for them: you don't know, actually, how much that cheered me up!

To the people who generously made connections for me, suggested books I should read, or sat down for long conversations only a fraction of which made it into print: Rebecca Burns, longtime comrade, made a key chapter's key conversation happen; Gemma Clarke made very generous introductions; Lena Solow, thank you for all the super-smart chats about retail and nonprofits, your influence is everywhere in those chapters; Amy Schiller, for all your insights on philanthropy and women's work and also for the jokes and the Beyonceder; Kate Bahn for sharing your dissertation and so many thoughts about teachers and caring workers; Eleni Schirmer for advice on teachers, recommended reading, and a perfect description of hegemony; Laura Sivert for art history recommendations, without which I would have been at a total loss; OK Fox for introductions and both OK and Lucia Love for long conversations about art and for your podcast, which has taught me so much about the art world; Marijam Didžgalvytė and Jamie Woodcock for all the video games; Amy Schur for advice and introductions in Los Angeles on some rainy picket lines; Andrea Dehlendorf for years of connections on Walmart and now Toys "R" Us; Chenjerai Kumanyika for suggestions on cultural workers and conspiring over cocktails; Matt Dineen for introducing me to Kate O'Shea—and Kate O'Shea, I've thanked you once but thank you again for the artists' tour of Ireland; Barb Jacobson for invaluable introductions and all the chats about UBI and so much more; Mary Ann Clawson, for leading me to Raymond Williams; Bill Mazza; Gabe Winant, Max Fraser, and Erik Loomis for book recommendations and patience with my amateur labor history when they are professionals.

To all the editors who assigned me pieces that helped lay groundwork for this book—Julia Rubin; Paula Finn and Steve Fraser at New Labor Forum; Lizzy Ratner, Chris Shays, and the whole crew at *The Nation*; Chris Lehmann and Katie McDonagh at the *New Republic*; David Dayen at *The American Prospect*; Tana Ganeva, who all the way back at AlterNet encouraged me in my weirdness; Natasha Lewis and everyone at *Dissent*; the good people of *The Progressive*, past and present; Richard Kim; Bob Moser; Matt Seaton; James Downie at the *Washington Post*; John Guida and Parul Sehgal at the *New York Times*; Maya Schenwar, Alana Price, and everyone at *Truthout*; David O'Neill at Bookforum; Alissa Quart and David Wallis at the Economic Hardship Reporting Project; Jessica Stites; Karin Kamp; Allegra Kirkland, everyone who's ever published me.

To endless inspirations, Eileen Boris, Angela Davis, Selma James, Silvia Federici, Frances Fox Piven, Arlie Russell Hochschild, Barbara Ehrenreich, Ruth Wilson Gilmore, Premilla Nadasen, and particularly Kathi Weeks for having been Kathi Weeks and her early interest in my work on this, a project I am incredibly grateful to share with such comrades. And Mark Fisher, whose work gave me a framework for thinking through the roots of this book and its conclusion: you are missed.

Dan Clawson, thanks for believing in me. I miss you and wish I could have handed you this book.

I just wrapped up this book with a call to spend more time caring about people and less about work and yet I am incredibly lucky to have comrades who are also friends, who shift from analyzing the conjuncture to crying together over heartbreak. I don't have space here to write what all of you mean to me, but thank you: Joe Guinan, Miya Tokumitsu, Tressie McMillan Cottom, Todd Wolfson for all the plotting, Victor Pickard, Nantina Vgontzas, Adam Kotsko for endless non-watercooler watercooler chats, Patrick Blanchfield for so much co-working, Abby Kluchin, Sean Collins, Connor Lewis, Ronan Burtenshaw, George Ciccariello-Maher, Viktoria Zerda, Sophie Lewis, Esther Kaplan, Edna Bonhomme, Dave Zirin, Jeremy Scahill, Matt Browner Hamlin, Astra Taylor, Joanne McNeil,

Susie Cagle, Sarah Nicole Prickett, Kali Handelman for an introduction and a lovely new friendship, Ajay Chaudhary, Isham Christie, Tobita Chow, David Stein, Greg Basta, Maurice BP-Weeks, Nelini Stamp for all the rebellions, Mary Clinton for that and also the hockey, Gregg Levine, Kate Aronoff, Alyssa Battistoni, Daniel Denvir, Thea Riofrancos, Travis Waldron, Ben Tarnoff, Moira Weigel, Laura Hanna, Matt Bors, Tanna Tucker, Shenid Bhayroo, Zack Lerner, Mike Konczal, Kendra Salois, Charlotte Shane, Zoé Samudzi, Michelle Chen for YEARS of podcastage, Lauren Kelley, Sarah Seltzer, Julianne Escobedo Shepherd, Kristen Gwynne, Mindy Isser, Kevin Prosen for always being an education, Meredith Clark for getting me into soccer, Samantha Corbin for a conversation in Ohio, Rory Fanning, Joshua Clover for a word on fascism, Arielle Cohen and Nooshin Sadeghsamimi for surviving lockdown with me and helping me finally learn to cook, Brenda Coughlin for being the power behind so many thrones, Matt Renner for starting the GSC with me, Raj Patel for reading an early chapter so closely and for encouragement that frankly makes me blush, Anne Rumberger, John McDonald, Molly Crabapple for sending me down a path of trying to think through art and for the letters, Sarah Feld for being the best reader and understanding all my weirdness.

To Laura Clawson, Samhita Mukhopadhyay, Angelica Sgouros, and Carinne Luck, for grieving alongside me.

To Terry Cramer and Rusti Poulette, for helping me keep it together.

To London, for loving me back. And all of the people here who've opened their arms and brilliant minds to me. Mona Nathan, for a place to hide and finish this book. Claire English, Adam Elliott-Cooper, Mathew Lawrence, Kyle Lewis, Callum Cant, Philip Proudfoot, John Merrick, Miriam Brett, Josh Gabert-Doyon, George Eaton, Jen Johnson, Dalia Gebrial, Archie Woodrow, Gary McQuiggin, James Butler, Michael Walker, Ash Sarkar, Clare Hymer, K. Biswas, Grace Blakeley, Barnaby Raine, Amelia Horgan, Adrienne Buller, Kulsoom Jafri, Duncan Thomas, Oonagh Ryder for a chat on abolition when I really needed it, Isaac Hopkins and Charlie Owen-Caw for putting me up and letting me obsess over your cat, Miranda Hall for talking about care and space, Nathalie Olah for reminding me that book-writing is crazy-making and it's not just me, Dalila Mujagic and the magpies.

Stephen Lerner and Marilyn Sneiderman, for opening your hearts and home to me and making me part of the family.

To Laura Flanders, I don't believe in bosses but you were the exception that proves the rule. Endlessly grateful that I got to work with and learn from you.

My sister, Amanda; my brother-in-law, John Vick; and once again, to Agnes Mae Vick: we're trying, kid, to keep this world around until you're big enough to fix it. Luckily you have wonderful parents who are there for you and for me while we both try to grow up.

Jessie Kindig for the witches, Sarah McCarry for a spell and a spread, and both of you for helping pick up the pieces of me at some of the worst moments of my life. To Nicole Aro for reminding me when I was falling apart that this is what friends are *for*. To Holly Wood for long socially distanced lockdown walks that helped me keep it together. To Sasha Josette: you know how I feel.

To Will Stronge for making me feel seen and known in a moment when I didn't know myself.

Brett Scott, whose fingerprints are on this book in surprising places.

Craig Gent for a correspondence that helped me not only survive lockdown but learn how to think better about loneliness, friendship, and other forms of connection.

To Cortney Harding, for over a decade now of a friendship that revolves around all of the best things in life: rock 'n' roll, good food, good politics, and always, always knowing I can rely on you.

To Julian Siravo for picking up the phone when I have a wild idea and you're the only one I can discuss it with, for the wombat communism, for talking me down from a ledge or two, and for always hugging me when I need it.

To Anna Lekas Miller and Salem Rezek for providing me the thing that has felt most like home in the past few years, and extra special thanks to Anna for ten years of camaraderie and cat jokes.

Ethan Earle: thank you for being there with wise and lovely words, the right poems, songs, and hippo videos, and a thing I don't quite have a word for, but maybe you can tell me how to say it in French.

Joana Ramiro, who talks to me pretty much every day about matters of the head and heart and the intersection of the two, who is here when work and love get me down, thank you for spending so much time thinking through the way we move in the world together.

Kieron Gillen, through the fun and games and deadly serious times, you have been there when I needed you, even with an ocean between us most of that time.

To Dania Rajendra, the root of our friendship might be that we've both gone through a similar kind of hell, but having you to help me through it has been everything and I wish I could go back in time to reciprocate.

Michael Whitney, last time I said "there are no words," and there still really aren't, but I'm going to try: you're my entire goddamn heart.

To my mother—I'm far away and it is hard but I am still who I am because of you. And my father, who I miss every single day.

Melissa Gira Grant and Peter Frase: this entire book grew from having the two of you in my life. I began to think through this topic with Melissa, in long emails and longer conversations over wine and cocktails, figuring out how to carve out space for the work we wanted to do in a world that too often doesn't consider that real work. And I clarified it (and so much else besides) with Peter, learning by arguing and challenging, and it's still your opinion I want first to check myself. I love both of you so much.

And to everyone in the streets, fighting for a better world: thank you for every risk you take and the love you bring forth.

NOTES

PREFACE TO THE PAPERBACK EDITION

1. According to University of California researchers, "When broken down by occupation, the researchers found that cooks had the highest risk of death from Covid-19 from March 2020 through October 2020, followed by packaging and filling machine operators and tenders and agricultural workers." Daily Briefing, "The Jobs Most At-Risk of Covid-19 Death, Charted," Advisory.com, February 10, 2021, www.advisory.com/en/daily-briefing/2021/02/10/covid-jobs.

2. Sarah Jaffe, "The Fight for $15 Confronts the 'Labor Shortage' Narrative," *The American Prospect*, May 19, 2021, https://prospect.org/labor/fight-for-15-confronts-the-labor-shortage-narrative.

3. Anthony Klotz, "The Covid Vaccine Means a Return to Work. And a Wave of Resignations." NBC News, May 30, 2021, www.nbcnews.com/think/opinion/covid-vaccine-means-return-work-wave-resignations-ncna1269018; Jessica Dickler, "'Great Resignation' Gains Steam as Return-to-Work Plans Take Effect," CNBC, June 29, 2021, www.cnbc.com/2021/06/29/more-people-plan-to-quit-as-return-to-work-plans-go-into-effect-.html; Ruchika Tulshyan, "Return to Office? Some Women of Color Aren't Ready," *The New York Times*, June 23, 2021, www.nytimes.com/2021/06/23/us/return-to-office-anxiety.html; Richard Partington, "UK Employers Struggle with Worst Labour Shortage Since 1997," *The Guardian*, July 8, 2021, www.theguardian.com/business/2021/jul/08/uk-employers-struggle-with-worst-labour-shortage-since-1997; Ross Lydall, "Londoners Are Flooding Back to Parks . . . but Not the Office," *Evening Standard*, June 22, 2021, www.standard.co.uk/news/london/londoners-flooding-back-royal-parks-not-office-b941925.html.

4. Elsie Chen, "These Chinese Millennials Are 'Chilling,' and Beijing Isn't Happy," *The New York Times*, July 3, 2021, www.nytimes.com/2021/07/03/world/asia/china-slackers-tangping.html.

5. "Four-Day Week 'an Overwhelming Success' in Iceland," BBC News, July 7, 2021, www.bbc.co.uk/news/business-57724779; Carl Shoben, "Public Support for Four Day Working Week Trial," Survation, June 22, 2021, www.survation.com/public-support-for-four-day-working-week-trial; Daniel Nettle, Elliott Johnson, Matthew Johnson, and Rebecca Saxe, "Why Has the COVID-19 Pandemic Increased Support

for Universal Basic Income?" *Humanities and Social Sciences Communications* 8, March 17, 2021, www.nature.com/articles/s41599-021-00760-7; Julia Horowitz, "Job Guarantees and Free Money: 'Utopian' Ideas Tested in Europe as the Pandemic Gives Governments a New aRole," CNN Business, November 23, 2020, https://edition.cnn.com/2020/11/23/economy/universal-basic-income-europe-pandemic/index.html; Will Hayward, "Plan Set Out for 5,000 People to Take Part in Universal Basic Income Trial in Wales," WalesOnline, June 9, 2021, www.walesonline.co.uk/news/wales-news/universal-basic-income-wales-ubi-20769221.

6. Sarah Jaffe and C.M Lewis, "Nurses Are Striking Across the Country Over Patient Safety," *The Nation*, May 6, 2021, www.thenation.com/article/activism/nursing-strike-massachusetts-covid.

INTRODUCTION: WELCOME TO THE WORKING WEEK

1. According to the United States Census, Current Population Survey, Annual Social and Economic Supplement, the median income for female workers aged thirty-five to forty-four with a master's degree in 2018 was $65,076. See www.census.gov/data/tables/time-series/demo/income-poverty/cps-pinc/pinc-03.html#par_textimage_54.

2. Derek Thompson, "Workism Is Making Americans Miserable," *The Atlantic*, February 24, 2019, www.theatlantic.com/ideas/archive/2019/02/religion-workism-making-americans-miserable/583441; Editorial Staff, "Do You Check Your Email After Work Hours? New Study Says Simply Thinking About It Could Be Harmful," BioSpace, August 13, 2018, www.biospace.com/article/do-you-check-your-email-after-work-hours-new-study-says-simply-thinking-about-it-could-be-harmful.

3. Thomas Piketty, *Capital in the Twenty-First Century* (reprint, Cambridge, MA: Belknap Press of Harvard University Press, 2017 [2014]), loc. 1930–1933, 2,806, 2807, 2809, 2811, Kindle; Guy Standing, *The Precariat* (London: Bloomsbury Academic, 2011), loc. 416, 421–423, 2806–2811, Kindle.

4. Vindu Goel, "Dissecting Marissa Mayer's $900,000-a-Week Yahoo Paycheck," *New York Times*, June 3, 2017, www.nytimes.com/2017/06/03/technology/yahoo-marissa-mayer-compensation.html; Sarah Leonard, "She Can't Sleep No More," *Jacobin*, December 27, 2012, https://jacobinmag.com/2012/12/she-cant-sleep-no-more; Dan Hancox, "Why We Are All Losing Sleep," *New Statesman*, November 6, 2019, www.newstatesman.com/24-7-jonathan-crary-somerset-house-losing-sleep-review. "Idleness and abundant leisure were once markers of the aristocracy," wrote Judy Wacjman. "Today a busy, frenetic existence in which both work and leisure are crowded with multiple activities denotes high status." Judy Wacjman, *Pressed for Time: The Acceleration of Life in Digital Capitalism* (Chicago: University of Chicago Press, 2014), 61. See also Ross Perlin, *Intern Nation: How to Earn Nothing and Learn Little in the Brave New Economy* (New York: Verso, 2011), 49.

5. William Morris, *Signs of Change: The Aims of Art*, Marxists Internet Archive, taken from 1896 Longmans, Green, and Co. edition, originally prepared by David Price for Project Gutenberg, www.marxists.org/archive/morris/works/1888/signs/chapters/chapter5.htm; Karl Marx and Friedrich Engels, *The Communist Manifesto* (1848), loc. 107–108, 111, 122–125, Kindle.

6. Antonio Gramsci, *Selections from the Prison Notebooks* (New York: International Publishers, 2012 [1971]), loc. 8082–8091, Kindle.

7. Ruth Milkman, *Farewell to the Factory: Auto Workers in the Late Twentieth Century* (Berkeley: University of California Press, 1997), 23.

8. Wacjman, *Pressed for Time*, 63–65; James Meadway, personal communication with author.

9. Emily Guendelsberger, *On the Clock: What Low-Wage Work Did to Me and How It Drives America Insane* (New York: Little, Brown, 2019). See also Eric Spitznagel, "Inside the Hellish Workday of an Amazon Warehouse Employee," *New York Post*, July 13, 2019, https://nypost.com/2019/07/13/inside-the-hellish-workday-of-an-amazon-warehouse-employee.

10. Michelle Chen, "6 Years After the Rana Plaza Collapse, Are Garment Workers Any Safer?," *The Nation*, July 15, 2019, www.thenation.com/article/rana-plaza-unions-world; Harrison Jacobs, "Inside 'iPhone City,' the Massive Chinese Factory Town Where Half of the World's iPhones Are Produced," *Business Insider*, May 7, 2018, www.businessinsider.com/apple-iphone-factory-foxconn-china-photos-tour-2018-5; Bertrand Gruss and Natalija Novta, "The Decline in Manufacturing Jobs: Not Necessarily a Cause for Concern," *IMFBlog*, April 9, 2018, https://blogs.imf.org/2018/04/09/the-decline-in-manufacturing-jobs-not-necessarily-a-cause-for-concern.

11. George Orwell, *The Road to Wigan Pier* (London: Penguin, 2001), loc. 320–323, 342–350, 551–553, 576–582, Kindle; Milkman, *Farewell to the Factory*, 11–12; Sarah Jaffe and Michelle Chen, "The GM Strike and the Future of the UAW," *Dissent*, November 8, 2019, www.dissentmagazine.org/online_articles/the-gm-strike-and-the-future-of-the-uaw.

12. Tamara Draut, *Sleeping Giant: How the New Working Class Will Transform America* (New York: Doubleday, 2016), 44.

13. Mark Fisher, *K-punk: The Collected and Unpublished Writings of Mark Fisher*, ed. Darren Ambrose (London: Repeater Books, 2018), loc. 7683, Kindle; Asad Haider, "Class Cancelled," August 17, 2020, https://asadhaider.substack.com/p/class-cancelled; Adam Kotsko, *Neoliberalism's Demons: On the Political Theology of Late Capital* (Stanford: Stanford University Press, 2018), loc. 230, Kindle. See also Mike Konczal, *Freedom from the Market: America's Fight to Liberate Itself from the Grip of the Invisible Hand* (New York: New Press, 2020).

14. David Harvey, *A Brief History of Neoliberalism* (Oxford: Oxford University Press, 2007), 1–2; Standing, *Precariat*, loc. 128; Philip Mirowski, *Never Let a Serious Crisis Go to Waste: How Neoliberalism Survived the Financial Meltdown* (New York: Verso, 2013), 23–24, 40, 56–57; Kotsko, *Neoliberalism's Demons*, loc. 741, 127, 132–133.

15. Fisher, *K-punk*, loc. 6984, 12617; Harvey, *Brief History*, 7–8, 14–15; Joshua Clover, *Riot. Strike. Riot.* (New York: Verso, 2019), loc. 1652–1654, Kindle; Mirowski, *Never Let a Serious Crisis*, 57. Orlando Letelier, "The 'Chicago Boys' in Chile: Economic Freedom's Awful Toll," The Nation, August 1976, www.thenation.com/article/archive/the-chicago-boys-in-chile-economic-freedoms-awful-toll. See also Naomi Klein, *The Shock Doctrine: The Rise of Disaster Capitalism* (New York: Metropolitan Books, 2010).

16. Harvey, *Brief History*, 23, 61; Fisher, *K-punk*, loc. 9308; Mirowski, *Never Let a Serious Crisis*, 130.

17. Fisher, *K-punk*, loc. 7548.

18. Harvey, *Brief History*, 25; Tim Barker, "Other People's Blood," *n+1*, Spring 2019, https://nplusonemag.com/issue-34/reviews/other-peoples-blood-2; Fisher, *K-punk*, loc. 7100; Clover, *Riot. Strike. Riot.*, loc. 1708–1710, 1861–1877, 2033–2036.

19. Nick O'Donovan, "From Knowledge Economy to Automation Anxiety: A Growth Regime in Crisis?," *New Political Economy* 25, no. 2 (2020): 248–266, https://doi.org.10.1080/13563467.2019.1590326.

20. Mirowski, *Never Let a Serious Crisis*, 63; Kotsko, *Neoliberalism's Demons*, loc. 170, 649, 707, 710; Harvey, *Brief History*, 5; Adam Kotsko, *The Prince of This World* (Stanford: Stanford University Press, 2016), 199–200; Fisher, *K-punk*, loc. 7674, 11308, 12574; Melinda Cooper, *Family Values: Between Neoliberalism and the New Social Conservatism* (Brooklyn, NY: Zone Books, 2019), loc. 2684–2687, Kindle.

21. Kotsko, *Neoliberalism's Demons*, loc. 71, 1823, 1831; Mirowski, *Never Let a Serious Crisis*, 110; Standing, *The Precariat*, loc. 995, 1001. See also Mark Fisher, *Capitalist Realism: Is There No Alternative?* (London: Zer0 Books, 2009).

22. Margaret Thatcher, Interview for *Women's Own*, 1987, Margaret Thatcher Foundation, www.margaretthatcher.org/document/106689; Eileen Boris and Rhacel Salazar Parreñas, "Introduction," in *Intimate Labors: Cultures, Technologies, and the Politics of Care*, ed. Eileen Boris and Rhacel Salazar Parreñas (Stanford: Stanford University Press, 2010), 9; Rene Almeling, "Selling Genes, Selling Gender," in Boris and Parreñas, *Intimate Labors*, 60; Fisher, *Capitalist Realism*, 33; Kristen Ghodsee, *Why Women Have Better Sex Under Socialism* (New York: Bold Type Books, 2018), 3; Laura Briggs, "Foreign and Domestic," in Boris and Parreñas, *Intimate Labors*, 49. In Japan, Guy Standing wrote, the company-as-family "was taken to its limit. . . . The company became a fictitious family so that the employment relationship became 'kintractship,' in which the employer 'adopted' the employee and in return expected something close to a gift relationship of subservience, filial duty and decades of intensified labour." Standing, *The Precariat*, loc. 512. UsTwo Games, "About Us," company website, www.ustwo.com/about-us; Harvey, *Brief History*, 53; Kathi Weeks, "Down with Love: Feminist Critique and the New Ideologies of Work," *Verso Blog*, February 13, 2018, www.versobooks.com/blogs/3614-down-with-love-feminist-critique-and-the-new-ideologies-of-work.

23. Weeks, "Down with Love"; Fisher, *K-punk*, loc. 8907; Kotsko, *Neoliberalism's Demons*, loc. 2622.

24. Fisher, *K-punk*, loc. 8222; Kotsko, *Neoliberalism's Demons*, loc. 1891; Sarah Jaffe, "The Post-Pandemic Future of Work," *New Republic*, May 1, 2020, https://newrepublic.com/article/157504/post-pandemic-future-work.

25. Fisher, *K-punk*, loc. 12661.

26. David Harvey, "Reading Capital with David Harvey," Episode 5, podcast audio, 2019, https://open.spotify.com/episode/6TFZkkswzQGAVcfizfWiJy?si=h42pT1HUSZuWEsykk9qfKA.

27. Selma James, *Sex, Race, and Class: The Perspective of Winning* (Oakland, CA: PM Press, 2012), 96; Tithi Bhattacharya, "How Not to Skip Class: Social Reproduction

of Labor and the Global Working Class," in *Social Reproduction Theory: Remapping Class, Recentering Oppression*, ed. Tithi Bhattacharya (London: Pluto Press, 2017), 70; Kathi Weeks, *The Problem with Work: Feminism, Marxism, Antiwork Politics, and Postwork Imaginaries* (Durham, NC: Duke University Press, 2011), 8.

28. Gramsci, *Selections*, 5083, 8338. Gramsci's concept of hegemony, education scholar Eleni Schirmer explains, is "the struggle to arrange the pieces of the world—the ideas and the images and the language and the culture and the politics and the music and the sexual norms." Eleni Schirmer, "Hello, We Are from Wisconsin, and We Are Your Future,'" *Boston Review*, April 7, 2020, http://bostonreview.net/politics /eleni-schirmer-wisconsin-primaries-scott-walker-act-10.

29. Harvey, *Brief History*, 39; Fisher, *K-punk*, loc. 8610–8617.

30. Max Weber, *The Protestant Ethic and the Spirit of Capitalism* (New York: Simon and Schuster Digital, 2013), loc. 690, 794–795, 891, 1891–1894, 2160, Kindle. The work ethic was built upon what Melinda Cooper called "an austere philosophy of desire." Cooper, *Family Values*, loc. 797–801; Weeks, *The Problem with Work*, 45.

31. Luc Boltanski and Eve Chiapello, *The New Spirit of Capitalism* (New York: Verso, 2018), loc. 1307–1313, 1403–1404, Kindle.

32. Boltanski and Chiapello, *New Spirit of Capitalism*, loc. 1453–1453, 1562–1564; Nancy Fraser, "Crisis of Care? On the Social-Reproductive Contradictions of Contemporary Capitalism," in Bhattacharya, *Social Reproduction Theory*, 25.

33. Weeks, *The Problem with Work*, 46–49, 59–60; Ronnie Schreiber, "Henry Ford Paid His Workers $5 a Day So They Wouldn't Quit, Not So They Could Afford Model Ts," The Truth About Cars, October 13, 2014, www.thetruthaboutcars.com/2014/10 /henry-ford-paid-workers-5-day-wouldnt-quit-afford-model-ts; Fraser, "Crisis of Care," 25; Boltanski and Chiapello, *New Spirit of Capitalism*, loc. 1339–1342.

34. Fraser, "Crisis of Care," 25; Boltanski and Chiapello, *New Spirit of Capitalism*, loc. 1376–1378, 2223–2225, 2344–2346, 2393–2395, 2484–2487, 2568–2569, 2660–2662, 2745–2748; Weeks, "Down with Love."

35. Boltanski and Chiapello, *New Spirit of Capitalism*, 2705–2708, 1809–1813, 1813–1815, 1824–1828; Ruth Wilson Gilmore, *Golden Gulag: Prisons, Surplus, Crisis, and Opposition in Globalizing California*, American Crossroads Book 21 (Berkeley: University of California Press, 2007); Ruth Wilson Gilmore, "What Is to Be Done," *American Quarterly* 63, no. 2 (June 2011): 245–265.

36. Harvey, *Brief History*, 41; Fisher, K-punk, loc. 2468, 7120; Boltanski and Chiapello, *New Spirit of Capitalism*, loc. 4037–4041, 4065–4068, 4112–4112.

37. Boltanski and Chiapello, *New Spirit of Capitalism*, loc. 4552–4552, 4376–4387, 2722–2724; Fisher, *K-punk*, loc. 12756–12764, 12944, 12959.

38. Weeks, "Down with Love"; Boltanski and Chiapello, *New Spirit of Capitalism*, loc. 3553–3556, 3889–3891, 3954–3959; Fraser, "Crisis of Care," 25–26; Weeks, *The Problem with Work*, 107–110.

39. Boltanski and Chiapello, *New Spirit of Capitalism*, loc. 4404–4406, 6201–6205, 2728–2730, 3434–3436; Fisher, *K-punk*, loc. 7676, 7122, 10690, 12750, 12959.

40. Silvia Federici, *Revolution at Point Zero: Housework, Reproduction, and Feminist Struggle* (Oakland, CA: PM Press, 2012), 2.

41. "Employment Projections," US Department of Labor, Bureau of Labor Statistics, Table 1.4: Occupations with the Most Job Growth, 2018 and Projected 2028, www.bls.gov/emp/tables/occupations-most-job-growth.htm.

42. Weeks, *The Problem with Work*, 76; Standing, *The Precariat*, loc. 3363–3366.

43. Chuckie Denison from Lordstown said that at work, decisions made by the bosses seemed to have less to do with producing good cars, and more to do with controlling the workforce. "Management did not like to see you smiling or having a good time. They would rather see you miserable and not producing than happy and producing." Sarah Jaffe, "The Road Not Taken," *New Republic*, June 24, 2019, https://newrepublic.com/article/154129/general-motors-plant-closed-lordstown-ohio-road-not-taken; Weeks, *The Problem with Work*, 20–23, 97; Gramsci, *Prison Notebooks*, loc. 7457, 7774–7843.

44. E. P. Thompson, *The Making of the English Working Class* (New York: Open Road Media, 2016), loc. 85–90, 624, Kindle.

45. The editors of *Notes from Below* describe class composition as "a material relation with three parts: the first is the organisation of labour-power into a working class (technical composition); the second is the organisation of the working class into a class society (social composition); the third is the self-organisation of the working class into a force for class struggle (political composition)." Jamie Woodcock, *Marx at the Arcade: Controllers, Consoles, and Class Struggle* (Chicago: Haymarket, 2019), loc. 979–983, Kindle. See also Notes from Below, "About," https://notesfrombelow.org/about; Weeks, *The Problem with Work*, 94; Marina Vishmidt, "Permanent Reproductive Crisis: An Interview with Silvia Federici," *Mute*, March 7 2013, www.metamute.org/editorial/articles/permanent-reproductive-crisis-interview-silvia-federici; Fisher, *K-punk*, loc. 8888.

46. Draut, *Sleeping Giant*, 5. If we, as Joshua Clover invites us to, expand our lens beyond the workforce, we can see the proletariat in its original sense, "those who are 'without reserves,' who are nothing, have nothing to lose but their chains, and cannot liberate themselves without destroying the whole social order," which includes those no longer useful to capital or those who labor, unwaged, in the home, doing the original labors of love. Clover, *Riot. Strike. Riot.*, loc. 2026–2031.

47. Draut, *Sleeping Giant*, 120, 155; Weeks, *The Problem with Work*, 62; Gabriel Winant, "The New Working Class," *Dissent*, June 27, 2017, www.dissentmagazine.org/online_articles/new-working-class-precarity-race-gender-democrats; Lois Weiner, *The Future of Our Schools: Teachers Unions and Social Justice* (Chicago: Haymarket Books, 2012), 137.

48. "The existence of exploitation always assumes some form of coercion," Boltanski and Chiapello wrote. "But whereas in pre-capitalist societies exploitation is invariably direct, in capitalism it passes through a series of detours that mask it." Boltanski and Chiapello, *New Spirit of Capitalism*, 7251–7255. Daisuke Wakabayashi, "Google, in Rare Stumble, Posts 23% Decline in Profit," *New York Times*, October 18, 2019, www.nytimes.com/2019/10/28/technology/google-alphabet-earnings.html.

CHAPTER 1: NUCLEAR FALLOUT

1. Tom Kelly and Harriet Crawford, "Terror of Farage Children as Mob Storms Pub Lunch: Leader Brands Anti-Ukip Protesters as 'Scum' After His Family Are Forced

to Flee Activists and Breastfeed Militants," *Daily Mail*, March 22, 2015, www.dailymail
.co.uk/news/article-3006560/Nigel-Farage-brands-anti-Ukip-protesters-scum-invaded
-pub-having-family-lunch-leaving-children-terrified.html.

2. "Single Parents: Claimant Commitment Under Universal Credit," Turn2Us,
www.turn2us.org.uk/Your-Situation/Bringing-up-a-child/Single-parents-and-Universal
-Credit.

3. bell hooks, *Communion: The Female Search for Love* (New York: William Morrow,
2002), xiii–xviii.

4. Stephanie Coontz, *The Way We Never Were: American Families and the Nostalgia
Trap* (reprint, New York: Basic Books, 2016); Michèle Barrett and Mary McIntosh, The
Anti-Social Family (New York: Verso, 2014), loc. 35–37, Kindle. French philosopher
Alain Badiou suggested, "Essentially, if you play with the word 'state' you could define
the family as the state of love." Alain Badiou with Nicolas Truong, *In Praise of Love* (Lon-
don: Serpent's Tail, 2012), 54; Angela Y. Davis, "JoAnn Little: The Dialectics of Rape," in
The Angela Y. Davis Reader, ed. Joy James (Hoboken, NJ: Blackwell, 1998), 158. See also
Raj Patel and Jason W. Moore, *A History of the World in Seven Cheap Things: A Guide to
Capitalism, Nature, and the Future of the Planet* (Berkeley: University of California Press,
2018).

5. Kathi Weeks, *The Problem with Work: Feminism, Marxism, Antiwork Politics, and
Postwork Imaginaries* (Durham, NC: Duke University Press, 2011), 63; Melinda Cooper,
Family Values: Between Neoliberalism and the New Social Conservatism (Brooklyn, NY:
Zone Books, 2019), loc. 29–30, Kindle; Friedrich Engels, *The Origin of the Family, Pri-
vate Property, and the State* (Kindle Edition, 2011 [1884]), 4. See also Selma James, *Sex,
Race and Class: The Perspective of Winning* (Oakland, CA: PM Press, 2012); Laura Briggs,
How All Politics Became Reproductive Politics (Berkeley: University of California Press,
2017), 2.

6. Stephanie Coontz and Peta Henderson, "Introduction: 'Explanations' of Male
Dominance," in *Women's Work, Men's Property: The Origins of Gender and Class*, ed.
Stephanie Coontz and Peta Henderson (London: Verso, 1986), loc. 66–205, 431–433,
Kindle; Stephanie Coontz and Peta Henderson, "Property Forms, Political Power, and
Female Labour in the Origins of Class and State Societies," in Coontz and Henderson,
Women's Work, Men's Property, loc. 2276–2279.

7. Coontz and Henderson, "Introduction," loc. 608–772; Lila Leibowitz, "In the
Beginning . . . : The Origins of the Sexual Division of Labour and the Development of
the First Human Societies," in Coontz and Henderson, *Women's Work, Men's Property*,
loc. 959–982; Nicole Chevillard and Sebastien Leconte, "The Dawn of Lineage Societies:
The Origins of Women's Oppression," in Coontz and Henderson, *Women's Work, Men's
Property*, loc. 1612–1642, 1799–1800.

8. Chevillard and Leconte argue, "The exploitation of man by man did in fact begin
as an exploitation of woman by man. But within this original exploitation lay the seeds
of the exploitation of humans of both sexes by the ruling human (who is again male)."
Chevillard and Leconte, "The Dawn of Lineage Societies," loc. 2135–2136. Coontz and
Henderson, "Property Forms," loc. 2659–2660, 2849–2890. Engels also rather acidly
noted that men "never . . . had the least intention" of being monogamous; monogamy was
for women. Engels, *Origin of the Family*, loc. 42–44, 49, 58.

9. "By Euripides," Engels wrote, "woman is designated as 'oikurema,' a neuter signifying an object for housekeeping, and beside the business of breeding children she served to the Athenian for nothing but his chief house maid." Engels, *Origin of the Family*, 61, 70; Luce Irigaray, "Women on the Market," originally published as "Le marche des femmes," in *Sessualita e politica* (Milan: Feltrinelli, 1978), https://caringlabor.wordpress.com/2010/11/10/luce-irigaray-women-on-the-market.

10. Silvia Federici, *Caliban and the Witch: Women, the Body, and Primitive Accumulation* (Brooklyn, NY: Autonomedia, 2004), 25, 31, 97. Unless otherwise noted, italics in quotations are reproduced from the original sources.

11. Federici explains: "Marx introduced the concept of 'primitive accumulation' at the end of *Capital* Volume 1 to describe the social and economic restructuring that the European ruling class initiated in response to its accumulation crisis, and to establish (in polemics with Adam Smith) that: (i) capitalism could not have developed without a prior concentration of capital and labor, and that (ii) the divorcing of the workers from the means of production, not the abstinence of the rich, is the source of capitalist wealth. Primitive accumulation, then, is a useful concept, for it connects the 'feudal reaction' with the development of a capitalist economy, and it identifies the *historical* and *logical* conditions for the development of the capitalist system, 'primitive' ('originary') indicating a precondition for the existence of capitalist relations as much as a specific event in time." Federici, *Caliban and the Witch*, 14, 17, 63–64, 88–89; Patel and Moore, *A History of the World*, 125. The witch hunters were obsessed with women's collective action, noted Barbara Ehrenreich and Deirdre English: "Not only were the witches women—they were women who seemed to be organized into an enormous secret society." Barbara Ehrenreich and Deirdre English, *Witches, Nurses and Midwives* (New York: Feminist Press, 2010), 42.

12. Federici, *Caliban and the Witch*, 135, 142.

13. Federici, *Caliban and the Witch*, 97, 149, 192. Patel and Moore wrote: "To make this system work, the state developed a keen interest in enforcing the categories of man and woman. Humans whose bodies didn't neatly fit were surgically altered to fit one category or the other." Patel and Moore, *A History of the World*, 117, 121, 128. Alan Sears, "Body Politics: The Social Reproduction of Sexualities," in *Social Reproduction Theory: Remapping Class, Recentering Oppression*, ed. Tithi Bhattacharya (London: Pluto Press, 2017), 173–174.

14. E. P. Thompson, *The Making of the English Working Class* (New York: Open Road Media, 2016), loc. 3881, 3974, Kindle.

15. Thompson, *Making of the English Working Class*, 4352, 4358, 4365–4376; Frances Fox Piven and Richard Cloward, *Regulating the Poor: The Functions of Public Welfare* (New York: Vintage, 1993), loc. 203, 358, 372, 417–429, 431, 442, Kindle; Cooper, *Family Values*, loc. 1080.

16. Cooper, *Family Values*, loc. 1080–1089, 1107–1109. Relief arrangements, Piven and Cloward argued, are part of the process of "defining and enforcing the terms on which different classes of people are made to do different kinds of work; relief arrangements, in other words, have a great deal to do with maintaining social and economic inequities." Piven and Cloward, *Regulating the Poor*, loc. 201, 217, 978.

17. Women who went to work, Thompson noted, often looked back wistfully at the home economy, which "supported a way of life centred upon the home, in which inner whims and compulsions were more obvious than external discipline." Thompson, *Making of the English Working Class*, 8587, 8617, 8634, 8643. Patel and Moore, *A History of the World*, 128. As just one example of reshaping indigenous lifeways, in the United States, the "Dawes Severalty Act of 1887 subdivided indigenous peoples' reserved lands into forty-acre plots, each distributed to a male-headed nuclear household." Salar Mohandesi and Emma Teitelman, "Without Reserves," in Bhattacharya, *Social Reproduction Theory*, 41.

18. Kelli Marìa Korducki, *Hard to Do: The Surprising Feminist History of Breaking Up* (Toronto: Coach House Books, 2018), 41, 53–54; Angela Y. Davis, *Women, Race and Class* (New York: Vintage, 1983), 12.

19. Laura Kipnis, *Against Love: A Polemic* (New York: Vintage, 2009), 60.

20. Angela Y. Davis, "Women and Capitalism: Dialectics of Oppression and Liberation," in *The Angela Y. Davis Reader*, 177.

21. Mohandesi and Teitelman, "Without Reserves," 39; James, *Sex, Race and Class*, 163–171, 177; Barrett and McIntosh, *Anti-Social Family*, loc. 266–267; hooks, *Communion*, 78.

22. Silvia Federici, *Revolution at Point Zero: Housework, Reproduction, and Feminist Struggle* (Oakland, CA: PM Press, 2012), 24; Barrett and McIntosh, *Anti-Social Family*, loc. 814–815; James, *Sex, Race and Class*, 153.

23. Amber Hollibaugh, interviewed by Kelly Anderson, Voices of Feminism Oral History Project, Sophia Smith Collection, Smith College, Northampton, Massachusetts, 2003–2004, 69; Nancy Fraser, "Crisis of Care? On the Social-Reproductive Contradictions of Contemporary Capitalism," in Bhattacharya, *Social Reproduction Theory*, 25.

24. Engels, *Origin of the Family*, 70.

25. Angela Y. Davis, "Surrogates and Outcast Mothers: Racism and Reproductive Politics in the Nineties," in *The Angela Y. Davis Reader*, 216; Andrew Cherlin, *Labor's Love Lost: The Rise and Fall of the Working-Class Family in America* (New York: Russell Sage Foundation, 2014), loc. 179, 186, 1422–1449, 1680, Kindle; Phyllis Palmer, *Domesticity and Dirt: Housewives and Domestic Servants in the United States, 1920–1945* (Philadelphia: Temple University Press, 1991), 22.

26. Fraser, "Crisis of Care," 25; Allan Carlson, *The Family in America: Searching for Social Harmony in the Industrial Age*, with a new introduction by the author (London: Routledge, 2017), 40; Cherlin, *Labor's Love Lost*, loc. 1109–1129, 1515, 1526; Palmer, *Domesticity and Dirt*, 13.

27. Barrett and McIntosh, *Anti-Social Family*, loc. 733–733; Cooper, *Family Values*, loc. 1149–1153, 1170–1175, 1186–1188, 1213–1214; Tera Hunter, *To 'Joy My Freedom: Southern Black Women's Lives and Labors After the Civil War* (Cambridge, MA: Harvard University Press, 1998), 37, 39–40.

28. Cherlin, *Labor's Love Lost*, loc. 1378, 1401; Mohandesi and Teitelman, "Without Reserves," 49; Cooper, *Family Values*, loc. 75–77.

29. Cooper, *Family Values*, loc. 47–50.

30. Cherlin, *Labor's Love Lost*, loc. 192–195, 247; Silvia Federici, "Preoccupying: Interview with Silvia Federici," *Occupied Times*, October 26, 2014, http://theoccupied times.org/?p=13482; Eva Kittay, *Love's Labor: Essays on Women, Equality and Disability* (London: Routledge, 1999), 41; Engels, *Origin of the Family*, 68–69; Cherlin, *Labor's Love Lost*, loc. 749–752, 811.

31. Selma James, "Child Benefit Has Been Changing Lives for 70 Years. Let's Not Forget the Woman Behind It," *The Guardian*, August 6, 2016, www.theguardian.com /commentisfree/2016/aug/06/child-benefit-70-years-eleanor-rathbone. See also Silvia Federici with Arlen Austin, eds., *Wages for Housework: The New York Committee, 1972–1977: History, Theory, Documents* (Brooklyn, NY: Autonomedia, 2017); Palmer, *Domesticity and Dirt*, 29–30, 76, 91, 101; Cherlin, *Labor's Love Lost*, loc. 1467.

32. Kristen Ghodsee, *Why Women Have Better Sex Under Socialism* (New York: Bold Type Books, 2018), 8, 62; Alexandra Kollontai, *The Autobiography of a Sexually Emancipated Communist Woman*, trans. Salvator Attansio (New York: Herder and Herder, 1971), transcribed for Marxists Internet Archive, 2001, www.marxists.org/archive /kollonta/1926/autobiography.htm.

33. Ghodsee, *Better Sex Under Socialism*, 58–59, 60–66, 121.

34. Ai-jen Poo, *Age of Dignity: Preparing for the Elder Boom in a Changing America* (New York: New Press, 2015), 100; Kipnis, *Against Love*, 93, 169.

35. Davis, "Women and Capitalism," 180; Barrett and McIntosh, *Anti-Social Family*, loc. 874–875; Cherlin, *Labor's Love Lost*, loc. 1510.

36. Palmer, *Domesticity and Dirt*, 64, 156; Barbara Ehrenreich, "Maid to Order," in *Global Woman: Nannies, Maids and Sex Workers in the New Economy*, ed. Barbara Ehrenreich and Arlie Russell Hochschild (New York: Metropolitan, 2004), loc. 1560, Kindle.

37. Kathi Weeks, "'Hours for What We Will': Work, Family, and the Movement for Shorter Hours," *Feminist Studies* 35, no. 1 (Spring 2009): 101–127; Federici, *Revolution at Point Zero*, 42–44, 56; Weeks, *The Problem with Work*, 65.

38. Shulamith Firestone, *The Dialectic of Sex* (London: Women's Press, 1979). Just the first chapter is reproduced at the Marxists Internet Archive, www.marxists.org /subject/women/authors/firestone-shulamith/dialectic-sex.htm.

39. Davis, *Women, Race and Class*, 205; Kristin Luker, *Abortion and the Politics of Motherhood* (Berkeley: University of California Press, 1985), 8, 118.

40. Luker, *Abortion*, 138, 145, 163, 202, 205, 206.

41. Federici, *Revolution at Point Zero*, 43; Premilla Nadasen, *Welfare Warriors: The Welfare Rights Movement in the United States* (London: Routledge, 2004), 204.

42. Nadasen, *Welfare Warriors*, 228, 395, 431, 441.

43. Nadasen, *Welfare Warriors*, 242, 249, 276, 300, 385.

44. Piven and Cloward, *Regulating the Poor*, loc. 2335, 2379, 2424, 2464, 3368; Kittay, *Love's Labor*, 124.

45. Piven and Cloward, *Regulating the Poor*, loc. 3254, 5569; Federici, *Revolution at Point Zero*, 43; Nadasen, *Welfare Warriors*, 1370, 1587, 1672.

46. Nadasen, *Welfare Warriors*, loc. 3456, 3667; Johnnie Tillmon, "Welfare Is a Women's Issue," *Ms.*, 1972, www.msmagazine.com/spring2002/tillmon.asp; Cooper, *Family Values*, loc. 1466–1467.

47. A few years later, discussing the Family Assistance Plan (FAP) proposal presented in 1971 by the Nixon administration, Senator Daniel Patrick Moynihan recognized that this demand was far from extravagant: "If American society recognized homemaking and child rearing as productive work to be included in the national economic accounts . . . the receipt of welfare might not imply dependency. But we don't. It may be hoped that the Women's Movement of the present time will change this. But as of the time I write it had not." Cited in Federici, *Revolution at Point Zero*, 43; Nadasen, *Welfare Warriors*, loc. 3611, 3672, 3973, 4302, 4330, 4038, 4079.

48. Nadasen, *Welfare Warriors*, loc. 4079, 4873; interview by Tony Brown, 1933–, in *Tony Brown's Journal: The President and Black America*, directed by Michael Colgan, Tony Brown Productions, 1982, 28 min.

49. Briggs, *Reproductive Politics*, 13, 48; Kittay, *Love's Labor*, 15, 119; Cooper, *Family Values*, loc. 381–383, 426–428, 439–441.

50. Federici, *Revolution at Point Zero*, 7.

51. Federici, *Revolution at Point Zero*, 7; James, *Sex, Race and Class*, 81.

52. James, *Sex, Race and Class*, 51, 82; Federici and Austin, *Wages for Housework*, 34, 203, 260; Mariarosa Dalla Costa, "The General Strike," in Federici and Austin, *Wages for Housework*, 275; Weeks, *The Problem with Work*, 130.

53. Federici and Austin, *Wages for Housework*, 34, 205.

54. Federici and Austin, *Wages for Housework*, 21, 125.

55. Nancy Folbre, ed., *For Love or Money: Care Provision in the United States* (New York: Russell Sage Foundation, 2012), xii; Federici and Austin, *Wages for Housework*, 113.

56. Federici and Austin, *Wages for Housework*, 23–24, 244; Cooper, *Family Values*, loc. 821–823.

57. Kittay, *Love's Labor*, 126; Tillmon, "Welfare Is a Women's Issue"; Cooper, *Family Values*, loc. 886–888; Weeks, *The Problem with Work*, 165; Erin Hatton, *Coerced: Work Under Threat of Punishment* (Berkeley: University of California Press, 2020), loc. 674–675, Kindle.

58. Ken Taylor, "The Reality of 'Welfare Reform,'" *Isthmus*, March 1, 2018, https://isthmus.com/opinion/opinion/welfare-reform-bill-walker-republican. As Melinda Cooper writes: "The opening preamble of PRWORA thus sets out the following extraordinary definition of public morality: '1) Marriage is the foundation of a successful society; 2) Marriage is an essential institution of a successful society, which promotes the interests of children'; and '3) Promotion of responsible fatherhood and motherhood is integral to successful childrearing and the wellbeing of children.'" Cooper, *Family Values*, loc. 1641–1644, 972–974, 989–996, 998–1001, 1497–1499, 1511–1513.

59. Premilla Nadasen, "How a Democrat Killed Welfare," *Jacobin*, February 9, 2016, www.jacobinmag.com/2016/02/welfare-reform-bill-hillary-clinton-tanf-poverty-dlc; Cooper, *Family Values*, loc. 1550–1557.

60. Fraser, "Crisis of Care," 25–26; Mark Fisher, *Capitalist Realism: Is There No Alternative?* (London: Zer0 Books, 2009); Ghodsee, *Better Sex Under Socialism*, 10, 68; Weeks, *The Problem with Work*, 159, 180.

61. Cherlin, *Labor's Love Lost*, loc. 3016; Cooper, *Family Values*, loc. 3279–3282; Federici, *Revolution at Point Zero*, 47, 97.

62. Cherlin, *Labor's Love Lost*, loc. 459, 465, 2839; Stephanie Coontz, "The New Instability," *New York Times*, July 26, 2014, www.nytimes.com/2014/07/27/opinion /sunday/the-new-instability.html; Naomi Cahn and June Carbone, "Just Say No," *Slate*, April 22, 2014, https://slate.com/human-interest/2014/04/white-working-class-women -should-stay-single-mothers-argue-the-authors-of-marriage-markets-how-inequality-is -remaking-the-american-family.html.

63. Folbre, *For Love or Money*, 4, 97. See also Arlie Russell Hochschild, *The Second Shift: Working Parents and the Revolution at Home* (New York: Viking, 1989); "Women Still Do More Household Chores Than Men, ONS Finds," BBC, November 10, 2016, www.bbc.co.uk/news/uk-37941191; Claire Cain Miller, "Nearly Half of Men Say They Do Most of the Home Schooling. 3 Percent of Women Agree," *New York Times*, May 6, 2020, www.nytimes.com/2020/05/06/upshot/pandemic-chores-homeschooling-gender .html; Reni Eddo-Lodge, "Women, Down Your Tools! Why It's Finally Time to Stop Do- ing All the Housework," *The Telegraph*, October 6, 2014, www.telegraph.co.uk/women /womens-life/11142847/Women-down-your-tools-Why-its-finally-time-to-stop-doing -all-the-housework.html; Suzanne M. Bianchi, John P. Robinson, and Melissa A. Milkie, *Changing Rhythms of American Family Life* (New York: Russell Sage Foundation, 2006); Patel and Moore, *A History of the World*, 32.

64. Heather Abel, "The Baby, the Book, and the Bathwater," *Paris Review*, January 31, 2018, www.theparisreview.org/blog/2018/01/31/baby-book-bathwater.

65. Annie Kelly, "The Housewives of White Supremacy," *New York Times*, June 1, 2018, www.nytimes.com/2018/06/01/opinion/sunday/tradwives-women-alt-right .html. Of the far right and the family, Jordy Rosenberg wrote, "Another way of putting this is that, unlike Bloch's midcentury Europe, we don't have the surplus libidinal en- ergies of mass communist movement for fascists to usurp, parody, or mimic. Rather, today's neofascism has a strange, parasitic relation to the affective surplus and the energies of the family. Actually, to be much more specific, it has a strange, parasitic relationship to the energies of the family's decomposition. . . . Contemporary neofascism harvests this splintering—this familial decomposition, which, like a collapsing star, emits a chaos of energy as it is vacuumed into oblivion. Note that, here, neofascism isn't about claiming the moral high ground for itself. Rather, it exults in performing its perversity. I'm not defending the nuclear family from these scavengers. I'm saying that the energies of the family's decomposition ought to be ours to harvest, to resignify—to kink. . . . What will become of us? I don't know, but I'm saying that fascism tries to usurp everything, including or especially unruliness, and I'm sorry, but no: the supernova of the family's destruction ought to be ours to redefine." Jordy Rosenberg, "The Daddy Dialectic," *Los Angeles Review of Books*, March 11, 2018, https://lareviewofbooks.org/article/the-daddy -dialectic.

66. Alexis C. Madrigal, "Two Working Parents, One Sick Kid," *The Atlantic*, Au- gust 12, 2014, www.theatlantic.com/business/archive/2014/08/two-working-parents -one-sick-kid/375909; Lindsay King-Miller, "Two Moms, Four Shifts: Queer Parents Are Overwhelmed Too," *The Guardian*, December 15, 2017, www.theguardian.com/us -news/2017/dec/14/two-moms-four-shifts-queer-parents-are-overwhelmed-too; Kat Stoeffel, "If You Cover Egg Freezing, You Better Cover Day Care," *The Cut*, October 15, 2014, www.thecut.com/2014/10/you-cover-egg-freezing-also-cover-day-care.html;

Briggs, *Reproductive Politics*, 10; Wednesday Martin, "Poor Little Rich Women," *New York Times*, May 16, 2015, www.nytimes.com/2015/05/17/opinion/sunday/poor-little -rich-women.html.

67. Julie Beck, "The Concept Creep of Emotional Labor," interview with Arlie Russell Hochschild, *The Atlantic*, November 26, 2018, www.theatlantic.com /family/archive/2018/11/arlie-hochschild-housework-isnt-emotional-labor/576637; Federici, *Revolution at Point Zero*, 23–24; Jane Miller, "The Ambiguities of Care," *In These Times*, April 29, 2014, http://inthesetimes.com/article/16532/the_ambiguities _of_care; Ghodsee, *Better Sex Under Socialism*, 152; Samantha Marie Nock, "Decrying Desirability, Demanding Care," *Guts*, January 24, 2018, http://gutsmagazine .ca/decrying-desirability-demanding-care.

68. Caleb Luna, "Romantic Love Is Killing Us: Who Takes Care of Us When We Are Single?," The Body Is Not an Apology, September 18, 2018, https://thebodyisnot anapology.com/magazine/romantic-love-is-killing-us; Folbre, *For Love or Money*, 13; Laura Anne Robertson, "Who Cares?" *New Inquiry*, December 5, 2014, https://thenew inquiry.com/who-cares.

69. Briggs, *Reproductive Politics*, 155, 168; Cooper, *Family Values*, loc. 2442–2444.

70. Silvia Federici points to "'communities of care' . . . formed by the younger generations of political activists, who aim at socializing, collectivizing the experience of illness, pain, grieving and the 'care work' involved, in this process beginning to reclaim and redefine what it means to be ill, to age, to die," as well as "solidarity contracts" created by the elderly, who pool resources to avoid being institutionalized. Federici, *Revolution at Point Zero*, 125; Bhattacharya, "Introduction," in Bhattacharya, *Social Reproduction Theory*, 8; Sunny Taylor, "The Right Not to Work: Power and Disability," *Monthly Review*, March 1, 2004, https://monthlyreview.org/2004/03/01/the-right-not-to-work -power-and-disability; John Tozzi, "Americans Are Dying Younger, Saving Corporations Billions," Bloomberg, August 8, 2014, www.bloomberg.com/news/articles/2017-08-08 /americans-are-dying-younger-saving-corporations-billions; Park McArthur and Constantina Zavitsanos, "Other Forms of Conviviality," Women and Performance, October 30, 2013, www.womenandperformance.org/ampersand/ampersand-articles/other-forms-of -conviviality.html?rq=other%20forms%20of%20conviviality. Writer Johanna Hedva suggested a radical potential in embracing illness and disability: "Because, once we are all ill and confined to the bed, sharing our stories of therapies and comforts, forming support groups, bearing witness to each other's tales of trauma, prioritizing the care and love of our sick, pained, expensive, sensitive, fantastic bodies, and there is no one left to go to work, perhaps then, finally, capitalism will screech to its much-needed, long-overdue, and motherfucking glorious halt." Johanna Hedva, "Sick Woman Theory," *Mask*, January 2016, www.maskmagazine.com/not-again/struggle/sick-woman-theory.

71. Matt Steib, "Texas Lt. Gov. Dan Patrick: 'Lots of Grandparents' Willing to Die to Save Economy for Grandchildren," *New York*, March 23, 2020, https://nymag.com /intelligencer/2020/03/dan-patrick-seniors-are-willing-to-die-to-save-economy.html.

72. Kittay, *Love's Labor*, 68.

73. Sophie Lewis points out, "Feminists used to draw a distinction between mothering (potentially good) and motherhood (bad). The former conjured an ensemble of practices (including Audre Lorde's 'we can learn to mother ourselves') that could

potentially destroy the latter institution." Sophie Lewis, "All Reproduction Is Assisted," *Boston Review*, August 14, 2018, http://bostonreview.net/forum/all-reproduction-assisted /sophie-lewis-mothering; Marina Vishmidt, "Permanent Reproductive Crisis: An Interview with Silvia Federici," *Mute*, March 7, 2013, www.metamute.org/editorial/articles /permanent-reproductive-crisis-interview-silvia-federici; James, *Sex, Race and Class*, 229; Kittay, *Love's Labor*, 103; Federici and Austin, *Wages for Housework*, 27; Silvia Federici, *Witches, Witch-Hunting, and Women* (Oakland, CA: PM Press, 2018), loc. 852, Kindle.

74. Weeks, *The Problem with Work*, 111; Patel and Moore, *A History of the World*, 135.

75. Patrick Butler, "Benefit Sanctions Found to Be Ineffective and Damaging," *The Guardian*, May 22, 2018, www.theguardian.com/society/2018/may/22/benefit -sanctions-found-to-be-ineffective-and-damaging.

76. Facundo Alvaredo, Bertrand Garbinti, and Thomas Piketty, "On the Share of Inheritance in Aggregate Wealth: Europe and the USA," *Economica* 84, no. 334, (2017): 239–260, available at Paris School of Economics, http://piketty.pse.ens.fr/files/Alvaredo GarbintiPiketty2015.pdf.

CHAPTER 2: JUST LIKE ONE OF THE FAMILY

1. Children's names have been changed to protect their identity.

2. Eileen Boris and Rhacel Salazar Parreñas, "Introduction," in *Intimate Labors: Cultures, Technologies, and the Politics of Care*, ed. Eileen Boris and Rhacel Salazar Parreñas (Stanford: Stanford University Press, 2010), 2.

3. Viviana Zelizer, "Caring Everywhere," in Boris and Parreñas, *Intimate Labors*, 269–270; Nancy Folbre, *For Love or Money: Care Provision in the United States* (New York: Russell Sage Foundation, 2012), 2; Boris and Parreñas, "Introduction," 8, 10.

4. Boris and Parreñas, "Introduction," 2; Eva Kittay, *Love's Labor: Essays on Women, Equality and Disability* (London: Routledge, 1999), 95, 110; Silvia Federici, *Caliban and the Witch: Women, the Body, and Primitive Accumulation* (Brooklyn, NY: Autonomedia, 2004), 99; E. P. Thompson, *The Making of the English Working Class* (New York: Open Road Media, 2016), loc. 4112, Kindle; Bridget Anderson, "Just Another Job? The Commodification of Domestic Labor," in *Global Woman: Nannies, Maids and Sex Workers in the New Economy*, ed. Barbara Ehrenreich and Arlie Russell Hochschild (New York: Metropolitan, 2004), 137; Andrew Cherlin, *Labor's Love Lost: The Rise and Fall of the Working-Class Family in America* (New York: Russell Sage Foundation, 2014), loc. 892, Kindle. Seemin Qayum and Raka Ray cite Mary Romero on "the proliferation of master-servant relationships in which race, ethnicity, and gender replace class as immutable social structures dictating a person's place in the hierarchy," where for white domestic workers, the occupation could catapult them up the social ladder, while women of color remained trapped in an "occupational ghetto." Seemin Qayum and Raka Ray, "Traveling Cultures of Servitude," in Boris and Parreñas, *Intimate Labors*, 101.

5. Boris and Parreñas, "Introduction," 2, 11; Lyz Lenz, "These 12 Apps Will Revolutionize Motherhood, Except They Won't," *Pacific Standard*, April 15, 2016, https:// psmag.com/news/these-12-apps-will-revolutionize-motherhood-except-they-wont;

Anderson, "Just Another Job," 135; Raj Patel and Jason W. Moore, *A History of the World in Seven Cheap Things: A Guide to Capitalism, Nature, and the Future of the Planet* (Berkeley: University of California Press, 2018), 24–25.

6. Angela Y. Davis, "Reflections on the Black Woman's Role in the Community of Slaves," in *The Angela Y. Davis Reader*, ed. Joy James (Hoboken, NJ: Blackwell, 1998), 116; Angela Y. Davis, *Women, Race and Class* (New York: Vintage, 1983), 12–23, 230; Nancy Fraser, "Crisis of Care? On the Social-Reproductive Contradictions of Contemporary Capitalism," in *Social Reproduction Theory: Remapping Class, Recentering Oppression*, ed. Tithi Bhattacharya (London: Pluto Press, 2017), 28; Carmen Teeple Hopkins, "Mostly Work, Little Play: Social Reproduction, Migration, and Paid Domestic Work in Montreal," in Bhattacharya, *Social Reproduction Theory*, 144–145; Patel and Moore, *A History of the World*, 130.

7. Tera Hunter, *To 'Joy My Freedom: Southern Black Women's Lives and Labors After the Civil War*, (Cambridge: Harvard University Press, 1998), 5, 16–17, 20. As Angela Davis noted, racism and sexism were mutually reinforcing: "As racism developed more durable roots within white women's organizations, so too did the sexist cult of motherhood creep into the very movement whose announced aim was the elimination of male supremacy." Davis, *Women, Race and Class*, 94, 96, 122. See also W. E. B. Du Bois, *Black Reconstruction in America: An Essay Toward a History of the Part Which Black Folk Played in the Attempt to Reconstruct Democracy in America, 1860–1880* (Oxford: Oxford University Press, 2014), Kindle.

8. Hunter, *To 'Joy My Freedom*, 3, 21–22, 27–32, 59–61, 228; Saidiya Hartman, *Wayward Lives, Beautiful Experiments: Intimate Histories of Riotous Black Girls, Troublesome Women, and Queer Radicals* (New York: W. W. Norton and Company, 2019), loc. 2986–3007, 3017, Kindle.

9. Hunter, *To 'Joy My Freedom*, 26, 50–53, 56–58, 60, 62, 74–88; Salar Mohandesi and Emma Teitelman, "Without Reserves," in Bhattacharya, *Social Reproduction Theory*, 46.

10. Hunter, *To 'Joy My Freedom*, 111, 148, 169, 185–186.

11. Hunter, *To 'Joy My Freedom*, 229, 231. Saidiya Hartman quotes the superintendent of the reformatory at Bedford Hills: "In placing a woman [in a reformatory] there is just one avenue open to her and that is domestic service. The present economic conditions are such that there is a larger demand for domestic help than we can supply. I usually have waiting lists for cooks, general housework girls and domestic servants of every kind. So great is the demand, particularly for general housework, that one lady said to me, 'I don't care if she has committed all the crimes in the Decalogue if she can only wash dishes.'" Hartman, *Wayward Lives*, loc. 3283–3301. Angela Y. Davis, "Race and Criminalization," in *The Angela Y. Davis Reader*, 70.

12. Historian Phyllis Palmer argued, "I hope to clarify the postulate that gender is never an identity formed in isolation from other identities that have significance in twentieth-century America, but is an amalgam of race and class with gender." Phyllis Palmer, *Domesticity and Dirt: Housewives and Domestic Servants in the United States, 1920–1945* (Philadelphia: Temple University Press, 1991), 5, 7, 14–15; Mohandesi and Teitelman, "Without Reserves," 44.

13. Hunter, *To 'Joy My Freedom*, 55; Palmer, *Domesticity and Dirt*, 58–59, 66; Premilla Nadasen, "Power, Intimacy and Contestation," in Boris and Parreñas, *Intimate Labors*, 207.

14. Phyllis Palmer wrote, "Over a third of women homemakers working as domestics were heads of households." Palmer, *Domesticity and Dirt*, 71–72, 75–77, 86–87.

15. Palmer, *Domesticity and Dirt*, 103, 119, 120.

16. Palmer, *Domesticity and Dirt*, 73, 122, 125, 134. See also Premilla Nadasen, *Household Workers Unite: The Untold Story of African American Women Who Built a Movement* (Boston: Beacon Press, 2015); Hartman, *Wayward Lives*, loc. 4214–4217; Ella Baker and Marvel Cooke, "The Slave Market," *The Crisis* 42 (November 1935), https://caring labor.wordpress.com/2010/11/24/ella-baker-and-marvel-cooke-the-slave-market.

17. Belabored Podcast #84: Domestic Workers Unite, with Premilla Nadasen, *Dissent*, August 21, 2015, www.dissentmagazine.org/blog/belabored-podcast-84-domestic -workers-unite-with-premilla-nadasen; Nadasen, "Power, Intimacy and Contestation," 206.

18. The intimacy of domestic work, Premilla Nadasen wrote, "fostered a work environment where employees' character, not only their ability to complete specified chores, became a measure of one's job performance." Nadasen, "Power, Intimacy and Contestation," 204, 207, 208; Belabored Podcast #84. See also Palmer, *Domesticity and Dirt*; Nadasen, *Household Workers Unite*.

19. Belabored Podcast #84; Nadasen, "Power, Intimacy and Contestation," 205–207, 211–212.

20. Nadasen, "Power, Intimacy and Contestation," 204.

21. Palmer, *Domesticity and Dirt*, 156; Barbara Ehrenreich, "Maid to Order," in Ehrenreich and Hochschild, *Global Woman*, 108.

22. Palmer, *Domesticity and Dirt*, 73–74, 99, 138, 139–144, 146–147.

23. Erin Hatton, *Coerced: Work Under Threat of Punishment* (Berkeley: University of California Press, 2020), loc. 685–689, Kindle; Angela Y. Davis, "Racialized Punishment and Prison Abolition," in *The Angela Y. Davis Reader*, 97; Angela Y. Davis, "Surrogates and Outcast Mothers: Racism and Reproductive Politics in the Nineties," in *The Angela Y. Davis Reader*, 218; Magdalene Laundry survivor Mary Norris told reporters: "We worked long hours every day, scrubbing, bleaching and ironing for the whole of Limerick—hotels, hospitals, schools, colleges—for which the nuns charged, of course, though we never saw a penny. It was an industry and they were earning a fortune from our labour. . . . When you went inside their doors you left behind your dignity, identity and humanity. We were locked up, had no outside contacts and got no wages, although we worked 10 hours a day, six days a week, 52 weeks a year. What else is that but slavery? And to think that they were doing all this in the name of a loving God! I used to tell God I hated him." "A Very Irish Sort of Hell," *The Age*, April 5, 2003, www.theage.com.au/world/a -very-irish-sort-of-hell-20030405-gdvhr9.html. Ed O'Loughlin, "These Women Survived Ireland's Magdalene Laundries. They're Ready to Talk," *New York Times*, June 6, 2018, www.nytimes.com/2018/06/06/world/europe/magdalene-laundry-reunion-ireland .html; Patsy McGarry, "Magdalene Laundries: 'I Often Wondered Why Were They So Cruel,'" *Irish Times*, June 6, 2018, www.irishtimes.com/news/social-affairs/religion-and

-beliefs/magdalene-laundries-i-often-wondered-why-were-they-so-cruel-1.3521600; "'I Wasn't Even 15. I Hadn't Even Kissed a Boy'—A Magdalene Survivor's Story," RTE, June 5, 2018, www.rte.ie/news/newslens/2018/0605/968383-magdalene-elizabeth -coppin.

24. Belabored Podcast #38: Caring for America, with Eileen Boris and Jennifer Klein, *Dissent*, January 24, 2014, www.dissentmagazine.org/blog/belabored-podcast-38 -caring-for-america-with-eileen-boris-and-jennifer-klein; Eileen Boris and Jennifer Klein, "Making Home Care: Law and Social Policy in the U.S. Welfare State," in Boris and Parreñas, *Intimate Labors*, 188–190. See also Eileen Boris and Jennifer Klein, *Caring for America: Home Health Workers in the Shadow of the Welfare State* (Oxford: Oxford University Press, 2012).

25. Boris and Klein, "Making Home Care," 188–197.

26. Boris and Klein, "Making Home Care," 192; Ai-jen Poo, *Age of Dignity: Preparing for the Elder Boom in a Changing America* (New York: New Press, 2015), 83; Eileen Boris and Jennifer Klein, "Organizing Home Care: Low-Waged Workers in the Welfare State," *Politics and Society* 34, no. 1 (March 2006): 81–107, https://caringlabor.word press.com/2010/11/11/eileen-boris-and-jennifer-klein-organizing-home-care-low-waged -workers-in-the-welfare-state.

27. Boris and Klein, "Making Home Care," 187, 188.

28. Boris and Klein, "Making Home Care," 188–197; Melinda Cooper, *Family Values: Between Neoliberalism and the New Social Conservatism* (Brooklyn, NY: Zone Books, 2019), loc. 2941–2943, 2936–2938, 3053–3056, Kindle; Kittay, *Love's Labor*, 116; Ronald Reagan, "Proclamation 5913—National Home Care Week, 1988," Reagan Library, November 19, 1988, www.reaganlibrary.gov/research/speeches/111988d.

29. Poo, *Age of Dignity*, 90; Kittay, *Love's Labor*, 65; Lynn May Rivas, "Invisible Labors: Caring for the Independent Person," in Ehrenreich and Hochschild, *Global Woman*, loc. 1323.

30. Rivas's full comment is worth including here: "I believe that the transfer of authorship is a negative phenomenon even for those who consciously work to make it happen. To be made invisible is the first step toward being considered nonhuman, which is why making another person invisible often precedes treating them inhumanely. To use Marxist terms, invisibility is the most extreme form of alienation—the ultimate manifestation of self-estrangement." Rivas, "Invisible Labors," loc. 1314, 1347, 1379, 1410, 1416.

31. Folbre, *For Love or Money*, 83; Boris and Klein, "Making Home Care," 197–200; Belabored Podcast #84; Tamara Draut, *Sleeping Giant: How the New Working Class Will Transform America* (New York: Doubleday, 2016), 135; Douglas Martin, "Evelyn Coke, Home Care Aide Who Fought Pay Rule, Is Dead at 74," *New York Times*, August 9, 2009, www.nytimes.com/2009/08/10/nyregion/10coke.html; Long Island Care at Home v. Coke, 551 U.S. 158 (2007).

32. Draut, *Sleeping Giant*, 136; Bob Woods, "Home Health-Care Workers in US at Tipping Point amid Coronavirus Outbreak," CNBC, April 14, 2020, www.cnbc .com/2020/04/14/home-health-care-workers-at-tipping-point-amid-coronavirus -outbreak.html. As I wrote in *In These Times* at the time: "The *Harris* case was brought

in 2010 by Pamela Harris, an Illinois homecare worker who received Medicaid money as wages for caring for her son, who has a disability. An executive order issued by Illinois governor Pat Quinn the previous year had designated personal assistants caring for disabled adults as state employees, allowing them to be represented by a collective-bargaining agent. Harris and the other plaintiffs were backed in the suit by the well-heeled anti-union group National Right to Work Legal Defense Foundation, and argued that she and other workers should not have to pay the costs of representing her to SEIU Healthcare Illinois & Indiana (SEIU–HCII), the union that represents homecare workers who are paid by the state for their work. The suit claimed that paying representation costs amounted to a forced association that is unconstitutional under the First Amendment." Sarah Jaffe, "Why Harris and Hobby Lobby Spell Disaster for Working Women," *In These Times*, June 30, 2014, https://inthesetimes.com/article/scotus-rules-against-female-workers; Harris v. Quinn, 573 U.S. 616 (2014).

33. Poo, *Age of Dignity*, 151; Andrea Marie, "Women and Childcare in Capitalism, Part 3," *New Socialist*, 2017, https://newsocialist.org.uk/women-and-childcare-in-capitalism-part-3; Bernadette Hyland, "From Factory Workers to Care Workers," Contributoria, March 2014, www.contributoria.com/issue/2014-03/52c98327a94a824a25000004.html.

34. Boris and Parreñas, "Introduction," 8; Belabored Podcast #84; Laura Briggs, *How All Politics Became Reproductive Politics* (Berkeley: University of California Press, 2017), 76; María de la Luz Ibarra, "My Reward Is Not Money," in Boris and Parreñas, *Intimate Labors*, 117.

35. Briggs, "Foreign and Domestic," in Boris and Parreñas, *Intimate Labors*, 50–51; Silvia Federici, *Revolution at Point Zero: Housework, Reproduction, and Feminist Struggle* (Oakland, CA: PM Press, 2012), 66–69; Briggs, *Reproductive Politics*, 81, 95; Rivas, "Invisible Labors," loc. 99; Ehrenreich, "Maid to Order," loc. 126.

36. Briggs, *Reproductive Politics*, 79.

37. Briggs, *Reproductive Politics*, 79.

38. Briggs, *Reproductive Politics*, 79; Joy M. Zarembka, "America's Dirty Work: Migrant Maids and Modern-Day Slavery," in Ehrenreich and Hochschild, *Global Woman*, 182; Anderson, "Just Another Job?," 132; Melissa Gira Grant, "Human Trafficking, After the Headlines," *Pacific Standard*, April 3, 2017, https://psmag.com/news/human-trafficking-after-the-headlines; Nicole Constable, "Filipina Workers in Hong Kong Homes: Household Rules and Relations," in Ehrenreich and Hochschild, *Global Woman*, 170–172; Hopkins, "Mostly Work, Little Play," 137. Arlie Russell Hochschild draws attention to the way love itself is alienated: "Just as we mentally isolate our idea of an object from the human scene within which it was made, so, too, we unwittingly separate the love between nanny and child from the global capitalist order of love to which it very much belongs." Arlie Russell Hochschild, "Love and Gold," in Ehrenreich and Hochschild, *Global Woman*, 33.

39. Hochschild, "Love and Gold," 33; Kittay, *Love's Labor*, 157–160.

40. Ehrenreich, "Maid to Order," 109; Qayum and Ray, "Traveling Cultures of Servitude," 114.

41. Rosa Silverman, "Does Asking Your Cleaner to Work Make You a Bad Feminist? Negotiating the Covid-19 Rule Change," *The Telegraph*, May 14, 2020, www

.telegraph.co.uk/women/work/does-asking-cleaner-work-make-bad-feminist-negotiating
-covid; Sarah Ditum, "The Underlying Sexism of the Conversation About Cleaners and
Covid," *The Spectator*, May 14, 2020, www.spectator.co.uk/article/the-underlying-sexism
-of-the-conversation-about-cleaners-and-covid.

42. Pierrette Hondagneu-Sotelo, "Blowups and Other Unhappy Endings," in Ehrenreich and Hochschild, *Global Woman*, 72; Constable, "Filipina Workers in Hong
Kong Homes," 167.

43. Roc Morin, "How to Hire Fake Friends and Family," *The Atlantic*, November 7, 2017, www.theatlantic.com/family/archive/2017/11/paying-for-fake-friends-and
-family/545060.

44. Federici, *Revolution at Point Zero*, 121.

45. Ehrenreich, "Maid to Order," 116; Miya Tokumitsu, *Do What You Love: And
Other Lies About Success and Happiness* (New York: Regan Arts, 2015), 6.

46. Lenz, "These 12 Apps."

47. Valerio De Stefano, "Collective Bargaining of Platform Workers: Domestic
Work Leads the Way," Regulating for Globalization, October 12, 2018, http://regulating
forglobalization.com/2018/12/10/collective-bargaining-of-platform-workers-domestic
-work-leads-the-way.

48. Dorothy Sue Cobble, "More Intimate Unions," in Boris and Parreñas, *Intimate
Labors*, 281.

49. Cobble, "More Intimate Unions," 281–286.

50. "Facts for Domestic Workers," New York State Department of Labor,
https://labor.ny.gov/legal/laws/pdf/domestic-workers/facts-for-domestic-workers
.pdf; Carney Law Firm, "New Massachusetts Law Expands Rights of Domestic
Workers," January 30, 2015, www.bostonworkerscompensationlawyerblog.com/new
-massachusetts-law-expands-rights-domestic-workers.

51. Sarah Jaffe, "Low Benefits, Temporary Jobs—Work Is Getting Worse . . . But
Hope for Labor Rights Is Emerging from a Surprising Place," AlterNet, August 28, 2012,
www.alternet.org/2012/08/low-benefits-temporary-jobs-work-getting-worse-hope-labor
-rights-emerging-surprising-place; National Domestic Workers Alliance homepage, accessed August 5, 2020, www.domesticworkers.org.

52. Alexia Fernández Campbell, "Kamala Harris Just Introduced a Bill to
Give Housekeepers Overtime Pay and Meal Breaks," *Vox*, July 15, 2019, www.vox
.com/2019/7/15/20694610/kamala-harris-domestic-workers-bill-of-rights-act.

CHAPTER 3: WE STRIKE BECAUSE WE CARE

1. John L. Rury, "Who Became Teachers? The Social Characteristics of Teachers in
American History," in *American Teachers: Histories of a Profession at Work*, ed. Donald
Warren (New York: Macmillan, 1989), 9–10; Megan Erickson, *Class War: The Privatiza-
tion of Childhood* (New York: Verso, 2015), 146.

2. Rury, "Who Became Teachers?," 11–12, 14; Dana Goldstein, *The Teacher Wars:
A History of America's Most Embattled Profession* (New York: Anchor, 2014), loc. 315,
Kindle.

3. Marjorie Murphy, *Blackboard Unions: The AFT and the NEA, 1900–1980* (Ithaca,
NY: Cornell University Press, 1992), 12–13; Goldstein, *The Teacher Wars*, loc. 402–428, 635.

4. Rury, "Who Became Teachers?," 15–27; Goldstein, *The Teacher Wars*, loc. 446–456, 717; Murphy, *Blackboard Unions*, 14.

5. Goldstein, *The Teacher Wars*, loc. 913–1037. Historian Michael Fultz wrote that African American teachers were "burdened with a spate of extracurricular expectations which they could not possibly fulfill." Michael Fultz, "African American Teachers in the South, 1890–1940: Powerlessness and the Ironies of Expectations and Protest," *History of Education Quarterly* 35, no. 4 (Winter 1995): 401–402.

6. Rury, "Who Became Teachers?," 23, 28–29; Murphy, *Blackboard Unions*, 1; Goldstein, *The Teacher Wars*, loc. 589, 631.

7. Murphy, *Blackboard Unions*, 12–15.

8. Murphy, *Blackboard Unions*, 20–24.

9. Murphy, *Blackboard Unions*, 36, 43–45.

10. Goldstein, *The Teacher Wars*, loc. 1283–1349; Murphy, *Blackboard Unions*, 46.

11. Murphy, *Blackboard Unions*, 47–59.

12. Murphy, *Blackboard Unions*, 59–60, 67, 72.

13. Murphy, *Blackboard Unions*, 90–95; Fultz, "African American Teachers in the South," 410–420.

14. Goldstein, *The Teacher Wars*, loc. 1616–1648; Eleni Schirmer, personal communication with author.

15. Murphy, *Blackboard Unions*, 97–98, 100, 102, 118, 119, 122.

16. Goldstein, *The Teacher Wars*, loc. 1716–1766.

17. Goldstein, *The Teacher Wars*, loc. 1840; Clarence Taylor, *Reds at the Blackboard: Communism, Civil Rights, and the New York City Teachers Union* (New York: Columbia University Press, 2013), loc. 87, Kindle; Murphy, *Blackboard Unions*, 133, 148, 154–157.

18. Rury, "Who Became Teachers?," 34.

19. Murphy, *Blackboard Unions*, 154–157; Taylor, *Reds at the Blackboard*, loc. 3, 12, 15–16; Goldstein, *The Teacher Wars*, loc. 1817.

20. Taylor, *Reds at the Blackboard*, loc. 29–33, 43, 73, 78, 287–288. Historian Marjorie Murphy points to an article by Howard University professor Doxey Wilkerson about segregation, which made a Black child feel "he is not an integral part of the social group with which he is thrown, but rather, that he is a thing apart, isolated, ostracized, somehow not quite like his classmates." Murphy, *Blackboard Unions*, 164.

21. Taylor, *Reds at the Blackboard*, loc. 277; Rury, "Who Became Teachers?," 37.

22. Murphy, *Blackboard Unions*, 184; Taylor, *Reds at the Blackboard*, loc. 104–115, 126, 151–153, 290.

23. Taylor, *Reds at the Blackboard*, loc. 104–115, 126, 151–153, 290; Murphy, *Blackboard Unions*, 190; Goldstein, *The Teacher Wars*, loc. 1945–1955.

24. Taylor, *Reds at the Blackboard*, loc. 153–173, 126, 151–153, 290.

25. Taylor, *Reds at the Blackboard*, loc. 204–213.

26. Murphy, *Blackboard Unions*, 181; Erickson, *Class War*, 126.

27. Murphy, *Blackboard Unions*, 200–204; Elizabeth Todd-Breland, *A Political Education: Black Politics and Education Reform in Chicago Since the 1960s* (Chapel Hill: University of North Carolina Press, 2018), 12, 24; Michael Fultz, "The Displacement of Black Educators Post-Brown: An Overview and Analysis," *History of Education Quarterly*

44, no. 1, A Special Issue on the Fiftieth Anniversary of the "Brown v. Board of Education" Decision (Spring 2004): 13–14, 20.

28. Goldstein, *The Teacher Wars*, loc. 214, 1592, 2271, 2332, 2402; Fultz, "The Displacement of Black Educators," 19, 25–26; Todd-Breland, *A Political Education*, 128.

29. Murphy, *Blackboard Unions*, 213–214, 239, 242, 243–245; Todd-Breland, *A Political Education*, 29, 52, 114; Goldstein, *The Teacher Wars*, loc. 2530, 2572–2627.

30. Lois Weiner, *The Future of Our Schools: Teachers Unions and Social Justice* (Chicago: Haymarket Books, 2012), loc. 1785–1800, Kindle.

31. Todd-Breland, *A Political Education*, 124–125; Taylor, *Reds at the Blackboard*, loc. 318; Goldstein, *The Teacher Wars*, loc. 2612–2751; Murphy, *Blackboard Unions*, 242; Jane McAlevey, *No Shortcuts: Organizing for Power in the New Gilded Age* (Oxford: Oxford University Press, 2016), 103.

32. Murphy, *Blackboard Unions*, 211; Goldstein, *The Teacher Wars*, loc. 2925.

33. Murphy, *Blackboard Unions*, 267–269, 271–272; Todd-Breland, *A Political Education*, 2, 164; Erickson, *Class War*, 53.

34. Josh Eidelson and Sarah Jaffe, "Defending Public Education: An Interview with Karen Lewis of the Chicago Teachers Union," *Dissent*, Summer 2013, www.dissentmagazine.org/article/defending-public-education-an-interview-with-karen-lewis-of-the-chicago-teachers-union.

35. Todd-Breland, *A Political Education*, 189, 198, 209, 215; Michael Powell, "Gilded Crusade for Charters Rolls Forward," *New York Times*, March 12, 2014, www.nytimes.com/2014/03/13/nyregion/gilded-crusade-for-charters-rolls-onward.html.

36. Goldstein, *The Teacher Wars*, loc. 3123, 3236, 3240; Todd-Breland, *A Political Education*, 159, 204–205.

37. Weiner, *The Future of Our Schools*, loc. 824, 1857–1864, 1916, 1995–1999, 2016, 2022–2029, 2045; Goldstein, *The Teacher Wars*, loc. 3160, 3510; Erickson, *Class War*, 45.

38. Goldstein, *The Teacher Wars*, loc. 3974–4081.

39. New York teacher and researcher Brian Jones explained the work that is still devalued: "Helping students find confidence, helping them to latch on to their passions, empowering them, that aspect of teaching and learning is greatly undervalued, and that's a very difficult thing to impose from above." Sarah Jaffe, "Taking the Caring Out of Teaching," *In These Times*, July 4, 2013, http://inthesetimes.com/article/15245/taking_the_caring_out_of_teaching_new_yorks_new_teacher_evaluation_system_i; Weiner, *The Future of Our Schools*, loc. 298, 344.

40. Erickson, *Class War*, 105; Malcolm Harris, *Kids These Days: The Making of Millennials* (New York: Back Bay Books, 2018), 119–120.

41. McAlevey, *No Shortcuts*, 107–109; Goldstein, *The Teacher Wars*, loc. 2886; Todd-Breland, *A Political Education*, 144; Eidelson and Jaffe, "Defending Public Education."

42. McAlevey, *No Shortcuts*, 20–29, 102.

43. Kate Bahn interview with author; see also Kate Bahn, "The ABCs of Labor Market Frictions: New Estimates of Monopsony for Early Career Teachers in the U.S. and Implications for Caring Labor" (PhD diss., The New School for Social Research University, 2015); Emma García and Elaine Weiss, "Low Relative Pay and High Incidence of

Moonlighting Play a Role in the Teacher Shortage, Particularly in High-Poverty Schools," Economic Policy Institute, May 9, 2019, www.epi.org/publication/low-relative-pay-and -high-incidence-of-moonlighting-play-a-role-in-the-teacher-shortage-particularly-in -high-poverty-schools-the-third-report-in-the-perfect-storm-in-the-teacher-labor-marke; Kevin Prosen, "A Letter to New York City's School Teachers," *Jacobin*, May 12, 2014, www.jacobinmag.com/2014/05/a-letter-to-new-york-citys-school-teachers.

44. Valerie Strauss, "Chicago Promised That Closing Nearly 50 Schools Would Help Kids in 2013. A New Report Says It Didn't," *Washington Post*, May 24, 2018, www .washingtonpost.com/news/answer-sheet/wp/2018/05/24/chicago-promised-that-closing -nearly-50-schools-would-help-kids-in-2013-a-new-report-says-it-didnt. The *Janus* case was officially between Mark Janus, a child support specialist who worked for the state of Illinois and contended that he should not have to pay representation fees, and the American Federation of State, County and Municipal Employees (AFSCME). The suit was originally filed by Bruce Rauner, the wealthy governor of Illinois, and shortly after the Supreme Court decision, Janus left his public-sector job to join the conservative think tank that had helped bankroll his suit. Mitchell Armentrout, "Mark Janus Quits State Job for Conservative Think Tank After Landmark Ruling," *Chicago Sun-Times*, July 20, 2018, https://chicago.suntimes.com/2018/7/20/18409126/mark-janus-quits-state -job-for-conservative-think-tank-gig-after-landmark-ruling; Sarah Jaffe, "With Janus, the Court Deals Unions a Crushing Blow. Now What?," *New York Times*, June 27, 2018, www.nytimes.com/2018/06/27/opinion/supreme-court-janus-unions.html; Heather Gies, "A Blow but Not Fatal: 9 Months After Janus, AFSCME Reports 94% Retention," *Salon*, April 6, 2019, www.salon.com/2019/04/06/a-blow-but-not-fatal-9-months-after -janus-afscme-reports-94-retention_partner.

45. Sarah Jaffe, "The Chicago Teachers Strike Was a Lesson in 21st-Century Organizing," *The Nation*, November 16, 2019, www.thenation.com/article/archive /chicago-ctu-strike-win; Sarah Jaffe, "Inside the Hard Road to Transform the Teacher's Movement into Real Power," *Medium*, October 19, 2018, https://gen .medium.com/inside-the-hard-road-to-transform-the-teachers-movement-into-real -power-f5932fc8ab6f; Samantha Winslow, "Saint Paul Teachers Strike for Their Stu-dents' Mental Health," *Labor Notes*, March 10, 2020, www.labornotes.org/2020/03 /saint-paul-teachers-strike-their-students-mental-health.

46. Sarah Jaffe, "How the New York City School System Failed the Test of Covid-19," *The Nation*, June 16, 2020, www.thenation.com/article/society/schools-teachers-covid.

47. Jacob Bogage, "Thousands of U.S. Workers Walk Out in 'Strike for Black Lives,'" *Washington Post*, July 20, 2020, www.washingtonpost.com/business/2020/07/20 /strike-for-black-lives.

48. Kyle Stokes, "After Deal with Teachers Union, LAUSD Students Can Expect (Some) Live Lessons Every Day," *LAist*, August 3, 2020, https://laist.com/2020/08/03 /coronavirus_distance_learning_lausd_los_angeles_teachers_union_live_video_lessons .php.

49. Zoie Matthew, "In a Dramatic Reversal, the L.A. City Budget Will Contain No New Funds for Police," *Los Angeles*, June 3, 2020, www.lamag.com/citythinkblog /garcetti-agrees-to-reductions-in-lapds-share-of-city-funds; United Teachers Los Angeles,

"UTLA Statement on LAUSD Vote to Defund School Police Budget by 35%," July 1, 2020, www.utla.net/news/utla-statement-lausd-vote-defund-school-police-budget-35.

CHAPTER 4: SERVICE WITH A SMILE

1. Bryce Covert, "The Demise of Toys 'R' Us Is a Warning," *The Atlantic*, July/August 2018, www.theatlantic.com/magazine/archive/2018/07/toys-r-us-bankruptcy-private-equity/561758; Sapna Maheshwari and Vanessa Friedman, "The Pandemic Helped Topple Two Retailers. So Did Private Equity," *New York Times*, May 14, 2020, www.nytimes.com/2020/05/14/business/coronavirus-retail-bankruptcies-private-equity.html.

2. Sarah Jaffe, "America's Massive Retail Workforce Is Tired of Being Ignored," *Racked*, June 20, 2017, www.racked.com/2017/6/20/15817988/retail-workers-unions-american-jobs.

3. European Commission, "Which Sector Is the Main Employer in the EU Member States?," Eurostat, October 24, 2017, https://ec.europa.eu/eurostat/web/products-eurostat-news/-/DDN-20171024-1; Bureau of Labor Statistics, "Charts of the Largest Occupations in Each Area," BLS.gov, May 2019, www.bls.gov/oes/current/area_emp_chart/area_emp_chart.htm; Bethany Biron, "The Last Decade Was Devastating for the Retail Industry. Here's How the Retail Apocalypse Played Out," *Business Insider*, December 23, 2019, www.businessinsider.com/retail-apocalypse-last-decade-timeline-2019-12; Derek Thompson, "What in the World Is Causing the Retail Meltdown of 2019?" *The Atlantic*, April 10, 2017, www.theatlantic.com/business/archive/2017/04/retail-meltdown-of-2017/522384; Abha Bhattarai, "'Retail Apocalypse' Now: Analysts Say 75,000 More U.S. Stores Could Be Doomed," *Washington Post*, April 10, 2019; Françoise Carré and Chris Tilly, *Where Bad Jobs Are Better: Retail Jobs Across Countries and Companies* (New York: Russell Sage Foundation, 2017), 1.

4. Peter Ikeler, *Hard Sell: Work and Resistance in Retail Chains* (Ithaca, NY: ILR Press, 2016), loc. 379, 385, 389, Kindle.

5. Ikeler, *Hard Sell*, loc. 395, 402.

6. Ikeler, *Hard Sell*, loc. 394, 410–411, 419, 421, 431.

7. Ikeler, *Hard Sell*, loc. 427, 433, 436, 442, 451–452; Tamara Draut, *Sleeping Giant: How the New Working Class Will Transform America* (New York: Doubleday, 2016), 44; Bethany Moreton, *To Serve God and Wal-Mart: The Making of Christian Free Enterprise* (Cambridge, MA: Harvard University Press, 2010), 54–55; Dana Frank, *Women Strikers Occupy Chain Stores, Win Big* (Chicago: Haymarket Books, 2012), 8, 29; Susan Porter Benson, *Counter Cultures: Saleswomen, Managers, and Customers in American Department Stores, 1890–1940* (Champaign: University of Illinois Press, 1987), 229.

8. Benson, *Counter Cultures*, 4, 26, 79, 125–126, 130, 187; Frank, *Women Strikers Occupy*, 19.

9. Benson, *Counter Cultures*, 20, 23, 125, 128, 209–210, 228, 230–233, 245.

10. Arlie Russell Hochschild, *The Managed Heart: Commercialization of Human Feeling* (Berkeley: University of California Press, 2012), loc. 144, 159, Kindle; Benson, *Counter Cultures*, 127.

11. Hochschild, *Managed Heart*, loc. 1410, 1421, 1445.

12. Martin Gelin, "The Misogyny of Climate Deniers," *New Republic*, August 28, 2019, https://newrepublic.com/article/154879/misogyny-climate-deniers; Jonas Anshelm and Martin Hultman, "A Green Fatwā? Climate Change as a Threat to the Masculinity of Industrial Modernity," *NORMA* 9, no. 2 (2014): 84–96, https://doi.org/10.1080/1890 2138.2014.908627; Frank, *Women Strikers Occupy*, 8, 29; Benson, *Counter Cultures*, 131, 155, 166, 180, 229.

13. Ikeler, *Hard Sell*, loc. 478–488; Frank, *Women Strikers Occupy*, 11–14; Benson, *Counter Cultures*, 236.

14. Frank, *Women Strikers Occupy*, 13–14, 19–20, 24, 37, 40–41.

15. Ikeler, *Hard Sell*, loc. 496–499, 525–527, 531, 550; Moreton, *God and Wal-Mart*, 8, 13; Nelson Lichtenstein, *The Retail Revolution: How Wal-Mart Created a Brave New World of Business* (New York: Metropolitan Books, 2009), 54, 83.

16. Lichtenstein, *Retail Revolution*, 54; Moreton, *God and Wal-Mart*, 5, 28, 37, 51.

17. Lichtentstein, *Retail Revolution*, 11, 14, 19–20, 24.

18. Lichtenstein, *Retail Revolution*, 36–38; Moreton, *God and Wal-Mart*, 5, 51, 54, 61, 65, 71–72, 76–77.

19. Moreton, *God and Wal-Mart*, 79–80; Lichtenstein, *Retail Revolution*, 41.

20. Lichtenstein, *Retail Revolution*, 83, 89–90, 126, 94; Moreton, *God and Wal-Mart*, 103, 106, 116; Hochschild, *Managed Heart*, loc. 2095.

21. Moreton, *God and Wal-Mart*, 50, 120.

22. Moreton, *God and Wal-Mart*, 184–186; Lichtenstein, *Retail Revolution*, 82; Valerie Strauss, "The 'Walmartization' of Public Education," *Washington Post*, March 17, 2016, www.washingtonpost.com/news/answer-sheet/wp/2016/03/17/the -walmartization-of-public-education; Walton Family Foundation, "2020 K-12 Education Strategic Plan," www.waltonfamilyfoundation.org/our-work/k-12-education; Moreton, *God and Wal-Mart*, 135.

23. Lichtenstein, *Retail Revolution*, 246; Frances Fox Piven and Richard Cloward, *Regulating the Poor: The Functions of Public Welfare* (New York: Vintage, 1993), loc. 6124, Kindle; Bethany Moreton, "On Her Book *To Serve God and Wal-Mart: The Making of Christian Free Enterprise*," Rorotoko, November 3, 2009, http://rorotoko.com /interview/20091104_moreton_bethany_serve_god_wal-mart_christian_free_enterprise /?page=2.

24. Lichtenstein, *Retail Revolution*, 205, 92; Ikeler, *Hard Sell*, loc. 580, 583, 586, 607, 609, 614, 654.

25. Piven and Cloward, *Regulating the Poor*, loc. 6120; Gabriel Winant, "Where Did It All Go Wrong?," *The Nation*, February 7, 2018, www.thenation.com/article /organized-labors-lost-generations; Lichtenstein, *Retail Revolution*, 99; Ikeler, *Hard Sell*, loc. 2041; Carré and Tilly, *Where Bad Jobs Are Better*, 219.

26. Ikeler, *Hard Sell*, loc. 331, 690, 767, 1478, 1511; James Cairns, *The Myth of the Age of Entitlement: Millennials, Austerity and Hope* (Toronto: University of Toronto Press, 2017), 66; Yasemin Besen-Cassino, *The Cost of Being a Girl: Working Teens and the Origins of the Gender Wage Gap* (Philadelphia: Temple University Press, 2017), 89, 92, 99–100; Carré and Tilly, *Where Bad Jobs Are Better*, 28.

27. Liza Featherstone, *Selling Women Short: The Landmark Battle for Workers' Rights at Wal-Mart* (New York: Basic Books, 2009), loc. 101, 137, 231–237, 420, 779, Kindle;

Liza Featherstone, "'Dukes v. Wal-Mart' and the Limits of Legal Change," *The Nation*, June 21, 2011, www.thenation.com/article/dukes-v-wal-mart-and-limits-legal-change; Wal-Mart Stores, Inc., v. Dukes, 564 U.S. 338 (2011).

28. Featherstone, *Selling Women Short*, loc. 1936, 1996, 2020; Besen-Cassino, *Cost of Being a Girl*, 104–105, 107, 109; Sofia Resnick, "Hobby Lobby Allegedly Fired Employee Due to Pregnancy," *Rewire*, July 29, 2014, https://rewire.news/article/2014/07/29 /hobby-lobby-allegedly-fired-employee-due-pregnancy; Sarah Jaffe, "Why Harris and Hobby Lobby Spell Disaster for Working Women," *In These Times*, June 30, 2014, http:// inthesetimes.com/working/entry/16894/scotus_rules_against_female_workers.

29. Featherstone, *Selling Women Short*, loc. 1936, 1996, 2020; Besen-Cassino, *Cost of Being a Girl*, 104–105, 107, 109; Catherine Ruetschlin and Dedrick Asante-Muhammad, "The Retail Race Divide: How the Retail Industry Is Perpetuating Racial Inequality in the 21st Century," *Demos*, June 2, 2015, www.demos.org/research/retail-race-divide-how -retail-industry-perpetuating-racial-inequality-21st-century; "Transgender Need Not Apply: A Report on Gender Identity Job Discrimination," Make the Road New York, March 2010, www.maketheroadny.org/pix_reports/TransNeedNotApplyReport_05.10 .pdf.

30. Besen-Cassino, *Cost of Being a Girl*, 82–85, 94, 97, 117; Daniel Lavelle, "Want a Shop Job? You've Got to Have the X Factor," *The Guardian*, February 27, 2018, www .theguardian.com/money/2018/feb/27/x-factor-want-a-shop-job-auditions.

31. Besen-Cassino, *Cost of Being a Girl*, 82–85, 94, 97, 117; Mindy Isser, "The Grooming Gap: What 'Looking the Part' Costs Women," *In These Times*, January 2, 2020, http://inthesetimes.com/article/22197/grooming-gap-women-economics-wage-gender -sexism-make-up-styling-dress-code.

32. Carré and Tilly, *Where Bad Jobs Are Better*, 38; Jaffe, "Massive Retail Workforce"; Aaron Braun, "Dispatches from the Labor Market," Full Stop, July 16, 2014, www.full-stop.net/2014/07/16/features/essays/aaron-braun/dispatches-from-the-labor -market.

33. Benson, *Counter Cultures*, 158; Lichtenstein, *Retail Revolution*, 112–114; Joseph Williams, "My Life as a Retail Worker: Nasty, Brutish, and Poor," *The Atlantic*, March 11, 2014, www.theatlantic.com/business/archive/2014/03/my-life-as-a-retail-worker -nasty-brutish-and-poor/284332; Graham Snowdon, "Get Happy!! Japanese Workers Face Smile Scanner," *The Guardian*, July 7, 2009, www.theguardian.com/money /blog/2009/jul/07/japanese-smile-scanning; Jaffe, "Massive Retail Workforce"; Ikeler, *Hard Sell*, loc. 1185.

34. Ikeler, *Hard Sell*, loc. 1408, 1418; Draut, *Sleeping Giant*, 155; Carré and Tilly, *Where Bad Jobs Are Better*, 29–30, 72; Jaffe, "Massive Retail Workforce."

35. Cairns, *Age of Entitlement*, 58; Office for National Statistics, "Contracts That Do Not Guarantee a Minimum Number of Hours: April 2018," www.ons.gov.uk /employmentandlabourmarket/peopleinwork/earningsandworkinghours/articles /contractsthatdonotguaranteeaminimumnumberofhours/april2018; Carré and Tilly, *Where Bad Jobs Are Better*, 1–2, 111, 149.

36. Jaffe, "Massive Retail Workforce."

37. Jaffe, "Massive Retail Workforce"; Carré and Tilly, *Where Bad Jobs Are Better*, 209.

38. Jaffe, "Massive Retail Workforce"; Bureau of Labor Statistics, "Retail Sales Workers: Summary," April 10, 2020, www.bls.gov/ooh/sales/retail-sales-workers.htm, Carré and Tilly, *Where Bad Jobs Are Better*, 18.

39. Emily Guendelsberger, "'The Most Physically Painful Experience of My Life': One Month Working in an Amazon Warehouse," *Philadelphia Inquirer*, July 11, 2019, www.inquirer.com/opinion/commentary/amazon-warehouse-on-the-clock-emily-guendelsberger-book-excerpt-20190711.html. See also Emily Guendelsberger, *On the Clock: What Low-Wage Work Did to Me and How It Drives America Insane* (New York: Little, Brown, 2019); Carré and Tilly, *Where Bad Jobs Are Better*, 215.

40. Hochschild, *Managed Heart*, loc. 3026.

41. Ikeler, *Hard Sell*, 1836, 1845, 2719–2720.

42. Abha Bhattarai, "Pandemic Bankruptcies: A Running List of Retailers That Have Filed for Chapter 11," *Washington Post*, August 3, 2020, www.washingtonpost.com/business/2020/05/27/retail-bankrupcy-chapter11; Charisse Jones, "Walmart Workers Will Call Out of Work, Use Tracker to Protect Themselves from COVID-19," *USA Today*, April 29, 2020, www.usatoday.com/story/money/2020/04/29/coronavirus-leads-some-walmart-workers-call-out-work/3047692001; Sarah Jaffe, "Belabored Stories: Will Workers' Gains Outlive the Crisis?," *Dissent*, April 7, 2020, www.dissentmagazine.org/blog/belabored-stories-will-workers-gains-outlive-the-crisis.

43. Michael Corkery, "Charles P. Lazarus, Toys 'R' Us Founder, Dies at 94," *New York Times*, March 22, 2018, www.nytimes.com/2018/03/22/obituaries/charles-p-lazarus-toys-r-us-founder-dies-at-94.html; Carré and Tilly, *Where Bad Jobs Are Better*, 47, 199.

44. Chavie Lieber, "Why Bankrupt Toys R Us Might Not Be Dead After All," *Vox*, October 3, 2018, www.vox.com/the-goods/2018/10/3/17932344/toys-r-us-liquidation-coming-back.

45. Vanessa Romo, "New Jersey Mandates Severance Pay for Workers Facing Mass Layoffs," NPR, January 22, 2020, www.npr.org/2020/01/22/798727332/new-jersey-mandates-severance-pay-for-workers-facing-mass-layoffs.

46. Eliza Ronalds-Hannon and Lauren Coleman-Lochner, "Toys R Us Workers Win $2-Million Settlement on Severance," *Los Angeles Times*, June 17, 2019, www.latimes.com/business/la-fi-toys-r-us-bankruptcy-pay-20190627-story.html.

CHAPTER 5: SUFFER FOR THE CAUSE

1. EJ Dickson, "How Nothing and Everything Has Changed in the 10 Years Since George Tiller's Murder," *Rolling Stone*, May 31, 2019, www.rollingstone.com/culture/culture-features/george-tiller-death-abortion-10-year-anniversary-842786; Carole Joffe and Tracy Weitz, "The Assassination of Dr. Tiller: The Marginality of Abortion in American Culture and Medicine," *Dissent*, November 10, 2009, www.dissentmagazine.org/online_articles/the-assassination-of-dr-tiller-the-marginality-of-abortion-in-american-culture-and-medicine.

2. Deb Gruver, "South Wind Women's Center Prepares to Open, Offer Women's Care," *Wichita Eagle*, February 6, 2013, www.kansas.com/news/article1108157.html; Rebecca Burns, "Planned Parenthood's Union Busting Could Have a Chilling Effect

for Workers Everywhere," *In These Times*, June 25, 2018, https://inthesetimes.com/working/entry/21237/planned_parenthood_union_busting_trump_labor; Aída Chávez, "Planned Parenthood Is Asking Donald Trump's Labor Board for Help Busting Its Colorado Union," *The Intercept*, May 23, 2018, https://theintercept.com/2018/05/23/planned-parenthood-union-nlrb.

3. Anna North, "The Trump Administration Is Demanding That Planned Parenthood Affiliates Give Back Their PPP Loans," *Vox*, May 23, 2020, www.vox.com/2020/5/23/21268539/planned-parenthood-80-million-ppp-loans-coronavirus.

4. Jesse Paul, "These Employees Survived the Planned Parenthood Shooting. They Say the Organization Could Have Done More to Help Them," *Colorado Sun*, December 2, 2019, https://coloradosun.com/2019/12/02/planned-parenthood-shooting-colorado-springs-employee-stories; Rachel Larris, "What You Need to Know About Indicted Anti-Choice Activist David Daleiden," Media Matters for America, January 26, 2016, www.mediamatters.org/james-okeefe/what-you-need-know-about-indicted-anti-choice-activist-david-daleiden.

5. Amy Schiller, "Caring Without Sharing: Philanthropy's Creation and Destruction of the Common World" (PhD diss., City University of New York, 2019), loc. 742–755, Kindle; Lester M. Salamon and Chelsea L. Newhouse, "The 2019 Nonprofit Employment Report," Johns Hopkins Center for Civil Society Studies, January 2019, http://ccss.jhu.edu/wp-content/uploads/downloads/2019/01/2019-NP-Employment-Report_FINAL_1.8.2019.pdf.

6. Schiller, "Caring Without Sharing," loc. 1163–1288.

7. Schiller, "Caring Without Sharing," loc. 1180–1182, 1306–1347; Frances Fox Piven and Richard Cloward, *Regulating the Poor: The Functions of Public Welfare* (New York: Vintage, 1993), loc. 302, Kindle.

8. Piven and Cloward, *Regulating the Poor*, loc. 358; Schiller, "Caring Without Sharing," loc. 1375–1376, 1408–1412, 1456–1457.

9. Piven and Cloward, *Regulating the Poor*, loc. 212; Schiller, "Caring Without Sharing," loc. 1166–1167, 1378–1379, 1398–1400.

10. Piven and Cloward, *Regulating the Poor*, loc. 417, 429, 431, 442, 469, 530, 552; Schiller, "Caring Without Sharing," loc. 1514–1518.

11. Ruth Wilson Gilmore, "in the shadow of the shadow state," in INCITE! Women of Color Against Violence, *The Revolution Will Not Be Funded: Beyond the Non-Profit Industrial Complex* (Durham, NC: Duke University Press, 2017), 45; Schiller, "Caring Without Sharing," loc. 1167–1170, 1526–1534; Alice Kessler-Harris, *Women Have Always Worked: A Concise History* (Champaign: University of Illinois Press, 2018), loc. 1702–1708, 1715–1719, Kindle; Salar Mohandesi and Emma Teitelman, "Without Reserves," in *Social Reproduction Theory: Remapping Class, Recentering Oppression*, ed. Tithi Bhattacharya (London: Pluto Press, 2017), 48.

12. Kessler-Harris, *Women Have Always Worked*, loc. 1731–1759.

13. Angela Y. Davis, *Women, Race and Class* (New York: Vintage, 1983), 59–66; Kessler-Harris, *Women Have Always Worked*, loc. 1774, 1846; Andrea Smith, "introduction: The Revolution Will Not Be Funded," in *Revolution Will Not Be Funded*, 3; Schiller, "Caring Without Sharing," loc. 1566–1567; Melissa Gira Grant, "The Unfinished

Business of Women's Suffrage," *New Republic*, August 10, 2020, https://newrepublic .com/article/158828/19th-amendment-women-suffrage-felony-vote-disenfranchisement.

14. Saidiya Hartman, *Wayward Lives, Beautiful Experiments: Intimate Histories of Riotous Black Girls, Troublesome Women, and Queer Radicals* (New York: W. W. Norton and Company, 2019), loc. 1654, Kindle; Kessler-Harris, *Women Have Always Worked*, loc. 1789–1798, 1830–1839, 1853–1856, 1864; Schiller, "Caring Without Sharing," loc. 1541–1554, 1579–1581.

15. Schiller interview with author; Schiller, "Caring Without Sharing," loc. 1556–1561, 1643–1673; Kessler-Harris, *Women Have Always Worked*, loc. 1883–1900; Eileen Boris, *Art and Labor: Ruskin, Morris, and the Craftsman Ideal in America* (Philadelphia: Temple University Press, 1986), 122, 126, 127, 131–132; Eva Kittay, *Love's Labor: Essays on Women, Equality and Disability* (London: Routledge, 1999), 126.

16. Boris, *Art and Labor*, 131–139, 180–182.

17. Kessler-Harris, *Women Have Always Worked*, loc. 1926, 1938–1948, 1953–1956; Boris, *Art and Labor*, 186–187.

18. Kessler-Harris, *Women Have Always Worked*, loc. 1929–1936, 1970, 1972, 1976–1982, 1987–2003, 2007–2019; Mohandesi and Teitelman, "Without Reserves," 49.

19. Schiller, "Caring Without Sharing," loc. 1563–1564, 1571–1573, 1583–1588, 1592–1612; Mohandesi and Teitelman, "Without Reserves," 48–50; Kittay, *Love's Labor*, 126–127.

20. Schiller interview; Schiller, "Caring Without Sharing," loc. 1149–1151, 1716–1743, 1799–1800, 1819–1822, 1827–1838; Leslie Albrecht, "Americans Slashed Their Charitable Deductions by $54 Billion After Republican Tax-Code Overhaul," Marketwatch, July 11, 2019, www.marketwatch.com/story/americans-slashed-their-charitable -deductions-by-54-billion-after-trumps-tax-overhaul-2019-07-09; Smith, "Introduction," 4.

21. Schiller, "Caring Without Sharing," loc. 1633–1637; Kessler-Harris, *Women Have Always Worked*, loc. 2037–2057, 2072.

22. Piven and Cloward, *Regulating the Poor*, loc. 1077–1232, 1336, 2710–2713; Boris, *Art and Labor*, 190; Mohandesi and Teitelman, "Without Reserves," 55.

23. Kessler-Harris, *Women Have Always Worked*, loc. 2145–2165; Smith, "introduction," 5, 7; Dylan Rodriguez, "the political logic of the non-profit industrial complex," in *The Revolution Will Not Be Funded*, 23.

24. Planned Parenthood, "Our History," 2020, www.plannedparenthood.org /about-us/who-we-are/our-history; Megan Seaholm, "Woman's Body, Woman's Right: Birth Control in America by Linda Gordon," Not Even Past, March 18, 2012, https:// notevenpast.org/womans-body-womans-right-birth-control-america-1976; Jill Lepore, "Birthright: What's Next for Planned Parenthood," *New Yorker*, November 7, 2011, www.newyorker.com/magazine/2011/11/14/birthright-jill-lepore.

25. Lepore, "Birthright."

26. Smith, "introduction," 5–7; Robert L. Allen, "from Black Awakening in Capitalist America," in *The Revolution Will Not Be Funded*, 54–58; Eric Tang, "non-profits and the autonomous grassroots," in *The Revolution Will Not Be Funded*, 218–219.

27. Tang, "nonprofits," 219; Paul Kivel, "social service or social change?," in *The Revolution Will Not Be Funded*, 138.

28. Piven and Cloward, *Regulating the Poor*, loc. 3986–4000, 4439–4570, 4698–5471, 3116.

29. Selma James, *Sex, Race, and Class: The Perspective of Winning* (Oakland, CA: PM Press, 2012), 127–128, 212.

30. Salamon and Newhouse, "2019 Nonprofit Employment Report"; Elizabeth Todd-Breland, *A Political Education: Black Politics and Education Reform in Chicago Since the 1960s* (Chapel Hill: University of North Carolina Press, 2018), 212; Smith, "introduction," 7–8; Gilmore, "shadow state," 45.

31. Nicolas Lemann, "Citizen 501(c)(3)," *The Atlantic*, February 1997, www.theatlantic.com/magazine/archive/1997/02/citizen-501c3/376777.

32. Tang, "non-profits and the autonomous grassroots," 220; Soniya Munshi and Craig Willse, "foreword," in *The Revolution Will Not Be Funded*, loc. 136, 255, 263, 272–283, 291, 311.

33. Tang, "non-profits and the autonomous grassroots," 224–226; Smith, "introduction," 7, 10; Tithi Bhattacharya, "Introduction: Mapping Social Reproduction Theory," in Bhattacharya, *Social Reproduction Theory*, 2; Nancy Fraser, "Crisis of Care? On the Social-Reproductive Contradictions of Contemporary Capitalism," in Bhattacharya, *Social Reproduction Theory*, 23, 33; Tithi Bhattacharya, "How Not to Skip Class: Social Reproduction of Labor and the Global Working Class," in Bhattacharya, *Social Reproduction Theory*, 75; James, *Sex, Race and Class*, 171.

34. Fiona Harvey and Anushka Asthana, "'Chilling' Lobbying Act Stifles Democracy, Charities Tell Party Chiefs," *The Guardian*, June 6, 2017, www.theguardian.com/politics/2017/jun/06/chilling-lobbying-act-stifles-democracy-write-charities-party-chiefs; "Lobbying: Union Anger over 'Cynical' Coalition Move," June 4, 2013, www.bbc.com/news/uk-politics-22760075.

35. Smith, "introduction," 7, 10; Rodriguez, "the political logic of the non-profit," 29–33; Gilmore, "shadow state," 45–47; Madonna Thunder Hawk, "native organizing before the non-profit industrial complex," in *The Revolution Will Not Be Funded*, 105–107; Adjoa Florência Jones de Almeida, "radical social change: Searching for a New Foundation," in *The Revolution Will Not Be Funded*, 187.

36. Mark Fisher, *Capitalist Realism: Is There No Alternative?* (London: Zer0 Books, 2009), 28; Mark Fisher, *K-punk: The Collected and Unpublished Writings of Mark Fisher*, ed. Darren Ambrose (London: Repeater Books, 2018), loc. 7422–7465, Kindle; Schiller, "Caring Without Sharing," loc. 1936–1937, 2205–2215; Tiffany Lethabo King and Ewuare Osayande, "the filth on philanthropy: Progressive Philanthropy's Agenda to Misdirect Social Justice Movements," in *The Revolution Will Not Be Funded*, 83; Ana Clarissa Rojas Durazo, "we were never meant to survive: Fighting Violence Against Women and the Fourth World War," in *The Revolution Will Not Be Funded*, 124.

37. Amara H. Pérez, Sisters in Action for Power, "between radical theory and community praxis: Reflections on Organizing and the Non-Profit Industrial Complex," in *The Revolution Will Not Be Funded*, 90–97.

38. Kayla Blado, "The Answer to Burnout at Work Isn't 'Self-Care'—It's Unionizing," *In These Times*, August 14, 2019, http://inthesetimes.com/working/entry/22017/burn-out-work-self-care-union-national-nonprofit.

39. Jonathan Timm, "The Plight of the Overworked Nonprofit Employee," *The Atlantic*, August 24, 2016, www.theatlantic.com/business/archive/2016/08/the-plight-of-the-overworked-nonprofit-employee/497081.

40. The Soros story has been repeated many times and can be found in Yael Fried-man, "Is Philanthropy Subverting Democracy?," *The Conversationalist*, October 25, 2019, https://conversationalist.org/2019/10/25/how-philanthropy-is-subverting-democracy, and also in Christine E. Ahn, "democratizing american philanthropy," in *The Revolution Will Not Be Funded*, 74; Stephanie Guilloud and William Cordery, "fundraising is not a dirty word: Community-based Economic Strategies for the Long Haul," in *The Revolution Will Not Be Funded*, 109–112; Pérez, "between radical theory and community praxis," 97; Al-isa Bierria, "pursuing a radical antiviolence agenda inside/outside a non-profit structure," in *The Revolution Will Not Be Funded*, 152.

41. Durazo, "we were never meant to survive," 115–116; Kivel, "social service or social change?," 142; Itzbeth Menjívar, "The Social Justice Sector Has an Inter-nal Racism Problem," *Sojourners*, June 11, 2019, https://sojo.net/articles/social-justice-sector-has-internal-racism-problem; Kimberly McIntosh, "Race Equality and Justice in the Charity Sector," Joseph Rowntree Foundation, October 1, 2019, www.jrf.org.uk/blog/race-equality-and-justice-charity-sector; Vanessa Daniel, "Philanthropists Bench Women of Color, the M.V.P.s of Social Change," *New York Times*, November 19, 2019, www.nytimes.com/2019/11/19/opinion/philanthropy-black-women.html.

42. Keeanga-Yamahtta Taylor, "Five Years Later, Do Black Lives Matter?" *Jacobin*, September 30, 2019, https://jacobinmag.com/2019/09/black-lives-matter-laquan-mcdonald-mike-brown-eric-garner.

43. Schiller, "Caring Without Sharing," loc. 1882–1916, 2069–2070, 2400–2402; "Normal Life: Administrative Violence, Critical Trans Politics, and the Limits of the Law, Dean Spade," book review, in *Lies: A Journal of Materialist Feminism* 1 (2012), https://libcom.org/library/lies-journal-marxist-feminism.

44. David Harvey, *A Brief History of Neoliberalism* (Oxford: Oxford University Press, 2007), 177; Schiller, "Caring Without Sharing," loc. 521–522, 582–585; Silvia Federici, *Revolution at Point Zero: Housework, Reproduction, and Feminist Struggle* (Oak-land, CA: PM Press, 2012), loc. 66, 70, 74–75, 81–85, Kindle; Hala Al-Karib, "The Dangers of NGO-isation of Women's Rights in Africa," Al Jazeera English, December 13, 2018, www.aljazeera.com/indepth/opinion/dangers-ngo-isation-women-rights-africa-181212102656547.html; Smith, "introduction," 11.

45. Jonathan Matthew Smucker, *Hegemony How-To: A Roadmap for Radicals* (Brook-lyn, NY: AK Press, 2017), 33–34, 38; Schiller interview; Daisy Rooks, "The Cowboy Mentality: Organizers and Occupational Commitment in the New Labor Movement," *Labor Studies Journal* 28, no. 33 (2003), https://doi.org/10.1177/0160449X0302800302; "Guide for the Exploited Nonprofit Workers," *Tituba's Revenge*, no. 1 (December 2011), https://titubasrevenge.files.wordpress.com/2011/12/tituba_newsletter_1_dec20111.pdf.

46. Yasmin Nair, "Fuck Love," YasminNair.com, November 1, 2011 https://yasminnair.com/fuck-love; Bethany Moreton and Pamela Voeckel, "Learning from the Right," in *Labor Rising: The Past and Future of Working People in America*, ed. Daniel Katz and Richard Greenwald (New York: New Press, 2012), 34–36.

47. "Guide for the Exploited"; Ann Goggins Gregory and Don Howard, "The Non-profit Starvation Cycle," *Stanford Social Innovation Review*, Fall 2009, https://ssir.org/articles/entry/the_nonprofit_starvation_cycle; Cory Doctorow, "Exploitation of Workers

Becomes More Socially Acceptable if the Workers Are Perceived as 'Passionate' About Their Jobs," BoingBoing, May 22, 2019, https://boingboing.net/2019/05/22/weaponized -satisfaction.html; Jae Yun Kim, Troy H. Campbell, Steven Shepherd, and Aaron C. Kay, "Understanding Contemporary Forms of Exploitation: Attributions of Passion Serve to Legitimize the Poor Treatment of Workers," *Journal of Personality and Social Psychology* 118, no. 1 (2020): 121–148, https://doi.org/10.1037/pspi0000190.

48. Bureau of Labor Statistics, "Nonprofits Account for 12.3 Million Jobs, 10.2 Percent of Private Sector Employment, in 2016," August 31, 2018, www.bls.gov /opub/ted/2018/nonprofits-account-for-12-3-million-jobs-10-2-percent-of-private -sector-employment-in-2016.htm; Rachel Swain, "Overview of the UK Charity Sector," *Prospects*, September 2019, www.prospects.ac.uk/jobs-and-work-experience/job-sectors /charity-and-voluntary-work/overview-of-the-uk-charity-sector; Ramsin Canon, "Nonprofit Workers Need Unions, Too," *Jacobin*, August 19, 2019, www.jacobinmag .com/2019/08/nonprofits-industrial-complex-socialist-organizing.

49. Stephanie Russell-Kraft, "The Aggressive Anti-Union Campaign at Story-Corps," *The Nation*, July 17, 2017, www.thenation.com/article/the-aggressive-anti-union -campaign-at-storycorps.

50. Sarah Jaffe, "Nonprofit Workers Join the Movement to Unionize," *The Progressive*, November 19, 2019, https://progressive.org/dispatches/nonprofit-workers -unionize-jaffe-191119; Nonprofit Professional Employees Union, "Nonprofit Professional Employees Union Files Unfair Labor Practice Against National Center for Transgender Equality Leadership for Retaliation Against Staff Organizing," November 15, 2019, https://npeu.org/news/2019/11/15/nonprofit-professional-employees-union-files -unfair-labor-practice-against-national-center-for-transgender-equality-leadership-for -retaliation-against-staff-organizing; Ellen Davis, "SPLC Management Won't Voluntarily Recognize Labor Union," *Nonprofit Quarterly*, November 15, 2019, https:// nonprofitquarterly.org/splc-management-wont-voluntarily-recognize-labor-union; Independent Workers of Great Britain, "IWGB Charity Workers Branch," 2020, https://iwgb .org.uk/page/iwgb-charity-workers-branch.

51. Kayla Blado, personal communication with author.

52. Independent Workers of Great Britain, "IWGB Charity Workers Branch Statement on COVID-19," 2020, https://iwgb.org.uk/page/iwgb-charity-workers -branch-covid-19-statement.

53. Canon, "Nonprofit Workers"; Sigal Samuel, "Racial Justice Groups Have Never Had So Much Cash. It's Actually Hard to Spend It," *Vox*, June 19, 2020, www .vox.com/future-perfect/2020/6/19/21294819/minnesota-freedom-fund-donations -police-protests; Samantha Cooney, "Planned Parenthood Has Received 300,000 Donations Since the Election," *Time*, December 27, 2016, https://time.com/4618359 /planned-parenthood-election-donations.

54. Gilmore, "shadow state," 51.

55. Cecile Richards (@CecileRichards), Twitter, June 27, 2018, 7:30 a.m., https:// twitter.com/cecilerichards/status/1011980006086578182; Caroline Lewis, "Kirk Adams & Cecile Richards," Crain's New York, accessed August 8, 2020, www.crains newyork.com/awards/kirk-adams-cecile-richards; Sarah McCammon, "After Years in

the Trenches, Planned Parenthood's Cecile Richards Will Step Down," NPR, January 26, 2018, www.npr.org/sections/thetwo-way/2018/01/26/580733009/after-years-in-the-trenches-planned-parenthoods-cecile-richards-will-step-down; Burns, "Planned Parenthood's Union Busting"; Natalie Kitroeff and Jessica Silver-Greenberg, "Planned Parenthood Is Accused of Mistreating Pregnant Employees," *New York Times*, December 20, 2018, www.nytimes.com/2018/12/20/business/planned-parenthood-pregnant-employee-discrimination-women.html.

56. Kitroeff and Silver-Greenberg, "Planned Parenthood"; Jessica Rubio, nurse practitioner, quoted in Erin Heger, "Planned Parenthood Has a History of Trying to Beat Back Labor Unions," *Rewire*, July 19, 2018, https://rewire.news/article/2018/07/19/planned-parenthood-history-trying-beat-back-labor-unions; Coworker.org, "Planned Parenthood Employees Need Paid Parental and Medical Leave," Coworker, www.coworker.org/petitions/planned-parenthood-employees-need-paid-parental-and-medical-leave.

57. Claude Solnik, "Planned Parenthood, ACLU, Refugee Charities Get 'Trump Bump,'" *Long Island Business News*, April 26, 2017, https://libn.com/2017/04/26/planned-parenthood-aclu-refugee-charities-get-trump-bump; Kitroeff and Silver-Greenberg, "Planned Parenthood"; PPRM Bargaining Unit, Facebook, June 17, 2018, www.facebook.com/PPRMBargainingUnit/photos/a.243437136213043/25580220 1643203.

58. Erin Heger, "'Frustrating,' 'Confusing': Planned Parenthood Workers Grapple with Organization's Union Fight," *Rewire*, June 14, 2018, https://rewire.news/article/2018/06/14/frustrating-confusing-planned-parenthood-workers-grapple-organizations-union-fight.

59. A report from the Economic Policy institute said of Trump's NLRB: "Under the Trump administration, the National Labor Relations Board (NLRB) has systematically rolled back workers' rights to form unions and engage in collective bargaining with their employers, to the detriment of workers, their communities, and the economy. The Trump board has issued a series of significant decisions weakening worker protections under the National Labor Relations Act (NLRA/Act). Further, the board has engaged in an unprecedented number of rulemakings aimed at overturning existing worker protections. Finally, the Trump NLRB general counsel (GC) has advanced policies that leave fewer workers protected by the NLRA and has advocated for changes in the law that roll back workers' rights." Celine McNicholas, Margaret Poydock, and Lynn Rhinehart, "Unprecedented: The Trump NLRB's Attack on Workers' Rights," Economic Policy Institute, October 16, 2019, www.epi.org/publication/unprecedented-the-trump-nlrbs-attack-on-workers-rights; Joey Bunch, "Lawmakers Back Denver Planned Parenthood Workers' Union Cause," *Colorado Politics*, June 13, 2018, www.coloradopolitics.com/news/lawmakers-back-denver-planned-parenthood-workers-union-cause/article_5f4df23c-d39a-5e9c-a840-615bfc46a422.html.

60. Chávez, "Planned Parenthood."

61. Dennis Carter, "Planned Parenthood Drops Its Fight Against Unionizing Workers in Colorado," *Rewire*, August 17, 2018, https://rewire.news/article/2018/08/17/planned-parenthood-drops-its-fight-against-unionizing-workers-in-colorado.

62. "Mass Exodus at Boulder Women's Health Center: Whistleblowers Disclose Damning Allegations That Contributed to Institutional Breakdown," *The Nation*

Report, September 17, 2019, www.thenationreport.org/mass-exodus-at-boulder-womens
-health-center-a-whistleblower-discloses-damning-allegations-that-contributed-to
-institutional-breakdown; Charlie Brennan, "Nearly Half of Boulder Valley Wom-
en's Health Center Staff Leaves, Citing Leadership," *Boulder Daily Camera*, August
27, 2019, www.dailycamera.com/2019/08/27/nearly-half-of-boulder-valley-womens
-health-center-staff-leaves-citing-leadership.

63. Alex Caprariello, "Planned Parenthood Employees Laid Off, Claim It's Retaliation for Voicing Concerns," KXAN News, April 10, 2020, www.kxan.com/news/local
/austin/planned-parenthood-employees-laid-off-claim-its-retaliation-for-voicing-con
cerns; Melissa Gira Grant, "A Worker Uprising at Planned Parenthood," *New Republic*, June
18, 2020, https://newrepublic.com/article/158224/planned-parenthood-covid-racism
-union.

CHAPTER 6: MY STUDIO IS THE WORLD

1. Megan Garber, "David Foster Wallace and the Dangerous Romance of Male Genius," *The Atlantic*, May 9, 2018, www.theatlantic.com/entertainment/archive/2018/05
/the-world-still-spins-around-male-genius/559925; Cristina Nehring, *A Vindication of
Love: Reclaiming Romance for the Twenty-First Century* (New York: Harper, 2009), 3.

2. Garber, "David Foster Wallace"; Miya Tokumitsu, *Do What You Love: And Other
Lies About Success and Happiness* (New York: Regan Arts, 2015), 2.

3. John Berger, *Landscapes: John Berger on Art*, ed. Tom Overton (New York: Verso,
2016), loc. 753, Kindle; Lewis Hyde, *The Gift: Creativity and the Artist in the Modern
World*, 25th Anniversary Edition (New York: Vintage, 2009), 186–189; Howard S.
Becker, *Art Worlds* (Berkeley: University of California Press, 1982), 14.

4. Berger, *Landscapes*, loc. 949–965; Hyde, *The Gift*, 249.

5. Raymond Williams, *Keywords: A Vocabulary of Culture and Society* (Oxford: Oxford University Press, 2014), 82–84, 143; John Patrick Leary, "How 'Creativity' Became
a Capitalist Buzzword," LitHub, March 11, 2019, https://lithub.com/how-creativity
-became-a-capitalist-buzzword. See also John Patrick Leary, *Keywords: The New Language
of Capitalism* (Chicago: Haymarket Books, 2019).

6. John Berger, *Ways of Seeing* (New York: Penguin, 2008), 4, 11; Walter Benjamin,
"The Work of Art in the Age of Mechanical Reproduction," in *Illuminations*, ed. Hannah
Arendt, trans. Harry Zohn (New York: Schocken Books, 1969 [1935]) 2, 6–7; Ben Davis,
9.5 Theses on Art and Class (Chicago: Haymarket Books, 2013), loc. 1318–1320, Kindle.

7. Becker, *Art Worlds*, 14–15, 353; Davis, *Art and Class*, loc. 1446–1448, 2906–
2909; Berger, *Ways of Seeing*, 30–31, 49, 51–52; Berger, *Landscapes*, loc. 2944–2946.

8. Becker, *Art Worlds*, 15, 100, 354; Berger, *Landscapes*, loc. 2750–2752, 2768–
2777; Berger, *Ways of Seeing*, 42; Julia Bryan-Wilson, *Art Workers: Radical Practice in
the Vietnam War Era* (Berkeley: University of California Press, 2011), 1–13; Williams,
Keywords, 41.

9. Berger, *Ways of Seeing*, 5–7; Frans Hals Museum, "Regents of the Old Men's Alms
House," www.franshalsmuseum.nl/en/art/regents-of-the-old-mens-alms-house.

10. Davis, *Art and Class*, loc. 1452–1461; Becker, *Art Worlds*, 109.

11. Becker, *Art Worlds*, 354; Raymond Williams, *Culture and Society: Coleridge to
Orwell, 1780–1950* (London: Vintage, 2017), 1, 4, 48–56, 66–67; Williams, *Keywords*,

41–42; Eileen Boris, *Art and Labor: Ruskin, Morris, and the Craftsman Ideal in America* (Philadelphia: Temple University Press, 1986), xii.

12. George Orwell, *All Art Is Propaganda: Critical Essays*, ed. George Packer (Boston: Mariner Books, 2009), 255; Berger, *Landscapes*, loc. 894–906; Williams, *Culture and Society*, 71.

13. Davis, *Art and Class*, loc. 2924–2925; Becker, *Art Worlds*, 182.

14. Williams, *Culture and Society*, 183–187, 207; Andrew Ross, *No Collar: The Hidden Cost of the Humane Workplace* (New York: Basic Books, 2002), 4; Boris, *Art and Labor*, xi–xv, 14–15, 138, 153, 156.

15. D. Anthony White, *Siqueiros: Biography of a Revolutionary Artist* (Charleston, SC: BookSurge Publishing, 2009), loc. 424–430, 722–723, 875–878, 930–933, 1058–1061, 1261–1298, 1351–1398, 2045–2047, 2149–2155, Kindle; Bryan-Wilson, *Art Workers*, 3–13.

16. Angela Y. Davis, "Art on the Frontline: Mandate for a People's Culture," in *The Angela Y. Davis Reader*, ed. Joy James (Hoboken, NJ: Blackwell, 1998), 235–239, 250–253; E. Doss, "Looking at Labor: Images of Work in 1930s American Art," *Journal of Decorative and Propaganda Arts* 24 (2002): 231–257, https://doi.org/10.2307/1504189; "The Future of America: Lewis Hine's New Deal Photographs," International Center of Photography, www.icp.org/browse/archive/collections/the-future-of-america-lewis-hines-new-deal-photographs; E. Doss, "Toward an Iconography of American Labor: Work, Workers, and the Work Ethic in American Art, 1930–1945," *Design Issues* 13, no. 1 (1997): 53–66, https://doi.org.10.2307/1511587; A. Joan Saab, *For the Millions: American Art and Culture Between the Wars* (Philadelphia: University of Pennsylvania Press, 2009), 2, 6–8, 15, 24–27.

17. Saab, *For the Millions*, 15–17, 20, 31–32, 34–38.

18. Saab, *For the Millions*, 40–42, 54–59, 61–63, 140–141; Doss, "Looking at Labor," 250.

19. Saab, *For the Millions*, 80, 44, 163, 165–166, 171–173; Berger, *Landscapes*, loc. 2536–2579.

20. Bryan-Wilson, *Art Workers*, 2–13; Leary, "How 'Creativity' Became a Capitalist Buzzword"; Saab, *For the Millions*, 173, 181. John Berger, typically, had a different understanding: "The majority of Russian painting is bad—the new developments are still embryonic. The majority of Western art is equally bad, but for the opposite reasons. In one case it is a question of art being too superficially literal; in the other of it being too profoundly remote. They have made art cheap. We have made it a luxury." Berger, *Landscapes*, loc. 2577–2579.

21. Mark Fisher, *K-punk: The Collected and Unpublished Writings of Mark Fisher*, ed. Darren Ambrose (London: Repeater Books, 2018), loc. 8650, 12654, 12706, 12777; Bryan-Wilson, *Art Workers*, 5–13; Luc Boltanski and Eve Chiapello, *The New Spirit of Capitalism* (New York: Verso, 2018), loc. 6692–6694, Kindle.

22. Bryan-Wilson, *Art Workers*, 1–13.

23. Bryan-Wilson, *Art Workers*, 1–13.

24. Bryan-Wilson, *Art Workers*, 1–13; Sarah Resnick, "Issues & Commentary: Organizing the Museum," *Art in America*, April 1, 2019, www.artnews.com/art-in-america/features/museum-unions-issues-commentary-organizing-the-museum-63617.

25. Bryan-Wilson, *Art Workers*, 4–13; Davis, *Art and Class*, loc. 283–285; Federica Martini, "Art History Cold Cases: Artists' Labour in the Factory," in Vanina Hofman and Pau Alsina, coords., "Art and Speculative Futures," Universitat Oberta de Catalunya, *Artnodes*, no. 19 (2017): 1–8, http://dx.doi.org/10.7238/a.v0i19.3099.

26. Martina Tanga, "Artists Refusing to Work: Aesthetic Practices in 1970s Italy," *Palinsesti* 1, no. 4 (2015): 35–49.

27. Bolanski and Chiapello, *New Spirit of Capitalism*, loc. 6692–6734, 8381–8386, 8711–8715, 9329–9331.

28. Davis, *Art and Class*, loc. 2956–2972.

29. David Harvey, *A Brief History of Neoliberalism* (Oxford: Oxford University Press, 2007), 47; Astra Taylor, *The People's Platform: Taking Back Power and Culture in the Digital Age* (New York: Metropolitan, 2014), 56–59, 66; Kate Oakley, "'Art Works'— Cultural Labour Markets: A Literature Review," *Creativity, Culture and Education*, October 2009, 29.

30. Berger, *Landscapes*, loc. 2668–2689; Becker, *Art Worlds*, ix–x, 23, 113.

31. Becker, *Art Worlds*, x, 1–5, 9–10, 13.

32. Kerry Guinan interview with author.

33. Becker, *Art Worlds*, 34–36, 52, 77–81, 91–97, 103–106, 172, 350.

34. Mark Fisher, *Capitalist Realism: Is There No Alternative?* (London: Zer0 Books, 2009), 76; Davis, *Art and Class*, loc. 210–213, 241–249, 274–275, 280–283, 438–441, 481–484, 492–497, 2917–2919; Oakley, "Art Works," 25–25.

35. Davis, *Art and Class*, loc. 298–300, 249–250, 1276–1297, 1298–1318, 1422–1431; Susan Jones, "By Paying Artists Nothing, We Risk Severing the Pipeline of UK Talent," *The Guardian*, May 19, 2014, www.theguardian.com/culture-professionals-network/culture-professionals-blog/2014/may/19/paying-artists-nothing-uk-talent; Susan Jones, "Rethinking Artists: The Role of Artists in the 21st Century," Seoul Art Space, Seoul Foundation for Arts and Culture International Symposium, November 4, 2014, https://sca-net.org/resources/view/rethinking-artists-the-role-of-artists-in-the-21st-century. The 2018 US study was done by researchers affiliated with crowdfunding site Kickstarter, which itself is a reminder that most working artists' lives involve asking other people for money. "A Study on the Financial State of Visual Artists Today," 2018, The Creative Independent, https://thecreativeindependent.com/artist-survey; Angella d'Avignon, "Got to Be Real," *The Baffler*, March 7, 2019, https://thebaffler.com/latest/got-to-be-real-davignon.

36. Claire McCaughey, "Comparisons of Arts Funding in Selected Countries: Preliminary Findings," Canada Council for the Arts, October 2005, www.creativecity.ca/database/files/library/comparisonsofartsfunding27oct2005.pdf; Drew Wylie Projects, "Scottish Parliament—Arts Funding Inquiry Comparative Analysis," May 2019, www.parliament.scot/S5_European/Inquiries/CTEEA_Arts_Funding_Research.pdf; Jones, "Rethinking Artists"; Danish Artist Union, accessed August 11, 2020, www.artisten.dk/Forside/The-Danish-Artist-Union; Oakley, "Art Works," 130.

37. Mark Brown, "Arts Industry Report Asks: Where Are All the Working-Class People?," *The Guardian*, April 16, 2018, www.theguardian.com/culture/2018/apr/16/arts-industry-report-asks-where-are-all-the-working-class-people; Jones, "Rethinking Artists"; Alexander Billet and Adam Turl, "The Ghost Ship Is Our Triangle Fire," *Red Wedge*

Magazine, December 12, 2016, www.redwedgemagazine.com/online-issue/ghostship; Jillian Steinhauer, "How Wealthy Are Artists' Parents?," *Hyperallergic*, March 21, 2014, https://hyperallergic.com/115957/how-wealthy-are-artists-parents.

38. Davis, *Art and Class*, loc. 1429–1490; Hito Steyerl, "If You Don't Have Bread, Eat Art!: Contemporary Art and Derivative Fascisms," E-Flux, October 2016, www.e-flux.com/journal/76/69732/if-you-don-t-have-bread-eat-art-contemporary -art-and-derivative-fascisms; Oakley, "Art Works"; Rachel Corbett, "Why Are Artists Poor? New Research Suggests It Could Be Hardwired into Their Brain Chemistry," ArtNet, July 2, 2018, https://news.artnet.com/art-world/why-are-artists-poor-research -suggests-it-could-be-hardwired-1310147.

39. Davis, *Art and Class*, loc. 1658–1721; Natasha Lennard, "New York City's Cops Are Waging War on Subway Performers," *Vice*, May 7, 2014, www.vice.com/en_us /article/nem9vm/new-york-citys-cops-are-waging-war-on-subway-performers.

40. Davis, *Art and Class*, loc. 1542–1544; Becker, *Art Worlds*, 260–267; d'Avignon, "Got to Be Real," 24–25; Tokumitsu, *Do What You Love*, 46–47.

41. Ben Davis and Sarah Cascone, "The New Museum's Staff Is Pushing to Unionize—and Top Leadership Is Not at All Happy About It," ArtNet, January 10, 2019, https://news.artnet.com/art-world/new-museum-union-drive-1436788; Resnick, "Organizing the Museum"; Frances Anderton, "Marciano Art Foundation and the Value of 'Art Labor,'" KCRW, November 12, 2019, www.kcrw.com /culture/shows/design-and-architecture/marciano-and-art-labor-shortlisted/marciano -art-foundation-and-the-value-of-art-labor; Benjamin Sutton, "An Online Spreadsheet Revealed Museum Workers' Salaries," Artsy, June 3, 2019, www.artsy.net/news /artsy-editorial-online-spreadsheet-revealed-museum-workers-salaries.

42. Stephen Tracy, "Milieu Insight Response and Clarification on The Sunday Times Essential Workers Poll," *Milieu*, June 15, 2020, https://mili.eu/insights /sunday-times-essential-workers-poll-response; Sarah Jaffe, "Belabored Stories: Someday the Museums Will Reopen," *Dissent*, March 30, 2020, www.dissentmagazine.org/blog /belabored-stories-someday-the-museums-will-reopen; Sarah Jaffe, "The Union Drive at the Philadelphia Museum of Art," *Dissent*, June 15, 2020, www.dissentmagazine.org /blog/the-union-drive-at-the-philadelphia-museum-of-art; Zachary Small, "Workers at Philadelphia Museum of Art Vote to Join Union," *New York Times*, August 6, 2020, www.nytimes.com/2020/08/06/arts/workers-at-philadelphia-museum-of-art-vote-to -join-union.html.

43. Bill Mazza, personal communication with author.

44. Heather Abel, "The Baby, the Book and the Bathwater," *Paris Review*, January 31, 2018, www.theparisreview.org/blog/2018/01/31/baby-book-bathwater; Rufi Thorpe, "Mother, Writer, Monster, Maid," *Vela Magazine*, n.d., http://velamag.com /mother-writer-monster-maid.

45. Davis, *Art and Class*, loc. 1778–1862.

46. Fisher, *K-punk*, loc. 8289–8297; Jeremy Lovell, "Hirst's Diamond Skull Sells for $100 Million," Reuters, August 30, 2007, www.reuters.com/article/us-arts-hirst -skull-idUSL3080962220070830; Davis, *Art and Class*, loc. 2074–2093, 2246–2248; Julia Halperin and Brian Boucher, "Jeff Koons Radically Downsizes His Studio, Laying

Off Half His Painting Staff," ArtNet, June 20, 2017, https://news.artnet.com/art-world/jeff-koons-radically-downsizes-his-studio-laying-off-half-his-painting-staff-998666; Pernilla Holmes, "The Branding of Damien Hirst," *ArtNews*, October 1, 2007, www.artnews.com/art-news/artists/the-branding-of-damien-hirst-176.

47. Becker, *Art Worlds*, 77; Lucia Love, Interview with author; Paddy Johnson and Rhett Jones, "Jeff Koons Lays Off Workers Amidst Reports of Unionization," Art F City, July 18, 2016, http://artfcity.com/2016/07/18/jeff-koons-lays-off-workers-amidst-reports-of-impropriety; Eileen Kinsella, "Jeff Koons Lays Off Over a Dozen Staffers After They Tried to Unionize," ArtNet, July 19, 2016, https://news.artnet.com/art-world/jeff-koons-lays-off-staff-members-563018.

48. Halperin and Boucher, "Jeff Koons Radically Downsizes"; Valeria Ricciulli, "Domino Sugar Factory: A Guide to the Megaproject's Buildings," Curbed, November 11, 2019, https://ny.curbed.com/2019/11/11/20954204/domino-sugar-factory-redevelopment-williamsburg-brooklyn-buildings; Dia: Beacon, "Richard Serra, Long-Term View, Dia Beacon," www.diaart.org/program/exhibitions-projects/richard-serra-collection-display; Doreen St. Félix, "Kara Walker's Next Act," *Vulture*, April 17, 2017, www.vulture.com/2017/04/kara-walker-after-a-subtlety.html; Christopher Beam, "Kehinde Wiley's Global Reach," April 20, 2012, https://nymag.com/arts/art/rules/kehinde-wiley-2012-4.

49. Benjamin, "Art in the Age"; Taylor, *People's Platform*, 44–66, 168–169, 175.

50. Molly Crabapple, interview with author; Malcolm Harris, *Kids These Days: The Making of Millennials* (New York: Back Bay Books, 2018), 179; Steven Rosenbaum, "Death of Vine Should Be a Lesson to Other Social Media Platforms," *Forbes*, November 2, 2016, www.forbes.com/sites/stevenrosenbaum/2016/11/02/death-vine-lesson-social-media.

51. Fisher, *K-punk*, loc. 8034; OK Fox and Love interview with author; Billet and Turl, "Ghost Ship."

52. Davis, *Art and Class*, loc. 2825–2827; Devyn Springer, "Cultural Worker, Not a 'Creative,'" *Medium*, October 23, 2018, https://medium.com/@DevynSpringer/cultural-worker-not-a-creative-4695ae8bfd2d; Alison Stine, "Why Art Matters, Even in Poverty," TalkPoverty, April 18, 2016, https://talkpoverty.org/2016/04/18/why-art-matters-even-in-poverty.

53. Art, Architecture, Activism, "Spare Room Project," 2019, www.spareroomproject.ie.

CHAPTER 7: HOPING FOR WORK

1. Imagine Canada, "Non-Profit Sector Continues to Grow," press release, March 5, 2019, www.imaginecanada.ca/en/360/non-profit-sector-continues-grow.

2. Ross Perlin, *Intern Nation: How to Earn Nothing and Learn Little in the Brave New Economy* (New York: Verso, 2012), loc. 94, Kindle, pp. 1–3, 196; Josh Sanburn, "The Beginning of the End of the Unpaid Internship," *Time*, May 2, 2012, http://business.time.com/2012/05/02/the-beginning-of-the-end-of-the-unpaid-internship-as-we-know-it.

3. Perlin, *Intern Nation*, 23–24.

4. Kathleen M. Kuehn, "Hope Labor as, Well, Hope Labor," KMKuehn.com, July 15, 2013; Kathleen Kuehn and Thomas F. Corrigan, "Hope Labor: The Role of Employment Prospects in Online Social Production," *Political Economy of Communication* 1, no. 1 (2013): 9–25.

5. Luc Boltanski and Eve Chiapello, *The New Spirit of Capitalism* (New York: Verso, 2018), loc. 3103–3104, Kindle; Kuehn and Corrigan, "Hope Labor."

6. Boltanski and Chiapello, *New Spirit of Capitalism*, loc. 3494–3496, 3932–3933, 3939–3940, 5091–5100; Miya Tokumitsu, *Do What You Love: And Other Lies About Success and Happiness* (New York: Regan Arts, 2015), 87.

7. Perlin, *Intern Nation*, 45, 46; Alexandre Frenette, "From Apprenticeship to Internship: The Social and Legal Antecedents of the Intern Economy," *TripleC* 13, no 2 (2015): https://doi.org/10.31269/triplec.v13i2.625; Olivia B. Waxman, "How Internships Replaced the Entry-Level Job," *Time*, July 25, 2018, https://time.com/5342599/history-of-interns-internships.

8. Frenette, "From Apprenticeship to Internship"; Perlin, *Intern Nation*, 46–48; Waxman, "How Internships Replaced the Entry-Level Job."

9. Frenette, "From Apprenticeship to Internship"; Perlin, *Intern Nation*, 47–51.

10. Perlin, *Intern Nation*, 51–53.

11. Perlin, *Intern Nation*, 53–56.

12. Lydia Dishman, "How I Made Ends Meet as an Unpaid Intern (and Why It Was Worth It)," *Fast Company*, January 16, 2019, www.fastcompany.com/90289973/how-i-made-ends-meet-as-an-unpaid-intern-and-why-it-was-worth-it.

13. Waxman, "How Internships Replaced the Entry-Level Job"; Frenette, "From Apprenticeship to Internship"; Perlin, *Intern Nation*, 30–31; Helen B. Holmes, "How the Unpaid Internship Became America's Favorite Corporate Scam," *Mel Magazine*, 2018, https://melmagazine.com/en-us/story/how-the-unpaid-internship-became-americas-favorite-corporate-scam; Sanburn, "Beginning of the End."

14. Perlin, *Intern Nation*, 31; Ryan Park, "Why So Many Young Doctors Work Such Awful Hours," *The Atlantic*, February 21, 2017, www.theatlantic.com/business/archive/2017/02/doctors-long-hours-schedules/516639; Sarah Jaffe, "16-Hour Shifts, But Not a Real Worker?," *In These Times*, October 23, 2013, http://inthesetimes.com/working/entry/15785/16_hour_shifts_but_not_a_real_worker.

15. Perlin, *Intern Nation*, 32–33; Sanburn, "Beginning of the End"; Karl E. Stromsem, "The Work of the National Institute of Public Affairs, 1934–1949: A Summary" (Washington, DC: National Institute of Public Affairs, 1949).

16. Perlin, *Intern Nation*, 32–33; Sanburn, "Beginning of the End."

17. Holmes, "The Unpaid Internship"; Perlin, *Intern Nation*, 65–72; Natalie Bacon, "Unpaid Internships: The History, Policy, and Future Implications of 'Fact Sheet #71,'" *Ohio State Entrepreneurial Business Law Journal* 6, no. 1 (2011): 67–96; Walling v. Portland Terminal Co., 330 U.S. 148 (1947).

18. Frenette, "From Apprenticeship to Internship"; Perlin, *Intern Nation*, 34–36, 90; Waxman, "How Internships Replaced the Entry-Level Job."

19. Perlin, *Intern Nation*, 68, 212.

20. Perlin, *Intern Nation*, 2–3, 14, 28, 36–39, 45, 96; Sanburn, "The Beginning of the End"; Frenette, "From Apprenticeship to Internship."

21. Guy Standing, *The Precariat* (London: Bloomsbury Academic, 2011), loc. 589, 3026, 2900, Kindle.

22. Perlin, *Intern Nation*, 26–27, 134; Malcolm Harris, *Kids These Days: The Making of Millennials* (New York: Back Bay Books, 2018), 91–94.

23. Tokumitsu, *Do What You Love*, 96; Harris, *Kids These Days*, 91; Madeleine Schwartz, "Opportunity Costs: The True Price of Internships," *Dissent*, Winter 2013, www.dissentmagazine.org/article/opportunity-costs-the-true-price-of-internships.

24. Kathi Weeks, "'Hours for What We Will': Work, Family, and the Movement for Shorter Hours," *Feminist Studies* 35, no. 1 (Spring 2009): 101–127; Schwartz, "Opportunity Costs."

25. Perlin, *Intern Nation*, loc. 203, pp. 85, 86, 89–90.

26. Perlin, *Intern Nation*, 80–82; Bacon, "Unpaid Internships"; Blair Hickman and Christie Thompson, "How Unpaid Interns Aren't Protected Against Sexual Harassment," ProPublica, August 9, 2013, www.propublica.org/article/how-unpaid-interns-arent-protected-against-sexual-harassment.

27. Perlin, *Intern Nation*, 100–106; Laurel Wamsley, "New Congresswoman Will Pay Her Interns $15 an Hour. Is That a Big Deal?," NPR, December 6, 2018, www.npr.org/2018/12/06/674378315/new-congresswoman-will-pay-her-interns-15-an-hour-is-that-a-big-deal; William Cummings, "Ocasio-Cortez Decries Congressional Pay, Vows to Give Interns 'at Least' $15 an Hour," *USA Today*, December 14, 2019, https://eu.usatoday.com/story/news/politics/2018/12/06/alexandria-ocasio-cortez-interns/2224892002; Sanjana Karanth, "Alexandria Ocasio-Cortez Explains Why Interns Should Be Paid with More Than Experience," *HuffPost*, July 25, 2019, www.huffingtonpost.co.uk/entry/alexandria-ocasio-cortez-paid-interns_n_5d3a061fe4b004b6adbd0edd.

28. Perlin, *Intern Nation*, 83–84, 118, 122, 132, 137–138; Kuehn and Corrigan, "Hope Labor"; Harris, *Kids These Days*, 22.

29. Lauren Lumpkin, "Coronavirus Blew Up Summer Internships, Forcing Students and Employers to Get Creative," *Washington Post*, May 3, 2020, www.washingtonpost.com/local/education/coronavirus-blew-up-summer-internships-forcing-students-and-employers-to-get-creative/2020/05/03/7f2708ae-83dd-11ea-a3eb-e9fc93160703_story.html; Perlin, *Intern Nation*, 45.

30. Perlin, *Intern Nation*, 61, 167–169; Christy Romer, "Almost 90% of Arts Internships Are Unpaid," *Arts Professional*, November 23, 2018, www.artsprofessional.co.uk/news/almost-90-arts-internships-are-unpaid; Hakim Bishara, "The Association of Art Museum Directors Calls on Museums to Provide Paid Internships," *Hyperallergic*, June 20, 2019, https://hyperallergic.com/506184/the-association-of-art-museum-directors-calls-on-museums-to-provide-paid-internships.

31. Perlin, *Intern Nation*, 152–155, 146–148; Standing, *The Precariat*, loc. 1877.

32. Perlin, *Intern Nation*, 163, 181–183; Trevor Smith, "How Unpaid Internships Reinforce the Racial Wealth Gap," *American Prospect*, February 4, 2019, https://prospect.org/education/unpaid-internships-reinforce-racial-wealth-gap. See also Nathalie Olah, *Steal as Much as You Can: How to Win the Culture Wars in an Age of Austerity* (London: Repeater, 2019).

33. Perlin, *Intern Nation*, 186, 194–196; Schwartz, "Opportunity Costs"; Standing, *The Precariat*, loc. 1856; Amalia Illgner, "Why I'm Suing over My Dream Internship,"

The Guardian, March 27, 2018, www.theguardian.com/news/2018/mar/27/why-im
-suing-over-my-dream-internship; Yuki Noguchi, "An Intern at 40-Something, and
'Paid in Hugs,'" NPR, April 1, 2014, www.npr.org/2014/04/01/293882686/an-intern
-at-40-something-and-paid-in-hugs; Dishman, "How I Made Ends Meet."

34. Susannah Cullinane, Deanna Hackney, and Kaylee Hartung, "Intern Killed
by Lion Died 'Following Her Passion,'" CNN, January 1, 2019, https://edition.cnn
.com/2018/12/31/us/lion-escapes-intern-family/index.html; Illgner "Why I'm Suing";
Sanburn, "Beginning of the End."

35. Sanburn, "Beginning of the End"; Waxman, "How the Internship Replaced the
Entry-Level Job."

36. Perlin, *Intern Nation*, 185, 199–200; Standing, *The Precariat*, 183–187; Rebecca Greenfield, "Unpaid Internships Are Back, with the Labor Department's Blessing," Bloomberg, January 13, 2019, www.bloomberg.com/news/articles/2018-01-10
/unpaid-internships-are-back-with-the-labor-department-s-blessing.

37. James Cairns, *The Myth of the Age of Entitlement: Millennials, Austerity and Hope*
(Toronto: University of Toronto Press, 2017), 84–87.

38. Eleni Schirmer, "Pay Your Interns Now," *Jacobin*, March 21, 2019, https://
jacobinmag.com/2019/03/quebec-unpaid-internships-strike-university.

39. Ingrid Peritz, "Quebec Students Stage Walkout over Unpaid Internships,"
Globe and Mail, November 21, 2018, www.theglobeandmail.com/canada/article-quebec
-students-stage-walkout-over-unpaid-internships; Caroline St-Pierre, "More Than
50,000 Quebec Students to Strike over Unpaid Internships," CTV News, November
19, 2018, www.ctvnews.ca/canada/more-than-50-000-quebec-students-to-strike-over
-unpaid-internships-1.4183316.

40. St-Pierre, "Students to Strike."

CHAPTER 8: PROLETARIAN PROFESSIONALS

1. Stanley Aronowitz, *The Last Good Job in America: Work and Education in the New
Global Technoculture* (Lanham, MD: Rowman and Littlefield, 2001); Philip G. Altbach,
"The Deterioration of the Academic Estate: International Patterns of Academic Work,"
in *The Changing Academic Workplace: Comparative Perspectives*, ed. Philip G. Altbach
(Chestnut Hill, MA: Center for International Higher Education, Lynch School of Educa-
tion, Boston College, September 2000), 11–33.

2. H. Perkin, "History of Universities," in *International Handbook of Higher Education*, ed. J. J. F. Forest and P. G. Altbach, Springer International Handbooks of Education, vol. 18 (Dordrecht: Springer, 2007).

3. Paula Young Lee, "The Musaeum of Alexandria and the Formation of the
Muséum in Eighteenth-Century France," *Art Bulletin* 79, no. 3 (September 1997): 385–
412, https://doi.org/10.2307/3046259; Sujit Choudhary, "Higher Education in India: A
Socio-Historical Journey from Ancient Period to 2006–07," *Journal of Educational En-
quiry* 8, no. 1 (2009); Lili Yang, "The Public Role of Higher Learning in Imperial China,"
Centre for Global Higher Education, Working Paper no. 28, October 2017; Raquel Lo-
pez, "Did Sons and Daughters Get the Same Education in Ancient Greece?," *National
Geographic*, August 28, 2019, www.nationalgeographic.com/history/magazine/2019/07
-08/education-in-ancient-greece.

4. Perkin, "History of Universities"; Altbach, "The Deterioriation of the Academic Estate"; Roberto Moscati, "Italian University Professors in Transition," in Altbach, *The Changing Academic Workplace,* 144–174.

5. Perkin, "History of Universities"; Moscati, "Italian University Professors in Transition," 144–174; Philip G. Altbach, "Academic Freedom: International Realities and Challenges," in Altbach, *The Changing Academic Workplace,* 261–277.

6. Perkin, "History of Universities"; University of Oxford, "Introduction and History," www.ox.ac.uk/about/organisation/history?wssl=1.

7. R. R. Palmer, "How Five Centuries of Educational Philanthropy Disappeared in the French Revolution," *History of Education Quarterly* 26, no. 2 (1986): 181–197; Heike Mund, "Knowledge Is Power: Humboldt's Educational Vision Resonates on 250th Birthday," DW, June 22, 2017, www.dw.com/en/knowledge-is-power-humboldts -educational-vision-resonates-on-250th-birthday/a-39363583; David Sorkin, "Wilhelm Von Humboldt: The Theory and Practice of Self-Formation (Bildung), 1791–1810," *Journal of the History of Ideas* 44, no. 1 (January–March 1983): 55–73, https://doi .org/10.2307/2709304; Altbach, "Academic Freedom," 261–277.

8. Perkin, "History of Universities"; Altbach, "Academic Freedom," 261–277; Jürgen Enders, "A Chair System in Transition: Appointments, Promotions, and Gate-Keeping in German Higher Education," *Higher Education* 41, no. 1 (2001): 3–25; Barbara Ehrenreich and John Ehrenreich, *Death of a Yuppie Dream: The Rise and Fall of the Professional-Managerial Class* (New York: Rosa Luxemburg Stiftung, February 2013), www .rosalux-nyc.org/wp-content/files_mf/ehrenreich_death_of_a_yuppie_dream90.pdf.

9. Perkin, "History of Universities," 568–592, 609–611, 595–597, 597–606; Ehrenreich and Ehrenreich, *Death of a Yuppie Dream;* Robert Lee and Tristan Ahtone, "Land-Grab Universities," *High Country News,* March 30, 2020, www.hcn.org/issues/52.4 /indigenous-affairs-education-land-grab-universities; Library of Congress, Primary Documents in American History: Morrill Act, www.loc.gov/rr/program/bib/ourdocs/morrill .html; Aronowitz, *Last Good Job,* 93.

10. Perkin, "History of Universities"; Joseph Thompson, "The GI Bill Should've Been Race Neutral, Politicos Made Sure It Wasn't," *Military Times,* November 9, 2019, www .militarytimes.com/military-honor/salute-veterans/2019/11/10/the-gi-bill-shouldve-been -race-neutral-politicos-made-sure-it-wasnt; Brandon Weber, "How African American WWII Veterans Were Scorned by the G.I. Bill," *The Progressive,* November 10, 2017, https://progressive.org/dispatches/how-african-american-wwii-veterans-were -scorned-by-the-g-i-b.

11. Ehrenreich and Ehrenreich, *Death of a Yuppie Dream*; Aronowitz, *Last Good Job,* 93–94; Ellen Schrecker, "Academic Freedom in the Age of Casualization," in *The University Against Itself: The NYU Strike and the Future of the Academic Workplace,* ed. Monika Krause, Mary Nolan, Michael Palm, and Andrew Ross (Philadelphia: Temple University Press, 2008), loc. 452–454, Kindle.

12. Ehrenreich and Ehrenreich, *Death of a Yuppie Dream;* Luc Boltanski and Eve Chiapello, *The New Spirit of Capitalism* (New York: Verso, 2018), loc. 1269–1273, Kindle.

13. Enders, "A Chair System," 36–60; Aronowitz, *Last Good Job,* 34–36.

14. Schrecker, "Academic Freedom," loc. 423–426, 429–444; Altbach, "Academic Freedom," 261–277.

15. Ashley Dawson and Penny Lewis, "New York: Academic Labor Town?," in Krause et al., *The University Against Itself*, loc. 238–251; Aaron Bady and Mike Konczal, "From Master Plan to No Plan: The Slow Death of Public Higher Education," *Dissent*, Fall 2012, www.dissentmagazine.org/article/from-master-plan-to-no-plan-the-slow-death-of-public-higher-education.

16. Dawson and Lewis, "New York," loc. 251–274. Historian Kim Phillips-Fein explains the crisis thus: "As is the case today, in the 1970s the city's economic problems were not solely of its own making: they had their roots in federal policies that favored suburbia and made it easy for manufacturers to relocate. The funding structure of Great Society programs such as Medicaid placed a heavy burden on New York's government. And as the financial sector was deregulated in the 1970s, banks became less inclined to hold municipal bonds. These were the background conditions that spurred the 1975 fiscal crisis, but the reason it became so charged was that under the pressures of default, the city had to reverse longstanding commitments the city had made to poor and working-class New Yorkers." Kim Phillips-Fein, "Rethinking the Solution to New York's Fiscal Crisis," *New York Review of Books*, NYR Daily, July 16, 2020, www.nybooks.com/daily/2020/07/16/rethinking-the-solution-to-new-yorks-fiscal-crisis. See also Kim Phillips-Fein, *Fear City: New York's Fiscal Crisis and the Rise of Austerity Politics* (New York: Metropolitan, 2017).

17. Angela Y. Davis, "Speech Delivered at the Embassy Auditorium," Los Angeles, California, June 9, 1972, http://americanradioworks.publicradio.org/features/blackspeech/adavis.html; Boltanski and Chiapello, *New Spirit of Capitalism*, loc. 4421–4423; Schrecker, "Academic Freedom," loc. 460–466; Barbara Ehrenreich, *Fear of Falling: The Inner Life of the Middle Class* (New York: Harper Perennial, 1990), 64; Aronowitz, *Last Good Job*, 91; Bady and Konczal, "From Master Plan to No Plan."

18. Altbach, "Deterioration of the Academic Estate," 11–33; Michael Shattock, "The Academic Profession in Britain: A Study in the Failure to Adapt to Change," *Higher Education* 41, no. 1/2 (2001): 27–47; Anne Applebaum, "Thatcher's Elimination of Tenure Leaves Professors in Outrage," Associated Press, July 11, 1988, https://apnews.com/940a913d0a84b91ff72512c4af09386a.

19. Ehrenreich and Ehrenreich, *Death of a Yuppie Dream;* Ehrenreich, *Fear of Falling*, 145, 152–153, 199; Gabriel Winant, "Professional-Managerial Chasm," *n+1*, October 10, 2019, https://nplusonemag.com/online-only/online-only/professional-managerial-chasm.

20. Ehrenreich, *Fear of Falling*, 12, 15, 200, 246; Winant, "Professional-Managerial Chasm"; Perkin, "History of Universities."

21. William Davies, *The Happiness Industry: How the Government and Big Business Sold Us Well-Being* (London: Verso, 2015), loc. 1765–1837, Kindle. Stanley Aronowitz noted in 2000 that the coming of the "knowledge economy" has been hailed many times: "Anticipating by nearly forty years the current mania over the 'new' economy in the wake of the broad application of automation and cybernation to the industrial and service workplaces, Andre Gorz and Serge Mallet similarly announced the birth of a new working class of qualified knowledge producers. . . . Unlike the assembly-line worker, the knowledge worker was fully qualified to run every aspect of the production process, from design to execution. What prevented this was simply the arbitrary authority of management and the power of capital." Aronowitz, *Last Good Job*, 16; Ehrenreich and Ehrenreich, *Death of a Yuppie Dream.*

22. Aronowitz, *Last Good Job*, 17, 39–40, 101; Ehrenreich and Ehrenreich, *Death of a Yuppie Dream*; Perkin, "History of Universities"; Henry A. Giroux, *Neoliberalism's War on Higher Education*, (Chicago: Haymarket Books, 2014), loc. 2166–2167, Kindle; Altbach, "Deterioration of the Academic Estate," 11–33.

23. Schrecker, "Academic Freedom," loc. 477–489; Abigail Hess, "The Cost of College Increased by More Than 25% in the Last 10 Years—Here's Why," CNBC, December 13, 2019, www.cnbc.com/2019/12/13/cost-of-college-increased-by-more-than-25percent -in-the-last-10-years.html; Robert Anderson, "University Fees in Historical Perspective," *History and Policy*, February 8, 2016, www.historyandpolicy.org/policy-papers/papers /university-fees-in-historical-perspective; Altbach, "Deterioration of the Academic Estate," 12–13.

24. Aronowitz, *Last Good Job*, 30–33.

25. Aronowitz, *Last Good Job*, 42; Sarah Jaffe, "'Injury to All' at Rutgers University," *Dissent*, June 22, 2020, www.dissentmagazine.org/blog/injury-to-all-at-rutgers-university.

26. Schrecker, "Academic Freedom," loc. 496–497; Altbach, "Deterioration of the Academic Estate," 11–33.

27. Monika Krause, Mary Nolan, Michael Palm, and Andrew Ross, "Introduction," in Krause et al., *The University Against Itself*, loc. 58–59; Dawson and Lewis, "New York," loc. 216–217, 220–221; Schrecker, "Academic Freedom," loc. 532–534; Aronowitz, *Last Good Job*, 40; Philip G. Altbach, "Introduction," in Altbach, *The Changing Academic Workplace*, ix–x; Altbach, "Academic Freedom," 273–274; Erin Hatton, *Coerced: Work Under Threat of Punishment* (Berkeley: University of California Press, 2020), loc. 168–169, 737–739, 750–753, Kindle; Adam Kotsko, "Not Persuasion, but Power: Against 'Making the Case,'" *Boston Review*, May 6, 2020, http://bostonreview.net/forum/higher-education-age-coronavirus /adam-kotsko-not-persuasion-power-against-%E2%80%9Cmaking-case%E2%80%9D.

28. Altbach, "Deterioration of the Academic Estate," 29.

29. Altbach, "Deterioration of the Academic Estate," 13–14, 27–28; "Faculty in the Global Network," New York University, www.nyu.edu/faculty/faculty-in-the-global -network.html.

30. Ehrenreich, *Fear of Falling*, 76, 81–82; Dawson and Lewis, "New York," loc. 230–231.

31. Hatton, *Coerced*, loc. 158–165, 191–194, 207–209, 228–242, 281–299, 305–307, 354–374.

32. Aronowitz, *Last Good Job*, 36; Schrecker, "Academic Freedom," loc. 553–554.

33. Aronowitz, *Last Good Job*, 22, 39–40, 43; Gwendolyn Bradley, "How Managerial Are Faculty?," American Association of University Professors, May–June 2014, www .aaup.org/article/how-managerial-are-faculty; Hatton, *Coerced*, loc. 154–155, 748–750, 756–758.

34. Krause et al., "Introduction," 26–49, 79–80, 90–93; Dawson and Lewis, "New York," loc. 305–306, 311–312; Giroux, *Neoliberalism's War*, loc. 341–344, 575–578.

35. Jeff Goodwin, "Which Side Are We On? NYU's Full-Time Faculty and the GSOC Strike," in Krause et al., *University Against Itself*, loc. 2365; "Joint Statement of New York University and GSOC and SET, UAW," November 26, 2013, www.nyu.edu /content/dam/nyu/publicAffairs/documents/20131126-JointStmntNYUgsocSETuaw.pdf.

36. Aronowitz, *Last Good Job*, 97–98; Krause et al., "Introduction," loc. 62–63; Dawson and Lewis, "New York," loc. 327–328; James Cairns, *The Myth of the Age of Entitlement: Millennials, Austerity and Hope* (Toronto: University of Toronto Press, 2017), 83; Mark Fisher, *Capitalist Realism: Is There No Alternative?* (London: Zer0 Books, 2009), 42.

37. Tressie McMillan Cottom, *Lower Ed: The Troubling Rise of For-Profit Colleges in the New Economy* (New York: New Press, 2017), 6–11, 84, 96, 180.

38. Ehrenreich and Ehrenreich, *Death of a Yuppie Dream*; Camilo Maldonado, "Price of College Increasing Almost 8 Times Faster Than Wages," *Forbes*, July 24, 2018, www.forbes.com/sites/camilomaldonado/2018/07/24/price-of-college-increasing-almost -8-times-faster-than-wages; College Tuition Inflation Calculator, In 2013 Dollars, www .in2013dollars.com/College-tuition-and-fees/price-inflation; Alex Press, "On the Origins of the Professional-Managerial Class: An Interview with Barbara Ehrenreich," *Dissent*, October 22, 2019, www.dissentmagazine.org/online_articles/on-the-origins-of-the -professional-managerial-class-an-interview-with-barbara-ehrenreich.

39. Angela Y. Davis, "Black Women and the Academy," in *The Angela Y. Davis Reader*, ed. Joy James (Hoboken, NJ: Blackwell, 1998), 222–224; Mark Fisher, *K-punk: The Collected and Unpublished Writings of Mark Fisher*, ed. Darren Ambrose (London: Repeater Books, 2018), loc. 5876, 7888–7889, Kindle; Giroux, *Neoliberalism's War*, loc. 1055–1103; Jeevan Vasagar and Jessica Shepherd, "Browne Review: Universities Must Set Their Own Tuition Fees," *The Guardian*, October 12, 2010, www.theguardian.com /education/2010/oct/12/browne-review-universities-set-fees; Sirin Kale, "An Oral History of the 2010 Student Protests," *Vice UK*, December 12, 2019, www.vice.com/en_uk /article/qjddzb/oral-history-2010-student-protests.

40. Paul Mason, *Why It's Kicking Off Everywhere: The New Global Revolutions* (London: Verso, 2012); Jodi Dean, *Crowds and Party* (New York: Verso, 2016), loc. 314, Kindle; Giroux, *Neoliberalism's War*, loc. 1130–1132, 2930–2931, 3481–3484.

41. Katerina Bodovski, "Why I Collapsed on the Job," *Chronicle of Higher Education*, February 15, 2018, www.chronicle.com/article/Why-I-Collapsed-on-the -Job/242537; Social Sciences Feminist Network Research Interest Group, "The Burden of Invisible Work in Academia: Social Inequalities and Time Use in Five University Departments," *Humboldt Journal of Social Relations* 39, Special Issue 39: Diversity & Social Justice in Higher Education (2017): 228–245; Tressie McMillan Cottom, "'Who Do You Think You Are?': When Marginality Meets Academic Microcelebrity," *Ada: A Journal of Gender, New Media, and Technology*, no. 7 (2015), https://adanewmedia.org/2015/04 /issue7-mcmillancottom.

42. Yasmin Nair, "Class Shock: Affect, Mobility, and the Adjunct Crisis," *Contrivers' Review*, October 13, 2014, www.contrivers.org/articles/8.

43. Jaffe, "Injury to All."

44. Kotsko, "Not Persuasion, but Power"; Ehrenreich, *Fear of Falling*, 262.

45. Gareth Brown and David Harvie, "2+ Years of Militancy in Universities: What Do We Know and Where Do We Go?" *Plan C*, February 17, 2020, www.weareplanc.org /blog/2-years-of-militancy-in-universities-what-do-we-know-and-where-do-we-go; Amia Srinivasan, "Back on Strike," *London Review of Books*, December 3, 2019, www.lrb.co.uk /blog/2019/december/back-on-strike; Interview with Claire English.

46. "Fordham Faculty Ratify First Contract, Win 67%–90% Raises for a Majority of Adjuncts," SEIU: Faculty Forward, July 2018, http://seiufacultyforward.org/fordham-faculty-ratify-first-contract-win-67-90-raises-majority-adjuncts; Daniel Moattar, "These Faculty Organizing Victories Show Labor Doesn't Need the Courts on Its Side," *In These Times*, August 31, 2018, https://inthesetimes.com/article/iowa-fordham-unions-seiu-trump-janus-faculty.

47. "Fordham Faculty Ratify First Contract."

CHAPTER 9: PLAYBOR OF LOVE

1. Studio Gobo Home Page, www.studiogobo.com.

2. Jamie Woodcock, *Marx at the Arcade: Consoles, Controllers and Class Struggle* (Chicago: Haymarket Books, 2019), loc. 1244–1247, Kindle; Chella Ramanan, "The Video Game Industry Has a Diversity Problem—But It Can Be Fixed," *The Guardian*, March 15, 2017, www.theguardian.com/technology/2017/mar/15/video-game-industry-diversity-problem-women-non-white-people; Eve Crevoshay, Sarah Hays, Rachel Kowert, Raffael Boccamazzo, and Kelli Dunlap, "State of the Industry 2019: Mental Health in the Game Industry," TakeThis, 2019, www.takethis.org/wp-content/uploads/2019/07/TakeThis_StateOfTheIndustry_2019.pdf.

3. Woodcock, *Marx at the Arcade*, loc. 1200–1209; David Jenkins, "Programmers Win EA Overtime Settlement, EA_Spouse Revealed," GamaSutra, April 26, 2006, www.gamasutra.com/view/news/100005/Programmers_Win_EA_Overtime_Settlement_EASpouse_Revealed.php.

4. Laura Sydell, "The Forgotten Female Programmers Who Created Modern Tech," NPR, October 6, 2014, www.npr.org/sections/alltechconsidered/2014/10/06/345799830/the-forgotten-female-programmers-who-created-modern-tech; Walter Isaacson, "Walter Isaacson on the Women of ENIAC," *Fortune*, September 18, 2014, https://fortune.com/2014/09/18/walter-isaacson-the-women-of-eniac. See also Walter Isaacson, *The Innovators: How a Group of Hackers, Geniuses, and Geeks Created the Digital Revolution* (New York: Simon and Schuster, 2014); Miss Cellania, "Ada Lovelace: The First Computer Programmer," Mental Floss, October 13, 2015, http://mentalfloss.com/article/53131/ada-lovelace-first-computer-programmer.

5. John Patrick Leary, "The Innovator's Agenda," *The Baffler*, March 2019, https://thebaffler.com/outbursts/the-innovators-agenda-leary. See also John Patrick Leary, *Keywords: The New Language of Capitalism* (Chicago: Haymarket Books, 2019); Judy Wacjman, *Pressed for Time: The Acceleration of Life in Digital Capitalism* (Chicago: University of Chicago Press, 2014), loc. 9.

6. Tasnuva Bindi, "Women Didn't Just Recently Start Coding, They Actually STOPPED Coding Decades Ago," *Startup Daily*, February 24, 2015, www.startupdaily.net/2015/02/women-didnt-just-recently-start-coding-actually-stopped-coding-decades-ago; Alyson Sheppard, "Meet the 'Refrigerator Ladies' Who Programmed the ENIAC," Mental Floss, October 13, 2013, http://mentalfloss.com/article/53160/meet-refrigerator-ladies-who-programmed-eniac; Isaacson, "Women of ENIAC"; Sydell, "Forgotten Female Programmers."

7. Brenda D. Frink, "Researcher Reveals How 'Computer Geeks' Replaced 'Computer Girls,'" Stanford Clayman Institute for Gender Research, June 1, 2011,

https://gender.stanford.edu/news-publications/gender-news/researcher-reveals-how-computer-geeks-replaced-computer-girls; Sydell, "Forgotten Female Programmers."

8. Sheppard, "Refrigerator Ladies"; Sydell, "Forgotten Female Programmers"; Bindi, "Women Didn't Just Recently Start Coding"; Frink, "Computer Geeks"; Astra Taylor and Joanne McNeil, "The Dads of Tech," *The Baffler*, October 2014, https://thebaffler.com/salvos/dads-tech.

9. Frink, "Computer Geeks"; Taylor and McNeil, "Dads of Tech."

10. Katie Hafner and Matthew Lyon, *Where Wizards Stay Up Late: The Origins of the Internet* (New York: Simon and Schuster, 1999), 10–11, 107.

11. Hafner and Lyon, *Wizards*, 12–14, 19–20.

12. Hafner and Lyon, *Wizards*, 44, 53.

13. In the United Kingdom, where Alan Turing's research laid the foundations for a digital computer that could hold programs in its memory, David Davies emerged from the team to put forth the concept that would be called "packet switching" at nearly the same time as American programmers. (Turing also invented an early version of a video game, a computer program that could play chess.) "Alan Turing: Creator of Modern Computing," BBC Teach, 2020, www.bbc.com/timelines/z8bgr82; Colin Drury, "Alan Turing: The Father of Modern Computing Credited with Saving Millions of Lives," *The Independent*, July 15, 2019, www.independent.co.uk/news/uk/home-news/alan-turing-50-note-computers-maths-enigma-codebreaker-ai-test-a9005266.html; Woodcock, *Marx at the Arcade*, loc. 262; Lyon and Hafner, *Wizards*, 79.

14. Hafner and Lyon, *Wizards*, 85.

15. Hafner and Lyon, *Wizards*, 123–190, 206–207.

16. Woodcock, *Marx at the Arcade*, loc. 185, 220, 250, 990–993; Astra Taylor, *The People's Platform: Taking Back Power and Culture in the Digital Age* (New York: Metropolitan, 2014), 18; Lyon and Hafner, *Wizards*, 214–218.

17. Woodcock, *Marx at the Arcade*, loc. 327.

18. Lyon and Hafner, *Wizards*, 113, 259; Woodcock, *Marx at the Arcade*, 232; Corey Pein, *Live Work Work Work Die: A Journey into the Savage Heart of Silicon Valley* (New York: Metropolitan, 2018), loc. 1705–1707, 1711, Kindle.

19. Alex Press, "Code Red," *n+1*, Spring 2018, https://nplusonemag.com/issue-31/politics/code-red.

20. Bindi, "Women Didn't Just Recently Start Coding"; Woodcock, *Marx at the Arcade*, loc. 2134–2137, 422–429, 2142–2165; Sydell, "Forgotten Female Programmers"; Miriam Posner, "Javascript Is for Girls," *Logic Magazine*, March 15, 2017, https://logicmag.io/intelligence/javascript-is-for-girls; Mark J. Perry, "Chart of the Day: The Declining Female Share of Computer Science Degrees from 28% to 18%," American Enterprise Institute, December 6, 2018, www.aei.org/carpe-diem/chart-of-the-day-the-declining-female-share-of-computer-science-degrees-from-28-to-18.

21. Pein, *Live Work Work Work Die*, loc. 1718–1723; Andrew Ross, *No Collar: The Hidden Cost of the Humane Workplace* (New York: Basic Books, 2002), 3, 9–10; Taylor, *People's Platform*, 11–12.

22. Ross, *No Collar*, 10–12; E. P. Thompson, *The Making of the English Working Class* (New York: Open Road Media, 2016), loc. 11160–11211, Kindle; Joanne McNeil, *Lurking: How a Person Became a User* (New York: MCD, 2020), loc. 837–839, Kindle.

23. J. K. Siravo, "The London Hackspace: Exploring Spaces of Integration and Transformation in a Hacker Community" (Architectural Design Year 3 History and Theory Dissertation, University College London, 2013).

24. As Andrew Ross wrote, "When elements of play in the office or at home/offsite are factored into creative output, then the work tempo is being recalibrated to incorporate activities, feelings, and ideas that are normally pursued during employees' free time." Ross, *No Collar*, 19–20; McNeil, *Lurking*, loc. 1038–1039.

25. McNeil, *Lurking*, loc. 196–198.

26. Moira Weigel, "Coders of the World, Unite: Can Silicon Valley Workers Curb the Power of Big Tech?," *The Guardian*, October 31, 2017, www.theguardian.com /news/2017/oct/31/coders-of-the-world-unite-can-silicon-valley-workers-curb-the-power -of-big-tech; Taylor, *People's Platform*, 14; Paolo Gerbaudo, *The Digital Party: Political Organisation and Online Democracy* (London: Pluto Press, 2018), loc. 1484, 1493, Kindle.

27. Kathi Weeks, *The Problem with Work: Feminism, Marxism, Antiwork Politics, and Postwork Imaginaries* (Durham, NC: Duke University Press, 2011), 60, 72–74, 82, 107; Leary, "Innovator's Agenda"; Dylan Love, "Steve Jobs Never Wrote Computer Code for Apple," *Business Insider*, August 29, 2013, www.businessinsider.com/steve-jobs-never -wrote-computer-code-for-apple-2013-8; Taylor and McNeil, "Dads of Tech"; Posner, "Javascript"; "The Smart, the Stupid, and the Catastrophically Scary: An Interview with an Anonymous Data Scientist," *Logic Magazine*, March 15, 2017, https://logicmag.io /intelligence/interview-with-an-anonymous-data-scientist/; McNeil, *Lurking*, loc. 1179– 1181; Pein, *Live Work Work Work Die*, loc. 983; Woodcock, *Marx at the Arcade*, loc. 1114–1115.

28. Jodi Kantor and David Streitfeld, "Inside Amazon: Wrestling Big Ideas in a Bruising Workplace," *New York Times*, August 15, 2015, www.nytimes.com/2015/08/16 /technology/inside-amazon-wrestling-big-ideas-in-a-bruising-workplace.html. Andrew Ross, too, had noted the similarity to "extreme sports," another innovation of the 1990s. Ross, *No Collar*, 12.

29. Kate Losse, "Sex and the Startup: Men, Women, and Work," Model View Culture, March 17, 2014, https://modelviewculture.com/pieces/sex-and-the-startup -men-women-and-work; Kate Losse, *The Boy Kings: A Journey into the Heart of the Social Network* (New York: Free Press, 2012), 5, 6, 9, 13–14, 25, 36, 38.

30. Losse, *Boy Kings*, 30, 36, 49, 53, 54, 58.

31. Losse, *Boy Kings*, 105, 109, 122.

32. Losse, *Boy Kings*, 74–75, 137; Losse, "Sex and the Startup"; McNeil, *Lurking*, loc. 1830–1831; Astra Taylor, "The Automation Charade," *Logic Magazine*, August 1, 2018, https://logicmag.io/05-the-automation-charade; Adrian Chen, "The Laborers Who Keep Dick Pics and Beheadings out of Your Facebook Feed," *Wired*, October 23, 2014, www.wired.com/2014/10/content-moderation; McNeil, *Lurking*, loc. 46–48, 247–249; Pein, *Live Work Work Work Die*, loc. 1081–1084, 1102; Miranda Hall, "The Ghost of the Mechanical Turk," *Jacobin*, December 16, 2017, www.jacobinmag.com/2017/12 /middle-east-digital-labor-microwork-gaza-refugees-amazon.

33. Losse, *Boy Kings*, 183; Kat Stoeffel, "If You Cover Egg Freezing, You Better Cover Day Care," *The Cut*, October 15, 2014, www.thecut.com/2014/10/you-cover -egg-freezing-also-cover-day-care.html; Ray Fisman and Tim Sullivan, "The Internet of

'Stuff Your Mom Won't Do for You Anymore,'" *Harvard Business Review*, July 26, 2016, https://hbr.org/2016/07/the-internet-of-stuff-your-mom-wont-do-for-you-anymore; Pein, *Live Work Work Work Die*, loc. 270; Taylor and McNeil, "Dads of Tech"; Geoff Nunberg, "Goodbye Jobs, Hello 'Gigs': How One Word Sums Up a New Economic Reality," NPR, January 11, 2016, www.npr.org/2016/01/11/460698077/goodbye-jobs-hello-gigs-nunbergs-word-of-the-year-sums-up-a-new-economic-reality; Susie Cagle, "The Sharing Economy Was Always a Scam," OneZero, March 7, 2019, https://onezero.medium.com/the-sharing-economy-was-always-a-scam-68a9b36f3e4b; Sarah Kessler, "Pixel & Dimed On (Not) Getting By in the Gig Economy," *Fast Company*, March 18, 2014, www.fastcompany.com/3027355/pixel-and-dimed-on-not-getting-by-in-the-gig-economy; Kevin Roose, "Does Silicon Valley Have a Contract-Worker Problem?," *New York*, September 18, 2014, http://nymag.com/intelligencer/2014/09/silicon-valleys-contract-worker-problem.html; Pein, *Live Work Work Work Die*, loc. 895. See also Emily Guendelsberger, *On the Clock: What Low-Wage Work Did to Me and How It Drives America Insane* (New York: Little, Brown, 2019).

34. Pein, *Live Work Work Work Die*, loc. 1130; Greg Bensinger, "'MissionRacer': How Amazon Turned the Tedium of Warehouse Work into a Game," *Washington Post*, May 21, 2019, www.washingtonpost.com/technology/2019/05/21/missionracer-how-amazon-turned-tedium-warehouse-work-into-game; Catie Keck, "Amazon Goes Full *Black Mirror* by Turning Grueling Warehouse Work into a Video Game," *Gizmodo*, May 22, 2019, https://gizmodo.com/amazon-goes-full-black-mirror-by-turning-grueling-wareh-1834936825; Noam Scheiber, "How Uber Uses Psychological Tricks to Push Its Drivers' Buttons," *New York Times*, April 2, 2017, www.nytimes.com/interactive/2017/04/02/technology/uber-drivers-psychological-tricks.html; Woodcock, *Marx at the Arcade*, loc. 1901–1903; Alberto Mora, "Does Gamification Work in the Software Development Process?," HCI Games, 2015, http://hcigames.com/gamification/gamification-work-software-development-process.

35. Wacjman, *Pressed for Time*, 62, 71; Miya Tokumitsu, *Do What You Love: And Other Lies About Success and Happiness* (New York: Regan Arts, 2015), 59.

36. Andrew Ross noted, "77.7 percent of companies acknowledged routine electronic monitoring of their employees, a figure that had doubled since 1997." Ross, *No Collar*, 11–12; Tokumitsu, *Do What You Love*, 57; Bryan Clark, "Facebook Employees Are Next-Level Paranoid the Company Is Watching Them," The Next Web, February 13, 2018, https://thenextweb.com/facebook/2018/02/13/facebook-employees-are-next-level-paranoid-the-company-is-watching-them; Nicholas Thompson, "Inside the Two Years That Shook Facebook—and the World," *Wired*, February 12, 2018, www.wired.com/story/inside-facebook-mark-zuckerberg-2-years-of-hell; Evgeny Morozov, "The Digital Hippies Want to Integrate Life and Work—But Not in a Good Way," *The Guardian*, December 3, 2017, www.theguardian.com/commentisfree/2017/dec/03/digital-hippies-integrate-life-and-work-wework-data-firms; Pein, *Live Work Work Work Die*, loc. 318, 474, 942, 947–953; Gerbaudo, *Digital Party*, loc. 1490; Lizzie Widdicombe, "The Rise and Fall of WeWork," *New Yorker*, November 6, 2019, www.newyorker.com/culture/culture-desk/the-rise-and-fall-of-wework.

37. Posner, "Javascript"; Clive Thompson, "The Next Big Blue-Collar Job Is Coding," *Wired*, February 8, 2017, www.wired.com/2017/02/programming-is-the-new-blue

-collar-job; Samantha Cole, "This Company Will Pay You to Learn to Code, and Take 15 Percent of Your Income Later," *Vice*, March 28, 2019, www.vice.com/en_us/article /yw878x/modern-labor-coding-bootcamp-will-pay-you-to-learn-to-code.

38. Toshio Meronek, "Mark Zuckerberg's Immigration Hustle," *Splinter*, March 12, 2015, https://splinternews.com/mark-zuckerbergs-immigration-hustle-1793846366.

39. Julia Carrie Wong, "Tesla Factory Workers Reveal Pain, Injury and Stress: 'Everything Feels Like the Future but Us,'" *The Guardian*, May 18, 2017, www .theguardian.com/technology/2017/may/18/tesla-workers-factory-conditions-elon-musk; Caroline O'Donovan, "Elon Musk Slams Tesla Union Drive, Promises Workers Free Frozen Yogurt," *BuzzFeed*, February 24, 2017, www.buzzfeednews.com/article /carolineodonovan/musk-slams-union-drive-in-email-to-employees.

40. Kate Losse, "Cults at Scale: Silicon Valley and the Mystical Corporate Aesthetic," 2015, http://dismagazine.com/discussion/72970/kate-losse-cults-at-scale; Taylor and McNeil, "Dads of Tech."

41. Pein, *Live Work Work Work Die*, loc. 1009.

42. Vivian Ho, "'It's a Crisis': Facebook Kitchen Staff Work Multiple Jobs to Get By," *The Guardian*, July 22, 2019, www.theguardian.com/us-news/2019/jul/22 /facebook-cafeteria-workers-protest; Weigel, "Coders of the World, Unite"; Press, "Code Red"; Sean Captain, "How Tech Workers Became Activists, Leading a Resistance Movement That Is Shaking Up Silicon Valley," *Fast Company*, October 15, 2018, www.fast company.com/90244860/silicon-valleys-new-playbook-for-tech-worker-led-resistance.

43. Ben Tarnoff, "Coding and Coercion," *Jacobin*, April 11, 2018, www .jacobinmag.com/2018/04/lanetix-tech-workers-unionization-campaign-firing; Sean Captain, "How a Socialist Coder Became a Voice for Engineers Standing Up to Management," *Fast Company*, October 15, 2018, www.fastcompany.com/90250388 /the-advocate-bjorn-westergard; Shaun Richman and Bill Fletcher Jr., "What the Revival of Socialism in America Means for the Labor Movement," *In These Times*, October 9, 2017, http://inthesetimes.com/working/entry/20587/labor-movement -workers-socialism-united-states; Tekla S. Perry, "Startup Lanetix Pays US $775,000 to Software Engineers Fired for Union Organizing," *Spectrum*, November 12, 2018, https://spectrum.ieee.org/view-from-the-valley/at-work/tech-careers/startup-lanetix -pays-775000-to-software-engineers-fired-for-union-organizing.

44. Wendy Liu, "Silicon Inquiry," Notes from Below, January 29, 2018, https:// notesfrombelow.org/article/silicon-inquiry; McNeil, *Lurking*, loc. 226–232, 240–242; Monica Torres, "As Tech Employees Party, Contract Workers Get Left Out," *Huff-Post*, August 1, 2019, www.huffingtonpost.co.uk/entry/contractors-holiday-party -employee-benefits_n_5c2c335ae4b0407e9085e368; Anonymous, "Organizing Tech: Insights into the Tech World's Sudden Rebellion," It's Going Down, October 16, 2018, https://itsgoingdown.org/organizing-tech-insights-into-the-tech-worlds-sudden -rebellion.

45. Sam Levin, "Google Accused of 'Extreme' Gender Pay Discrimination by US Labor Department," *The Guardian*, April 7, 2017, www.theguardian.com/technology /2017/apr/07/google-pay-disparities-women-labor-department-lawsuit; Kate Conger, "Exclusive: Here's the Full 10-Page Anti-Diversity Screed Circulating Internally at Google [Updated]," *Gizmodo*, August 5, 2017, https://gizmodo.com/exclusive-heres-the-full-10

-page-anti-diversity-screed-1797564320; McNeil, *Lurking*, loc. 232–234; Daisuke Wak-abayashi and Katie Benner, "How Google Protected Andy Rubin, the 'Father of An-droid,'" *New York Times*, October 25, 2018, www.nytimes.com/2018/10/25/technology/google-sexual-harassment-andy-rubin.html.

46. Emily Sullivan and Laurel Wamsley, "Google Employees Walk Out to Protest Company's Treatment of Women," NPR, November 1, 2018, www.npr.org/2018/11/01/662851489/google-employees-plan-global-walkout-to-protest-companys-treatment-of-women; Claire Stapleton, Tanuja Gupta, Meredith Whittaker, Celie O'Neil-Hart, Stephanie Parker, Erica Anderson, and Amr Gaber, "We're the Or-ganizers of the Google Walkout. Here Are Our Demands," *The Cut*, November 1, 2018, www.thecut.com/2018/11/google-walkout-organizers-explain-demands.html.

47. Johana Bhuiyan, "Google Workers Demand the Company Stop Selling Its Tech to Police," *Los Angeles Times*, June 22, 2020, www.latimes.com/business/technology/story/2020-06-22/google-workers-demand-company-stop-selling-tech-to-police; Annie Palmer, "Amazon Employees Plan 'Online Walkout' to Protest Firings and Treatment of Warehouse Workers," CNBC, April 16, 2020, www.cnbc.com/2020/04/16/amazon-employees-plan-online-walkout-over-firings-work-conditions.html.

48. Weigel, "Coders of the World Unite"; Seth Fiegerman, "Google's Parent Com-pany Now Has More Than 100,000 Employees," CNN Business, April 29, 2019, https://edition.cnn.com/2019/04/29/tech/alphabet-q1-earnings/index.html; "Facebook: Num-ber of Employees, 2009–2020 | FB," MacroTrends, www.macrotrends.net/stocks/charts/FB/facebook/number-of-employees.

49. Cecilia D'Anastasio, "Striking Voice Actors Didn't Get Everything They Wanted, But It Was a Start," *Kotaku*, September 16, 2017, https://kotaku.com/striking-voice-actors-didnt-get-everything-they-wanted-1818822686; Woodcock, *Marx at the Arcade*, loc. 1325–1341.

50. Allegra Frank, "Pro-Union Voices Speak Out at Heated GDC roundta-ble," *Polygon*, March 22, 2018, www.polygon.com/2018/3/22/17149822/gdc-2018-igda-roundtable-game-industry-union; Allegra Frank, "This Is the Group Using GDC to Bolster Game Studio Unionization Efforts," *Polygon*, March 21, 2018, www.polygon.com/2018/3/21/17145242/game-workers-unite-video-game-industry-union.

51. "Fire Activision CEO Bobby Kotick for Pocketing Millions While Laying Off 800 Workers," Coworker.org, petition, 2019, www.coworker.org/petitions/fire-activision-ceo-bobby-kotick-for-pocketing-millions-while-laying-off-800-workers; Jeff Grubb, "Game Workers Unite Org Calls for Activision CEO's Job After Layoffs," *Venture Beat*, February 13, 2019, https://venturebeat.com/2019/02/13/fire-bobby-kotick.

52. Game Workers Unite, UK, union homepage, www.gwu-uk.org.

53. Tom Ley, "They Turned Spider-Man into a Damn Cop and It Sucks," *Dead-spin*, September 10, 2018, https://theconcourse.deadspin.com/they-turned-spider-man-into-a-damn-cop-and-it-sucks-1828944087.

54. Ben Quinn, "'Unlawful and Vicious': Union Organiser Sacked by Games Company," *The Guardian*, October 3, 2019, www.theguardian.com/politics/2019/oct/03/ustwo-austin-kelmore-union-organiser-sacked-games.

55. GamesIndustry Staff, "Games Industry Donates to Black Lives Matter and More to Support US Protests," GamesIndustry.biz, June 24, 2020, www.gamesindustry.biz

/articles/2020-06-03-games-industry-donates-to-black-lives-matter-and-more-in-support-of-us-protests.

CHAPTER 10: IT'S ALL FUN AND GAMES

1. Western Collegiate Hockey Association, "WCHA 20th Anniversary Team: Meghan Duggan, Wisconsin," WCHA.com, www.wcha.com/women/articles/2018/12/wcha-20th-anniversary-team-meghan-duggan-wisconsin.php.

2. Seth Berkman, "Women Get a Spotlight, but No Prize Money, in New N.H.L. All-Star Event," *New York Times*, January 24, 2020, www.nytimes.com/2020/01/24/sports/hockey/nhl-skills-competition-women.html; Sportsnet Staff, "CWHL Announces It Will Pay Players in 2017–18," Sportsnet, September 1, 2017, www.sportsnet.ca/hockey/nhl/cwhl-announces-will-pay-players-2017-18; D'Arcy Maine, "How Much Will the Top Players in the NWHL Make This Season?," ESPN, September 30, 2015, www.espn.com/espnw/athletes-life/the-buzz/story/_/id/13778661/how-much-top-players-nwhl-make-season.

3. Maine, "How Much."

4. Berkman, "Women Get Spotlight."

5. Mary Bellis, "A Brief History of Sports," ThoughtCo., August 23, 2019, www.thoughtco.com/history-of-sports-1992447.

6. Bellis, "Brief History"; Mark Perryman, *Why the Olympics Aren't Good for Us, and How They Can Be* (New York: OR Books, 2012), loc. 159–162, Kindle; Dave Zirin, *A People's History of Sports in the United States: 250 Years of Politics, Protest, People, and Play* (New York: New Press, 2008), 1–2; Garth Vaughan, "The Colored Hockey Championship of the Maritimes," Birthplace of Hockey Museum, October 3, 2001, www.birthplaceofhockey.com/hockeyists/african-n-s-teams/segr-integr; Associated Press, "Canada Stamps Honor on Pre-NHL All-Black Hockey League," AP, January 23, 2020, https://apnews.com/db727ad26c7f8c74cc6c2debb3b98ea1; National Hockey League (@NHL), Twitter, June 19, 2020, 4:24 p.m., https://twitter.com/NHL/status/1274000088034168834.

7. Perryman, *Olympics Aren't Good*, loc. 97–98, 162–167, 597–602.

8. Perryman, *Olympics Aren't Good*, loc. 167–172; Dave Zirin, *What's My Name, Fool? Sports and Resistance in the United States*, loc. 274–284, Kindle; Robert J. Szczerba, "Mixed Martial Arts and the Evolution of John McCain," *Forbes*, April 3, 2014, www.forbes.com/sites/robertszczerba/2014/04/03/mixed-martial-arts-and-the-evolution-of-john-mccain.

9. Zirin, *What's My Name*, loc. 284–293, 2722–2724.

10. Zirin, *What's My Name*, loc. 293–298, 777–784; Zirin, *People's History*, 26–27.

11. Zirin, *What's My Name*, loc. 360–469.

12. Zirin, *What's My Name*, loc. 805–810, 298–302; Perryman, *Olympics Aren't Good*, loc. 151–159. See also Robert McChesney, *The Political Economy of Media: Enduring Issues, Emerging Dilemmas* (New York: Monthly Review Press, 2008).

13. Zirin, *What's My Name*, loc. 543–665.

14. Taylor Branch, "The Shame of College Sports," *The Atlantic*, October 2011, www.theatlantic.com/magazine/archive/2011/10/the-shame-of-college-sports/308643.

15. Branch, "The Shame of College Sports"; Timothy Michael Law, "Football's Cancer," *Los Angeles Review of Books*, September 10, 2015, https://lareviewofbooks.org

/article/footballs-cancer-exploitative-labor-in-americas-favorite-sport; Chuck Slothower, "Fort Lewis' First 'Student-Athlete,'" *Durango Herald*, September 25, 2014, https://durangoherald.com/articles/79431.

16. Chris Koentges, "The Oracle of Ice Hockey," *The Atlantic*, March 2014, www.theatlantic.com/magazine/archive/2014/03/the-puck-stops-here/357579; Zirin, *What's My Name*, loc. 305–308; John Molinaro, "From Humble Beginnings: The Birth of the World Cup," Sportsnet, June 9, 2018, www.sportsnet.ca/soccer/from-humble-beginnings-the-birth-of-the-world-cup; Vaughan, "The Colored Hockey Championship"; Associated Press, "Canada Stamps Honor," https://apnews.com/db727ad26c7f8c74cc6c2debb3b98ea1.

17. Branch, "Shame of College Sports"; Zirin, *People's History*, 113, 127; Howard Bloom, "NFL Revenue-Sharing Model Good for Business," *Sporting News*, September 14, 2014, www.sportingnews.com/us/nfl/news/nfl-revenue-sharing-television-contracts-2014-season-business-model-nba-nhl-mlb-comparison-salary-cap.

18. Zirin, *What's My Name*, loc. 1430–1440.

19. Zirin, *What's My Name*, loc. 1502–1562.

20. Zirin, *What's My Name*, loc. 1440–1497, 1574–1576; Zirin, *People's History*, 194, 205; Dave Zirin, *Welcome to the Terrordome: The Pain, Politics and Promise of Sports* (Chicago: Haymarket Books, 2007), loc. 552–557, Kindle; Perryman, *Olympics Aren't Good*, loc. 177–178; William C. Rhoden, "Early Entry? One and Done? Thank Spencer Haywood for the Privilege," *New York Times*, June 29, 2016, www.nytimes.com/2016/06/30/sports/basketball/spencer-haywood-rule-nba-draft-underclassmen.html; Business & Economics Research Advisor: A Series of Guides to Business and Economics Topics, "The Sports Industry," Summer 2005 (updated December 2016), www.loc.gov/rr/business/BERA/issue3/football.html.

21. Perryman, *Olympics Aren't Good*, loc. 545–552; Zirin, *What's My Name*, loc. 338–339, 762–764, 1033–1037.

22. Zirin, *What's My Name*, loc. 771–902.

23. Zirin, *What's My Name*, loc. 911–913.

24. Zirin, *What's My Name*, loc. 1037–1258; John Wesley Carlos and Dave Zirin, *The John Carlos Story: The Sports Moment That Changed the World* (Chicago: Haymarket Books, 2013).

25. Zirin, *What's My Name*, loc. 2714–2742.

26. Zirin, *People's History*, 95, 119; Lindsay Parks Pieper, "They Qualified for the Olympics. Then They Had to Prove Their Sex," *Washington Post*, February 22, 2018, www.washingtonpost.com/news/made-by-history/wp/2018/02/22/first-they-qualified-for-the-olympics-then-they-had-to-prove-their.sex.

27. Zirin, *What's My Name*, loc. 2793–2820, 2696–2702.

28. "Title IX Frequently Asked Questions," NCAA.org, www.ncaa.org/about/resources/inclusion/title-ix-frequently-asked-questions#title; Zirin, *What's My Name*, loc. 2576–2590; Britni de la Cretaz, "Almost Undefeated: The Forgotten Football Upset of 1976," Longreads, February 2019, https://longreads.com/2019/02/01/toledo-troopers.

29. Eric Anthamatten, "What Does It Mean to 'Throw Like a Girl'?" *New York Times*, August 24, 2014, https://opinionator.blogs.nytimes.com/2014/08/24

/what-does-it-mean-to-throw-like-a-girl; Autumn Whitefield-Madrano, "The Beauty in Watching Women Want," *HuffPost*, July 2, 2015, www.huffpost.com/entry/the-beauty-in-watching-women-want_b_7712570.

30. Perryman, *Olympics Aren't Good*, loc. 93–95, 977–979, 1231–1243.

31. Dave Zirin elaborates, "In 1984, Los Angeles Police Chief Daryl Gates oversaw the jailing of thousands of young Black men in the infamous 'Olympic Gang Sweeps.' As Mike Davis has written, it took the reinstatement of the 1916 Anti-Syndicalism Act, a law aimed at the revolutionary union, the Industrial Workers of the World, to make these Stalinesque jailings a reality. The 1916 bill forbade hand signals and modes of dress that implied IWW membership. The L.A. politicos of the '80s modernized the bill to include high fives and bandanas, making the case that Blood and Crip Joe Hills were overrunning the city. It was in the Gates sweeps that the seeds for the L.A. Rebellion of 1992, as well as the first music video by a fledging rap group called N.W.A., were planted. The Atlanta Games in 1996 were no different." Zirin, *Welcome to the Terrordome*, loc. 2007–2013; Perryman, *Olympics Aren't Good*, loc. 977–987, 180–195, 1016–1017; Judy Celmer, "1984 Olympics Gets Auto Sponsor," United Press International, August 19, 1981, www.upi.com/Archives/1981/08/19/1984-Olympics-gets-auto-sponsor/7234367041600. See also Mike Davis, *City of Quartz: Excavating the Future in Los Angeles* (New York: Verso, 2018 [1990]).

32. Branch, "Shame of College Sports"; Perryman, *Olympics Aren't Good*, loc. 193–199; Erin Hatton, *Coerced: Work Under Threat of Punishment* (Berkeley: University of California Press, 2020), loc. 1870–1877, Kindle.

33. Perryman, *Olympics Aren't Good*, loc. 1209–1230, 965–977; William Davies, *The Happiness Industry: How the Government and Big Business Sold Us Well-Being* (London: Verso, 2015), loc. 1883–1940, Kindle; Malcolm Harris, *Kids These Days: The Making of Millennials* (New York: Back Bay Books, 2018), 173.

34. Zirin, *What's My Name*, loc. 1417–1418, 2986–2998, 3095–3096. See also Dave Zirin, *Bad Sports: How Owners Are Ruining the Games We Love* (New York: Scribner, 2010); Hillary Hoffower and Taylor Borden, "The 20 Richest Billionaires Who Own Sports Teams, Ranked," *Business Insider*, January 30, 2020, www.businessinsider.com/richest-billionaire-sports-team-owners-2018-9.

35. Sheiresa Ngo, "Alex Rodriguez Net Worth and How He Makes His Money," Showbiz CheatSheet, March 10, 2019, www.cheatsheet.com/entertainment/alex-rodriguez-net-worth-and-how-he-makes-his-money.html; Teddy Mitrosilis, "Alex Rodriguez and the 15 Richest Contracts in MLB History," Fox Sports, October 20, 2016, www.foxsports.com/mlb/gallery/new-york-yankees-alex-rodriguez-contract-richest-baseball-deals-of-all-time-080716; Forbes America's Richest Families List, "#75 Steinbrenner Family," 2015, www.forbes.com/profile/steinbrenner/#ce5c7a45854f; Travis Waldron, "Minor League Baseball Players Allege Wage Violations in Lawsuit Against MLB," ThinkProgress, February 13, 2014, https://archive.thinkprogress.org/minor-league-baseball-players-allege-wage-violations-in-lawsuit-against-mlb-196348b96335; Associated Press, "Minor League Baseball Players Can Seek Wage Increases, Appeals Court Rules," August 17, 2019, www.si.com/mlb/2019/08/17/minor-league-baseball-wages-appeals-court; Zirin, *What's My Name*, loc. 1427–1429.

36. Zirin, *Welcome to the Terrordome*, loc. 736–870; Ian Gordon, "Inside Major League Baseball's Dominican Sweatshop System," *Mother Jones*, March/April 2013, www .motherjones.com/politics/2013/03/baseball-dominican-system-yewri-guillen.

37. Zirin, *What's My Name*, loc. 3229–3323, Zirin, *Welcome to the Terrordome*, loc. 2241–2243.

38. John Branch, "Derek Boogaard: A Brain 'Going Bad'" *New York Times*, December 5, 2011, www.nytimes.com/2011/12/06/sports/hockey/derek-boogaard-a-brain -going-bad.html; Law, "Football's Cancer."

39. Mark Fainaru-Wada and Simon Baumgart, "'Who Does This to People?'" ESPN, August 25, 2017, www.espn.com/espn/feature/story/_/page/enterpriseNFLWives /wives-former-nfl-players-left-navigate-concussion-settlement.

40. Harris, *Kids These Days*, 132–143.

41. Branch, "Shame of College Sports"; John Duffley, "In 40 States, Sports Coaches Are the Highest Paid Public Employees," *FanBuzz*, December 31, 2019, https://fanbuzz .com/national/highest-paid-state-employees.

42. Branch, "Shame of College Sports"; Zirin, *What's My Name*, loc. 3156–3215; ESPN News Services, "Clowney: Pay College Athletes," ESPN, February 13, 2014, www.espn .com/nfl/draft2014/story/_/id/10449257/jadeveon-clowney-says-college-athletes-paid.

43. Hatton, *Coerced*, loc. 197–200, 226–227, 739–748, 942–946, 970–981, 1272– 1280, 1294–1297, 1729–1734.

44. Lester Munson, "NLRB Decision Very Well-Reasoned," ESPN, March 26, 2014, www.espn.com/espn/otl/story/_/id/10678393/nlrb-director-decision -follows-road-map-laid-northwestern-quarterback-kain-colter-legal-team; Ben Strauss, "N.L.R.B. Rejects Northwestern Football Players' Union Bid," *New York Times*, August 17, 2015, www.nytimes.com/2015/08/18/sports/ncaafootball/nlrb-says-north western-football-players-cannot-unionize.html.

45. Tom Farrey, "Jeffrey Kessler Files Against NCAA," ESPN, March 17, 2014, www.espn.com/college-sports/story/_/id/10620388/anti-trust-claim-filed-jeffrey -kessler-challenges-ncaa-amateur-model; Jemele Hill, "The NCAA *Had* to Cut Athletes a Better Deal," *The Atlantic*, October 30, 2019, www.theatlantic.com/ideas/archive /2019/10/ncaa-had-cut-student-athletes-better-deal/601036; Steve Berkowitz and Jori Epstein, "NCAA's $208.7 Million in Legal Settlement Money Finally Reaching Athletes' Mailboxes," *USA Today*, December 15, 2019, https://eu.usatoday.com /story/sports/2019/10/04/ncaas-208-7-million-legal-settlement-reaching-athletes-mail boxes/3859697002; Marc Tracy, "The N.C.A.A. Lost in Court, but Athletes Didn't Win, Either," *New York Times*, March 11, 2019, www.nytimes.com/2019/03/11/sports /ncaa-court-ruling-antitrust.html.

46. Ross Dellenger, "Coronavirus Liability Waivers Raise Questions as College Athletes Return to Campus," *Sports Illustrated*, June 17, 2020, www.si.com/.amp /college/2020/06/17/college-athletes-coronavirus-waivers-ohio-state-smu; Anya van Wagtendonk, "Covid-19 Is Exposing Inequalities in College Sports. Now Athletes Are Demanding Change," *Vox*, August 2, 2020, www.vox.com/2020/8/2/21351799 /college-football-pac-12-coronavirus-demands; Lia Assimakopoulos, "College Football Players Attempt to Unionize as Hope for a Season Dies Out," NBC

Washington, August 10, 2020, www.nbcwashington.com/news/sports/nbcsports/college
-football-players-attempt-to-unionize-as-hope-for-a-season-dies-out/2386941.

47. Sarah Jaffe, "Why Are US Women's World Cup Champs Paid Like Chumps?"
Dame, July 6, 2015, www.damemagazine.com/2015/07/06/why-are-us-womens-world
-cup-champs-paid-chumps; Rachel Grozanick, "Women's Soccer Shouldn't Be Expected
to Redeem FIFA," bitch media, June 23, 2015, www.bitchmedia.org/post/womens
-soccer-shouldnt-be-expected-to-redeem-fifa; Sara Hendricks, "The Entire U.S.
Women's Soccer Team Sued the Soccer Federation for Gender Discrimination," Re-
finery29, March 9, 2019, www.refinery29.com/en-us/2019/03/226544/us-womens
-soccer-lawsuit-world-cup; Travis Waldron, "On Equal Pay Day, U.S. Women's Soccer Players Finally Strike a Deal," *HuffPost*, May 4, 2017, www.huffpost.com/entry
/us-womens-soccer-players-pay_n_58e4faf4e4b03a26a3682a42.

48. Associated Press, "Colin Kaepernick, NFL Settle Collusion Lawsuit," *Hollywood Reporter*, February 15, 2019, www.hollywoodreporter.com/news/colin
-kaepernick-nfl-settle-collusion-lawsuit-1187235; Dave Zirin, "Colin Kaepernick's
Message to Chicago Youth: 'Know Your Rights,'" *The Nation*, May 10, 2017, www
.thenation.com/article/archive/colin-kaepernicks-message-to-chicago-youth-know
-your-rights; Kofie Yeboah, "A Timeline of Events Since Colin Kaepernick's National
Anthem Protest," *The Undefeated*, September 6, 2016, https://theundefeated.com
/features/a-timeline-of-events-since-colin-kaepernicks-national-anthem-protest.

49. Aaron McMann, "Jim Harbaugh: Colin Kaepernick 'Is Right,' Like Muhammad Ali, Jackie Robinson," Mlive, June 23, 2020, www.mlive.com/wolverines
/2020/06/jim-harbaugh-colin-kaepernick-is-right-like-muhammad-ali-jackie-robinson
.html; Joanne Rosa, "Spike Lee Calls NFL Commissioner's Apology Excluding Colin
Kaepernick 'Weak,'" ABC News, June 12, 2020, https://abcnews.go.com/Entertainment
/spike-lee-calls-nfl-commissioners-apology-excluding-colin/story?id=71203109;
Brakkton Booker, "Roger Goodell on Colin Kaepernick's Possible Return to
NFL: 'I Welcome That,'" NPR, June 16, 2020, www.npr.org/sections/live-updates
-protests-for-racial-justice/2020/06/16/878810674/roger-goodell-on-colin-kaepernicks
-possible-return-to-nfl-i-welcome-that.

50. Sarah Jaffe, "Don't Call It a Boycott: NBA Players Are Inspiring a Strike Wave,"
The Progressive, August 27, 2020, https://progressive.org/dispatches/dont-call-it-a-boycott
-jaffe-200827; Dave Zirin, "The Sports Strikes Against Racism Have Not Been Coopted,"
The Nation, August 31, 2020, www.thenation.com/article/society/nba-blm-strike.

51. Sarah Jaffe, "The Subversive Brilliance of Marshawn Lynch," *The Week*, January
28, 2015, https://theweek.com/articles/536184/subversive-brillianceof-marshawn-lynch;
Zirin, *What's My Name*, loc. 3980–3981, 3983–3985.

52. Sarah Jaffe, "Why the U.S. Women's Hockey Players Are Planning to Strike,"
Dissent, March 17, 2017, www.dissentmagazine.org/blog/u-s-womens-hockey-players
-planning-strike.

53. OlympicTalk, "Meghan Duggan, Following a Trailblazer's Path, Plans Post-
Pregnancy Return to U.S. Hockey Team," NBCSports, October 4, 2019, https://olympics
.nbcsports.com/2019/10/04/meghan-duggan-pregnancy-comeback-hockey; Seth Berkman, "Contract Fight with U.S.A. Hockey Over, Hard Work Begins for Women's

Team," *New York Times*, April 1, 2017, www.nytimes.com/2017/04/01/sports/hockey/usa
-hockey-womens-team.html.

54. Berkman, "Contract Fight Over"; Seth Berkman, "U.S. Women's Team
Strikes a Deal with U.S.A. Hockey," *New York Times*, March 28, 2017, www.nytimes
.com/2017/03/28/sports/hockey/usa-hockey-uswnt-boycott.html; Barry Svrluga,
"The U.S. Women's Hockey Team Fights the Good Fight—and Wins," *Washington Post*, March 29, 2017, www.washingtonpost.com/sports/olympics/the-us-womens
-hockey-team-fights-the-good-fight—and-wins/2017/03/29/28bce0ce-1432-11e7-ada0
-1489b735b3a3_story.html; Todd Kortemeier, "Hockey Gold Medalist Meghan Duggan Gives Birth to Son, with Wife Gillian Apps, on Leap Day," TeamUSA.org, March
6, 2020, www.teamusa.org/News/2020/March/06/Hockey-Gold-Medalist-Meghan
-Duggan-Gives-Birth-To-Son-With-Wife-Gillian-Apps-On-Leap-Day.

55. Emily Kaplan, "Sorting Out the Current Landscape of Professional Wom-
en's Hockey," ESPN, September 20, 2019, www.espn.com/nhl/story/_/id/27643375
/sorting-current-landscape-professional-women-hockey.

56. Rick Maese, "Women's Hockey Stars Announce Boycott of North American
Pro League," *Washington Post*, May 2, 2019, www.washingtonpost.com/sports/2019
/05/02/womens-hockey-stars-announce-boycott-north-american-pro-league; Cindy
Boren, "As They Seek a New League, Women's Hockey Stars Form Players Association,"
Washington Post, May 20, 2019, www.washingtonpost.com/sports/2019/05/20/they
-seek-new-league-womens-hockey-stars-form-players-association.

57. Greg Wyshynski, "PWHPA Postpones Weeklong Hockey Tour in Japan Due
to Coronavirus," ESPN, February 24, 2020, www.espn.com/nhl/story/_/id/28771533
/pwhpa-postpones-weeklong-hockey-tour-japan-due-coronavirus; John Wawrow, "Pro
Women's Hockey Association Unveils Five-City Regional Plan," AP, May 13, 2020,
www.theoaklandpress.com/sports/pro-womens-hockey-association-unveils-five-city
-regional-plan/article_9ac847cc-9552-11ea-8064-630e10c266f2.html.

58. Greg Levinsky, "US Women's Hockey Captain Meghan Duggan Subs
in for Danvers Gym Teacher Battling Coronavirus," Boston.com, April 11, 2020,
www.boston.com/sports/local-news/2020/04/11/meghan-duggan-subs-in-danvers
-gym-teacher-coronavirus.

CONCLUSION: WHAT IS LOVE?

1. Silvia Federici, "Wages Against Housework," Power of Women Collective and Falling Wall Press, 1975, https://caringlabor.wordpress.com/2010/09/15
/silvia-federici-wages-against-housework.

2. Mark Fisher, *K-punk: The Collected and Unpublished Writings of Mark Fisher*, ed.
Darren Ambrose (London: Repeater Books, 2018), loc. 8971, Kindle.

3. Adam Kotsko, *Neoliberalism's Demons: On the Political Theology of Late Capital*
(Stanford: Stanford University Press, 2018), loc. 1891, Kindle; Paul Mason, *Why It's Kick-
ing Off Everywhere: The New Global Revolutions* (London: Verso, 2012); Linda Jacobson,
"Strike Tracker: Tentative Agreement Reached in St. Paul Public Schools," Education
Dive, March 13, 2020, www.educationdive.com/news/tracker-teachers-on-strike/547339.

4. Antonio Gramsci, *Selections from the Prison Notebooks* (New York: International
Publishers, 2012 [1971]), loc. 6023, 7398, Kindle; Fisher, *K-punk*, loc. 6897, 7015, 10054.

5. Alyssa Battistoni, "Alive in the Sunshine," *Jacobin*, January 12, 2014, https://jacobinmag.com/2014/01/alive-in-the-sunshine; Phillip Frey and Christoph Schneider, "The Shorter Working Week: A Powerful Tool to Drastically Reduce Carbon Emissions," Autonomy, May 2019, http://autonomy.work/wp-content/uploads/2019/05/Fridays 4FutureV2.pdf; Philipp Frey, "The Ecological Limits of Work: On Carbon Emissions, Carbon Budgets and Working Time," Autonomy, May 2019, http://autonomy.work /wp-content/uploads/2019/05/The-Ecological-Limits-of-Work-final.pdf; Fisher, *K-punk*, 10054.

6. Guy Standing, *The Precariat* (London: Bloomsbury Academic, 2011), loc. 416, 421, 423, 2806–2809, 2811–2813, Kindle.

7. George Orwell, *The Road to Wigan Pier* (London: Penguin, 2001 [1937]), loc. 3774–3777, Kindle; Karl Marx, *Grundrisse: Foundations of the Critique of Political Economy*, trans. Martin Nicolaus (New York: Penguin, 2005), 690–712.

8. Silvia Federici, *Revolution at Point Zero: Housework, Reproduction, and Feminist Struggle* (Oakland, CA: PM Press, 2012), loc. 2, Kindle.

9. Selma James, *Sex, Race, and Class: The Perspective of Winning* (Oakland, CA: PM Press, 2012), 149; Andrew Cherlin, *Labor's Love Lost: The Rise and Fall of the Working-Class Family in America* (New York: Russell Sage Foundation, 2014), loc. 3225–3281.

10. Cristina Nehring, *A Vindication of Love: Reclaiming Romance for the Twenty-First Century* (New York: Harper, 2009), 3; bell hooks, *All About Love: New Visions* (New York: William Morrow, 2018), 178; Naomi Cahn and June Carbone, "Just Say No," *Slate*, April 22, 2014, https://slate.com/human-interest/2014/04/white-working-class-women -should-stay-single-mothers-argue-the-authors-of-marriage-markets-how-inequality-is -remaking-the-american-family.html. See also Naomi Cahn and June Carbone, *Marriage Markets: How Inequality Is Remaking the American Family* (Oxford: Oxford University Press, 2014); Laura Kipnis, *Against Love: A Polemic* (New York: Vintage, 2009), 19.

11. Alexandra Topping, "One in 10 Do Not Have a Close Friend and Even More Feel Unloved, Survey Finds," *The Guardian*, August 12, 2014, www.theguardian.com /lifeandstyle/2014/aug/12/one-in-ten-people-have-no-close-friends-relate; Tim Balk, "More Than 20% of Millennials Claim to Have No Friends, Poll Finds," *New York Daily News*, August 3, 2019, www.nydailynews.com/news/national/ny-millenials -no-friends-yougov-poll-20190804-ek5odkrxmvbfhex7ytvp2p6rwy-story.html; Sarah Jaffe, "The Cost to Connect," *Rhizome*, December 20, 2012, https://rhizome.org /editorial/2012/dec/20/instagame/; Keir Milburn, Nadia Idle, and Jeremy Gilbert, #ACFM Trip 11: Friendship, podcast, June 26, 2020, https://novaramedia.com/2020 /06/26/acfm-trip-11-friendship.

12. Sarah Jaffe, "The Relational Economy," *Dissent*, Summer 2020, www.dissent magazine.org/article/the-relational-economy.

13. Samhita Mukhopadhyay, *Outdated: Why Dating Is Ruining Your Love Life* (Seattle: Seal Press, 2011), 15; Kathi Weeks, "Down with Love: Feminist Critique and the New Ideologies of Work," *Verso Blog*, February 13, 2018, www.versobooks.com/blogs/3614 -down-with-love-feminist-critique-and-the-new-ideologies-of-work; Nancy Fraser, "Crisis of Care? On the Social-Reproductive Contradictions of Contemporary Capitalism," in *Social Reproduction Theory: Remapping Class, Recentering Oppression*, ed. Tithi Bhattacharya (London: Pluto Press, 2017), 23.

14. Gramsci, *Prison Notebooks*, loc. 7816–7987; Michael Ballaban, "When Henry Ford's Benevolent Secret Police Ruled His Workers," *Jalopnik*, March 23, 2014, https://jalopnik.com/when-henry-fords-benevolent-secret-police-ruled-his-wo-1549625731; Kipnis, *Against Love*, 37.

15. Cherlin, *Labor's Love Lost*, loc. 3318–3325; Kipnis, *Against Love*, 21, 154.

16. James, *Sex, Race and Class*, 229; Kathi Weeks, *The Problem with Work: Feminism, Marxism, Antiwork Politics, and Postwork Imaginaries* (Durham, NC: Duke University Press, 2011), 36; Merri Lisa Johnson, ed., *Jane Sexes It Up: True Confessions of Feminist Desire* (Seattle: Seal Press, 2002), 50.

17. Nadia Idle, Jeremy Gilbert, and Keir Milburn, #ACFM Trip 8: Acid Urbanism, podcast, February 16, 2020, https://novaramedia.com/2020/02/16/acfm-acid-urbanism; Luc Boltanski and Eve Chiapello, *The New Spirit of Capitalism* (New York: Verso, 2018), loc. 9514–9519, Kindle; Federici, *Revolution at Point Zero*, 4.

18. Kipnis, *Against Love*, 36.

19. William Morris, *Signs of Change: The Aims of Art*, Marxists Internet Archive, taken from 1896 Longmans, Green, and Co. edition, originally prepared by David Price for Project Gutenberg, www.marxists.org/archive/morris/works/1888/signs/chapters/chapter5.htm; Kipnis, *Against Love*, 40.

20. Tera Hunter, *To 'Joy My Freedom: Southern Black Women's Lives and Labors After the Civil War* (Cambridge, MA: Harvard University Press, 1998), 3.

21. Edwidge Danticat, *Create Dangerously: The Immigrant Artist at Work* (New York: Vintage, 2011), 18; Fisher, *K-punk*, loc. 9755–9759; Caroline Knapp, *Appetites: Why Women Want* (Berkeley: Counterpoint, 2011), 41.

22. Judy Wacjman, *Pressed for Time: The Acceleration of Life in Digital Capitalism* (Chicago: University of Chicago Press, 2014), loc. 166–167, Kindle.

23. Wacjman, *Pressed for Time*, 170; Kathi Weeks, "'Hours for What We Will': Work, Family, and the Movement for Shorter Hours," *Feminist Studies* 35, no. 1 (Spring 2009): 115.

24. Ben Davis, *9.5 Theses on Art and Class* (Chicago: Haymarket Books, 2013), loc. 3008–3026, Kindle; Kipnis, *Against Love*, 114; Standing, *The Precariat*, loc. 3072.

25. Tithi Bhattacharya, "Introduction: Mapping Social Reproduction Theory," in Bhattacharya, *Social Reproduction Theory*; Boltanski and Chiapello, *New Spirit of Capitalism*, loc. 8557–8559.

26. Federici, *Revolution at Point Zero*, loc. 112; Barbara Ehrenreich, *Dancing in the Streets: A History of Collective Joy* (New York: Holt, 2007), 259–260; James, *Sex, Race and Class*, 101.

27. Joshua Clover, *Riot. Strike. Riot.* (New York: Verso, 2019), loc. 1233–1240, Kindle; Amia Srinivasan, "Back on Strike," *London Review of Books*, December 3, 2019, www.lrb.co.uk/blog/2019/december/back-on-strike.

28. Elijah Walker and Pierre-Antoine Louis, "After a Week of Turmoil, a Community Rallies," *New York Times*, June 3, 2020, www.nytimes.com/2020/06/03/us/george-floyd-protest-minneapolis-community.html; Mariame Kaba, "Yes, We Mean Literally Abolish the Police," *New York Times*, June 12, 2020, www.nytimes.com/2020/06/12/opinion/sunday/floyd-abolish-defund-police.html; Shane Burley, "Life and Times at the Capitol Hill Autonomous Zone," *Roar Magazine*, June 16, 2020, https://

roarmag.org/essays/life-and-times-at-the-capitol-hill-autonomous-zone; Viewpoint Staff, "'A Political Form Built out of Struggle': An Interview on the Seattle Occupied Protest," *Viewpoint Magazine*, June 17, 2020, www.viewpointmag.com/2020/06/17/a-political -form-built-out-of-struggle-an-interview-on-the-seattle-occupied-protest.

29. Fisher, *K-punk*, loc. 10039–10147, 12912.

30. Sarah Katherine Lewis, *Sex and Bacon: Why I Love Things That Are Very, Very Bad for Me* (Seattle: Seal Press, 2008), 256.

31. Angela Y. Davis, "Women and Capitalism: Dialectics of Oppression and Liberation," in *The Angela Y. Davis Reader*, ed. Joy James (Hoboken, NJ: Blackwell, 1998), 179.

INDEX

A4 Sounds, 179, 204–205
Abbate, Janet, 273
Abel, Heather, 45, 197
abolitionists, 146
abortion
    legalization of in USSR, 35
    political fight over, 36–38
    regulation of labor supply and,
        44
academia
    accountability in, 243, 248
    adjunct professors in, 231–233,
        246–247, 256, 258–262
    Black women in, 253, 255
    coronavirus pandemic and,
        235–236, 255–256
    personal example from, 231–236,
        246–247, 257–262
    polarization in, 244
    politicians, 246
    power struggles in, 237–238
    rising costs in, 245
    specialization within, 238–239
    unions/organizing and, 242, 249,
        250–252, 256, 257–262
    wages in, 258
    See also education; schools;
        teachers
academic freedom, 238, 240–241
accountability, 243, 248
acculturation benefits, 264–265
#ACFM, 329–330
Acid Communism, 334
ACT UP, 190
Activision-Blizzard, 286
Addams, Jane, 147, 148

adjunct professors, 231–233, 246–247,
    256, 258–262. *See also* academia;
    Wilson, Katherine
adolescence, 213–214
Advanced Research Projects Agency
    (ARPA), 270
Advanced Research Projects Agency
    Network (ARPANET), 270–271
Adventure, 272
aesthetic labor, 127
affirmation trap, 8
AFL-CIO, 251
Against Equality, 161
Against Love (Kipnis), 326
Age of Dignity, The (Poo), 71
Agwaze, Kevin, 263–267, 281, 285–289
Aid to Families with Dependent Children
    (AFDC), 38–39, 43, 70
AIDS crisis, 47, 190
Ali, Muhammad, 302–303
alienation, 10
Alito, Samuel, 71
All-American Girls Professional Baseball
    League, 304
Allen, Paul, 307
Allen, Robert L., 152
Allende, Salvador, 7
Alliance of Californians for Community
    Empowerment (ACCE), 106, 130
"amateur" athletics, 299–300, 305–306.
    See also Olympics
Amazon
    coronavirus pandemic and, 284
    distribution center of, 5, 131
    gamification and, 279
    success of, 132

Amazon (*continued*)
    Trump administration and, 282
    Walmart and, 124
    work culture of, 276–277, 278
American Association of University
    Professors (AAUP), 241, 247
American Civil Liberties Union, 167
American Federation of Labor (AFL),
    91–92
American Federation of Teachers (AFT),
    91–92, 99
American Institute of Architecture
    Students, 217
American Medical Association, 214
Americanization, 149
amyotrophic lateral sclerosis (ALS), 309
"Analytical Engine," 268
Anshelm, Jonas, 119
Anthony, Susan B., 146
anti-chain-store movement, 121–122
anti-choice protesters, 142
Antiterrorism and Effective Death Penalty
    Act (1996), 73
anti-union campaigns, 166–170, 196
app-based work, 76
Apple, 276, 278
apprentices, 212–214, 248
Aronofsky, Darren, 224
Aronowitz, Stanley, 236, 241, 246, 248,
    249
Art + Feminism, 335
Art and Labor podcast, 198, 200
Art Architecture Activism, 203
Art Workers' Coalition (AWC), 187–189,
    193
Art Workers' Guild, 184
art worlds, 191–192
Art Worlds (Becker), 191
artistic critique, 13, 187, 189, 191, 334
artists
    conceptions of, 179–180, 181–183
    outsider, 195–196
    working conditions of, 193
Artists' Union, 185
arts
    capitalism and, 198
    coronavirus pandemic and, 178–179,
        196–197, 205
    during the Depression, 185–186

    digital distribution and, 199–200
    education for, 177
    funding for, 177
    Industrial Revolution and, 182–183
    internships and, 222
    labor and, 183–184
    "mystery" of, 180–181
    neoliberalism and, 189–191
    parenting and, 197
    patronage of, 181–182
    personal example from, 175–178,
        202–205
    state support for, 193–194
    support workers for, 188, 196, 198–199
    as tourist commodity, 189–190
    unions/organizing and, 185–186,
        187–188, 194, 196–197, 198,
        201–205
arts and crafts movement, 184
Asawa, Ruth, 197
Ashley, Mike, 307
Association of Art Museum Directors, 222
Atari, 272, 273
attachment parenting, 45
"Austerity U.," 252
automation, 325
autonomia, 189
autonomy, 279
Autonomy (think tank), 324

Babbage, Charles, 268
Babies "R" Us, 114, 133
bachelor's degrees, 237
"bad mothers"/"bad women," 25, 29
Bady, Aaron, 243
Bahn, Kate, 101
Bain Capital, 115, 133, 135
Baker, Ella, 66
Bangladeshi garment workers, 5–6
Baran, Carl, 271
barcode scanners, 124
"Bargaining for the Common Good,"
    102–103
baseball "academies," 308
Basic Income House, 51–52
Battistoni, Alyssa, 324
Bayh-Dole Act (1980), 247
Becker, Howard, 191–192
Beecher, Catharine, 88–89

begging, 144–145
Bell, Callum, 307
Benjamin, Walter, 199
Berger, John, 180–181, 182
Beutner, Austin, 106
Bianco, Karn, 280
Bilas, Frances, 269
Billet, Alexander, 201
birth rate, decrease in, 44
Black athletes, 296–297, 298–299,
    302–303, 304, 313–314. *See also* sports
Black Codes, 64
Black Lives Matter movement, 106–107,
    109, 159, 170, 288
Black Panthers, 243
Black Swan case, 224
Black teachers, 89, 92, 96–98
Black veterans, 239–240
Black women
    in academia, 253, 255
    domestic work and, 63–64, 67–68
    freedom and, 330–331
    home care and, 69
    nonprofits and, 158–159
    slavery and, 62
    welfare reform and, 43–44
    welfare rights movement and, 38–39
Black workers
    enforcement of family structure on, 33
    family wage system and, 34
    welfare rights movement and, 40
Blado, Kayla, 163–164
Blake, Jacob, 314
Bloomingdale's, 128
Boal, Augusto, 49
bohemian ethic, 191
Bolden, Dorothy, 64, 66, 80
Bolt, Beranek and Newman, 271–272
Boltanski, Luc, 11, 13, 187, 190
Bono, 156
Boogaard, Derek, 309
Boothe, Travis, 132
Boris, Eileen, 60, 68, 148, 184
Boston Blades, 294
boundary struggles, 12
Boy Kings, The (Losse), 277
Branch, Taylor, 300, 310
Braun, Aaron, 128
Brett, Marie, 178–179, 202

Brexit, 23, 288, 289
Briggs, Laura, 44, 46, 73
Brink, Ashley, 139–143, 146, 165–171
Britain First, 22
Bronx Slave Markets, 66
Brown v. Board of Education, 94, 96
"Browne Report," 254
Brundage, Avery, 303, 304
Bryan-Wilson, Julia, 188
Bunten, Natasha, 201–202, 205
burnout, 9, 131–132, 157, 161
Bush, George W., 100

Cabral, Chloe, 225, 227
Cairns, James, 252
call centers, 279
Callings: The Purpose and Passion of Work
    (Isay), 162
cameras, in-home, 57
Canadian Women's Hockey League
    (CWHL), 294, 317
Canon, Ramsin, 162, 164
capitalism
    artistic critique of, 13, 187, 189, 191,
        334
    arts and, 198
    changes in, 13
    domination and, 15
    family and, 26
    faults in, 323–324
    home-workplace division, 27–28
    housework and, 41
    justification of, 11–12
    late, 6–7
    marriage and, 31–32
    social critique of, 13, 334
    women and, 31
capitalist realism, 8, 156, 323–324
capitalist retail, 116–117
captive audience meetings, 166
Caputo-Pearl, Alex, 104
Care.com, 76
caring work, 14–15, 18, 47–48, 68–74. *See
    also* domestic work
Carlos, John, 302, 303
Carnegie, Andrew, 149
Carré, Françoise, 129–130
Carrier plant, 4–5, 16
casualized workers, 256–257

chain stores
    backlash against, 121
    rapid growth of, 120
Chaos Computer Club, 275
charity
    church and, 144–145
    conditions on, 147
    politics and, 155, 156
    power and, 143
    tax deductions for, 149–150
charter schools, 99, 123
Cherlin, Andrew J., 33, 327–328
Chiapello, Eve, 11, 13, 187, 190
Chicago Federation of Men Teachers, 92
Chicago Teachers Federation (CTF), 91
Chicago Teachers Union (CTU), 98, 99,
    101, 105
child care
    costs of, 24–25
    nannies and, 55–59
    tensions surrounding, 64–65
child labor, 33, 148
child support/benefits, 43, 51
child-rearing, 35. See also parenting
Christian family values, 121, 123, 126
chronic traumatic encephalopathy (CTE),
    309
church, charity and, 144–145
citizenship status, 72–73
Citron, Alice, 95
City College of New York, 239
civil rights movement, 66, 151
Civil Service Commission, 215
Civil War, 62
Clarke, John Cooper, 23
Clarkson University, 294
class, solidarity and, 16
class composition, 16
class shock, 255
class-action lawsuits, 125–126, 136
climate crisis, 324, 334
Clinton, Bill, 43, 70, 274
Clinton, Hillary, 126
"clopening," 129
Clover, Joshua, 8
Cloward, Richard, 39, 145
coal miners, 6
Coalition for Educational Justice, 105
Cobble, Dorothy Sue, 77
Code of Hammurabi, 212

coding. See programming
Coke, Evelyn, 71
collective households, 47
college sports, 299–300, 310–312
Colorado Springs Planned Parenthood,
    142
Colter, Kain, 311, 313
Columbia University, 247
Comités unitaires sur le travail étudiant
    (Student Work Unitary Committees;
    CUTEs), 225–228
Committee of Interns and Residents, 214
Communism, 92, 93–94, 95, 243, 298
Communist International, 184
Communist Party, 185, 186
community art centers, 186
community colleges, 247
community schools, 84–87, 104, 107, 109
Community Schools Steering Committee,
    109
companion robots, 75
competition, 306–307
computer hackers, 270
computer programmers/programming
    as blue-collar job, 280–281
    gender stereotypes and, 273
    history of, 267–273
    job growth and, 14–15
    See also tech industry
Congress, US, internships and, 215, 216,
    220–221
Congress of Industrial Organizations
    (CIO), 185
Congress of Racial Equality (CORE), 152
connection, 329–330, 332
Connolly, James, 204
contingent control, 125
Cook, Bryan, 196
Cooke, Marvel, 66
Coontz, Stephanie, 26, 27
Cooper, Melinda, 43–44
cooperative system, 214
Cork Printmakers, 176
Cork Women's Travellers Network, 203
Cornell University, 239
coronavirus pandemic
    academia and, 235–236, 255–256
    Amazon and, 284
    art workers and, 196–197
    arts and, 178–179, 205

child care and, 53
domestic work and, 45, 59–60, 74
domestic workers and, 81–82
education and, 108–109
essential workers and, 9, 18
health-care system and, 323
internships and, 221, 229
isolation and, 326
manufacturing jobs and, 5
nonprofits and, 163–164
Planned Parenthood and, 170
retail work and, 132
self-sacrifice and, 48
sports and, 312
teachers and, 103
tech industry and, 267, 288–289
Corrigan, Thomas F., 211–212
Council on Medical Education, 214
cowboy mentality, 161
Crabapple, Molly, 199, 200, 279
Crawford College of Art and Design,
175–176, 179
creative, as term, 181
creative class, 190–191, 251
creative work, 15, 18
creativity, 331–332
crunch times, 266, 287
Cultural Workers Education Center,
201–202
Cunningham, Imogen, 197
CUNY system, 242–243
customer interactions, 112–114, 118

Damore, James, 283
dance, 63
Dancing in the Streets (Ehrenreich),
333
D'Angelo, Josephine, 304
Daniel, Vanessa, 159
Davies, William, 307, 323
d'Avignon, Angella, 195
Davis, Angela, 31, 62, 64, 146, 195, 243,
253, 256, 335
Davis, Ben, 182, 192–193, 332
Davis, Stuart, 185, 186
Dawson, Ashley, 242
Dead Giraffe Society, 134, 136–137
"Death of a Yuppie Dream" (Ehrenreich
and Ehrenreich), 252–253
deindustrialization, 8

Deliveroo, 286
Dellenger, Ross, 312
Denison, Chuckie, 6, 12
Dennison, Ray, 300
department stores, 117–118
depression, competition and, 307
destination internships, 222
Detroit Woolworth Five and Dime strike,
119–120
Dialectic of Sex, The (Firestone), 37
Didžgalvytė, Marijam, 286
digital artisans, 274
Digital Atelier, 199
digital distribution, 199–200
disabilities, people with, 47–48
Discord, 285
discrimination
education and, 94
internships and, 220
nonprofits and, 163, 166
in Olympics, 296
Planned Parenthood and, 170
in retail work, 125–127
in sports, 298–299, 313
in tech industry, 285–286
Disney World, 217–218
Dissent, 243
distance learning, 108–109
distribution center jobs, 5, 131
Ditum, Sarah, 74
diversity, internships and, 223
divesting and investing, 107
Division I hockey, 292
Dixon, Lorraine, 309
Dixon, Rickey, 309
Do What You Love (Tokumitsu), 280
Dodd, Bella, 94
Domencich, Loretta, 39–40
domestic violence, 34, 51
domestic work
app-based work and, 76
Black women and, 63–64, 67–68
challenges regarding, 79–81
coronavirus pandemic and, 45, 59–60,
74
invisibility and, 70–71
personal example from, 55–60, 78–79,
80–82
schedules of, 65
unions/organizing and, 65–67, 76–81

domestic work (*continued*)
   workshops for, 78–79
   See also caring work; home care work;
     housework
Domestic Worker Bill of Rights, 77, 78,
   80–81
Domestic Workers United, 77
dot-com boom, 273–274
doulia, concept of, 48
Du Bois, W. E. B., 62
Duggan, Meghan, 291–295, 305, 306,
   315–319
Dukes, Betty, 126
Duncan, Arne, 100
Dunn, Crystal, 313

Earned Income Tax Credit, 42
e-commerce, 131
Economic Policy Institute, 102
education
   coronavirus pandemic and, 108–109
   internships and, 207–210, 213–214,
     218–220. *see also* academia; schools;
     teachers
Education Amendments Act (1972),
   304–305
education reform movement, 98–101
egg freezing, 46
Ehrenreich, Barbara, 74, 76, 240, 244,
   252–253, 333
Ehrenreich, John, 240, 244, 252–253
elder boom, 68, 71–72, 75
Electronic Arts (EA), 266
Electronic Numerical Integrator and
   Computer (ENIAC), 268–269
Emanuel, Rahm, 101, 102
emotional labor, 118–119, 235–236
Enactus, 123
Engels, Friedrich, 26, 32
English, Claire, 256–257
English Collective of Prostitutes, 153
Equal Employment Opportunity
   Commission, 126
Erickson, Megan, 88, 96
Eruzione, Mike, 316
e-sports leagues, 287
essential workers, 9, 18, 323
eugenics, 151
exploitation, description of, 17

Facebook, 276, 277–278, 279, 280, 282,
   284
Facebook Video, 277–278
facial-recognition software, 282
factory workers, 5–6
Faculty Forward campaign, 258
Fair Labor Standards Act (FLSA), 34, 65,
   67, 69, 216
fair workweek ordinance, 130
Fallout Club, 49–50
family
   after welfare reform, 44–45
   capitalism and, 26, 31–32
   challenges to "traditional," 37–38
   Fordist compromise and, 33–34
   imposed structure of, 30–31
   as institution, 26–27
   nuclear, 26, 32
   personal example from, 21–25, 29, 30,
     32, 49–54, 325–326
   socialism and, 35
   welfare rights movement and, 39
   See also parenting
Family Allowance, 35
Family Assistance Plan, 40
family ethic, 26
family narrative, 75
family responsibility, 30
Family Romance, 75
family wage, 12, 32–34, 92, 213
"fampany," 288
Farage, Nigel, 22
Fauxtomation, 278
Fear of Falling (Ehrenreich), 244
Featherstone, Liza, 126
Federal Art Project (FAP), 185–186
Fédération Internationale de Football
   Association (FIFA), 300
Federici, Silvia, 14, 28, 29, 44, 160, 321,
   325, 335
feminine mystique, 13–14
Feminine Mystique, The (Friedan), 36
feminist movement/revolution
   early, 146
   impact of, 327
   Planned Parenthood and, 151
feminization of teaching, 88
Fight for $15, 283
financial crisis (2008), 126, 323, 324

Financial Reform Committee, 136
"Fire Bobby Kotick," 286
Firestone, Shulamith, 37–38
Fisher, Mark, 8, 253, 331, 334
Fisher Phillips, 166
Florida, Richard, 190, 201
Floyd, George, 108, 284, 314, 323
Folbre, Nancy, 42
food service, 14
Forbush, A. R., 65–66
Ford, Gerald, 242
Ford, Henry, 33, 327
Ford Foundation, 151, 152
Fordham, 257–259
Fordham Faculty United (FFU), 257
Fordism, 272
Fordist compromise, 3–4, 12, 33–34
for-profit colleges, 252
foster parents, 42
foundations, 149–151, 152, 154
Fox, OK, 200
"Fragment on Machines" (Marx), 325
Frank, Dana, 120
Fraser, Nancy, 12
free time, 324–326
Freedman's Bureau, 33
freedom, 7, 330–331, 332
French Revolution, 89, 182, 238
Frenette, Alexandre, 212–213
Friedan, Betty, 13–14, 36, 67
"friendly visitors," 147, 149, 150
friendships, 326–327
furloughed workers, 164
FWD.us, 281

Game Developers Conference, 285,
    288–289
Game Workers Unite (GWU),
    285–288
Gamergate movement, 287–288
gamification, 279
Garber, Megan, 179–180
gender
    changes in understanding of, 32
    creation of, 28
    Fordist compromise and, 34
    pay gap and, 45
    of teachers, 269–270
    See also women

gender roles
    development of, 32–33
    family and, 25
    housework and, 41
General Motors workers, 6, 119
Ghodsee, Kristen, 35
Ghost Ship, 201
GI Bill, 239–240
gig economy, 76, 279, 286
Gilmore, Ruth Wilson, 13, 154, 156, 165
Glatt, Eric, 224
globalization, 12–13, 248
Goldstein, Dana, 93
Goldwater, Barry, 122
Goodell, Roger, 314
Google, 275, 282, 283–284
Graduate Student Organizing Committee
    / United Auto Workers (GSOC-UAW)
    Local 2110, 251
graduate students, 247–249, 250–252,
    255–256
"graduates with no future," 323
graffiti, 195
Gramsci, Antonio, 11, 327
Gran Fury, 190
Granger, Richard, 130–131
Grant, Melissa Gira, 335
grassroots donations, 164–165
Great Depression, 150, 185–186
Great Domestication, 29
Great Society, 152
Greek civilization, ancient, 324–325
Green Bay Packers, 298
grief, 328–329
grooming gap, 127
Groundswell Fund, 159
guaranteed income proposals, 39–40,
    51–52, 53–54
Guendelsberger, Emily, 5, 131
Guerrilla Girls, 197
Guggenheim Museum, 196, 202
guild system, 212–213, 237
Guinan, Kerry, 192, 197–198, 201,
    202–203, 204–205
Gutride, Minnie, 95

H1-B visas, 281
hackerspaces, 274–275
Hafner, Katie, 270

Haider, Asad, 6–7
Haley, Margaret, 91, 101
Hals, Frans, 182, 183
Happiness Industry, The (Davies), 307
Harbaugh, Jim, 314
Harper's Bazaar, 223–224
Harris, Malcolm, 200, 219, 221, 310
Harris, Pamela, 71
Harris v. Quinn, 71, 102
Hartman, Saidiya, 63, 147
Hatton, Erin, 68, 249, 311
"having it all," 38, 46
health care, access to, 47
health insurance, 1, 47, 112, 136
Hearst, 224
heartbreak, 329
hegemony, 11
Henderson, Peta, 27
Higer, Amy, 246–247
higher education
    access to, 239, 242
    cost of, 245, 253
    hierarchical structure of, 236–237
    spread of, 147
    for women, 149
    See also academia; education
Hine, Lewis, 185
Hirst, Damien, 198
historically Black colleges and universities
    (HBCUs), 240
*History of the World in Seven Cheap Things,
    A* (Moore and Patel), 29
Hobby Lobby, 126
Hochschild, Arlie Russell, 45, 46–47, 73,
    118, 131
Holland, Donal, 205
home, labor of love ideology and, 26
home care work, 14, 68–74. *See also* caring
    work; domestic work
Home Depot, 126
home economics movement, 67
homemaker (term), 32
Homestead Steel Plant, 115–116
home-workplace division
    capitalism and, 27–28
    development of, 32–33
    domestic work and, 60–61
    See also work-life balance
hooks, bell, 31
hope labor, 211–212, 218, 222, 249, 254

"hope of rest," 3, 4
Hopkins, Carmen Teeple, 73
Hopper, Grace, 269
hospitals, charity and, 145
housecleaning, 58
Houser, Kathy, 128
housewife (term), 32
housework
    capitalism and, 41
    family wage and, 33
    gender disparity in, 45
    labor of love ideology and, 26
    proposed compensation for, 34–35,
        40–42, 49
    terminology changes and, 32
    See also domestic work
housing costs, 25
Hull House, 147, 148
Hultman, Martin, 119
human traits, desirability of, 6
Humboldt, Wilhelm von, 238
Humboldtian university, 238, 241, 246
Hunter, Tera, 33, 62, 63, 64, 330–331
Hunzru, Hari, 198
Hyde, Lewis, 181

IBM, 282
ICE (intellectual, cultural, and
    educational) sector, 251
ice hockey, 291–295
Idle, Nadia, 329–330
Ikeler, Peter, 125
Illegal Immigration Reform and
    Immigrant Responsibility Act (1996),
    73
Illgner, Amalia, 223
immigration
    Americanization of, 149
    home care work and, 68, 69, 70, 71,
        72–74
    tech industry and, 281, 289
    Trump administration and, 86, 108
Immigration and Customs Enforcement
    (ICE), 282
INCITE! Network, 154–155
indentured servants, 61
Independent Workers Union of Great
    Britain (IWGB), 163, 286, 289
industrial breadwinner masculinity, 119
industrial capitalism, 145, 146–147

industrial ethic, 12
industrial jobs, decline in, 4–5
Industrial Revolution, 182–183
Industrial Workers of the World, 12, 93
industrialization of bohemia, 274
inequality, nonprofits and, 144–145
Information Processing Techniques Office,
    270
Intel, 273
intellectual property, universities' control
    of, 247
Intern Nation (Perlin), 214
International Ice Hockey Federation
    (IIHF) Women's World Championship,
    316–318
International Olympic Committee, 300
Internet, 199–200, 270–272, 275–276
internships
    coronavirus pandemic and, 221, 229
    description of, 210–212
    history of, 212–217
    internship auction and, 222
    lawsuits related to, 217, 223–224
    personal example from, 207–210,
        218–219, 220, 225, 226–229
    politicians and, 215, 216, 220–221
    strikes and, 225–228
    unions/organizing and, 219, 224–225
    See also education
interpersonal relationships, 326. *See also*
    family; marriage
intimate labor, 60–61, 77
invisibility, 70–71
Isay, Dave, 162
isolation, 326
Isser, Mindy, 127

J. Crew, 132
Jacobin, 162
Jacobson, Barb, 52
Jaffe, Louis, 95
James, Selma, 31–32, 41, 48–49, 153, 325,
    328
Janus v. AFSCME, 102, 107
Jennings, Jean, 269
Jimenez, Rosa, 83–87, 104–110
Job Retention Scheme, 164
Jobs, Steve, 276
John Reed Club, 185
Johnson, Boris, 289

Johnson, Izzy, 196
Johnson, Jack, 298
Johnson, Lyndon, 97, 152, 216, 302
Jordan, Josh, 258, 259
Josipović, Ivo, 193–194
Julien, Allison, 78
just-cause protections, 258
just-in-time labor, 9

Kaba, Mariame, 334
Kaepernick, Colin, 297, 313–314, 315
Kelley, Florence, 148
Kelmore, Austin, 288
Kennedy, John F., 122
Kessler, Jeffrey, 312
Kessler-Harris, Alice, 148–149
Kids These Days (Harris), 219, 310
King, Billie Jean, 304, 318
Kipnis, Laura, 326, 330
Kittay, Eva, 48, 49, 74
Klein, Jennifer, 68
Knight, Hilary, 319
"Know Your Rights" camps, 314
knowledge economy, 8, 244, 251
Kohlberg Kravis Roberts (KKR), 115, 135
Kollontai, Alexandra, 35
Konczal, Mike, 243
Koons, Jeff, 198, 201
Korducki, Kelli María, 30–31
Kotsko, Adam, 8, 99, 256
Krasner, Lee, 186
Kresge's, 120
Krieger, Ali, 313
Kroenke, Stanley, 307
Kroger, 132
Ku Klux Klan, 63
Kuehn, Kathleen, 211–212

labor of love ideology
    cracking of myth of, 322–323
    critiques of, 13
    exploitation and, 17
    gender roles and, 25–26
    impact of, 9–10
    shift to, 12
labor-community alliances, 106
Land Grant Act (1861), 214
land grant universities, 239
Lanetix, 282–283
Lange, Dorothea, 186

late capitalism, 6–7
laundry workers, 63, 66
law enforcement, tech industry and, 283–284
Lazarus, Charles, 112, 133
League of Their Own, A, 304
learn-to-code boot camps, 280–281
Leary, John Patrick, 181
Lee, Spike, 314
Lemann, Nicholas, 154
Lepore, Jill, 152
lesbianism, 42
Lewis, Karen, 99, 101
Lewis, Penny, 242
Liberty Hall, 178
Lichtenstein, Nelson, 121
Lichterman, Ruth, 269
life expectancy, declining, 48
Lippard, Lucy, 189
Lloyd, Betty, 128
Lloyd, Carli, 316
Lobbying Act, 155
lone artist, image of, 179, 187
loneliness, rise in, 326–327
Lordstown plant, 6, 13
loss prevention, 128
Losse, Kate, 277–278, 281
Louis, Joe, 298–299
love
    housework and, 30–31
    importance of, 335
    marriage and, 30–31
    reciprocity of, 15–16
    work and, 326–328
Love, Lucia, 198, 200
Lovelace, Ada, 267–268
Lower Ed (Cottom), 252
loyalty oaths, 92
Luce, Stephanie, 131
Lucky Stores, 126
Luker, Kristin, 37
Luxemburg, Rosa, 333
Lynch, Marshawn, 315
Lyon, Matthew, 270

Machete, El, 184
Magdalene laundries, 68
magic, eliminating belief in, 28
Maier, Vivian, 195–196
Major League Baseball (MLB), 299, 301

male genius, image of, 179–180
Malone, John, 23
Malone, Ray, 21–25, 29, 30, 32, 49–54, 325–326
manufacturing jobs, decline in, 116
Marciano Art Foundation, 196
Marcoux, Camille, 207–210, 218–219, 220, 225, 226–229
marriage
    capitalism and, 31–32
    labor of love ideology and, 30–31
    welfare reform and, 43
"marriage promotion" programs, 43
Martin, Wednesday, 46
Marx, Karl, 26, 184, 325, 332
Marx at the Arcade (Woodcock), 272
Mason, Paul, 254, 323
mass incarceration, 44
mass media, sports and, 298, 300–301
Massachusetts Institute of Technology (MIT), 239, 271
Master Plan (University of California system), 242
master's degrees, 237
maternity leave, 35
Mazza, Bill, 197
McDowell, Mary Stone, 93
McLaren, Cheyenne, 106
McMillan Cottom, Tressie, 252, 255
McNeil, Joanne, 270, 275
McNulty, Kay, 269
McQuade, Laura, 170
Meadway, James, 4
Mechanical Turk, 278
Medicaid, 69–70, 71
medical interns and residents, 214–215
#MeToo movement, 283–284
Mexican muralists, 184–185
Microsoft, 282
Milkman, Ruth, 6
Miller, Marvin, 301
Milwaukee Bucks, 314
minimum income proposals, 39–40, 51–52, 53–54
minimum-wage laws, 32–33, 121, 122, 130
Minnesota Freedom Fund, 159, 164
Monocle, 223
Montgomery bus boycott, 66
Moore, Jason W., 29, 49
"more intimate unions," 77

MORENA party (Mexico), 49
Moreton, Bethany, 117, 124
Morrill Act (1862), 239
Morris, William, 3, 4, 183–184, 330
Mothers for Adequate Welfare (MAW), 39
Movement of Asylum Seekers in Ireland, 203, 205
Mukhopadhyay, Samhita, 327
Murch, Donna, 256
Murphy, Isaac, 298
Murphy, Marjorie, 90, 98
muses, 179
Museum of Modern Art (MoMA), 188, 196
museums, artists challenges to, 188, 196
Musk, Elon, 281

Nadasen, Premilla, 38, 66, 72
Nair, Yasmin, 161, 255
nannies, 55–60, 79–82. *See also* caring work; domestic work; Seally, Adela
Nash, Ciaran, 203
Nation, The, 224
Nation at Risk, A, 99–100
National Center for Transgender Equality, 163
National Collegiate Athletic Association (NCAA), 294, 300, 310, 311, 312–313
National Consumers League (NCL), 148
National Domestic Workers Alliance (NDWA), 69, 77–78
National Domestic Workers Union, 66
National Education Association (NEA), 91
National Endowment for the Arts, 188–189
National Football League, 301
National Hockey League (NHL), 293–294, 317, 318
National Institute of Public Affairs, 215
National Labor Relations Act (NLRA), 34
National Labor Relations Board (NLRB), 163, 168–169, 250–251, 283, 311–312
National Nanny Training Day, 78
National Organization for Women (NOW), 67
National Recovery Administration (NRA), 65
National Welfare Rights Organization (NWRO), 38, 39–40
National Women's Football League, 305

National Women's Hockey League (NWHL), 294, 316
National Women's Soccer League, 313
Native populations, enforcement of family structure on, 30
NBA (National Basketball Association), 314
Neff, Gina, 221
neoliberalism
    academia and, 242, 248, 251, 252
    arts and, 189–191, 195
    domestic work and, 46
    elder boom and, 72
    family and, 44
    financial crisis (2008) and, 323
    freelancers and, 280
    labor of love ideology and, 10
    nonprofits and, 154
    overview of, 6–8
    retail work and, 124
    schools and, 101
    sports and, 306
    teachers and, 98–99
    welfare reform and, 40, 42–43
neoliberalism and, 10 not sure what this means?
"Never Again" pledge, 282
New Deal, 33–34, 65, 68–69, 152, 185–186
New Left, 187
New Museum, 196
New Right, 242
New York University (NYU), 248, 251–252
NewsGuild, 282–283
Nixon, Richard, 40, 254
No Child Left Behind Act (2002), 100
"no-collar" work, 274
Nonni, Ella, 170
nonprofit industrial complex (NPIC), 154–155
Nonprofit Professional Employees Union (NPEU), 163–164
nonprofits
    coronavirus pandemic and, 163–164
    funding for, 154, 158–160
    inequality and, 143–145
    internships and, 210, 221
    personal example from, 139–143, 146, 165–171

nonprofits (*continued*)
    unions/organizing and, 162–164,
      165–170
    wages in, 157–158
    work conditions in, 162, 164
Northwestern University football,
    311–312
nuclear family, 26, 32
nursing, 14

Obama administration, 100, 157
Ocasio-Cortez, Alexandria, 221
Occupy Wall Street, 224, 332–333
Ocean Hill–Brownsville, 97–98
O'Connor, Bridget, 220
Olney, Eve, 176, 203
Olympic Charter, 296
Olympic ice hockey, 292, 295
Olympic Project for Human Rights
    (OPHR), 303
Olympics, 295, 296–297, 298, 302, 303,
    304, 305
On the Clock (Guendelsberger), 131
on-call shifts, 129
online gaming culture, 287–288
Open Society Foundation, 158
operaismo (workerism) movement, 40–41,
    189
Organization United for Respect at
    Walmart (OUR Walmart), 133–134
organized abandonment, 13
Ornstein, Severo, 272
Orozco, José Clemente, 184
Ortiz, David, 308
Orwell, George, 6, 325
Osaka, Naomi, 314
O'Shea, Kate, 175–178, 202–205
Other Criteria, 198
outsider artists, 195–196
Ouvrage, 228
overidentifying with job, 131
overtime pay, 157
Owens, Jesse, 298
Oxford, 238, 256

Palmer, Phyllis, 68
pandemic (2020). *See* coronavirus
    pandemic
Parent Community Organizing
    Committee, 106

parenting
    arts and, 197
    attachment, 45
    child support/benefits and, 43, 51
    foster, 42
    single mothers, 44–45, 49–50, 52
    See also family
Parks, Gordon, 186
Parreñas, Rhacel Salazar, 60
part-time work
    women and, 219
    See also gig economy
Patel, Raj, 29, 49
patriarchy
    rise of, 27–28
    stigma on lesbianism and, 42
    See also gender
Patrick, Dan, 48
patronage, art and, 181–182
Patterson, Floyd, 302
Patty Kazmaier Award, 294
PayPal, 281
Pearson, Ralph, 185
Pein, Corey, 281–282
People's Budget, 109
People's Kitchen, 203, 204
Pérez, Amara H., 156–157
performance-enhancing drugs, 308–309
Perlin, Ross, 214, 216, 222
Perryman, Mark, 296, 305
personal protective equipment, lack of, 170
personal relationships, 326. *See also* family;
    marriage
Personal Responsibility and Work
    Opportunity Reconciliation Act (1996),
    43–44
Philadelphia Museum of Art (PMA),
    196–197
Pinkerton detectives, 115
Pinochet, Augusto, 7
Piven, Frances Fox, 39, 145
Planned Parenthood Federation of America
    (PPFA), 142, 151–152, 164, 166–167
Planned Parenthood of the Rocky
    Mountains (PPRM), 140–143, 165–170
playbor, 272, 274
police funding, 109
political organizations, 326–327
politicians, internships and, 215, 216,
    220–221

Pollock, Jackson, 186, 187
Poo, Ai-jen, 69, 71–72, 78
Poor Laws, 29–30
poor relief, 29–30
Poor Relief Act (1662), 145
poorhouse, 145
Portland Terminal Company, 216
post-Fordism, 6–7
praxis, 324–325
precariat, 218
pregnancy
    discrimination and, 166
    firing due to, 126
Primates of Park Avenue (Martin), 46
printmaking, 175–178
private education reform industry, 100
privatization, 8–9
pro-choice movement, 140
Professional and Administrative Staff
    Association, 188
professional development funds, 258,
    259
Professional Staff Congress (PSC), 242
Professional Women's Hockey Players
    Association (PWHPA), 317–318
professional-managerial class (PMC), 240,
    244, 252–254, 255
profitability crisis, 40
programming
    as blue-collar job, 280–281
    gender stereotypes and, 273
    history of, 267–273
    job growth and, 14–15
    See also tech industry
Progressive Educators for Action, 105
Project (RED), 156
Project Maven, 283
property taxes, 99
Prosen, Kevin, 102
protest movements, 332–334. *See also*
    strikes
Protestant Ethic and the Spirit of Capitalism
    (Weber), 11
Protestant Reformation, 238
Protestant work ethic, 43
public service work, 145–146
public space, reclamation of,
    332–334
public universities, 241–242
punitive neoliberalism, 323

Qayum, Seemin, 74
quality assurance (QA) testing, 287
queer relationships
    family structure and, 47
    "having it all" and, 46
queer women, patriarchy and, 42

race
    concept of, 28–29
    discrimination and, 126
    domestic work and, 61–62
    retail work and, 126–127
    See also Black athletes; Black teachers;
        Black veterans; Black women; Black
        workers
Race to the Top, 100
racial justice movements, 287–288. *See also*
    Black Lives Matter movement
racial segregation, 239–240
racism
    Planned Parenthood and, 170
    in sports, 298–299
    See also discrimination
Rana Plaza garment factory collapse, 5
Rapinoe, Megan, 305, 313, 315
Ray, Raka, 74
Reagan, Ronald
    AIDS crisis and, 190
    Davis and, 243, 253
    deindustrialization and, 8
    deregulation and, 274
    education and, 254
    family and, 70
    immigration and, 73
    Olympics and, 306
    retail work and, 124
    teachers and, 99–100
    welfare reform and, 40, 43
Reclaim Our Schools LA, 106
Reclaim the Block, 159
Red Scare, 92, 94–95
Red Wedge Magazine, 201
Reed, Carolyn, 67
Regulating the Poor (Piven and Cloward),
    145
Reinhart, Ann Marie, 111–115, 125, 130
relief programs, 185
reproductive labor, 26–27, 28, 37, 45
research journals, 238
residency, 214

Retail, Wholesale and Department Store
    Union (RWDSU), 120, 128
Retail Action Project, 130
retail apocalypse, 130, 134
Retail Clerks International Association
    (RCIA), 120–121
retail work
    burnout and, 131–132
    class-action lawsuits and, 125–126, 136
    as cornerstone of economy, 116
    coronavirus pandemic and, 132
    customer interactions and, 112–114,
        118
    e-commerce and, 131
    explosion of, 117
    high-end/low-end split in, 124
    hiring practices in, 127
    low pay for, 118, 119
    personal example from, 111–115, 125,
        130
    race and, 126–127
    recession and, 124–125
    schedules of, 129
    surveillance and, 128
    unions/organizing and, 119–121, 125,
        130, 133–134
Revolution Will Not Be Funded, The
    (INCITE! Network), 154–155
Revolutionary Union of Technical
    Workers, Painters, and Sculptors, 184
RFK Community Schools, 104
Richards, Cecile, 165–166
Riggs, Bobby, 304
Riot, Strike, Riot (Clover), 8
Rise Up Retail, 135–136
Rivas, Lynn May, 70
Rivera, Diego, 184
Roberge, Jean-François, 225, 228
Robertson, Laura Anne, 47
Robinson, Jackie, 299
robots, 75
Rockland Psychiatric Center, 220
Rodney, Lester, 298
Rodriguez, Alex, 307
Roe v. Wade, 37
Rometty, Ginni, 282
Romney, Mitt, 133
Roosevelt, Theodore, 297
Rosenberg, Jordy, 46
Ross, Andrew, 194, 274, 280

Ruskin, John, 183–184
Rutgers, 256

Saab, A. Joan, 186
Sacco, Nicola, 93
sacrificial labor, 194
Salon des Refuses, 182
same-sex marriage, 44
sanctuary schools, 87, 108
Sanders, Bernie, 134–135, 136
Sanger, Margaret, 151
scheduling software, 129
Schiller, Amy, 143, 149
Schmeling, Max, 298
school reconstitutions, 105
schools
    charter, 99
    desegregation of, 96–97
    funding of, 98–99
    segregated, 89, 92, 94
    See also academia; education; teachers
Schrecker, Ellen, 241
Schweitzer, Ellen, 103
Science Ltd., 198
scientific charity, 149
Screen Actors Guild–American Federation
    of Television and Radio Artists (SAG-
    AFTRA), 284–285
scripts for retail workers, 132
Sculpture House Casting, 199
Seally, Adela, 55–60, 78–79, 80–82
Sears, 121
Seattle General Strike (1919), 333–334
"second shift," 45, 65
secret shopping, 128
self-sacrifice, 160–161
self-scanners, 131
self-service model, 122, 124
separate spheres ideology, 32
Serra, Richard, 199
Service Employees International Union
    (SEIU), 71, 165–166, 169, 214, 258
service proletariat, 124
service shopping, 128
"service with a smile," 116
settlement house movement, 147–148
severance pay law, 136
sex, nonreproductive, penalizing of, 29
sex discrimination lawsuit, 125–126
sex testing, 304

sex workers, 153
sexual harassment, 80, 220, 283–284
sexuality, capitalism and, 31–32
Shanker, Al, 97
Shaw, Sarah, 197
shorter hours movement, 297
short-termism, 164
Silicon Alley, 274
Silicon Valley, 273, 278
single mothers, 44–45, 49–50, 52
Siqueiros, David Alfaro, 184–185
Siravo, Julian, 274
Sisters in Portland Impacting Real Issues
    Together (SPIRIT), 156–157
slavery, 33, 61–62, 66, 213
slum reform, 147
smile scanner, 128
Smith, Adam, 213, 217, 239
Smith, Tommie, 302, 303
Snyder, Betty, 269
social conservatism, 42–43
social critique, 13, 334
social housekeepers, 148
social justice schools, 84–85
social media, 255, 275–278
social protests (2020), 332–334
social reproduction, 325
Social Security, 65, 68
social welfare policy, 29–30
social work, 150
social-distancing protocols, challenges
    regarding, 60
socialism, 35
Sociological Department, 33
solidarity, 16, 335
Soros, George, 158
South Wind Women's Center, 140
Southeastern Conference, 310
Southern Poverty Law Center, 163
Soviet realism, 187
Spare Room (O'Shea and Olney), 203
sports
    Black athletes and, 296–297, 298–299,
        302–303, 304, 313–314
    college, 299–300, 310–312
    coronavirus pandemic and, 312
    earliest, 295–296
    health risks in, 308–310, 312
    in late nineteenth century, 296–298
    mass media and, 298, 300–301

personal example from, 291–295, 305,
    306, 315–319
as political, 296–297
professionalization of, 298
team owners and, 307
television and, 300–301
unions/organizing and, 301–302,
    311–313
wages in, 294, 307–308, 313
Srinivasan, Amia, 256–257
standardized testing, 92, 100
Standing, Guy, 218, 324–325
Stanton, Elizabeth Cady, 146
Starr, Ellen Gates, 148
startup founders, 281–282
state university system, 239
status coercion, 249
Statute of Artificers, 213
Steinbrenner family, 307
Stella, Milou, 50, 52
steroids, 308–309
Steyerl, Hito, 194
Stillman, Charles, 92
Stine, Alison, 201
StoryCorps, 162–163
street art, 195
stress, increase in, 245
strikes
    academia and, 251–252, 256–257
    at Detroit Woolworth Five and Dime,
        119–120
    at Homestead Steel Plant, 115–116
    length of working day and, 3
    in Lordstown, 13
    in sports, 314–316
    student, 224–225
    teachers,' 84, 102–105, 107, 109–110,
        323, 333
    in tech industry, 283–285
    time and, 333–334
student debt, 164
student loans, 242
student movement (Britain; 2010), 254
student protests, 254
student strikes, 224–225
student-athletes, 300, 310–312
Students Deserve, 106–107, 108–109
Students in Free Enterprise (SIFE), 123
Studio Gobo, 264–266
suburban housewives, 13–14

Sugar Sphinx (Walker), 199
surveillance, 280
Svanoe. Anya, 130
Sweeney, John, 251

Tahrir Square, 332
Talk Poverty, 201
Tang, Eric, 152
Target, 124, 126, 132
Target distribution center, 5
TaskRabbit, 76
tax laws, 149–150, 158
Taylor, Astra, 190, 199–200, 270, 278
Taylor, Breonna, 108, 323
Taylor, Frederick Winslow, 92
Taylor, Keeanga-Yamahtta, 159–160
Taylor, Sunuara, 48
Teach for America, 100
Teacher Wars, The (Goldstein), 93
teachers
    Black, 89, 92, 96–98
    challenges regarding, 85–86
    changing gender profile of, 269–270
    during the Depression, 93
    deskilling of, 100
    education reform movement and,
        98–101
    low pay for, 83
    loyalty oaths for, 92
    pandemic and, 108–109
    pay penalty and, 101–102
    personal example from, 83–87,
        104–110
    Red and, 94–95
    social justice schools and, 84–85
    strikes and, 84, 102–105, 107, 109–110,
        323, 333
    traditional perceptions of, 87–88
    unions/organizing and, 90–93, 97–98,
        105–106, 110
    women, 88–90, 94
    See also academia; education; schools
Teachers Union (TU), 94, 95, 98
tech industry
    coronavirus pandemic and, 267,
        288–289
    as cult, 281
    personal example from, 263–267, 281,
        285–289
    strikes and, 283–285

surveillance and, 280
turnover and, 265
unions/organizing and, 272–273,
    282–289
    See also programming
Tech Solidarity, 282
Tech Workers Coalition (TWC), 282
television, sports and, 300–301
tenure laws, 96
tenure protections, 240–241, 243
Terkel, Studs, 162
Thatcher, Margaret, 7–8, 9, 124, 190, 243,
    248
Theater of the Oppressed techniques, 49
Thiel, Peter, 281
Thompson, Clive, 281
Thompson, E. P., 16
Till, Emmett, 107
Tiller, George, 139–140
Tillmon, Johnnie, 39, 43
Tilly, Chris, 129–130
TINA, 8
Title IX, 304–305, 310
To 'Joy My Freedom (Hunter), 330–331
Tokumitsu, Miya, 76, 219, 279–280
Torqued Ellipses (Serra), 199
Toys "R" Us, 111–115, 124, 133–136
"tradwives," 46
transgender workers, protections for, 163
traumatic brain injuries, 309
Trilling, Lionel, 241
triple-A-games, 264–265
Trump, Donald, 4–5, 16, 86, 108, 164,
    167, 168–169, 282
Turl, Adam, 201
Twitter, 200, 276, 278

United Auto Workers (UAW), 196
Uber, 279, 286
UK Independence Party (UKIP), 21–22
Ulion, Gretchen, 292
Unemployed Artists' Group, 185
union avoidance, 166
Union Power, 105
unions/organizing
    academia and, 242, 249, 250–252, 256,
        257–262
    arts and, 185–186, 187–188, 194,
        196–197, 198, 201–205
    campaigns against, 166–170, 196

domestic work and, 65–67, 76–81
family wage and, 33
home care work and, 71
industrial breadwinner masculinity
    and, 119
internships and, 219, 224–225
Janus v. AFSCME and, 102
layoffs and, 5–6
neoliberalism and, 7
nonprofits and, 162–164, 165–170
Planned Parenthood and, 165–170
retail work and, 119–121, 125, 130,
    133–134
sports and, 301–302, 311–313
teachers and, 90–93, 97–98, 105–106,
    110
tech industry and, 272–273, 282–289
Walmart and, 122
UNITE HERE, 104
United Federation of Teachers (UFT),
    97–98
United Food and Commercial Workers
    (UFCW), 130–131, 133–134
United for Respect, 133–135
United Teachers Los Angeles (UTLA), 83,
    103–104, 105, 107, 108
universal basic income, 51–52, 53–54
Universal Credit, 24–25, 30, 50
universities
    British, 243, 253–254
    early, 237–238
    intellectual property and, 247
    land grant, 239
    public, 241–242
    research at, 247–248
    in United States, 239–242
    working conditions of, 249–250
    See also academia; education
University and College Union, 256
University of Berlin, 238
University of California system,
    242–243
University of Dreams, 222
University of Naples, 238
University of Wisconsin, 292
University of Wisconsin at Madison,
    239
urbanism, 330
US Equal Employment Opportunity
    Commission, 220

USA Hockey, 291–295, 315, 317
USA Soccer, 313
Ustwo, 288

vagrancy, 62–64
Vanzetti, Bartolomeo, 93
venture capitalists, 281–282
venture labor, 221
video-game programmers, 263–267
Vine, 200
voice actors, 284–285
Volcker, Paul, 8
Vornado Realty Trust, 115, 135

wage labor, exploitation and, 29
wages
    in academia, 258
    comparisons of, 323
    family wage and, 12, 32–34, 92, 213
    minimum-wage laws and, 32–33, 121,
        122, 130
    in nonprofits, 157–158
    overtime pay and, 157
    in sports, 294, 307–308, 313
    stagnation in, 322–323
    wage gap and, 36
Wages for Housework Campaign, 40–42,
    46, 49, 52, 189, 225
Waiters and Waitresses Union, 120
Waldron, Travis, 308
Walker, Kara, 199
Walker, Scott, 254
Walling vs. Portland Terminal Co., 216
Walmart, 121–125, 128, 130, 132, 135
Wal-Mart Stores, Inc., v. Dukes, 125–126
Walton, Ann, 307
Walton, Sam, 121–122
Walton family, 123
Walton Family Foundation, 123
Wambach, Abby, 313
Wang, Diana, 223–224
Wang, Lily, 135
War on Poverty, 68–69, 152–153, 216
War Services Subdivision, 187
warehouse jobs, 5
Warren, Elizabeth, 136
Washington Mystics, 314
We Dream in Black, 79
"We Only Want the Earth" project, 179,
    204–205

Weber, Max, 11
Weeks, Kathi, 10, 15, 44, 328
Weigel, Moira, 284
Weiner, Lois, 97, 100
Weinstein, Harvey, 284
welfare capitalism, 124–125, 149
"welfare queen" stereotype, 40
welfare reform, 43–44, 126
welfare rights movement, 38–40, 153
welfare state, 150, 177
Wescoff, Marlyn, 269
Westergard, Björn, 283
WeWork, 280
Where Bad Jobs Are Better (Carré and Tilly), 129–130
Where Wizards Stay Up Late (Hafner and Lyon), 270
"white baby challenge," 46
white supremacy, 46
Whitefield-Madrano, Autumn, 305
Why the Olympics Aren't good for Us, and How They Can Be (Perryman), 296
"wife bonuses," 46
wildcat strikes, 13
Wiley, Kehinde, 199
Williams, Justin, 163
Williams, Raymond, 181, 183
Williams, Serena, 305
Wilson, Katherine, 231–236, 246–247, 257–262
Winant, Gabriel, 17
Wipper, Janette, 283
witch-hunts, 28, 49
WNBA (Women's National Basketball Association), 314
women
    capitalism and, 31
    in early computing fields, 267–269
    exploitation of, 27–29
    higher education for, 149
    home care work and, 68, 69, 70, 71, 72–74
    housework and, 26
    limitations on work hours of, 33
    part-time work and, 219
    single mothers, 44–45, 49–50, 52
    in sports, 303–305. see also Duggan, Meghan
    See also gender

Women and Capitalism (Davis), 31
women of color. *See* Black women
women's club movement, 147
Women's High Performance Advisory Group, 317
Women's March (2017), 316
Women's Strike, 316
Women's Tennis Association, 304
Women's Trade Union League (WTUL), 148
women's work
    devaluing of, 42
    as love, 26
    subordination of, 27–29
    See also gender; *individual areas of work*
Women's World Cup, 305
Woodcock, Jamie, 272
Woolworth's, 121
work
    brief history of, 2–3
    as empowerment, 36
    enjoyment from, 3
    necessity of, 321–322
    as source of fulfillment, 11
work ethic, 26, 28, 30
work-as-liberation ideology, 36
workerism movement, 40–41
work-for-labor, 218
workhouses, 30
Working Artists in the Greater Economy (W.A.G.E.), 193
working class, description of, 16–17
working day, length of, 3
work-life balance, 26, 44, 326. *See also* home-workplace division; *individual areas of work*
workplace realism, 15, 47
Works Progress Administration (WPA), 185, 187
World Cup, 300, 313
World Health Organization, 157
World War II, 298, 304

Yeshiva University, 250
YMCA, 298
Yuichi, Ishii, 75

zero-hours contract, 129, 287
Zirin, Dave, 298, 301, 308
Zuckerberg, Mark, 277–278, 281

READING GROUP GUIDE

1. Throughout this book, Jaffe discusses how much of what we love about work is not the work itself, but rather the quality of life afforded by it, our coworkers, or rare moments of pleasure. Do you like your job? Did reading this book change your feelings toward work?

2. Have you experienced burnout? How did you deal with it?

3. Jaffe writes widely about different kinds of unions, as well as their historical victories and losses. Do you belong to a union? How has it protected you and your coworkers?

4. Jaffe writes that when work "demand[s] our love along with our time, our brains, and our bodies," our relationships and lives suffer. Can you relate? When have you had to sacrifice personal well-being or social time in order to be seen as a good worker or to survive?

5. In the introduction, Jaffe writes about the process of outsourcing jobs from the United States and western Europe into poorer countries, as well as the flows of migrants from colonized nations into the United States seeking work. How did neoliberal capitalism shape these global patterns? Does this argument change how you think about working conditions outside the United States?

6. Throughout the book, Jaffe calls readers toward collective action and organizing. After reading this, what kinds of actions do you want to take to make your working conditions better for you and fellow workers?

7. In Chapter 1, Jaffe writes that the family is an economic and political institution and that women do "reproductive labor" within and

outside the home. Growing up, who did the maintenance work of cleaning, cooking, and providing care in your family? What have you observed about reproductive labor in your current household?

8. Jaffe discusses the various ways that anti-Blackness, white supremacy, and misogyny harm the most marginalized workers in every field, from service work to social work, from academia to athletics. What are some of the ways you've experienced or witnessed these dynamics in your own workplace? Have you been able to combat them, whether collectively or individually?

9. Throughout the book, Jaffe challenges the distinctions made between "skilled" and "unskilled" labor, especially as it relates to the qualities we tend to believe are innate for "women's work" or for "men's work." What are some skills you have had to learn, or unlearn, to do your job? Where do you see these binaries enforced in your own life? Whose labor do these binaries view as more or less valuable?

10. In the conclusion, Jaffe points to the reclamation of public space in the spirit of liberation as essential to contemporary social movements. Have you ever been in spaces where you get to slow down, be present, and connect with other people—where you can begin to glimpse a vision of society outside of, or after, capitalism? How did it make you feel?

11. What surprised you most in this book?

12. Consider what Jaffe asks in the conclusion to this book: What would you do with your time if you didn't have to work?

Amanda Jaffe

Sarah Jaffe is a Type Media Center Fellow and an independent journalist covering the politics of power, from the workplace to the streets. She is the author of *Necessary Trouble: Americans in Revolt*. Her work has appeared in the *New York Times*, *The Nation*, *The Guardian*, the *Washington Post*, *The American Prospect*, and many other publications. She is the cohost, with Michelle Chen, of *Dissent* magazine's *Belabored* podcast, as well as a columnist at *The Progressive* and *New Labor Forum*. You can find out more about her at sarahljaffe.com.